I Saw Our Moon
== Last Night ==

The Correspondence Between Howard Shenton and Glorious Andrews During WWII

Compiled and edited by

JACQUELINE ANDREWS GRACE

ISBN: 978-1-62429-279-8

Front cover photo credit:
Beverly Studios, Inc.
Manchester's Quality Photographers
24 Hanover Street
Manchester, New Hampshire

Printed through Opus Self-Publishing Services
Located at:
Politics and Prose Bookstore
5015 Connecticut Ave. NW
Washington, D.C. 20008
www.politics-prose.com / / (202) 364-1919

Dedicated to Uncle Howard & Auntie Glorious

*and to all the members of the Greatest Generation who fought for our
freedoms during WWII*

Table of Contents

PROLOGUE

Howard Carl Shenton was born in Baltimore, Maryland on January 19, 1919 to a tugboat captain and his wife. He had one older brother who they called Shim. Sadly, the boys' mother died when Howard was only three years old and Shim was five. That left Shim to take care of Howard whenever their widowed father was out on the tugboat or drinking in the local bars.

You can only imagine the trouble the two boys could get into without proper supervision. One day they were playing "Jack Be Nimble" while jumping over a fire and Howard fell into the hot coals and burned his knee. Little Shim held him all the rest of the day as he cried in his arms until their father returned home.

When the boys were 10 and 12, their father remarried. Shim didn't get along with the new wife, so their dad sent the brothers away to separate foster homes. At the beginning of the Depression this was a common practice and state supervision of foster care barely existed back then. Howard ended up in Shady Side working on the farm of Cap'n Charlie Hartge and Miss Grace located on West River at the end of

Steamboat Road. He lived in the attic with no heat or electricity. He missed his older brother Shim sorely and despaired of ever seeing him again.

On the first day of school in Shady Side, Howard was playing first base on the school grounds when Glorious Legna Andrews walked up with her friend. She turned to her friend and asked, "Who is that new boy?" When she didn't get an answer she said, "I'm going to marry that boy."

Miss Ethel Andrews, Glorious's mother, who was the teacher at Shady Side Elementary School, recognized Howard's sharp mind and paid special attention to his education. If he wasn't allowed to go to school because he had to work on the farm on the day of standardized testing, she would send Mr. Andrews to go fetch Howard out of the fields to come take the test so the school's achievement scores would be higher.

Glorious' parents owned the Rural Home Hotel, later known as the Andrews Hotel, one of several summer boarding houses in Shady Side. Howard could often be seen driving the farm's horse cart to deliver eggs to various places in Shady Side. Glorious knew when he'd be passing by, so she planned to be out playing tennis on the Rural Home Hotel courts as often as possible. Howard later commented, "That Andrews gal sure does play a lot of tennis."

Howard was forced to drop out of school after the 8th grade so he could work on the farm. He longed for an education more than anything else, except for love.

EDITOR'S NOTE

Dear Reader,

As you begin reading these letters, don't be surprised if you experience the sensation of jumping into a time machine and finding yourself plunked smack dab in the undertow of the Second World War. These letters are original source material, written in 1941-1945. They are the actual correspondence between Howard C. Shenton and Glorious Legna Andrews, both of Shady Side, Maryland, after Howard was drafted into the Army. This is not a memoire written many years after the fact, nor is it a fictional fabrication in the form of letters. I transcribed them directly from the original handwritten letters with minimal changes. Fortunately, Howard was an excellent speller and had a firm grasp of proper grammar which made my job much easier. I have merely made minor changes here and there to clarify meaning and to protect the innocent. These are personal letters with a unique narrative voice, handy abbreviations, military acronyms, and use of contemporary slang. As this poignant love story unfolds, we are plunged into an earlier era and treated to an inner view of life and culture during WWII.

Only a few of the 359 letters Glorious wrote to Howard survived the war. They begin with August 7, 1942 and end with her November 16, 1942 letter, plus a letter from May 29, 1943. Her letters give us a taste of the situation on the Homefront during WWII and give us insight into her first year of teaching high school math at Glen Burnie High School after graduating from Hood College. She rented a room in Annapolis during the school week so she could carpool with other teachers or ride the train to and from school. Her letters reveal her own voice, personality, and emotions as the reader is forced to imagine what she may have written in subsequent letters based on Howard's response.

Included in this publication is a smattering of correspondence to and from other people in Howard's life, as well as some of the photographs that survived for many decades stored in an old suitcase where Glorious kept all of Howard's letters in chronological packets tied daintily with pastel silk ribbon.

As you read these letters bear in mind they were written in an earlier time when society held some different standards to those of present day. Depending on your own age, you may feel more of a jolt from the paradigm shift than someone who lived through the changes. You will encounter attitudes about women that may give you pause. You may notice how staunchly held moral codes were often compromised by the uncertainty of war, yet you may be astonished by the innocence that held forth. The ubiquity of tobacco products may surprise you. Slang words you've never heard before may puzzle you. You may feel the urge to watch an old movie or two, or listen to songs from the early 1940s to find out why they meant so much to those serving in the armed forces and their loved ones left at home.

You may need to come to terms with the fact that nations, who are now our allies, were once our enemies. Nicknames for those enemies may not be politically correct now, but they were used commonly during the Second World War and were not considered slurs. Unspeakable atrocities were committed during this brutal war so trust and forgiveness did not come quickly, but healing eventually paved a way towards friendship.

If you as the reader glean one thing from these letters, it is my hope that you discover for yourself the reason this band of brave men and women are forever to be known as the Greatest Generation.

I Saw Our Moon
== Last Night ==

BOOT CAMP

Over hill, over dale
As we hit the dusty trail.

The Caisson Song
Edmund L. Gruber
1908

Camp Wheeler, Georgia

June 21, 1941

Dear Glorious,

I finally made up my mind to write. It's really quite a job. You probably realize that by now —since you haven't received any letters from me. Maybe I'll be able to overcome that. I hope so.

Things have certainly changed around since I saw you last. For better or worse I don't know. This Army life isn't too bad after you're in it a few weeks. The hardest job is keeping within the rules and regulations. They are very strict around here. One thing I have learned since my induction in the Army, and that is how to keep house. We are forever sweeping, mopping, cleaning windows and dusting in the barracks. They inspect them three times a week. The worst thing is in the morning after "Reveille", the whole company is marched in a line covering our area. Then we break loose and pick up matches, cigarette butts and paper off the ground. If someone would see us and didn't know what it was all about, they would think we had lost something, or else that we were crazy.

I am in a "heavy weapons battalion". Meaning, we use machine guns of all calibers. We also use the pistol and rifle, but we don't get much training with those. Our instructors are regular Army men. We have two sergeants and three corporals. The other platoons have a lieutenant in charge. Evidently they didn't have enough for all. These fellows are very strict and don't stand for any foolishness. After you get to know them, they are fairly decent fellows. Our sergeant has made me an "acting sergeant". This doesn't mean much now but it may be all right later on. I will get a chance to handle the platoon. If I do all right, I'll probably get a rating. It means a lot more work and some of the boys are pretty hard to handle. But in the Army you have to take it and make the best of it.

This country down here isn't much. There isn't a thing to see but sand and pine trees. The heat is terrible. Two boys passed out yesterday when we went for a hike. Georgia is supposed to be a peach state. I haven't seen a peach tree since I've been here. The camp is located about ten miles from the city of Macon. This is one of the dirtiest towns I have ever seen. It is about twice the size of Annapolis. We don't go in much, as there are lots of ways to spend your spare time around the camp. Baseball and volleyball are the favorite sports. Then, we have three different theatres in the camp.

The food is good and you get plenty of it. We have chicken, roast beef and all other kinds of meat. They get up some pretty good deserts, too! Friday is the only day I don't enjoy the meals. That's because I hate fish.

The schedule is a fairly tough one. In the morning we drill for three hours with ten-minute breaks every hour. Then we get a lecture which lasts an hour. In the afternoon we march three or four miles out in the country. There we get more lectures. This schedule is interrupted with special details. When you go on detail you do anything from unloading freight cars to planting grass.

This is about all I can think of to write about now. I miss playing tennis. They don't go in for it much down here.

Love and good luck,
Howard

Company "D" 3rd Training Battalion

Camp Wheeler, Georgia

Camp Wheeler, Georgia

July 26, 1941

Dear Glorious,

I don't quite understand all this controversy about your letter. I did get one letter from you. The one today being the second I've received. The apology should be the other way around. Seems as if I was trying to get two for one. But, don't get the idea that I don't want to write to you. I think it's swell writing you. In fact I could say better than that, but not in a letter. Your letters are the best ones I've received. So <u>please</u> keep writing! I'll answer them.

When you went to Norfolk you should have kept right on down the coast to Georgia. Camp Wheeler would be fine with you around. Glad you had a nice time. Your going swimming in the ocean sounded good. We have a few lakes to swim in down here but it's not as good as salt water. I still remember the first and last time you and I went swimming. Fishing too!

Speaking of tennis. Keep me posted on your tournament playing. I thought I had a match last Sunday. But, the people down here are too lazy. They said it was too hot. I'll probably get up a game before my thirteen weeks are up or finished. Bowling and dancing are the favorite pastime pleasures here. There is a dance going on about every other night. I don't enjoy them much, though. Guess I'm too particular who I dance with. Then, they are so darn crowded it isn't much fun. The "fifteenth battalion" had a "farewell" dance last night at the service club. They are leaving Monday for Camp Dix, New Jersey. I'd like to be in that outfit. Another fellow and I crashed it and we had a fairly good time. We had to bribe the guard. At that he wouldn't let us in until it was almost over. I danced with one of the captains' wives. She was very nice. Our battalion is having a dance next Friday. They are getting the girls from some college near Macon. The orchestra plays "Stardust" pretty good.

You talk about going "domestic". Join the Army and you will get very good training. I've been lucky though. The acting sergeants only do K.P. once while here. I had it last week so that's over for me. K.P. is the hardest job in the Army. You go on at six in the morning and work until eight-thirty in the evening.

We are getting more work now. I go on guard tomorrow and Monday I'm "charge of quarters". The guard detail is tough. There are eleven "general orders" and we have to know these. I'm an acting corporal of the guard and this means I go on for two hours and get four off, for twelve hours. The privates are only on two hours in the twelve. However, I won't have to walk a post.

This past week we've been firing the 30 caliber machine gun for record. Our platoon made up a "kitty" of five dollars for the highest score. One fellow beat me by two points to win it. He made 178 out of a possible 200 and I made 176. Our lieutenant gave me two packs of cigarettes for being a close second. Their guns are the fastest firing things in the world. The bullets cut the trees down behind the targets. It looked as though a terrible hurricane had passed through the woods. I hate to think of what this gun would do to a man. Next week we go out in the field with these guns and study problems. Somebody is going to have sore shoulders from carrying the guns. They are very unhandy to carry.

The first, second and 3rd battalions put on a parade this morning. Honestly, our company was terrible. Since we've been working with the guns, they haven't given us "close order" drilling and it really showed up today. I think we'll get it more often now, and that's hot work. You are wet with perspiration after the first ten minutes. When you perspire like this they fill our drinking water with salt. Then nobody wants to drink it. It doesn't taste very nice.

Pat certainly has a time. Imagine not wanting to go and see the northeastern part of the country. I think that would be a wonderful trip. However, Shady Side is still more wonderful to me. Maybe Pat sees something much better in Shady Side or should I say Jack, then she could see elsewhere. You asked if he liked her. I think so. He has quite a few girlfriends but I think he likes Pat the best. He mentioned her in his letter. So you think Jack is a "kidder". I don't know whether you could call me that or not. Glorious, I do like to fool and play. But, I can be serious when the occasion demands it. That occasion came almost a year ago. Does that answer your question? That's a lot of stuff about you not understanding some people. You understand everything.

As September draws near you are more scared. I'm surprised! I hope you're not worrying over this teaching business. If other people do it there is no reason why you can't. These old army sergeants could help you there. The first two days we spent in the army we were fairly wild, but before a week was over these boys had us eating out of their hands. We didn't like them at first but now we think they are fine fellows and would do anything they asked us without hesitation. I'd like to have you for a teacher. Please stop worrying about it. You'll do alright. Another thing. About you being blue. I can't understand that either. You should be having a swell time. This is the time of the year when everything blossoms forth. Not only that, you have something to look forward to. You know people aren't very nice to be around when they are blue. I'm going to eat "chow" now. "Be back in a flash."

The chow wasn't so good. We didn't have any dessert.

I must tell you about a prank we pulled on a fellow the other night. He went to a movie so we knew he wouldn't be back until after "lights out" (9 PM). We took his pants and shirt, stuffed them full of paper. Then we rigged up his shoes and leggings on the stuffed trousers, so it looked like a man. Then we placed this on his bunk, used a canteen for the head and placed a hat over this. Really, it looked like a soldier asleep. This boy came in about ten o'clock and of course right away he thought he was in the wrong barracks. They all look alike and someone is always going into the wrong one. So, he went next door, as soon as he got in that barracks he knew he was wrong. Then he counted all the barracks in the block—He came back to where he started out and started raising Cain with this fellow for being in his bunk (the dummy). Well, we were wide awake and couldn't hold back any longer. I laughed so hard. The guard had to come in and quiet us down. We still laugh about it.

Glorious, I have no idea where we will go when our thirteen weeks are up. I'm being good, I think. Hope to see you in about two months. Don't forget to write and I will answer your letters.

Love, (not like in tennis)

Howard

Camp Wheeler, Georgia

August 4, 1941

Dear Glorious,

The reason I didn't say anything about the pictures, was because I had to hurry and finish the letter, so some of the boys that were going to town could mail it. The mail goes out quicker that way. I think the pictures are very good. You look as though you were very happy and satisfied. I see no reason why you expected me to send them back. I expect "very much" to keep them.

It's so hot here tonight! The perspiration is just rolling. We are supposed to work cleaning up the barracks, as the "general" of the camp is inspecting tomorrow morning. I am taking time out to write this letter. Last Saturday our company didn't pass the inspection, so we had to work until 3:00 o'clock in the afternoon cleaning up. We'll pass tomorrow!

Our dance really came off swell Friday night. I was on the reception committee. Introducing three hundred girls to five hundred soldiers is quite a job. Some of the boys wanted nothing less than "Cleopatras" to dance with. However, everybody had a good time. The Colonel said it was the nicest dance he had attended since being in the service. Every girl received a rose bud and they thought it was a splendid gesture. The boys are still talking about what a good time they had.

I had quite a surprise today. A letter came postmarked Orono, Maine. It was from Pat. She seems to be in about the same situation I'm in. Too far from Shady Side! She also said to send you her love. But, I think she had better save it for Jack. More than likely she is.

Yesterday three of us went swimming in a lake about ten miles from camp. We stayed in the water all afternoon. Then we went in town and had dinner. I still haven't been able to get a tennis game. Guess I'll have to give it up.

Talking about you discussing the war situation. We are learning how to make war, yet you hardly ever hear a word said about the present conflict. Girls are the chief topic for conversation around here.

We are studying the 81-millimeter trench mortar now. Don't know whether we'll get a chance to fire it or not. It's nothing more than a stove pipe with a gun sight mounted on it.

There's been a rumor going around that we will leave here in three weeks. I don't think there is any truth in it. We have plenty of things yet to learn that would fill in our thirteen weeks. I wish we were leaving in three weeks. Then maybe I would see you before you become an old maid schoolteacher. That wouldn't make any difference, though. You could take any part in a show and still be the "leading lady".

Well, Buttercup, guess I had better close with that.

Love,

Howard

P.S. It isn't that I'm afraid to write about all the nice things you mentioned. I just think of them but don't seem able to put them in writing or to say them. Lots of them are there. Don't forget to write.

Love again,
Howard

Camp Wheeler, Georgia

August 16, 1941

Dear Glorious,

I am sitting right in a beehive writing this letter. The 1st sergeant had to pick me for "charge of quarters" today. All the boys are running in and out getting their mail and signing out to go in town. The company clerk is running around singing our battalion song at the top of this voice. I'm afraid I'll have to gag him if he keeps on. He is also the company's jitterbug. I don't think he's missed a dance since being here. He says the same thing about me. But, it's not true. We've been working so hard lately that I haven't felt like going out.

This U.S.O. you speak of. I'm afraid I don't know much about it. You have to explain it a little more. We hardly ever know what's going on outside. If it's for the soldiers, do a good job and we'll all love you for it.

Last Sunday six of us went to Savannah. I didn't think much of the place. All the towns down here are alike. The best part of the trip was the bathing in the ocean. We stayed in the water for three hours. Honestly, this country is terrible. We rode 180 miles and didn't see anything but the ocean. On the way home we stopped in a town for dinner. While standing in front of a restaurant trying to decide whether to eat there or somewhere else, a very lovely lady came along and wanted to buy our dinner for us. There being six of us we thought it a rather expensive gesture, so we refused. The people down here are the most wonderful I have ever come in contact with. They treat you as though you were a lifelong friend.

Yesterday was the hardest day we've had so far. In the morning we marched four miles to the mortar range. We fired the mortars, had lunch and got home about 2:30. Inspection was at 3:30; we passed that! From 4:30 till 6:00 we had a review on the week's work. Then at 7:30 we went on a ten mile hike. This was over at 11 o'clock. They fed us doughnuts and coffee, then tucked us in. There were a lot of stiff and sore boys around here this morning. They slept as long as they wanted to but <u>me</u>, I had to go on duty at 7:00 this morning. (There ain't no justice.) We have another one coming up next week. It's pretty tough on the muscles, but we do have a lot of fun.

I'm glad to hear you took cute Mimi over the hurdles in your tennis match. Just keep up the fight and maybe you'll win a cup. I'm rooting for you 100 per cent. Still trying to get a game up down here. (No success.) Guess I'll have to wait and play with you.

So Mr. Fox thinks Glen Burnie is the place for you. That should be a nice spot. You will be close to home and I think it is a nice town. I'll bet you can hardly wait until the day when you will be teaching.

It is definite that we won't leave here before the 15th of Sept. No one has any idea where we will be sent. (Camp Meade would be nice). Just when the weather will be getting nice we will have to "take off". I think cool weather would kill us all.

The Cleopatra I had at the dance was a cute black haired school teacher. Her name is "Peggy" and she's a good dancer. She's much too short for me to dance with though. I like to dance with girls tall enough for me to rest my chin on their head. It keeps them from jumping around so much. Speaking of dancing brings to mind some of those recordings you spoke of. Listen to "Yours" played by Benny Goodman. "Stardust" by Tommy Dorsey is better than Lombardo's rendition.

The discussion of girls —we talk about girls from all points of the compass. You never hear much about the girls from home. You keep those lovely thoughts to yourself. The "leading lady" —I won't comment on that anymore. I was honest with myself when I said it and still am.

I wish you would send me Pat's address so I can answer her letter. If she and Jack have split up I guess it isn't Shady Side. I also wish you "good luck and success" with your U.S.O. committee.

Love,

Howard

Camp Wheeler, Georgia
Sunday Morning
August 31, 1941

Dear Glorious,

I can't understand why you haven't written. It has been three weeks since I've heard from you. Maybe you didn't get my last letter, so many of the boys say their mail doesn't get through. I'm really starting to worry about you. So, for "Gosh sakes" answer this one right away. Will you?

Everything is kind of dead around here. Most of the boys have gone home for the holiday. There are only about fifteen of us here in the barracks, so there isn't much commotion. I expect to come home after we get to our next post. We leave here on the 16th of Sept. It's not definite, but we are supposed to get leave then. I've been thinking about all the boating and tennis I've been missing. The closest I can come to doing any of these things, is to go swimming in a two by four lake or else rent a rowboat and row around. I never was much of a rower. A bunch of us are going swimming this afternoon.

The acting non-commissioned officers received a little honor Friday. The "Colonel" presented us with a certificate stating "Due to this trainee's diligent and faithful services, I hereby present this certificate." It was almost like getting a diploma. Our battalion also had a tragedy. A corporal in Company A was killed in an auto crash Thursday night. We gave him a military funeral before sending him home. He was from Alabama. I also hear "Ole Black Grace" is dead. Gosh, it's going to seem strange at home without her around.

The battalion went out on night-problems last week. We hiked about three miles from camp and pitched tents. Then we set up our guns to throw back an enemy attack. Then the area which we occupied was gassed. We couldn't see much at first without the gas masks and with our masks on we couldn't see anything. I was going around getting a detail to relieve the men on the guns, I woke two boys [who were] asleep in their tent. While trying to crawl out the tent fell on them. It took them five minutes to get untangled. I laughed so much that I became weak and wasn't a bit of help to them. We got back to camp at midnight and found out six fellows were missing. The captain and one of the lieutenants took a truck and went back where we had been. They found the boys asleep in their tents. It was a lot of fun.

The weather is getting pretty nice now. We sleep under sheets instead of the shower. About two weeks ago everyone broke out with a heat rash. We looked like a bunch of monkeys with everybody scratching. The durn stuff sets you crazy. Most of us are over it now.

They tell me Stanley Trott was called for his physical exam. His heart was beating so fast he had to go back. He laughed at me but I guess he was nervous, too.

Well Glorious, I guess you will be teaching pretty soon. I wish you "Good Luck" and don't be too hard on the "little ones". Keep your eye peeled for spit balls, they sting like bullets. If you catch the culprit, make him stand at attention for 15 minutes.

Love,

Howard

Camp Wheeler, Georgia
September 12, 1941

Dear Glorious,

I can't understand why you didn't answer that letter. It being a silly whim of yours doesn't go. You told me once you were a practical person, so there must have been a good reason. I feel as though I did something wrong and we can't have that. If it concerns, "you and I can't ever be more than friends", forget it. I can be a pretty good friend and I can write without becoming involved. Nothing gives me more pleasure than corresponding with you, but if you think it's harmful to you in any way by writing, (Please don't!) If and when you write give me an explanation. Will you? I felt pretty rotten about the whole thing.

Well Glorious, last night we finished our thirteen weeks of basic training. We left camp at 7:00 o'clock last night and got back 7:30 this morning. First we went on a five mile hike to the field where we took up defensive positions. We had to dig in the gun positions and it was tough work. Lunch was served at midnight and work was continued until 3:00

o'clock. After that most of the boys went to sleep. We got back to camp around 7:30, ate breakfast and went to bed.

The boys are disappointed; we know for sure where our next home will be. South Carolina is the furtherest north any of us will get. Some are going to Florida and some to southern Georgia. I drew Camp Jackson, S.C. There is talk of going on maneuvers in Tennessee. If this happens, I won't get home until around Christmas. We leave Tuesday for the new camp.

I could have stayed here. They wanted me to be an M.P. However, an M.P.'s job is a tough one; they are disliked very much by the soldiers. Another thing, I've been in this state long enough, I want to have a change of scenery.

A bunch of us went to Atlanta last Sunday. I must say it is a very nice city. It's more like the cities up north. We went to a show and it wasn't too bad. (When Ladies Meet.)

Glad to hear your U.S.O. committee did all right. I should say it is for a worthy cause. There is a drive on down here now. Guess the southern folks are a bit slow going in action. But I can tell you, if all the people were like the Georgians there wouldn't be a need of the U.S.O. The different clubs and churches have been supplying entertainment for the boys ever since this camp opened.

I heard about Capt. Perry. Too bad Derwill lost in the tournament; he has plenty of time to win one. I'm enclosing a couple of pictures taken on the mortar range. Don't work too hard and be a nice teacher.

Sincerely yours,
Howard

P.S. I'll write you from S.C.

PILLROLLER TRAINING

Aspirin and a little castor oil is the antidote for a cold in the army.

Pvt. Howard C. Shenton

120th Infantry Medical Detachment,

Fort Jackson, South Carolina

January 30th, 1942

Fort Jackson, South Carolina

Sept. 20, 1941

Dear Glorious,

I have a new home and frankly, I don't think much of it. This place is entirely different from Camp Wheeler. We live in tents and they are awful. The roof is full of holes, the darn things are lopsided and you can't keep your bed clothes clean with all the dust and dirt blowing around. The only good thing is that it's a little closer to home (Shady Side).

The more I see of the army the more disgusted I get. This is a National Guard unit, 30th Division. The men act no more like soldiers than civilians. There is an absolute lack of military discipline. Everybody does pretty much as they please. Quite the contrary of what we were taught at Wheeler.

To make things more disgusting: We put in our basic training learning heavy weapons. They bring us here and of all things to put a machine gunner in —the Medical Detachment. Our thirteen weeks was just that much time wasted. I was asked to join the M.Ps, but refused so here I am a pillroller. That's what the Med. Det. is known as to the rest of the infantry. My morale is below sea level.

We leave Thursday for maneuvers in North and South Carolina. They are to last two and a half months. The boys here have just come back from Tennessee. We've heard some tall stories about these maneuvers. They say you walk your legs off and don't get much to eat. This is supposed to be the biggest maneuver of any peace time army.

So many of the boys here are getting discharges. You should see their faces when they get that discharge paper. It makes me kind of homesick.

A couple of us went to Columbia yesterday. It's a fairly nice town. But the people aren't a bit like they were in Georgia. These people don't think much of the soldiers. However, I guess the soldiers brought it on themselves. Some of these boys are pretty bad. This army's enough to drive you nuts. We had two fellows that went crazy while in Wheeler. One got a discharge and the other was in the hospital when we left. He waited until the last week there, then blew up. I think if he was sent home he would snap out of it. But, he probably has to stay in the hospital at least two months before they'll release him. He was from Mississippi and a darn good boy when he came in the army.

With these maneuvers going on I won't get home until Christmas. I'm going to try and get a fifteen day furlough then. It seems like years since I've seen Shady Side. Jack Nowell wrote me and said I hadn't missed anything by not being home this summer. But, I think he was just trying to make me feel good. Believe me; I was sure surprised to get a letter from him.

Well Legna, I suppose you are working hard now. Stick with it kid and do a good job. I'm rooting for you.

Don't know when I'll be able to write again. But you can write me as we get our mail while on maneuvers.

Truly yours,
Howard

120 Inf. Med.Det.

A.P.O. #30

Fort Jackson, South Carolina

Woods of South Carolina

October 31, 1941

Dear Glorious,

You want to know what the maneuvers are like. Personally, I don't think they are worth a damn. I think a bunch of kids playing "Cowboys and Indians" use more strategy then this army. The only thing we learned so far is how to sleep in the woods and do without food for sixteen or twenty hours. The only time you see any real action is when you've marched all night and don't get any breakfast. Then to come in contact with the enemy in the afternoon. Everybody is 'mean' as can be. Sometimes we have hand to hand fights, then. The umpires have a tough job trying to stop these fights. One unit fixed bayonets and came at us one day. They were mad about the umpires' decision. You would be surprised how lack of food and sleep can affect a man. The only big thing I can see the army is learning on these maneuvers is how to transport soldiers by truck at night in "blackouts". One night when the roads were dusty we had five trucks turn over. All of them were full of men. No one was killed and only a few hurt. It's surprising how few accidents we have on these blackouts. Some nights we ride all night long and sometimes we walk all night. I think walking is better than riding. There are so many of us in one truck that you can't breathe. But we do have some good times —when the "problem" is over and we go back to the base camp and sit

19

around the fire at night. That's when you can hear some wonderful stories. I have a new name now, all the boys in the Med.Det. call me "damn Yankee". Most of the fellows are from N.C. and you should hear us arguing about which is the better state, Maryland or N.C. I usually have six or eight against me but I hold my own. I wouldn't take a million dollars for the wonderful friendships I've found in this army. Every time things quiet down you can hear the boys calling for that Yankee to start an argument so we can have something to do. We also have some nice poker games. The boys can hardly wait now to get paid so we can get one going.

I'll have to tell you a little bit about what the Med. Det. has to do in these maneuvers. First we have sick call in the field as at the "post" every morning at 8:00 o'clock. The umpires are giving tags to pass out to the soldiers which have the nature of the wound written on it. We have to come around and dress their wounds and get them back to the "Aid Station". We've had as many as twenty a day to fix up. Nothing will make a pillroller cuss quicker than a "simulated casualty". They have broken up more than one good poker game. Once in a while we give these tags out ourselves. The goldbrickers in the Companies make a dive for them. When you get one of these tags you're out of action for a whole day and man do those boys love that. The boys from the regiment band are with us acting as litter bearers. Whenever we get a broken leg, simulated of course, we make the casualty walk within a hundred feet of the "Aid Station", then splint his leg and carry him in on the stretcher.

I have been out in the woods for two weeks now. I haven't been near a town or come in contact with any civilians. But I guess we will all go in town this afternoon, today being payday.

So you would like for me to go to school with you and beat a few bad boys. Well I don't know about that. You see I wasn't such a good boy and maybe I wouldn't feel right about it. As I told you once before you should take a few lessons from some of these old army sergeants. They would have them straightened out in no time. Don't let them get you down and when you tell them to do something make sure they do it. If they don't, there should be some way to punish them. But don't ever let them get away without punishment, or let them think they are putting something over on you. And be calm; Goodness yes, "do be calm". I think you were right when you said you take things too seriously. Simmer down and don't try so damn hard.

Well Glorious, when I got your letter, the one before this last one, I said I wasn't going to write you anymore. What that man said over the radio about soldiers needing letters is quite true. But I don't suffer from want of letters. I have enough things right here in camp to occupy my mind and to keep me amused. I'm not trying to be sarcastic or anything like that, but why don't you stop writing. Writing is a lot of trouble anyway. I never did like to do it.

The maneuvers will be over around the 1st of December. I expect to get ten days leave for Christmas.

Good bye now,
Howard

Fort Jackson, South Carolina
December 1, 1941

Dear Miss Andrews,

I am just as happy as a jay bird. To think! I'll be home in a few short weeks. There is another one of those rumors going around that we will get fifteen days leave. The trouble is some of us will have to take it before or after Christmas. I'm hoping and praying I'll get mine at Christmas.

The maneuvers ended last Thursday night. We didn't get back to Jackson till 11:00 o'clock Saturday night. I crawled into a bed the first time in ten weeks. Darn if I didn't dream I was sleeping in the bed that night. That's one dream that was true. Some of the boys had to get up and get on the floor so they could sleep. This place looked almost like home after ten weeks in the woods. I think if the maneuvers had lasted much longer a lot of boys would have been A.W.O.L. It sure was getting cold out there. The last two weeks were pretty tough. I think we walked more in those two weeks than we did the other eight. Sometimes I would fall asleep while on the march. We had a lot of work on those hikes. So many of the boys fell out with bad feet. I'm telling you some had blisters big as a half dollar. I would fall out with them, patch their feet then run for a mile to catch up with the company again. The worst hike was one we took one night in sand up to our ankles. We had walked twelve miles that day and this was a ten miler. To top this off it started raining after we finished the hike. I just unrolled my blankets fell in them and let the rain give me a massage. Sorry to hear you've been sick. Maybe a "pillroller" could have helped you. We always give patients aspirin or soda pills no matter what the trouble is. Haven't lost a man yet.

Gosh, I wish I could have seen the Navy/Notre Dame game. I've been bragging about the Navy team. The boys haven't given me a moment's peace since that game. But, did I lord it over them after Army's defeat last Saturday. I teased them about it for a while then walked away singing, "Anchors Aweigh". These boys take their football seriously. All I hear now is Duke's going to the "Rose Bowl". I keep telling them the only reason Duke got the invitation was because Navy turned it down. Damn if a bunch didn't come in the tent last night, woke me up and started another argument about football.

Ah, my little Greta Garbo, "you want to be alone". I can't understand that. I should think a little company would be swell. Why don't you "break down" and mix a little with your fellow countrymen. You don't know what they are missing. About that "one night" when I come home —maybe it wouldn't be good for me. I might run a temperature!

Glad to hear about the church. A <u>good</u> church is surely nice. It's been quite a while since I've been to a church. The last time was in Great Falls, S.C. and I was invited to dinner afterward. Well Glorious, take good care of yourself. I'll bring you a soda pill when I come home.

Sincerely yours,

Howard

P.S. Any similarity between that stamp being upside down and anything you have in mind is purely a coincidence.

Fort Jackson, South Carolina

"New Year's Eve"

Dear Glorious,

Your letter certainly came at a very good time. I guess I was a little despondent but your letter made me feel fine. All the fellows have been feeling low since we come back from leave. We haven't been doing much work as half the boys are still away and we have too much time to think about all the "good times" we are missing by not being home. They almost remind you of a bunch of "old maids". (Always squabbling over something.) If we don't get something to do pretty soon, the whole bunch will go nuts (crazy).

I celebrated Christmas on the 26th. All the boys brought cake, fruit and candy back with them. Everybody pooled his stuff and we had a party in our tent. The only thing missing was a tree and a little of the spirit. However, we had a good time.

I went to church in Washington Christmas Eve. A crowd of us went and after church we went out. (Places I mean). I didn't particularly like the service. It was an Episcopal Church. Everything was conducted with pomp and dignity and was very spectacular but the sermon wasn't so good. The preacher wasn't a very good talker. When he wanted to bring out a point he'd repeat two or three times. I almost fell asleep. I heard a good sermon in the Methodist Church last Sunday. Another fellow and I went to Columbia so I suggested going to church. Imagine!

Sorry to hear about those boys not showing up for Mrs. Chews' dinner. I didn't think the army would let you down. Maybe they were confined or something like that. Wish I could have made that dance. I went to one in camp Monday night. I tried the same thing you did. (Imagination.) It didn't work here either.

So you don't like the S.S. & Galesville crowd and you think the feeling is mutual. Maybe they don't recognize a nice person when they see one. I can! Perhaps you were incognito. Not fixing your hair different now, are you? It was a little damp last time I saw it. No Glorious, I'm only kidding. To tell the truth you're just a little bit different from the rest of them. You don't drink or smoke and raise h-ll like they do. But I guess you have just as much fun. Not getting too personal, I hope.

Glorious, if I seemed unappreciative of your "present", please forgive me. At the time I wanted one thing from you and it wasn't cigarettes. I just forgot myself. "Thanks, buttercup."

I went to see a "big name" band last night. They played "This Love of Mine". I thought it a swell tune and there's no "ruts" around either. Try and hear it sometime.

"A Happy New Year"

Yours,

Howard

Fort Jackson, South Carolina
January 13, 1942

Dear Glorious,

This army is really stepping to a war time cadence. Every hour of the day is taken up with drilling and lectures. I like it, though. This outfit can stand plenty of training. I've learned more first-aid in the past two weeks than I did in six months previous. First-aid is very interesting when you get into it. I worked in the infirmary last week and experience is the best teacher, after all. I learned a lot about bandaging and applying dressings. One of the "doctors" is having a heck of a time. The army puts out stuff for us to be lectured on and learn. He says it's all obsolete and disagrees with everything he has to teach us. He tells us to do it the army way then gives his ideas on the subject with so much disgust in his tone, we have to laugh at him. The "ole boy" is a good doctor, too. The discipline is more strict now. We have to check out, state where we are going and be back by midnight. Of course, I realized all hard working people should be in bed by 12:00 but sometimes it's hard to get back to camp that early. Then if you're a little late it's extra duty for a couple of days.

"If imagination is too vivid then the real thing doesn't amount to much." That sounds like you, but that's not the way I meant it. I can't imagine anybody like you, anyway. Not that you are so different but the way I see you. Sounds like I'm going off the deep end but while I am touching this subject I'll tell you what it was I wanted when you gave me the cigarettes. I wanted to "kiss" you, of course. Those "dry runs" aren't so good where there's deep feeling. Glorious, you remind me of the "moon". ("Pretty as can be, yet so damn far out of reach.") Someday I'll get me a rocket ship and climb up there. Don't worry about me getting hurt if I fall. I'll be packing a parachute.

Guess I'd better write about something else. The weather has been very cold down here, too. We've had a little snow and sleet. Too bad little Ivan [Glorious's Model A Ford] can't take the cold. Maybe you'd better get him a fur coat. The 44th Division was transferred from Fort Dix, New Jersey to some camp in Louisiana. They traveled in trucks and two boys froze to death riding in them. They camped at Jackson last Saturday night and pulled out early Sunday morning. We will probably be maneuvering around in two or three months' time. I wouldn't care if we started right now. I'm just about as ready now as I'll ever be.

Enclosing some snapshots taken after Christmas furlough.

Good luck to you in your "first-aid" course.

Yours,

Howard

P.S. If you think your last letter was silly, make them all silly. I thought it very nice.

Love,

Howard

Fort Jackson, South Carolina
January 24, 1942

Dear Glorious,

Your choice of writing to me instead of marking the test was certainly a break for me. I was beginning to think maybe you didn't get my last letter. So my last letter was very, very. I hope it wasn't "much, too much". Getting a letter from you is the best thing that happens to me down here.

So you don't like living with a roommate. Gosh, Legna! [Legna is Glorious' middle name —"Angel" spelled backwards —made up by her mother]. You almost have me believing you're a "female hermit". Maybe you should take up jitterbugging, if your roommate likes swing music. Then you two could get together and have a "jam session" to pass away monotonous time. I'd like to see *you* cutting a rug. Speaking of music, right now I am listening to the "Hit Parade". Remember that rainy Saturday night? It was a bigger 'hit" with me then. (Anyhow <u>something</u> hit me.) I'm still down for the count.

The army is still putting us through the "paces". I haven't had first-aid classes lately. We've been doing small problems in the field two and three days a week. Thank goodness we don't have to stay out overnight. One day we missed the kitchen truck and didn't get any lunch. (I made a short reconnaissance and "rounded up" me a store.) Everything was lovely after that. Since we've been on these problems I've been staying with the Aid-Station. This eliminates all walking, which is nice too.

I don't know about being transferred yet. If I am I won't leave Fort Jackson. There is a training cadre being made up to take care of the new recruits. There's a possibility I will be selected for this.

Don't work too hard with the exams and do take care of your throat. I had a teacher in Baltimore that lost her voice one day. She had a h-ll of a time. We enjoyed it. Imagine!

Was that a question mark after "me" in the end of your letter or a slip of the pen? Sure looked like a question mark. I do, Glorious. Definitely!

Love,

Howard

P.S. If you were my teacher I would bring you an apple every day.

Howard

January 30, 1942

Dear Glorious,

I knew you should have taken care of that sore throat. You must have been very sick, I'm sorry! Just think, I missed an opportunity to show you how good a pill-roller I've become. Aspirin and a little castor oil is the antidote for a cold in the army. So Derwill was good to you. That's an accomplishment for a brother. Drilk's a pretty good boy, though. His sister's a swell person too!

Today has really been tough. We went on an eighteen mile jaunt. Everybody had to walk from the "Colonel" down to a private. The boys are dead tonight. This is the first long hike we've pulled for a month. The band was playing to receive us when we came back. The "funeral march" would have been very appropriate. Tomorrow we have a parade. This makes the second this week. I hate parades; you have to stand at attention too long. Marching to music is nice though. Everybody usually stays in step then.

The way things are shaping up I don't think I'll ever be transferred. There were vacancies in a heavy weapons Co. in our regiment. Some high ranking officer tried to transfer the pill-rollers with heavy weapons training. It was knocked in the head some way and the vacancies were filled by new recruits.

Glorious, you want to know, "How I think of you." Well, that's quite a confession for me. The first thing I remember when thinking of you is your face. It has a pair of blue grey eyes, which makes the smile pretty because they laugh. These eyes are also very serious and determined

29

looking. Especially when that chin is stuck out. The face shows good and strong character. This is topped by light-brown hair which is always being washed. You have cute bangs but keep them piled on top with a ribbon. (Usually blue). Or is it pink? Then I think of you as a person who doesn't make friends easily but is a good friend to have. A girl that doesn't drink or smoke and one you would be proud of. She's practical but worries too much about the future. I admire her sense of humor and good conversation. Then I think of how I'd like to hold her tight and kiss her. This is where I stop thinking. Glorious, I don't know whether this makes sense or not. I've never explained thoughts like these before. Don't worry about me sharing with anyone the things you say in your letters. I value them too much to share them with anyone.

Whitey wrote me. He and Herbert seemed to have had a good time in New York. Personally, I hate the place. Too many people. He sent me a picture of a "cute little de-icer" named Dorothy Johnson. (First time I've ever heard a girl called "de-icer".)

Too bad you couldn't see Ellsworth when he was home on furlough. I'm just hoping we will get a furlough in a couple of months. It seems like six since I've been home.

George and I were thinking of going to a show tonight. "How Green Was My Valley" doesn't sound so good though. Don't know whether I've told you about George or not. He's my foster-mother. Tucks me in bed and gets me up for "reveille". Gives me h-ll when I stay out late and always wants to know where I'm going when I leave. He's a Pennsylvania Dutchman, a swell fellow.

Tell me what it is you want me to do for you in your next letter. Stay out of drafts; I can prove there's nothing like a draft. Don't have many colds, either.

Love,
Howard

February 8, 1942

Dear Glorious,

I saw the most wonderful sight in my life yesterday. The "30ᵗʰ Division" paraded for the "Divisional Commander" and his staff. It was a great spectacle! The regimental colors flying alongside "Old Glory" and each regiment's band playing its theme song as their regiment passed the reviewing stand was beautiful. Everybody was in the best of military form. Seeing all these men in uniform and knowing what they stand for, made you feel glad you were a part of it. (Even though we darn near froze waiting for the parade to get under way.)

We are still maneuvering in the field three days a week. When this first started we had it fairly easy. Now every time the troops set up a new line we set up the aid-station. The sergeant will pick out a spot for the station, then we set up the station and camouflage everything including ourselves. Just about this time the Colonel will come around, inspect everything then tell us to put the stuff back on the truck and take up a new position. (We set the aid-station up five times one day.) All of this is dull and monotonous when you are simulating warfare. In actual battle it would be a little different; at least you wouldn't mind camouflaging. Still can't see why the aid-station should be set up. Before, we just opened one of the medical chests and left it on the truck. Then when the troops moved we could take off after them without losing any time. Besides we never have any patients.

How about your last letter? I thought it was all right. I still "love you", there wasn't anything in the letter that could make me feel differently. Glorious, don't worry about the outcome of our affair. I know you are a practical person and think before you do a thing. The "outcome" is too far away to think about yet. Writing like we've been doing lately may be foolish, but if so, then "foolishness" sure gives me a "wonderful feeling". Another thing, all these letters you write and then tear them up. I can't believe the letters are that terrible, especially with you "pushing the pen". Think of all the stationery wasted.

So you are reading "Dry Guillotine", terrible heading: don't you think? I'll read it if I run across it. I'm reading "The Sun is My Undoing" by Marguerite Steen. It's kind of raw too. One thing about it is, it's too long a story (1200 pages). If the Colonel keeps coming around and tells us to take up a new position, I'll never finish it.

Tell your roommate I said "thanks" for sending her love. She had better save it for someone who will appreciate it more. I'll send you my love and you can give her any part of it you don't want. Bet she has Glen Miller's recording of "Blues in the Night". It's sure a hit tune down here.

Glorious, I may just as well keep Whitey's girl's pictures. I've never seen her and don't know anything about her. Whitey's alright! I always thought he was a pretty good boy. Let's don't argue about it.

Love, (all my love)

Howard

February 15, 1942

Dear Glorious,

This has been a very trying week-end. All week-end leaves and passes were canceled. An order came out Friday saying everyone in the 120th had to be inoculated for yellow-fever Sunday morning. When the boys heard this there was a grand rush for the telephone. These fellows had planned to go home and with something like this happening it was a terrible let-down. Honestly, if someone mentions a shot in the arm to me I'll go crazy. I don't think there is a disease we aren't immune from [to] now. Next we'll be taking shots for bullet-poisoning. Well, the boys who didn't get to go home were disappointed. So most of them went to town last night and did a little drinking. This morning there was a lot of sick boys in camp especially after being in the hospital while waiting to be <u>shot</u>. Guess the smell was too much for them. It didn't bother me so much. I went to town this afternoon and took in a show and had dinner. Then went to church!

Glorious, I don't agree with you at all when you say your letters are boring. I'd be interested in anything you say. But . . . here's what they do to me. First you write me and the letter is wonderful. Kind of makes me believe the feeling I have for you is mutual. Then, maybe two or three letters later (We are on "letter time" now) I'll get a letter and it's just like letting the air out of a tire. That's what I feel like, a flat tire. The letter you wrote me when you were sick was worth all the rest put together. (Don't worry I've burned it.) I would still rather get a letter from you then eat three meals a day. From now on we'll write about the weather and the practical things in life. (Mushy letters sound silly any way, I guess.) <u>Please</u>

33

don't misinterpret this paragraph. I want to write you and receive your letters. That flat tire is fixable.

Tomorrow is a big day. We go out on a three day problem. This means "the sky for a ceiling" for two nights. Hope it's raining in the morning; maybe we won't have to go. The boys are asking "Little David" to send it down. (He's the soldiers' rain-god.)

The Pennsylvania Dutch are pretty nice people. I went to town with one today. He was in my platoon at Wheeler. They put him in the 118th up here. Doesn't drink, smoke or like girls but a swell friend. He differs from George in one thing. George plays poker once in a while. We really had a party yesterday afternoon. George's Ma sent him a box, roast chicken, cake and candy.

Legna, the bugle is sounding off (Taps). Write me and remember, don't waste any stationery.

Good Luck,

Howard

P.S. It's probably just as well you didn't tell your roommate about the love. I don't think I know the meaning of the word.

Howard

February 20, 1942

Dear Glorious,

I stepped out of line in my last letter, "I'm sorry". Maybe it's me that is moody. I'm not angry with you and please don't think I ever was. A letter from you is a grand event for me, regardless of its contents. Just think of the pleasure you would deprive the boys if you didn't write.

Whenever one of them brings the mail to the tent I always know when there is a letter from you. They say, "No mail, Howard. G. Andrews didn't write you." Right then I hold out my hand. After ten minutes of fuming and fussing, I'll get it. Seems they can't understand why a girl would write me. Of course, I have never tried to make them understand. Glorious, you could write me a thousand letters and never mention the word love, I would still appreciate them. No more "flat tires". Your last letter put me back on the beam and cleared the fog.

Remember "Little David", our rain god? He was good to us. It rained Monday & Tuesday so we didn't go on our overnight problem. But we weren't idle. Classes in first-aid are still in order and gas-mask drill is always good for an hour of unscheduled time.

Don't know positive about the connection of being inoculated and shipped out. I was quoting one of our "Lieutenants". However there seems to be an awful rush to immunize the men against disease. Some of the men are taking shots, two at a time. I worked in the infirmary today and a lot of these "two at one timers" hit the dirt after being shot. (Sounds almost like gunnery).

You shouldn't stay up so late to write letters. I don't blame your roommate for wanting the lights out. Think of your health, Buttercup.

I'm sorry about that last letter. Try and forget I ever wrote it.

Love,
Howard

February 27, 1942

Dear Glorious,

The weather today is cloudy and damp. Your letter arrived and the stamp wasn't upside down. Don't mind this pitter, patter, Legna. Tonight I am a very happy boy. Five day furloughs are being granted to the men from Pennsylvania and Maryland. Mine starts next Friday (6th) and "Buttercup" I'm coming home.

If I sing "Maryland, My Maryland" one more time today, the boys will go nuts. There is one thing I am not forgetting and that is "this army". Anything can happen between now and next Friday to keep me from going but it's swell just thinking about coming home. If everything goes alright I should be in S.S. Saturday noon (7th).

Life has been quite dull for me the past week. I've been on K.P. duty; we pull it a week at a time here. You go on at 6:00 in the morning and get off 7:00 or 7:30 at night. One thing about this job is you get all you want to eat and I might say anything you want to eat. The boys in my tent fared pretty well. I kept them supplied with fruit. My locker looked like a fruit stand. I did get a break though. The regiment went on an overnight problem Monday and it rained that night. The boys looked and felt miserable Tuesday when they came in. The kitchen force stayed at the Fort. The meals were cooked here then carried to the field on trucks. I was all set to do a little "gibing" with the boys when they came in but they took one look at me and said, "Don't open your damn mouth." Guess I'm sympathetic; I just sighed and walked away. It isn't often I pass up an opportunity to do a little ribbing.

Yes, I saw the picture "Johnny Eager". He was a hard man, McGee. I thought it pretty good. The "love bug's sting" was too much for him though, poor fellow. I figured he would break down sooner or later. It's a wonder the army hasn't found a vaccine for this disease. (We are still taking shots.)

The way you used the word "visiting" sounded like you were disgusted. What's the matter, Legna? Don't you like your colleagues? I don't know how teachers act together but it seems to me in social life or contact with outsiders they don't act natural. They always say the right thing at the right time and are much too pleasant. Don't take this serious, Glorious; I don't know anything about teachers. Do you stamp your foot and point your finger when you get mad in class, like Miss Ethel does or did? Boy, it was like a storm coming when she did that. (I always had my umbrella.)

What in the world has happened to your pal, Jack? I haven't heard from him since Christmas.

Don't worry about finding something to entertain you. It will come along sometime.

Love,

Howard

P.S. The boys asked me what the L. stood for. I told them "lovely". They left me with a blank look. See you soon.

Totch

March 11, 1942

Dear Glorious,

The trip back to camp wasn't too bad. I met some boys on the train from my "division". We had a fairly pleasant time. Arrived in Columbia at 3:30 Tuesday morning and made camp in time to have a fire going for my bunkmates when they got up. The mornings are a little chilly yet. George came dragging in at 5:30. I told him he should have spread his ears and flown back. Uncle Sam is likely to draft him any day now as a dive bomber.

When I called you from the station Monday evening, there were many things I wanted to say but . . . as usual when I talk to you my mind doesn't work right. I told you about calling Pat but forgot to tell you she is thinking of getting married. (If our corporal doesn't hurry and get hitched we will have to put him in a strait jacket. He's to get married Thursday and darned if he isn't a nervous wreck now.) Then Glorious, I wanted to say, "I love you". I thought about saying it but didn't know how to go about bringing the words forth.

The fellows down here wouldn't believe that I could be speechless at any time. I said I was sorry about you being awakened but that wasn't the truth. The sound of your voice made me feel so glad that I wouldn't have cared if the whole neighborhood has been disturbed. Miss Ethel said you needed lots of sleep. "Your Mama is right!" (Quoting from the song, Blues in the Night).

The army is teaching me how to drive a truck now. For the next two weeks I go to school from 8:00 in the morning till 11:00. I don't expect to be a truck driver but by going to this school I'll get a government permit.

Then in case of an emergency I can drive a truck with "my little permit". The first thing we learned was we didn't know how to drive (the army way). We have nothing special to do in the afternoon. Yesterday the top-kick almost went crazy trying to find something for us to do. (Eight of us are going to school). Today he had a schedule all mapped out. I still found time to write you with interruptions of course.

Gosh Legna! Two letters from you in one day. Why I can hardly believe it. It's wonderful! Your last letter came in the evening's mail. Those little ones were swell. I wasn't as far away as you thought when you wrote the "first little letter". We had company at home so about eight-thirty (8:30) they sent me to the store to get some cigarettes. I went to Luther's [store] but on my way back I thought I would ride past the Rural Home Hotel and maybe I'd get a glimpse of you passing by. However, I didn't, that's when I thought of calling you from Union Station. Glorious, that call was worth every cent it cost and more besides. Sure I would have wanted you to see me off but trains pulling out give one a very empty feeling. Don't you think? It would have been better having you see Glenn Miller's show with me. That was something we could have enjoyed. So I scared you for a minute Sunday. Don't ever be scared of me, Glorious, not even for a minute. My control is perfect even if I can't think of what I want to say.

Did I say your hat wasn't nice looking? My error. Most women's hats look as though they've been run over by a truck. Must take an awful strong imagination or else a fantastic mind to create some of the styles I've seen. I'd say your fur trimmed bonnet was a bit on the conservative side. I was only kidding you.

39

Tomorrow night the "First Baptist Church" of Columbia is inviting thirty boys over for supper. Entertainment and a girl companion for each boy. For the 120th Med. Det. Exclusively. I didn't realize we carry so much weight around the city of Columbia, especially with the church.

Glorious, I didn't tell you over the phone but here goes in writing. "I love you with all my heart".

Love,
Howard

March 19, 1942

Dear Glorious,

School was called off today so in between the "top-kick's" whistle blowing I'll attempt to answer your letter. He will blow us out not less than three times an hour, maybe more. One of these days I'm going to hide that whistle so we can have a little peace.

Yesterday was pretty tough for the students of the truck school. We had a stiff eye examination and a test to see how steady your nerves are. My eyesight was perfect but when I was handed a ball of different colored strings and told to pick out a red and green, I thought they had me. Then the sergeant picked out a couple of strings and asked me what they were. I made a perfect score. We have a written exam coming up tomorrow, then we drive the trucks. If I didn't know what this course was for I'd think we were going "in" for aviation.

I'll take a chance and answer that question about the church entertainment. I had a nice time but the feminine companion for each boy was the "bunk". There were fifty boys and about twenty girls. We

40

played a game called "squirrel in the cage". The girls (squirrels) were caged up all evening.

I don't know who Pat's fiancé is, she didn't' tell me. While on the subject of matrimony, Speedy or Breezy as you call her is getting married. Everybody seems to be taking the high dive. (Must be seasonal.)

Buttercup, I didn't tell the boys I was speechless when facing you. I said they wouldn't believe it's possible for me to be speechless anywhere at any time.

Wish I could go to the dance with you Friday night, "June Bug". However I'm afraid the chaperone job wouldn't work. More than likely someone would have to chaperone me. I'd like to dance with you and hold you so tight till people would think it was someone dancing with their shadow. Schoolteachers and dancing shadows wouldn't go well together. (Most unconventional.) I'd still like to dance with you, Legna, even if we dance a yard stick apart.

Bob Wilde wrote me again last week. I was surprised to hear from him so soon. I think Bobby's a little lonesome and homesick. He thinks when this "mining course" is over, they'll ship him out. Sure wish I was in the Navy. If inspections and parades would win the war we'd have the Japs and Hitler beat to death by now.

Glorious, you didn't enjoy the week-end I was home any more than I did. If I could have one week-end every two months like that, army life or any kind of life would be easy and wonderful.

Honey, it's ten-thirty (10:30) and we have a first-aid class coming up. Goodbye now.

Love,

Howard

P.S. Send me any kind of pictures. Ones of you preferred. Howard

41

March 27, 1942

Dear Glorious,

I wanted to answer your letter right away but I sprained my thumb playing volleyball the other day. It was so swollen I couldn't hold a pen. A great game, two sprained fingers, a sprained thumb and our faces were all scratched. These soldiers must get rough before they can have any fun. The boys at the infirmary though we had a free-for-all. It was, sort of.

"Culp versus Andrews" must have been a great battle. Personally, I dislike Rev. Culp. George Rogers' funeral brought about that feeling. I was mad enough that day to straighten Mr. Culp's crooked mouth. Rev. Culp might make a good Holy Roller but as a "minister" of a church, he's a "flop". Glorious, you shouldn't entertain thoughts of dying. Wait until you get around 70 or 80 years old. It would be more becoming to you then.

P on my soul, Legna, your last letter is a "masterpiece". Can't for the life of me see why you thought it wasn't fit for the mail. I hope you didn't chew all your fingernails. (Try gum sometime, it's better for the digestive system.)

Life is rather dull here now. I've finished Truck School and passed A.1. Out of a hundred boys, twenty-eight got their permits. Next week I'll go out with the aid station again. There is more talk of us leaving Fort Jackson. I think we are going to Tennessee this time. We've been going to every state on the Atlantic Coast so now it's Tennessee. I don't think we are going anywhere. Looks to me like we are here for the duration.

I was invited to another church party Wednesday night but didn't go. A bunch of us went to Columbia to see a stage show instead. The game "Squirrel in the Cage" isn't a thing like Post Office. That is I don't think so, but I never played Post Office. It was mentioned that night at church but the chaperones were in favor of the squirrel game.

Glorious, it's hard for me to say what I think of you. The words kind of gang up on me and won't come out. I will say, to me, you are an intelligent, conservative and practical person, maybe a bit too practical, but it's alright. You are stubborn in your convictions, which I think is a good thing. I do know I love you and you are the only girl I've ever loved. Why? Well there are reasons, of course, but I don't think love is something that can be analyzed. The "promise" is out. Glorious, I couldn't promise that. Why don't you ask me to cut off my arm or something like that? It would be the same as *that "promise"*.

Your roommate should read the "Advice to the Lovelorn" column in the paper. She must have a highly-geared mind to switch her thoughts and intentions so quick.

What was it you started to say about "Speedy"? (Windy and Breezy as you call her.) She's probably married by now.

Hope the dance came off alright. Don't be too strict a chaperone. Listen for a new tune on the Hit Parade called "I Remember You".

Bye Buttercup,

Love,

Howard

April 1, 1942

Dear Glorious,

Hope my last letter explained why I didn't write you sooner. I wrote Whitey's letter before spraining my thumb. The darn thing is still sore and a little swollen.

The southern papers gave your blizzard plenty of write-ups. Outside of a few cool mornings, the weather has been like summer here. Which is a good thing because tomorrow we move out of our semi-tents and huts. "Uncle" is going to build us barracks to live in. While the building is going on we will live in squad-tents. (With all the conveniences, "running cold water when it rains").

The cookies came yesterday. (Today they are gone.) The boys and I really enjoyed them. Sure was swell of the little girls. Mary Lee must be quite a cook. She's a sweet kid. One of my girl friends. I'll have to send her an Easter card for the cookies. They tasted something like some I ate at your house. Toll-house cookies I believe you called them.

Saw a good show last night, "The Male Animal". Don't miss it, you will laugh yourself sick. The song "I Remember You" wasn't on the Hit Parade. It's a new song that I've picked to make the H.P. Maybe it will be on next week.

The word you and Derwill argued about is "bo-hog". A fine piece of slang. No one could say it like a soldier though.

We have a new "medical officer" on our staff. He is a psychiatrist, one of the seemingly craziest people I have ever met. He can ask his patients some of the darnedest questions. I think he is a Jew but I've already named him "The Mad Russian". It doesn't make any difference whether you have athletes foot or a stomach ache. He will always ask if you or your family had hay fever or asthma. With all this questioning you'd think the infirmary was a courtroom instead of a place for sick people.

Your spring afternoon bumming around must have been pleasant. I like to bum around too, on spring afternoons. Shady Side is so pretty in the spring.

The paragraph in your letter about "our point" reminds me of some poem I've heard. I only remember one line. "The dashing waves splashed high; On a rock-bound coast." (Two lines) Do you know what poem it is? Funny but I just can't remember more of it or even the title. Miss Ethel probably knows what it is. So "the point" is washing away. Guess it can't take the consequences. (I can though).

George is running around here like an old woman, packing his stuff for the move tomorrow. Any day now I expect him to start a flower garden around our tent. A great guy but he has funny, or I might say peculiar ideas sometimes. I'm always teasing him and he gets mad and starts cussing (mildly). One day a bunch of us were getting on the bus going to town. I said something to him and he started swearing. Just when he finished he looked around and saw a girl sitting on the bus. The poor fellow was so embarrassed he like to dropped in his tracks. Took about two days for him to get over it.

Keep on writing me. I'll take time to answer! We aren't playing volleyball now. We bursted [*sic*] the ball.

Love,
Howard

Fort Jackson, South Carolina

April 9, 1942

Dear Glorious,

Your imagination isn't working so good. I'm not angry with you. Just the contrary. My thoughts of you have been *and are* quite pleasant. I've had plenty of time for thinking lately too.

Glorious your letter didn't come until this evening and there isn't time for you to get an answer by Saturday. I'm sorry if you are disappointed or was disappointed Saturday. Just because Uncle mails our letters free is no reason why I should write you every day. I can think of lots of better reasons. I don't think it would work. I would probably go stale and you would be bored. I couldn't think of anything to write about every day. Can you?

So you're an "advisory to the lovelorn" now. I think you told your roommate right. If it's true that the boy loves her. How about the roommate, she seems to be a sort of "fickle person" according to one of your letters. It would be a shame if he were to marry someone else and loved her (Roomy). Think of the girl he's to marry. He couldn't very well love both of them. Could he? I think you gave some good advice, "My Little Lady". I'm coming around to see you about a month before I get married and see what you have to offer.

"The Landing of the Pilgrims", nice poem. Did you recognize it or did you ask Miss Ethel? Wonder how I remember that first line and not the title or the rest of it. It did bring out a "point" anyway.

A couple of the boys and I went to Columbia Sunday for "church". The church was jammed and packed. The minister wanted to know where everybody had been since last Easter. He told them to come around next Sunday; they could wear the same hats and outfits. He preached on "Immortality". After church we had dinner and went to a show. The show was great, "The Fleets In". My song "I Remember You" was taken from it. Has it hit the Hit Parade yet? Since we've been living in tents I haven't heard a radio. When the show was over we sat in the park and watched the Easter Parade.

I started writing this letter in my tent but rain came up and drove me out. I'm in the Service Club and someone just played "Stardust" on the juke box. Gosh! That's a pretty tune.

The Med. Det. is on the carpet. The "Division commander" is anxious to know how much his pillrollers know about militarism in general. Today we had exams on Military Courtesy, Field Sanitation and Chemical Warfare. They were fairly simple. We have four more coming up tomorrow. Everybody is taking them, from the top-kick down. If and when we pass these exams we take a surgeons' technician course. No doubt, we'll all come out doctors. Looks like my school days are just starting. But it's alright with me, I like school. Anything, just to be doing something different to relieve the monotony.

Wish you had climbed aboard Ivan and rushed to S.C.; I could have admired your bonnet. If I could have seen you "Darling" your bonnet would have looked like a "halo". Too bad I wasn't home at Easter. I would have enjoyed helping with the dishes. After a week's K.P. dishwashing is a minor chore.

Love,
Howard

I'll write you next week so you'll get the letter on Saturday at S.S. even if your letter doesn't come on time. Love, Howard.

April 13, 1942

Dear Glorious,

Your letter was a surprise. Writing while riding in a car must be quite a job. It was sweet of you and I could read every word of it. I guess Maryland is blooming now. This is the time of year when Shady Side is <u>most</u> beautiful. South Carolina according to your clipping and what I read in the paper is supposed to be pretty. I haven't seen any of its beauty so far. We soldiers don't get around much. I'll still take "My Maryland".

Glorious I thought of writing a "thank you" to the girls for the cookies. Somehow I haven't been keeping up with my correspondence lately. "Thanks" for the reminding, "I just wrote them". If it hadn't been for you I'd probably have kept putting it off and never gotten around to it. I couldn't think of any phase of camp life that would be interesting to the girls though. Think they'll be disappointed? I can't have Mary Lee "let down" like that. Maybe you can think of something. If you do, let me know. I'll write and tell them about it.

We finished our exams last week and quite a few didn't pass. Those boys are going to school now to brush up on all the subjects they failed. You should have heard the language around here this morning when they "took off" for school. The rest of us stayed home and caught detail all day. Some General is coming to visit us tomorrow and everything must be in "top-shape". (General Lear) He is the guy who made the boys walk 15 miles for yoo-hooing some girls.

"I Remember You" made the Hit Parade last week. It was #8. Did you hear it? If you did let me know how you liked it. I saw Captains of the Clouds about three weeks ago. I enjoyed it a lot. "Cagney sure gets around the block".

Seems I have a couple of champions in Luther and Amy. I didn't know I was such a nice boy!

I'm sorry to hear about Miss Ethel being sick. She's almost my favorite teacher.

Glorious you said you wanted a Caduceus. I'm sending you one along with a 120th insignia pin. Hope you like it.

Well I have another letter to write this week so it will get to S.S. by Saturday. Maybe I'd better sign off.

Legna (angel backwards or frontwards, it's "angel" to me.) I think about you too, an awful lot. When you write and say you love me, I get kind of weak inside. Is that good or bad? It's a wonderful feeling!

All My Love,
Howard

April 15, 1942

Dear Glorious,

If you don't get this letter Saturday I will be very disappointed.

This has been one of the longest days I've spent in the army. Three of us went out with the regiment this morning on a problem. We were riding of course. After we found where the Command Post was placed, we went for a ride. The aid-station is always near the C.P. Only today we didn't take the aid-station out. Most of the boys are going to school and

49

what was left was put on detail before the Med.Det. knew the regiment was going out. There were only three of us around when the order came down. We represented the Med.Det. in the field today. (Fine representation) Since we didn't have enough men to set up the aid-station, we toured the country. With ten-minute breaks every hour for Pepsi-Colas. Around eleven o'clock we drove up to the C.P. and found out the regiment was going into camp. None of us liked this because we knew our top-kick would put us to work in the afternoon. He did! We had litter drill. A pillroller hates drilling with a litter next to "pulling" K.P. I thought the afternoon would never pass. I forgot to mention it; we did have one patient this morning. His tummy was hurting; he had been operated on for appendicitis. I threw a bandage around his middle to give him support and to keep his clothes from irritating the incision. (Doctor Kildare.)

Tomorrow we have the afternoon off. A crowd of us are going to Columbia to see Tony Pastor's Orchestra on the stage. Tony played for Artie Shaw a long time ago, before Artie gave up his first band. He has most of Shaw's old band and it's pretty good.

There's a U.S.O. show at our theatre tonight. They give us one about every other week and there are some mighty fine acts. These shows are about the best work the U.S.O. does.

The weather has been ideal for tennis. I suppose you have been playing some. Wish I could get in a few sets now and then. It's been such a long time since I've played. I'd probably have to learn the game over again. Since we bursted the volleyball the boys have gone in for baseball. I must say it's much better for the anatomy then volleyball. You know Legna, tennis is a great game. If it hadn't been for you and me playing, we wouldn't be so well acquainted. It sure was a good excuse for me to come over to the Rural Home. I had a better excuse or reason but you didn't know about it —at first anyway. Wish I could give the top-kick an excuse to go to the Rural Home now. But he wouldn't understand. He's immune to love. (Poor fellow.)

Hope Mama's cold is better.

I'm not promising a letter for next Saturday and "please" don't be disappointed.

I love you, Buttercup!

Howard

April 18, 1942

Dear Glorious,

Your crack about being glad I finally wrote to you wasn't so good. I answered your letter the very day it came. It will probably be a week or more before I will be able to write you again. Six of us are detailed to the firing range next week. We leave tomorrow afternoon and won't get back until Friday or Saturday. The range is located about twenty miles out from camp. We won't receive any mail or be able to mail any letters while out there. Our job is to take care of anyone that gets hurt but I hope we get a chance to do some shooting. I won't mind it so much then. Wish I hadn't passed my exams, then I'd be going to school instead of the range. The top-kick either dislikes me or likes my work. He sure sees that I keep busy.

Glorious do you realize what you said when you said I just didn't love you? That hurt me. How do you arrive at such conclusions? Is it because I would go stale writing to you every day? Get some other reason; Buttercup, that one is no good. Darling, I love you so much it hurts and you know I do. You are the one person in my life whom I can say I love. There never was anyone else and I don't think there ever will be. Don't go saying things like that. It sounds like you are trying to talk me into believing I don't love you. I started to answer your letter right away but thought I'd better think the situation over. I stepped out of line once and promised I wouldn't do it again. You said you could write every day and yet you didn't answer your Hood roommate's letter. (How about "you" now?) Maybe this is different though. Please Glorious, I do love you and I'm sure you know it.

Wish I could see your yellow and black outfit. No doubt it would knock my eye out. You had a white tennis outfit that brought my eyes out. It's a wonder I ever returned the ball playing with you. Legna, you could wear a burlap sack and still get a "reading" from me. Don't spill any cocktails on your yellow and black suit at the reception. The stain is awfully hard to get out. You've been to so many weddings lately till I bet you could perform the ceremony yourself. No, I'm not contemplating marriage soon but I'll still come around and seek your advice before diving off the deep-end. It's too bad about Phyllis but she did find out the boy didn't love her. I figured <u>that</u> as soon as you told me about the affair. There isn't anything like finding out the truth though.

Glorious you can write me while I'm on the range. I'll get my mail when I come in next week.

Yours,

Howard

P.S. You can call me Sweetheart or anything you like. It's bound to sound good coming from you.

Love,

Howard

Fort Jackson, South Carolina
April 28, 1942

Dear Glorious,

We came off the range yesterday. One of the sergeants brought the mail to us Saturday. I wanted to answer your letter and send it in then but there wasn't time. We were scheduled to stay out until Wednesday afternoon, but something came up. We are having all our property checked, they are taking up all but necessary clothing and equipment. Looks as though we might go on a little trip. I'm in a traveling mood so it can't happen too soon.

The 120th moved into their new barracks yesterday. I got in just in time to pick up my bed and lug it a ¼ of a mile to the barracks. The barracks are really swell after living in tents for the past month. My bed is excellently located, right beneath a double window with a good view of the road that runs in front of all the mess halls Every once in a while though soot blows in the windows from their chimneys.

It was kind of dull on the range but I didn't mind that so much. I stayed in the aid-station while the other pillrollers went on the firing line. The Lt. and I slept most of the time. We had a small epidemic of the mumps and sent seven boys into the hospital. One boy was shot through the chest, accidentally of course. According to the latest reports he is getting over it very nicely. It was so cold out there we couldn't sleep. The days were hot and the nights cold. We had the ambulance to bring us more blankets from camp. One of the cooks kept me supplied with hot coffee at night. (In exchange for a few aspirin.) I wanted to go up on the firing line and shoot some but couldn't get away from the aid-station. Lt. Pomper, the psychiatrist, was the medical officer with us. We psycho-analyzed one another; I still think he is a little crazy. He gets some of the boys so "het-up" questioning them till they start crying.

Norman Linton wrote me. He is at Fort Logan, Colorado. I didn't even know about him being drafted. We both agree in what we think of the army.

There was a shake-down in the Med.Det. Monday. Seems three of our sergeants went on a binge Saturday night and forgot to report for "Reveille" Sunday. The Major confined them to the Co. area for seven days. Imagine our sergeants setting such an example for their men. If it had been a Pvt, "The Major" would have been on his back yet. From all reports the whole Med.Det. went on the loose. Even George put one on; he won't talk about it, guess he's kind of ashamed. Maybe it's a good thing for me, I wasn't in camp.

Glorious, of course I don't know whether I get all your letters but I get quite a few. What's wrong though? Does it seem as though I've missed a few points or you don't get an answering letter?

I can't sing the song, "I've got a girl and she has freckles on her nose." (Don't know the words or the music.) I didn't think your freckles were so prominent.

So Ivan is giving you a little trouble. I thought you had him well-trained.

Goodbye "freckle nose".

Love,
Howard

Fort Jackson, South Carolina

April 29, 1942

Dear Glorious,

We have the afternoon off so I'm answering your letter right away. You should get this by Saturday. I wrote you last night too.

I went to school this morning but didn't think much of the class. The teacher gave a small lecture on first-aid then showed us motion pictures on the darn stuff. That makes three times I've seen those pictures. The class was supposed to start at 9:30 and the officer didn't show up until 10:35. I had a good time waiting though, there was a problem on arithmetic in the paper this morning and I was working it. I got the correct answer but couldn't explain how I did it to the other boys. At least they couldn't see it my way. I got them arguing then sat back and laughed at the fuss they were making. The thing that gets me is the fact that the War Department puts these pictures out with specific treatments for the pillrollers to learn. When we get back to the infirmary our officers say, don't do that, it's wrong. Then give us their treatments. One doctor says one thing and another will contradict him. On one of our quizzes I asked the officer in charge if he wanted what the book said or what our officers told us was right. He said follow the book. It's a very confusing mess.

Our new barracks are really swell. I suggested hauling topsoil to put around them so we could plant some flowers. The top-kick didn't think much of that idea. Instead we had to dig ditches around them. (Much more practical idea.) I think George wants to put up curtains.

I think it's fine, you working as a registrar for Uncle. You know Glorious; sometimes I get in a rut thinking there is so much to be done and here we are, down here doing the same thing every day. It seems like a waste of time but we will probably get a chance to do our part before long. Lately Washington seems interested in the 30th Division. The Chief of Staff is down here now inspecting.

The pictures were very good. "Thanks" for sending them.

Legna, it's true about a young man's fancy turning to love in the spring. Just think of how much more I could enjoy spring if I were home. I don't have any one here to love. Maybe I should make a reconnaissance and locate something or someone. Shady Side is too far to go though for a trip like that. Wish I knew when I'll get another furlough. The furloughs have been discontinued for the Med.Det. I think they will start giving them again pretty soon but it will be at least two months before my turn comes. We were supposed to get one every ten weeks but the army is always changing things.

No Glorious, my love for you isn't just a fair-weather affair. I feel it too often and it affects me too deeply.

Bye now,

Love,

Howard

Fort Jackson, South Carolina
May 5, 1942

Dear Glorious,

Your letter today is the most thrilling thing I've seen or heard. Gosh Glorious, if you can only make it. That was a pretty big "might" you wrote. I'm keeping my fingers crossed and am hoping you make it.

I've talked to the sergeant and he said there was no reason why I couldn't get a week-end pass. The "passes" start at noon Saturday and end Sunday midnight. We have a new Division Commander and he is going to inspect the 120th on Thursday. If anything happens and we get confined or something like that, I will wire you after I get your letter saying you are coming. If the letter says you are not coming, of course I won't wire whether we get confined or not. I'm not worrying about being confined though; we had this afternoon and will have all day tomorrow to get ready for this inspection.

The best place I know to meet you in Columbia is the lobby of the hotel Wade Hampton. This hotel is very prominently located. It is on the corner of Main and Gervais Streets, right across the street from the Capitol (State House); you can't miss it. If you are awfully late showing up and I'm not there, (thinking something happened so you couldn't make the trip) call Regimental Headquarters of the 120th and they will notify me at the Med.Det. They will get the number of the phone where you called from and I can call back and we can get together from there. "How am I doing Legna, if things get murkier" sounds kind of complicated to me.

Harry's outfit must be Med.Det. 305th or 307th Inf. of the 77th Division. We have the 320th Tank Destroyer Regiment in our Division (30th) but the 77th is a new division composed of recruits. They are getting their basic training now, so if Harry has only been in the army three or four weeks he must be with the 77th. I can see no reason for his not being able to get off for the week-end. The 77th was certainly running the streets of Columbia over last Saturday. I'm sure he can get off.

I have the addresses straight about where to send the wire. I hope your letter comes Thursday though, then I'll have plenty of time to get you.

Glorious I can't say I won't be disappointed if you don't come, because that's not true. It's something nice to look forward to and it wouldn't be the first time I've been disappointed. So remember, if you can't make it, don't feel bad about it. Just think about what a swell idea it was. I can hardly wait until Thursday to hear from you. "See you Saturday, Buttercup". (Maybe!)

Love and luck,
Howard

Fort Jackson, South Carolina
May 10, 1942

Dear Glorious,

Needless to say, but I was disappointed Saturday. Since I've been in the army though I've learned to take disappointments in my stride. I had thought about seeing you ever since last Tuesday. So you see it was a "little let-down". But don't let it worry you. Maybe I'll get a furlough in a couple of months. I was in town last night and there were soldiers running around with their girlfriends' bags, trying to find a place for them to stay. Honest, there were so many soldiers in Columbia last night you couldn't walk on the street. You just had to push your way around. I would have found a place for you to put up even if I had to pitch my tent. (You would love that, no!) Since the 77th Division has been at Jackson, Columbia is jammed and packed on Saturday nights. About the Wade Hampton, it's a high-priced place, I don't know about the class. Speedy works there and incidentally she didn't get married. She doesn't date anymore though; maybe the wedding was just postponed. If you ever decide to come down let me know a little ahead of time and I'll make reservations somewhere.

Glorious, you say you think of me often. I want you to know it's the same way with me. Since that Saturday night (August 29, 1940) we never saw much of one another, so guess there wasn't much left to do but think. Dan Cupid wasn't shooting "blanks" that night. Sometimes I think if I could just be with you, for a few hours, everything would be lovely. I guess it wouldn't though; I'd have to be a little hoggish and want a few more. Maybe we'll be shipwrecked on a deserted island sometime.

Last week was about the toughest one I've had in the army. The new Commanding General inspected the 120th Thursday. We put on all kinds of demonstrations. I put on a leg-splint and was in the close-order drill platoon. We really knocked their eyes out with the close order drill. I think the inspection in general was satisfactory. It should have been, we worked until 11 o'clock Wednesday night getting ready for it. Every piece of equipment including the aid-stations had to be washed. I was supposed to stand the inspection with the truck. After washing and cleaning the darn thing our sergeant decided he needed me at the aid-station. So somebody else took the truck after I had whipped it in shape.

If there are any mistakes in this letter blame it on Sleepy (one of my bunkmates). He's telling me stories of his civilian life. I'm hearing about every other word and saying yes and no once in a while.

Glorious if I was down-hearted because you couldn't come, that last letter perked me up. It was very sweet, Darling. My morale is 100 percent.

Rumors are really flying around about us moving out. The boys are even betting as to when it will happen.

Bye Legna,

Love,

Howard

Fort Jackson, South Carolina

May 14, 1942

Dear Glorious,

Your "last hello" sounded mighty low. What's the matter Buttercup, are you down in the dumps or in the doghouse for some reason? You should be able to beat *that hello* especially on the fourth try. If it's because you couldn't make it last week, forget it. Seeing you last week would have been the most wonderful thing in the world for me. But you couldn't make it, so that's all there is to it. Let's don't talk about you coming down later though. I don't like to think of that happening so long before it's possible. If we are here by the 1st of July, I should get a furlough. (How I could use one!) Every once in a while I get homesick and feel like going over-the-hill. (A.W.O.L.) That's a nice way to commit suicide now.

Life here is getting to be like it was at Camp Wheeler. The discipline is very strict. We have a new Division Commander and also a Company Commander. The Division Commander wants to make his Division the best in the 2nd Army and Co. Commander wants to make the 120th Med. Det. the best in the pillroller outfit in the Division. So you can see grass isn't growing under our feet. When the big boys inspected the 120th last week they found our knowledge of Chemical Warfare was satisfactory, but the Regimental Chemical Officer wants us to rate excellent. Therefore we now have a school on how to use protection against gas attacks. It is really for non-commissioned officers. Three from each Co. or Detachment were to attend. Two Pvts and one Sgt. got under the gun in the Med.Det and I'm one of the P.V.Ts. I never miss a detail. We do have a good instructor though; I took one look at him and told our sergeant, that guy must be a school teacher. Sure enough, we found out later he was a teacher in civilian life. It was the way he walked around the class room while talking that made me think of him as a genuine teacher. Legna, do you walk around the class room with your hands clasped behind your back and look as though you are going to pounce on a pupil if he so much as bats an eyelid? Also observing whether what you are saying is sinking in or flying through the windows with the greatest of ease. That's the way this Lt. does, every now and then we reach up and grab some of that hard lecturing going through the window. I've learned more about gas from him in two days than all my previous instructions together.

A new order came out; all personnel must have hair cut within one inch of the noggin. We look wonderful, just like a bunch of escaped convicts. George's ears are more prominent than ever. Our hats are too large for us with the new hairdo. George doesn't have to worry about his slipping over the ears though.

Say, who said anything about being shipwrecked on a deserted island with Mrs.R? How did she get into it?

Bye now and remember: "You are always in my heart."

Love,

Howard

Fort Jackson, South Carolina

May 16, 1942

Dear Glorious,

The clipping is very cute. I have my doubts about that soldier getting back to camp on time. A soldier's morale is lowest when riding back to camp after a furlough. It makes you feel like you've left everything that means the most to you behind. You feel kind of all alone in the world. But oh! How wonderful it is to get one and get away from it all for a few days. The way things are shaping I should get one by July. I've been in the army one year (May 31) and have had only five days. We are supposed to get thirty. (Christmas was a leave.)

Well Buttercup, I graduated today, even received a diploma. Our gas training was a twenty hour course and I mean they threw it at us. We were lucky to have such a good teacher. The Second Army Chemical Officer inspected our class one day. The Division Officer told us today the big shot was much impressed by our teacher. We told the Division Officer our instructor acted as though he might have been a schoolteacher. So you see my first impression was right, I knew he was a schoolteacher after the first five minutes in class. We were thanked for our cooperation; he said we did a fine piece of work. Four privates attended and only one flunked, five N.C.Os. failed. Our work has just started though, we have to instruct and drill our respective Companies in Chemical Warfare. The Colonel (D.C.O.) said today was Commencement Day, our work was just commencing. Our Company Commander sent for me and my diploma this afternoon. He thought it was a mighty fine piece of work. It kind of reminded me of Camp Wheeler, when I got my certificate for acting sergeant. Our Co. Commander took a course under the D.C. O. and all he got was a slip of paper with the Colonel's name on it.

So Mrs. Johnson tried to pull a fast one on you. I hope she didn't get away with it. Things like that get under my skin. I had a terrible argument with one of the boys the other day. He was complaining about there being so many young fellows in civilian life when he thinks they should be in the army. Then he started raving about how a soldier's life is like a slave's. From the way he talked you would have thought the Government had something against him and was making him suffer by drafting him in the army. He made me sick and the rest of the boys felt the way I did. (This guy had just come off furlough, so I made allowances.)

Does Phyllis have the recording "Skylark" with vocals by Dinah Shore? Hoagy Carmichael wrote it. Another good one is Sleepy Lagoon by Harry James' Orchestra. Glenn Miller played "I Don't Want to Walk Without You Baby" on his Sunset Serenade this evening. "Johnny Doughboy Found a Rose in Ireland" is good too. I'll still take "Stardust" by Tommy Dorsey's Orchestra. Have you heard "Now and Forever", a real ear tingler?

Well Legna, I've run out so bye now. I still "love you". That goes without telling.

Love,

Howard

P.S. I mailed last letter to S.S. Don't know whether it got there by Saturday . . .

Howard

Fort Jackson, South Carolina
May 20, 1942

Dear Glorious,

I hope you get this Saturday. I hoped that same thing last week but evidently it didn't happen. If today hadn't been your birthday I wouldn't have written. Here it is 10 o'clock at night and we just finished working. We've been cleaning and shining Med. Det. equipment all day. I think some visiting "General" is going to inspect the 120th. I couldn't get a card to send you so I'll take it out in writing. How about it, is that all right? "Happy Birthday to you, Darling." Too bad I couldn't help you celebrate it. (Did you need any help?) I could have at least proposed a toast, with a Coca Cola or Milk Shake anyway, don't you think? Or do you go in for the stronger beverage? (No! I know the answer to that one.)

Glorious, do you mean to say, that Jack Neiman is thinking of getting married? I can hardly believe that. Why he seems so young. Did getting his questionnaire have anything to do with bringing forth such thinking? Fellows get some peculiar ideas sometimes, when that little form comes around. They think well, I'm leaving home and maybe never get back. That attitude makes me very disgusted. Thank goodness, we don't have many boys whom have that feeling here. I like to be a little "optimistic" anyway.

The Division Commander has a new order out. We get up at five in the morning, instead of six. He told us the other night why he issued the order on having our hair cut short. Seems there were too many short-haired women in the Division. He must have thought some of the boys were getting permanent waves. We found out though that the "ole boy's" noggin is bare as Mother Hubbard's cupboard. I think he was jealous.

Glorious I'd better stop now, the boys are raising h_ _ _ about the light being on. I'm going to cut Georgie's ears down yet.

All my love,
Howard

Fort Jackson, South Carolina

May 22, 1942

Dear Glorious,

From your last letter I would say you have all the symptoms of spring fever. Of course, a pillroller's diagnosis isn't always correct. The treatment is always the same though. (Aspirin and soda pills with an occasional dose of castor oil.) I know a good treatment for spring fever but it's a military secret. I can't understand you losing ten pounds though. Glorious, I believe you work too hard.

I don't know as it was such an honor to attend the Chemical Warfare School. At the time it seemed like a drab and monotonous detail. That Company Commander was proud of the marks we made. There was some talk flying around about making me gas non-com for the Company but it hasn't been settled yet. I would be only too glad to get a rating in this outfit. I have more worries added to my mind now. I put in an application for Officers' Candidate School. If you make above 110 on your I.Q. you are allowed to do this. Today I was called before the Division Board for an oral examination. This Board is composed of a Colonel, Captain, and Lieutenant. They ask questions on current events, arithmetic and a few other things. This evening the report came down from Regimental H.Q. and I passed. I put in for Ordnance and the Ordnance School is at Aberdeen, Maryland. So if I pass my physical and a few other minor details work out alright, I should be in Maryland sooner or later. But I'm not counting too much on this, what I know is just rumors. I will know more definite what the set-up is next week. They certainly didn't lose much time in telling me to take my physical and get my papers ready. I might be a Lt. yet. The boys are on my neck; they are calling me Lt and Captain Shenton and salute when I walk by. They sure like to razz a fellow, but we, or they, are having a good time so that's the difference. I can take it.

About me coming to Shady Side from Washington with Warden. That's another confession for me. Can you think of a better reason for me to come to Shady Side other than to see you? (Lots of "to's") My real reason was to see you even though I did have, or made, other excuses. Glorious, I fell in love with you long before that rainy Saturday night (August 29). I kept fighting against it though; I didn't want it to happen. Sometime I will tell you why. It's a long story. Look now, don't you get to thinking about this and worry yourself. Promise me that, please! You have other things to work that brain on so don't let this bother you.

I went to the dentist day before yesterday for some fillings. He and I had a jitterbug contest all our own, when he started grinding. I even hate the smell of a dentist's office. Tomorrow I go back to get my fillings shined or something like that. From the way I was grabbed around the neck during one of the drillings I deducted the dentist must be a tough guy in a clinch. (Romantic clinch) I asked him once if he had struck oil but his sense of humor was no good. All I got was a black look for that one.

"See you in my dreams, tonight."

Love,
Howard

Officer's Training School Explanation
May 27, 1942

Dear Glorious,

I'm going to try explaining how this Officer's Candidate School affair came about. If you make a grade of 110 or above on the intelligence quiz the army gives each man when he's inducted, you are eligible to put in an application for O.C.S. I made 123 but didn't know it until a month ago. The Company clerk had been going over the service records and told me about it. A few others boys became interested and had their grades looked up. Our names were submitted to Division H.Q., there they were put on file, for a rest, I guess. Then we were sent applications to fill out and these went back to Division H.Q. again. If these were O.K. you were called before a Board. (There's a special Board for each branch of service.) This Board observes your appearance and the way you answer their questions. The questions were on arithmetic and current events mostly. I was asked to define the words *character* and *reputation*. After you've been before the Board you wait a couple of days to hear from them. If you've passed you are notified to take a physical exam and get the necessary papers together. The latter is plenty of red-tape. This report goes to Regimental H.Q. then Division H.Q. and if O.Kd you go to School for three months. When the fire and smoke has cleared away after these three months and you are still alive, you are a Commissioned Officer in Uncle's Armed Forces. I've had my physical but the report hasn't come in yet. The only thing I see that can hold me up is not graduating from High School. This may have a bearing on whether or not I get the appointment. I'm not worried about it; I'm still a pretty good pillroller.

But the Maryland part <u>gets</u> me. Aberdeen is only 25 miles from Baltimore and S.S. is right next door. "How about me for a neighbor, Buttercup?"

Glorious, I realize that long story was a mistake. But remember, please don't think about it or let it worry you. I'll tell you the story, next time I come home.

Glorious we are going for a six-week jaunt sometime soon, "according to rumors". I don't know if the whole Co. or Det. is going. Maybe I won't have to go if the Officer's School report is O.Kd. I'll write you whenever I can if we go. You can write to the same address. The mail will be forwarded to us. So if you don't get as many letters from me as usual, you will know the reason. Maybe I'll know something definite by Friday or Saturday. I hope this doesn't interfere with the furloughs —that would be drastic for us.

I drew a swell picture in my mind of that gathering at Rural Home last Sunday. Had a place reserved for myself too. Daydreaming some people call it, a swell pastime when you're a little lonesome. Ninety-six boys in the Med.Det. and I get lonesome. Is that hard to believe?

Aunt Annie Nowell wrote to me the other day. You didn't know she was my aunt too, did you? She's a swell person! I like her a lot.

Well Darling, if anybody should drive up in a hack and lean out and ask you, "I love you with all my heart".

Howard

Fort Jackson, South Carolina

May 31, 1942

Dear Glorious,

Today is my anniversary. It seems like I've been in the army more than a year. A lot has happened in the past year but I can't see where it has changed me. (The new hairdo has changed my looks a little.) When I think of all the places I've been and the people I've met, it has been quite an experience. I've learned a lot too, mostly about people.

Haven't heard any more about the O.C.S. I wish they would let me know something soon; I have Maryland on my mind. The worst thing that can happen now is for them to send me to an O.C.S. not in Md. That would be a terrible let-down. My passing the Board exam for Officer's Training has started a movement in the Med.Det. Everybody wants to try for it now. Only three of us have made the grade so far. Every evening the boys collect in my barracks and we have quite a session discussing current events. We have the world situation well in hand.

The regiment is moving out on their six week problem today. The pillrollers were lucky, we are using a skeleton force and only nineteen go out at a time for the week. I'll probably go next week or maybe the following.

What makes you think you are writing me too often? You can't realize how much I look forward to getting your letters. One every day wouldn't be too often but that's too much to expect. Another thing Glorious, I can't remember a single incident when you forced yourself on me, so forget about that. Write me whenever you have the chance and feel like writing. I'll always appreciate your letters and will answer them. I'd never let you down, Honey.

Aunt Annie Nowell sent me a box of caramels yesterday. I told you she was "swell", didn't I? When I opened it there was a small riot in camp. I yelled "attention", and said, look boys, let's do this in a military manner, "fall in" on the right. Sometimes your box will be opened before you know you have one. (Nice family.)

The U.S.O. had a good show at our theatre last night. These shows are better than the ones I've seen on the stage at home. I really enjoyed the one last night even though I had to stand up all through it.

Glorious, I can't tell as yet when I'll get a furlough. If I stay here I should get one around the first of July. If I go to O.C.S. it will be a long time before I get one. I think you get a seven day furlough after the three months of schooling is up. Of course Aberdeen is so close I should be able to slip in a week-end or a Sunday at home. I'd give anything for a few days in Shady Side. I'm homesick.

Legna, would you run into my arms if I came knocking at Mrs. Shipley's door? I doubt it; you would be worried about what Mrs. Shipley thought about such a procedure. I'd love that. Wish I could prove whether you would or not. (Maybe I'll get the chance.)

Bye now, and I hope all your pupils made the "grade". You made A+ on my report.

Love,
Howard

Fort Jackson, South Carolina

June 3, 1942

Dear Glorious,

"Thanks" for the pictures, they are alright. I like to have pictures of you, because then I can look at them when I think of you. You're not funny looking. I think you are beautiful, Buttercup. I didn't know whether the thing on your head was a hat or a doughnut left from breakfast. You really don't see much of it, perched on the back of the head like that. It's cute though! Derwill certainly has a serious look on his face. Must have been thinking about the dance he was taking you to. Wish I could have traded places with him. I haven't danced much lately; we've been working so hard a fellow stays off his feet as much as possible. I'd still try a few whirls though, if you were around. Maybe I had better stick to the subject of pictures. I didn't mean to take the pictures dancing Legna, but I like both, especially with you. Send me some more and I'll try to send you a few.

The six-week jaunt I spoke about is just like maneuvers. The regiment goes in the field on Sunday afternoon and stays out until the following Friday. This goes on for six weeks. The Med.Det. is using a skeleton force, only nineteen men go out at one time. They stay one week and a new force goes out the following week. I will go next week or the following more than likely. So far this set-up hasn't interfered with furloughs. Unless the furloughs are stopped, my turn should come around the first week of July. A lot can happen between now and then though.

The song "You are Always in My Heart" was taken from the picture of the same name. I saw it quite some time ago. In the picture the song was played sort of semi-classical and it's a very pretty tune. The picture was good too. Have you heard "Sleepy Lagoon" played by Harry James? That's the best yet. You will always be in my heart Glorious. Those words didn't have to be set to music for an etching in my memory. I've known it for quite some time.

Haven't heard any more about O.C.S. One of the Lieutenants is going to investigate a little for me. It may be a couple of months before I get any action on the darn thing. The army is slow when it comes to things like that.

Four of us were detailed for an experiment yesterday. We took a litter, bandages and a couple of tents and hiked to one of the nearby lakes. The idea was to ferry a patient across on the litter. We tried making a boat with the litter and tents or shelter-halfs as the army calls them. We failed there, the patient was very damp. Finally we decided to build a raft. That worked swell. I was the patient on the first experiment so of course I was wet. This made me suggest a swim that was the best part of the experiment. We had a lot of fun. I feel sorry for the litter patients on river crossings. The litter squads must learn to take patients over all sorts of obstacles. The guys acting as patients during some of the drill became actual casualties. (Shock mostly.)

Hope you get your boat licenses. I want to take a cruise with you as the "Skipper".

Bye now!

Love,

Howard

Fort Jackson, South Carolina

June 8, 1942

Dear Glorious,

The "good ole summer" time has come to S.C. It is really hot here, almost as bad as Georgia was last year. The boys are raging this evening. They put on a parade for some "big shots" from Washington this afternoon. I had an appointment with the dentist and didn't get to go. The boys are calling me a goldbricker (One who tries to get out of work). That's not true though. I was a victim of circumstances. They say a few boys passed out before the parade started.

The pillrollers had a swell party Saturday. We rented a place on one of the lakes for the afternoon. Everybody went swimming. We had a lot of fun. After the swim we had a steak fry. There was corn on the cob and potato salad to go with the steak. Then we had refreshments, this was when the party hit a high note. I was elected bartender and some of the boys tried to make a hog of themselves. Nobody was drunk and the party was a success. The Company Commander said we will have another in three or four weeks.

The regiment isn't going in the field until tomorrow because of the parade today. I don't have to go today but I'll get the detail next week, more than likely.

A few of us went to Columbia Saturday night after our party was over. The town was so full of soldiers you couldn't walk. We couldn't even buy a Coca-Cola, every store and café was jammed. It took us two hours to get back to camp. I never saw such a mob of people in my life. We made up our minds never to go in town on Saturday night again.

Too bad so many of your pupils failed. I guess you're glad school is over. A teacher does get a "break" in having a long vacation. They need one after ten months of teaching. Especially if kids now are like they were when I went to school. We had a lot of fun though. I'd like to do it over.

Your talking about the bugs at Mrs. Shipley's reminds me of a soldier standing at attention. When attention is called, there is sure to be a few gnats flitting around your nose or eyes. You dare not take your hand and brush them away either. If you do there is a sergeant or corporal on your neck and that's much worse than a few gnats.

About that A+ "measure" as you call it. I'd explain it but I would get in too deep. My heart took that "reading", Buttercup. (The doctors say your heart never lies.) Maybe the adage, "love is blind" is true. Could be, but I can see pretty good. I'd better go now.

Goodnight Legna!

Love,

Howard

P.S. If this letter isn't so good, blame it on the weather. I don't seem to be able to think right tonight. Your last letter was great.

So long, Angel,

Howard

Fort Jackson, South Carolina
June 10, 1942

Dear Glorious,

The 30th Division is kind of on the spot. I told you about the parade Monday and it being so hot. Well the Commanding-General is thoroughly disgusted about all the men falling out. The Med. Det. is in the clear though, not one of our men dropped out. The great Lord Louis Mountbatten, Commander of the British Commandos reviewed the troops. He was the guest of General Marshall. Of course, with all these muck-a-mucks around our General wanted us to make a good showing. I'm afraid we didn't do so well. He said anyone not physically fit to take a five-mile hike and then stand a parade wasn't fit for combat fighting. It was a tough detail, the boys told me it was tougher than anything we had done on maneuvers. The hike and passing in review wasn't hard, it was the heat that mowed the boys down. Even officers fell out. An officer doesn't fall out of ranks because he is feeling bad. (They pass out on their feet.) I'm kind of sorry I missed the affair.

We had a big day yesterday. The Med. Det. put on a demonstration for the Division Surgeon and the Chaplains of the 30th. Don't know why the Chaplains were interested. Guess they wanted to see what kind of medical attention a soldier gets in combat. Our Detachment Commander was kind of proud to think the 120th pillrollers have quite a reputation at Fort Jackson. The demonstration came off swell, everybody was on their toes. That's what counts in the army, "spirit and teamwork". We had both yesterday.

Honey, I couldn't let you know where we were going if we left Jackson. Even if I would now, which I am sure none of us will. But if it happens, you will hear from me. Today I had a letter from Jim Hale. The P.S. said, "I'm in Australia." (It was censored too; of course he didn't say where in Australia.) So you'll hear from me in case we should go. A sea cruise wouldn't surprise any of us now. We are getting too much attention from Washington.

Certainly I remember the night we sat on the lawn chair near the tennis court. You and Derwill and I had been over Elsie Hartge's playing tennis that afternoon. I was in shorts and you told me to go home and change, you would wait there for me. I didn't want to leave you though even for that little while. I haven't forgotten any of the times you and I were together. That's how deep an impression you made on me, Buttercup.

What enlightened Mother's mind to the fact "that you love me"? (I'm hoping it's a fact.) You don't have to answer that one Legna.

If I don't get to see you in July, Uncle is going to have a very disappointed nephew. Yes Glorious, we can take it if it has to be that way. But I'm being very optimistic about that furlough.

Haven't heard any more about O.C.S.

"Bye Darling"

Love,

Howard

P.S. Enclosing picture taken by one of the boys on Carolina maneuvers last fall.

Howard

Fort Jackson, South Carolina
June 14, 1942

Dear Glorious,

The pillrollers had a little excitement today. One of the boys in the rifle company was cleaning his rifle and shot himself in the foot. You never heard such shouting for "pillrollers" in your life. We grabbed a litter and went after him. The bullet went through his shoe, foot and the floor. The doctor (Lt.) called it a nice clean wound. I don't know what was nice about it. It was very careless of this boy not to make sure his rifle was empty after coming off guard. This was one time when he suffered from his own carelessness. He could have shot any one of his bunkmates, cleaning that rifle in the barracks. The Lt. was kind of exasperated about the whole thing. I think we called him away from a party at the "officers' club".

We put on another demonstration for the Chaplains. They were the casualties this time. The Division Chaplain weights 350 lbs. and I was in the litter squad that picked him up. I had to get some men from another squad to help get him on the litter. We were arguing how much the old boy weighed. He said, don't worry boys, I still ride a train on the single ticket. Of course I had to pipe up and say, what kind, a freight train? I must have said it in a morbid tone because he got off and walked to the aid-station after we carried him about 100 yards. (Maybe he thought the litter was going to break.) Our demonstrations have gone over very good. The Division surgeon was very pleased.

Sue Smith's shower must have been quite an occasion. What's going on? Is everybody diving off the deep-end? I have never heard of so many people getting married.

I've been trying to get a little information on my furlough. It may be the 27th of this month or the 4th of next and then it might be the 11th of July. (Kind of definite, isn't it?) More than likely it will be the 11th. I would rather have it beginning the 4th. Guess it doesn't matter, just so I get one. I need a change of scenery.

Just read a good book, "All That Glitters" by Frances Parkinson Keyes. It deals with lives (private and public) of our senators and diplomats in and around Washington. It wanders to France and Mexico for a little while. I think you would enjoy it.

George got a box from home. We haven't been to the mess hall for two days. If his mother keeps on, the government will be paying us ration money.

We are having an inspection tomorrow by the General's staff. The boys have been cleaning and scrubbing their equipment and the barracks all day. We have been warned about what will happen if the Med.Det. doesn't pass. Everything is really shining tonight. It takes us a day to get ready and the inspection will take about an hour. (But o-h, what an inspection officer can do in an hour.)

Well Honey, take care of S.S. till I get there. S.C. would be a lovely state if it had a Shady Side and one more thing but I better not talk about that.

Love,

Howard

Fort Jackson, South Carolina
June 17, 1942

Dear Glorious,

Your letter came this morning and I'm taking time out to answer it this afternoon. We have the afternoon off but we are going to eat supper early and put on another demonstration this evening. It will probably be 10:00 or 10:30 when we get back to camp and I wouldn't be able to write you then. (Lights go out at 10:00) This demonstration work is kind of tough. It is another job added to the usual routine. We had one yesterday, one today and another tomorrow. Too bad we are such good pillrollers. The army doesn't let you rest on your "laurels", a good reputation is hard to maintain. Our inspection last Monday by the Division Staff was excellent. It should have been, we were ready for the inspection at 7:30 in the morning. The "officers" came around 3:30 in the afternoon; the boys were on pins and needles all day. We walked around and looked at our displays at least twenty times. (Making changes and cursing all inspection officers.

A pleasant Sunday in S.S. isn't something hard for me to understand. I can't remember one that was unpleasant. Glorious, it would surprise you to know how I wish for Shady Side sometimes. It's a "grand ole place" and I'll always like it. The army will never get me to change my mind about that.

I was asleep when that picture was taken. One of the "band boys" took it after a night march. The band was attached to the Med.Det. as litter-bearers, while on maneuvers. They didn't walk, which is why they were up so early the next morning. I had my feet or <u>legs</u> doubled up because when I straighten them, my feet stick out and get cold. Three of us would sleep like that when it was very cold. The man in the middle would be as snug as a bug in a rug. We usually pitched a coin for that position. If a sergeant was sleeping with us he would try and "throw his rank on us". (We would then throw him out.)

Legna, if the 120th moves out I'll be able to write. It may be some time before I could let you know where we were. We probably wouldn't know ourselves for a little while.

I'm sorry to hear about "ole gray", the cat. Maybe he was drafted. He will show up around Rural Home sooner or later.

My furlough is still "dangling". I know it will be soon but there is nothing definite yet.

79

The top-kick is tooting his whistle (Chow call). "Good day, Buttercup".

Love,

Howard

Fort Jackson, South Carolina
June 22, 1942

Dearest Glorious,

I'm sorry my letter left you so cold. (Maybe you need a little S.C. climate.) I thought it was a bit cool too, army life leaves one rather numbed and another thing, I can't express my sentiments on that particular subject. I have beautiful thoughts but they jam on me when I try to let them out. (Congesting isn't it or would you say "disgusting"?) Sure I love you Honey, more than anything in the world. Aren't you aware of the "<u>fact</u>" by this time? Maybe I had better call you and as we say in the army, "put you in the <u>know</u> about his thing." I know you were only kidding about this in your last letter but I don't like cool letters either, especially from someone you love. How is the temperature "Angel"? Rising any yet?

Well, the pillrollers have to put on another demonstration this evening. They should take a movie of us in action and then we could rest once in a while. We will work till about ten tonight and tomorrow we are going on an all day hike, carrying litters with 100 lb. sand bags on them. I have a feeling the hike is going to end at some pond or lake where we can go swimming. Last week we had an all-night problem. (Evacuating casualties) On the way to the field we passed a large group of men that had been hiking all day. They were the saddest sight I've ever seen. Half of them had fallen out and some were in very bad shape. A few were so bad off till they were screaming at the top of their voice. But what "got" me was the fact we couldn't stop and help. We had six trucks with which we could have hauled the very sick ones back to camp. But oh no! We had to go on and set up our aid-stations and simulate evacuating casualties at night. We've only done this at least ten times already. The only thing we had to show for the night's work was chiggers. We were absolutely covered with the darn things. If we had stopped and helped those men it would have been a good night's work. (I was rather disgusted with the army for a while.)

So your pal Jack has departed from the ranks of the <u>free</u> and the brave. I didn't think Jack had it in him. I'm like you though Legna; they are both terribly young for such a big step. Maybe it will work out alright, I hope so. Jack is likely to regret it though if he is "drafted". I think that is what drove one of the boys crazy at Camp Wheeler. (He married about two months before being drafted.)

Glorious, you don't think I could come home and not stop by Rural Home Hotel. Why that would be sacrilegious. I don't know about tennis though, it has been such a long time since I've played. However, I would like a try at it, with you anyway.

The bugler is blowing "chow call". I have to eat and get ready for work. Still can't say definite when I'll get my furlough.

Don't tell anyone Buttercup, but "I love you".

Yours,

Howard

81

P.S. The clipping was alright—reminds me of some of the sergeants—they are always passing the "buck" to the corporals.

Howard

Fort Jackson, South Carolina
June 24, 1942

Dear Glorious,

What's this you say about being mixed up? Don't tell me you and Rev. Culp have crossed wires again. Well, whatever it was don't let it worry you. I get "mixed up" a lot, but I just let things take their course. It usually comes out alright.

Of course I wouldn't let you down. I like to get letters on Saturday too (or any other time). What made you think I wouldn't write last week? The letter "fringed with ice" must have had something to do with it. I didn't realize it was all that freezing, it wasn't meant to be that way. You occupy a warm place in my heart, Legna. Blame it on the dull routine; a soldier goes stale once in a while.

I like your descriptions of the boat rides. They sound wonderful. Guess it's because I've always liked boats and the water. I should have been drafted for the Navy instead of the Army. I'm not complaining though, I'm proud of the 120th Med. Det. even though life is dull at times.

Remember the hike we were to have Tuesday and I said it would probably end at some pond or lake where we could swim. Well we didn't take the hike but we did go swimming. Guess working late Monday night made the Det. Commander a little generous. We practiced treatment of gas casualties in the morning and got the afternoon off. We managed to get a couple of trucks and go swimming. The best lakes are about ten miles from camp. I'd like to do this every afternoon but it wouldn't help the war effort any. Course we could simulate a few drownings and practice artificial respiration. That hike will be sometime this week though; we get tired thinking about the darn thing. One hundred lbs. dead weight is a nice load for any litter squad on a 15 or 16 mile hike.

The latest news is that we will go on maneuvers in August. The object is to study desert and jungle fighting. We will be gone for two months. They could skip the desert fighting. We've always worked in sand ankle deep around here. (S.C. is a grand state.)

It is certainly fine of you and Miss Ethel to give Jack a shower. (I was under the impression he was "all wet" when he got married. Isn't that a terrible pun?) I just can't picture Jack married, it seems like a very few years since he used to run around the school, eating a sandwich and his fat tummy shaking when he laughed.

Isn't the "Skip Jack" the boat belonging to the Major or did it belong to the fellow from Avalon Shores? I wasn't thinking about boat names that day. That Major was certainly a sloppy sailor; I thought he was never going to get the boat docked at Kline's pier.

I should know by the first of next week when I'll get my furlough. I'm still hoping to get it on the 3rd.

Win one set of tennis for me over the week-end. I'll be thinking of you.

Love,
Howard

Fort Jackson, South Carolina

June 28, 1942

Dear Glorious,

I've put in for my furlough but won't know until tomorrow if it will be accepted. The worst part of it is though I have to go in the field tomorrow morning and won't be back until Friday evening. (The furloughs start Friday night.) Being in the field it is doubtful I will be able to write and let you know for sure whether I'll be home Saturday or not. The only thing I can say is, if I don't make it this Friday I will the following. If there is any way possible, I'll write or let you know about this coming Friday. The furlough starts around 8 o'clock Friday and I should get to Washington Saturday morning and Shady Side should be showing on the horizon by late afternoon. I'll see you Saturday night, I hope. It's too bad I can't say more definite when I'll be home but that's the way with the army, you can never plan anything.

Glorious, don't pay any attention to what Whitey says. He always did like to tease and kid people. He will see enough of me. I don't think he stays in one place very long so no doubt he won't see much of me. (I expect to be in Shady Side most of the time.)

The U.S.O. had a very good show here last night. Rubinoff and his violin was the main attraction. He played "Intermezzo" and it was beautiful. These shows are really worth seeing. They are much better than the ones we see in Columbia's leading theatres for $.65 [65 cents].

Honey, it is certainly wonderful of you to save your gas so we can go to Beverly Beach. You shouldn't do it though; maybe you will need it for a necessity. Any place is alright with me when you are around. I don't

84

have to go to B.B. to enjoy your company. The idea of you thinking of it gives me a fine feeling, whether we go or not. (You're tops.)

I almost worried our Captain to distraction today, trying to get a truck so we could go swimming. He finally said "yes" and signed the trip ticket. I knew he was going to let us go when I first asked him but he wanted to argue about it. We have a swell group of officers even though they are not "so military".

See you Saturday evening, Legna,

Love,

Howard

Fort Jackson, South Carolina
July 5, 1942

Dear Glorious,

I can't begin to tell you how disappointed I was last Friday night. All week long I had been thinking about going on my furlough and then to come in camp and find out I couldn't go, well, I just about blew a fuse. The top-kick crossed me up. I called him every name under the sun. (Under my breath of course.) I had a feeling that not being in camp, somebody was going to get my furlough but I was still hurt about it. If my section sergeant hadn't been in the field I would have gotten it. But the top-kick picked the men he wanted to go and I didn't figure in his selection. The worst of it is though, the sun-fish said I could have mine on the 3rd. He told me this on Friday before we went in the field but he said he forgot about me when I took the matter up with him. I felt like climbing his frame and giving him something to remember me by.

Unless something unusual comes up, I'll be in Shady Side next Saturday. I'll heckle the top-kick into giving me that furlough, if I have to remind him of it every ten minutes. He will be glad to get rid of me for a week. Keep your fingers crossed for me, "Buttercup". I'll write you Wednesday and let you know whether or not I get the furlough. It should be rather definite by that time.

We had a very unpleasant time in the field last week. It rained every day or I should say night. It was hot as blazes during the day and it would rain at night. Everything was a mess; our equipment became filthy before the week was out. The first day fixed me, I was covered with chiggers, and they almost set you crazy. We looked like a bunch of monkeys, everybody was scratching for dear life. The doctor made up a mixture to kill them but it wasn't very effective. The boys in the rifle Co. took the "beating" though. They had to get down and crawl through the grass and bushes. The chiggers had a picnic on the poor fellows. They didn't seem to mind it so much though; they've been out for five straight weeks and kind of toughened up. We managed to get the truck one night and went to the store. (The closest one was six miles.) We stocked up on candy, cake, watermelon and Pepsi Colas. (That made us feel fine.)

I made "corporal" while in the field and didn't find it out till we came in Friday. The news left me cold; I was too disappointed about the furlough. At that time I felt like a yard-bird. Two of my buddies also made corporal, they were having a swell time talking about it and I was sitting on my bunk moaning about the furlough. It's a wonder they didn't dig a hole and put me in it. I snapped out of it after a bit though. We went to town and had a steak dinner to celebrate.

Well Honey, I have another week to look forward to seeing you and dear ole Shady Side. (It's going to be a long one for me.) Again I'll say "See you Saturday".

Love,
Howard

Cpl. Howard C. Shenton
120th Infantry, Med.Det.
Fort Jackson, South Carolina
APO #30
U.S. Army
July 8, 1942

Dear Glorious,

The top-kick and I finally hashed things out. I leave here Friday evening around 7 o'clock and my train leaves at 8:00. The train should get in Washington 7:00 or 8:00 Saturday morning. Gosh! I can hardly wait till Friday. A furlough is something a soldier dreams about and seldom becomes a reality.

Your last letter was mighty sweet, "Buttercup". Letters like that really boost a fellow's morale.

I will call you soon as I get home Saturday. I may be lucky enough to get home in the afternoon. I'll see you Saturday night.

Love,
Howard

Fort Jackson, S.C.

July 18, 1942

Dearest Glorious,

This place is certainly a terrific let-down after seven days in Shady Side. We are sweltering in the heat; the temperature is about 105° in the shade. Most of the fellows stayed in camp this afternoon, which is very unusual for Saturday. It's too hot to do anything, no wonder people in the South are inclined to be lazy. Wish I had West River to dive in and cool my heels.

The train ride back wasn't so bad. We made good time and I had a seat all the way. I got to camp around 3:30 this morning and was able to get a couple hours of sleep before reveille. There was quite a reception committee around my bunk when I awoke. I think they wanted to heckle me a little though; these boys delight in waking people out of a sound sleep. I knew all the latest happenings before breakfast. The boys kind of made me feel glad to be back. I needed a little cheer. Last night on the train I saw our moon (it is ours, we saw it first, Wednesday night remember) and longed for you so much it hurt. I'm going to look at it every night until it is full and think of you. Not that I need a reminder though; we can share it even though five hundred miles separate us. It's prettier here, the sky is full of clouds and that makes a nice background. I could enjoy it more in Shady Side, of course!

There was a little good news awaiting me: O.C.S. is cooking again. An order came down for me to take another physical exam with some others that are up for the school. It seems a physical is only good for sixty days so I will have to take another before being called. This is rather encouraging; it kind of makes me think I might be leaving soon. They certainly aren't going to have me taking an exam every sixty days for nothing. I tried to see the Major today and learn something definite but we were busy and when I got a chance to see him, he was busy. I should know something soon. You never know anything about what goes on in the army until it's about to happen. If I'm going, I hope they take me before we go on maneuvers.

We have a tough schedule for next week —three night problems. This means staying up all night and working in a blackout. One thing, it won't be so hot at night and "our moon" will be giving off quite a bit of light by then. So it shouldn't be too bad.

I want to mention my phone call; maybe it didn't make sense to you. If it didn't, "forgive me". I'll never forget last week; it was the most wonderful week in my life and "you" made it that way. "Legna, you are tops", you're my "very very high particular."

Love,

Howard

P.S. Give "Ivan" a toot on his horn for me.

Howard

July 20, 1942
11:00 A.M.

Dear Darling Glorious,

I just received your letters; both arrived in the morning mail. They gave me quite a thrill, I love them. We are taking things easy this morning. The regiment is moving out at 1:00 o'clock on an all-night problem. I have to go with the aid-station; we will get back sometime tomorrow afternoon and probably have to go out again in the evening. This may be my only chance to write for three or four days, this is going to be a tough week. I'm in good shape for it though; I caught up with my sleep over the week-end.

Our happy family was disrupted somewhat over the week-end. One of the regiments in the 30th Division is shipping out and their Med.Det. wasn't up to full strength. They took ten men out of our Det. to fill in. We didn't know a thing about it until Sunday morning about 8:00. By 10:00 o'clock the boys were on their way. Some of them took it pretty hard. It wouldn't be so bad if we had all left together. It just goes to show how quick things can change in the army. With these men leaving and some that left before, we have plenty of work coming up. There should be 126 men in the Det. and now we have 75. Somebody is going to do a little overtime.

I took a reading on "our moon" last night. It is getting full very quick. Looking at it made me realize more than ever how wonderful last week was and I wished for you with all my heart. Honey, there is no doubt in my mind about loving you; last week cleared that up. I had been thinking maybe I was wasting your time and mine in thinking and hoping for something that might never happen. Glorious, even if we "never merge as one" I'll be able to look back and see it all as something very beautiful and worthwhile.

Well Darling, I must get ready to leave. I'll write again, soon as possible. So long, Buttercup*.

Love, (with all that's in me)

Howard

*Reserved for Glorious.

July 22, 1942

Dearest Glorious,

This is really the first opportunity since coming back to Jackson for me to sit and think about what to write you. The top-kick detailed me as "Charge of Quarters" today and all it requires is to be present at all times. We came off the field late yesterday and I was to go out again this morning and stay until tomorrow. There is another night problem coming up Friday so more than likely I'll catch that one.

Maybe we didn't talk about the kind of letters I like, but the two you wrote are good enough for me. They are superb—kind of made me feel I was still with you and "inspiring" too. After reading them, two weeks of field duty wouldn't have bothered me. You are quite a "lady", Legna and I am glad "I love you". (I don't think anybody could feel sorry about loving someone though, could they? That is, if they really loved <u>that someone</u>.)

Glorious, please don't worry about taking up too much of my time, when I was on furlough. I wasn't with you one minute more than I wanted to be. I lived four months and three days for that week and you made it worth living for. I wanted to be with you as much as possible. That wonderful week will stay with me a long time "Buttercup", I'll never forget it. There will come a day (I'm hoping) when all our weeks will be like that. Maybe not exactly like it, but we will be just as happy.

Say, you are kind of early with the "Christmas present", aren't you? You can give me anything. All I want is a chance to see you and be with you—that would be my best gift. If I get that it will be a "Great Christmas".

Going in the field Monday for our night problem, 67 men fell out. Walking in the sun and the temperature around 110° played havoc with the men. The pillrollers had their work "cut out" that day, but I'm proud to say not one of our boys fell out. I was driving up and down the road with the Captain (Medical Officer) all afternoon. He was very disgusted and didn't give the men any sympathy. A lot of them fell out just because they were hot but some really hit the dirt. We sorted them out and sent the sick ones back to camp. The others we collected and the Colonel make them march to the area we occupied before the problem started. We had supper around 9:30 that night and then grabbed a little sleep. (("Ole Man Moon" was pretty that night.)) Breakfast was at 2:00 A.M. then after eating we drove about six miles in a blackout and then worked the problem on foot for the rest of the day. The troops rode in camp so we weren't bothered with treating heat exhaustion. My sufferings amounted to a few chigger bites. (They sure like me.)

The first time I go in town I'll see about the picture. It will probably take two weeks to get it.

Goodbye now, Angel,

I Love You

Howard

P.S. The hugs and kisses are sweet. Hold me tight when you hug me.

Howard

July 25, 1942

Dearest Glorious,

If writing a boy three letters before you received one makes a forward huzzy... "Then I love huzzies." I think you are very sweet, Buttercup.

How about this: I'm restricted to the regimental area. An order came out yesterday stating, I am on the priority list for O.C.S. and until all my papers are turned in I will be restricted. It should be lifted this afternoon. I went to the office of the O.C.S. Board this morning to find out the possibilities of my going and when I would. They told me my chances of going are excellent and that I would leave on August 13. I couldn't find out for sure if I was being sent to Aberdeen. The fact that I live in Maryland may make them send me to some other state. The army does things like that.

Legna, I've had a problem on my mind since this order came out on O.C.S. I may be doing the wrong thing by accepting it. You see, there is an opening for Staff sergeant in the Det. and the Det. Commander wanted me to take it, on trial of course. This is a mighty fine offer and quite a temptation for me. I was slightly overcome when the Captain told me about it, because last Monday & Tuesday was the first time he and I had ever worked together in the field. Then again there are five or six boys in the Det. who exceed me in seniority (Buck sergeants and tech sergeants), they are the logical ones to pick from, but the Captain wouldn't consider them. I thought it over and decided on O.C.S. It is quite true my chances of passing the school are a little doubtful but I'm willing to take the risk. You don't get such opportunities in the army very often. I know some boys who have been to the Ordnance school and "washed out". They say it is <u>plenty</u> tough. I am sure I could handle the Staff sergeant's job even with the few difficulties I would run against at first. When the Captain places me over these boys, (my seniors) there would be a lot of talk and ill-feeling. I could cope with this situation but it would be rather uncomfortable for a while. These boys will be sore any way because the Captain said if I didn't take the job he was going to "import" a staff sergeant from the 105th Medical Bn. The 120th Med. Det. is detached from the 105th. I gave the problem much thought and decided on the O.C.S. Even if I wash out I can work for staff sergeant; it may take a long time but I may never get another chance for Ordnance O.C.S.

If my restriction is lifted this afternoon I'm going to town with one of my Camp Wheeler buddies. He is in an outfit that is <u>moving out</u> next week. (Destination unknown) You may remember me writing about him. (P.A. I nicknamed him at Wheeler and the name still sticks. He's more Pennsylvania Dutch than George.) We will have dinner and probably go to a show. "No drinking; P.A. doesn't drink." I'll have to toast him with a "coke", I guess.

Honey, I have to close now, we are shooting a hundred & fifty men with typhoid vaccine and I'm to help. See you in Maryland soon?

Love,

Howard

P.S. Hope my problem didn't bore you. I wanted to kind of get it "off my chest". (If you know what I mean.)

Howard

July 29, 1942

Dearest Glorious,

The pillrollers are saying today, "Shenton got a letter from G. Andrews". They like to see me get letters from you; I get such a happy look on my face, I guess. Honey, I love to get them too. You spoiled me last week by writing four; I was sort of expecting one yesterday. I'm quite satisfied with the one today though.

I'm on duty at the infirmary this week, first time since December. It isn't hard work but the hours are rather long. We are on duty from 7:30 in the morning till 9:00 at night and one "detail" catches it for seven days. The work is interesting and you can learn a lot about first-aid. When things get slow we have a good time, taking our blood pressure and fooling around. I wouldn't mind working there all the time if the hours weren't so long. The stories that some of these soldiers can tell when they have a minor ailment, you would think they were about to die. They make them real good if there's a long hike coming up but they can't fool the "medical officers". I had one guy pass out on me today; he's allergic to the smell of hospitals and such. He got my sympathy for I was the same way before my pillrolling days. (Remember?)

Look Buttercup, when you talk about my being with you, don't say I <u>seem</u> to enjoy it. Say, "<u>I enjoy it</u>". There isn't anything I would rather do than to be with you. I wish we could go "sailing" every day, we should have gone at least once more when I was home. You're a nice "shipmate", Legna.

Talk about religious literature, I heard some the other day from one of our chaplains. (I'm always running into them at the wrong time, it seems.) This one had an ear ache and came over to get treatment. I washed it out and put some "drops" in the darn thing. He was damning and helling all around the place while I was working on him. (Not very religious, but <u>literature</u>.) The ole boy was grateful though, even if I did hurt him a little.

Glorious, I don't know when I'll get the picture taken. Not before Saturday anyway because I can't get off, but I will have it taken, that's a "promise".

No, I don't think the 120th will ever move out. They have transferred a lot of men out of this regiment in the last two weeks and I believe we will be a training outfit. We couldn't move now because we don't have enough men. You can't tell though, when we get some new men and after they are trained, anything can happen.

Haven't seen our moon the last two nights; it's not up when I go to bed. But I see it every morning at reveille. It's still high in the sky then and just as pretty. It was full yesterday morning.

So long, "Darling".

Love,
Howard

August 2, 1942
9:30 A.M.

Dearest Glorious,

Sunday morning is a swell time to write letters. It's not so hot and everything is quiet after Saturday night's activities. Most of the boys go back to bed after roll call and sleep till dinner time. I was thinking of you last night and started to write but perspiration and ink were running together, so I had to quit. I stayed under the shower for a couple of hours trying to get cool.

The 120th Med. Det. is still putting on demonstrations. We had one in the field Friday night for the doctors and nurses of the Post hospital. I was relieved of infirmary duty so as to help put the darn thing on. The nurses had a terrible time; they were either penned in a briar patch or else thought they saw a snake. We worked until 10:00 at night on this one and be damned if we didn't have to go out again yesterday morning and practice for another Monday. The one Monday is interesting though. The troops are to demonstrate a river crossing "under fire". Bombers are going to drop flour or powder of some sort in sacks to get the bombing effect. All of this gun fire and bombing is going to produce casualties so then the pillrollers put on their show. We have to swim out and pull in some men that were wounded while swimming across and hike them back to the aid-station on litters. I like this demonstration; at least you can keep cool while you are in the water. After this is over we are going to an assembly area, rest and eat supper and start on a "twenty mile night hike". (Everybody doesn't finish.) We will have Tuesday off, I guess. The hike should be over around 4:00 Tuesday morning.

No Legna, it's not chemistry that would hold me back in O.C.S. There are any number of things that can wash you out. Why I know a boy who flunked the Ordnance school and he is a college graduate. He is very smart and passed his tests but they said, "He wasn't officer material". (Has no personality and "get-up"). I'm not going to enter with the idea of failing. I'll give it all I've got; if I fail I can take it. There's nothing to lose and everything to gain. I can still serve Uncle in the ranks and be proud of it. He's a "grand ole guy" and I wouldn't let him down, no matter what!

Honey you are right about "being loved" gives one a secure feeling. It makes you feel as though you have a grip on life and no matter what happens you can take it in your stride and never falter. I'm glad you understood about me wanting "to kind of get that problem off my chest". You're sweet Buttercup and I love you with all there is "in me" to love.

The picture still hasn't been taken. I wanted to go in town yesterday afternoon but we didn't get in until 2:00 and then we had to wait around and get paid. By that time it was too late.

Thanks for the hugs and kisses. I like those deep-ringed hugs.

Love to you Angel,

Howard

P.S. I hope Miss Ethel is feeling better.

H.

August 5, 1942

Hello Buttercup,

An extraordinary thing has happened. The temperature has dropped to 90°. At least you can sit still and perspiration won't pour out like a shower. I had a very restful afternoon, catching up on my sleep. We took a twenty-mile hike Monday night and got to bed around 3:30. Last night I worked at the infirmary until 2:30 getting the vaccine records straight. Four hundred boys are being transferred and their vaccine records must be accurate before they leave. We immunize the boys from all diseases but lead poisoning before they leave. After working last night

I had to work sick-call this morning and that lasted until noon. I was ready for bed after lunch. The Captain has placed me on permanent duty at the infirmary. (Permanent until the 13th) Field duty is harder but I like it much better.

Gosh, that day-dream was alright but the foreign country part doesn't appeal to me. Let's make it come true in the U.S. Darling, I didn't realize you day-dreamed like that. I think it's great though. There is a song out called "Day Dreaming". Glenn Miller has a fine arrangement of it. My dreams are centered around you but they concern the past and what I would do if you were with me at the present. (We've done some wonderful things Legna.) I'm sorry the night dream was unpleasant; kind of made me feel like a villain. That one had better not come true.

The glorious sunset trip must have been swell. I'm glad you told me about it. I've a swell picture of that Rhode River shore-line in my mind. The only thing I didn't like was you taking off your shoes. Then I couldn't carry you around the old tree laying on the shore, when we walked back to the boat. (Remember?) That day makes me know we will have a sailboat, "Shipmate".

Legna, please don't feel bad about taking up so much of my time while I was on furlough. I was happy about it; after all I've only seen you three times in almost two years. I got a good look every time though. (Taking "readings" again.) If I could get another week right now, I would want it to be just like that last. That "love claim" is mutual Honey and I can't think of any better reason for taking up one another's time. (In case "that fellow" drives up and asks you, I love you Glorious!)

Sorry to hear about Miss Ethel. Give her my best wishes for a quick recovery. She will be in that classroom, pointing her finger and stomping the left foot in September, I'll bet.

Maybe I'll know something about O.C.S. by Saturday. I will write Sunday anyway. "Goodnight Buttercup". Try and have a pleasant dream so you can tell me about it.

Love, Howard

August 7, 1942
9:40 P.M.

Dear Howard,

There are so many things that come to me during the day that I should tell you, but when I sit down to write they are gone. As a result I just ramble on and on saying nothing.

Today has been tough for me. The weather has been showery and cold and hot, very unsettled, I'd say. Now with that as a set-up here are my activities. Drilk [Glorious's younger brother, Derwill] awakened me at 6:45, I got dressed, ate my breakfast, got aboard the boat for a fishing trip. The party was quite large and was composed of a few grownups and many children. We fished in, at least, 10 different places and caught only a few. In the meantime I was hot, sleepy, cold and irky girky. At 12 noon we started in and got caught in a shower. After washing off the boat (which brought back memories even though it wasn't the same boat, pleasant memories??) I ate my dinner. Then I was compelled to play two sets of tennis with Mr. Chesney, Drilk and another guy. All the while I was rocking as if I were still on the boat. Immediately upon completing our tennis I had to go on a swimming trip. I went in and I got wet, I hate to get wet, Ha ha! Then I was cold and I had to sit around and wait for everyone to decide to go in. Upon getting home I found that Grace's oldest boy was sick and I had to take her home. I got into some clothes and did that. Then came two more sets of tennis, a shower, dressed again, supper eaten standing up in the kitchen (we're so crowded that our table is taken). It was raining and I thought I wouldn't have to see that boat again today but it stopped and the people wanted to go, I went—Thus my tough day which would probably seem quite a nice one to you, but Honey, I am not made like you are nor have I had your training. As a result I am exhausted! Wish you were here to rub my back. Would you do it? Howard, I am afraid that if we got married you wouldn't want to do it for me anymore. I am an awful baby where you're concerned. I'd always be wanting you to "pet" me. I think you'd grow awfully tired of it. Then if you were no longer kind, thoughtful and gentle to me as you are now, I couldn't stand it. I'd die, 'cause I love you partly for those things.

I worked at our rationing board here in Shady Side on Wednesday and Thursday nights, we were very busy. We really issued the sugar certificates, but we can accept only applications for gasoline and tires. I enjoyed the work though for I like that sort of thing.

Love to my darling,
Glorious

August 7, 1942

11:00 A.M.

Dearest Legna,

Sick-call was small this morning and we finished early so I thought I'd write to the "sweetest girl in the world". (Hope you don't mind 'cause she's a wonderful person.) I think about "her" an awful lot and wish she was here so I could look at her and talk to her. Let me describe her. She has blue-grey eyes that have a kind of piercing look but at times sparkle and reflect with warmth. Then that "grin", it gets me, makes you smile whether you want to or not. Whenever you see it, there's humor or a joke forthcoming. Her height is just right; she can nestle her head on my shoulder very comfortably. I enjoy being with her regardless of where we are or what we are doing. I like to dance with her because then I can hold her close and I feel contented then.

A pillroller just brought me a letter from her and she is knitting me a sweater. I know the sweater will keep me warm because when I wear it I'll think of her and then my love will make me all aglow. "I told you she was wonderful, didn't I?" If you ever see her, give her my love and tell her she's beautiful.

Well Glorious, I had better cut this short. It's almost dinner time and we have to examine a bunch of fellows for insurance this afternoon and I'm on duty till 11:00 tonight.

Maybe you had better hold on to the sweater for a while. At least till I find out more about O.C.S. The picture had better wait till then too, that is, if you don't mind.

I'll write again Sunday.

> All my love to the sweetest girl in the world,
>
> Howard

Saturday—9:40 A.M.

August 8, 1942

Dearest,

It is raining here this morning. I am afraid it is a northeaster for the wind is from that direction and it is sighing as only a northeaster does. I like the rain, it is so restful, but of course it is very bad for business.

I had a short conversation with Mrs. Edward Petherbridge the other day. She wants me to tell you that Norman Linton has been make a Sergeant which I was going to tell you anyway for I had just talked to his mother that same morning. I didn't inform Mrs. Petherbridge that you refused the offer to become a Staff Sergeant. Now I am not a bit nice am I? It isn't the fact that Norman is a Sergeant that irks me 'cause Norman is bright and a sweet boy, he deserves all he can get but it is Mrs. Petherbridge's attitude that I don't like. Honey, I shouldn't talk like this, but perhaps it is just as well that you realize what a nasty person I am. You see Margaret Vialli Petherbridge has always seemed to me to be such an awful person and when you are brought into the picture I shudder, because she has always seemed to have a bit of a possessive attitude about you. The wind was taken from my sails the day you left when she went down with George Harry to get you and it seemed to me in saying good-bye you held her hand a bit too long. The going down with George was all right, but the good-bye got me. Oh well, skip it. I am crazy to even mention it. You know that I am insanely jealous of anyone who looks at you 'cause I love you so dearly. Thus you know I am a terrible person but tell me you love me anyhow, will you? Further, I am mean to write anything to make you uncomfortable when you write such sweet adorable letters to me.

Norman Wilde is coming home for the weekend. He made his solo flight last week, that's pretty good, isn't it?

Guess what? We found a big possum in the hollow of our cherry tree. I haven't looked today so I don't know whether he is still there or not.

Mother is much better, she has completed the quinine dose and she has skipped her chill and fever twice so I guess the malaria is gone. She has to have another blood test on Monday to make sure.

Chix, (Jack's wife) thinks you have the personality and brains to become an officer so there's one more added to those who stand behind you.

Darling, we do have a "grip on life and we can feel as if no matter what happens we can take it in our stride". I love you Howard, no matter what.

Love,

Your awful, terrible, Glorious

OOOOOO XXXXXXXX

August 9, 1942
Fort Jackson, S.C.

Dearest Glorious,

I still don't know definitely whether or not I'm leaving Wednesday. The "order" hasn't come to regimental headquarters yet. Some fellows have left here though with only two hours' notice. The Captain said, if I don't leave, he's going to transfer me to Northern Africa. I asked him, why do that, when South Carolina is a very reasonable facsimile. He was only kidding but anything is possible. Almost half of the 120th has been transferred this week. The 120th is evidently going to be used for training purposes only. I don't see how they are going to "pull maneuvers" with such few men. The maneuvers won't start until the middle of September and maybe they will have some new men by that time. We already have 45 new men and we are not at "full strength" yet. The "old pillrollers" are being transferred; there are only fifty of the "old boys" left. It is really tough being transferred after you've been in an outfit for a long time.

Sure I was thinking about you last Tuesday, Darling. I think of you every day, Buttercup. We have a rendezvous every night, just before I go to sleep. It's especially nice when I'm out in the field and the night is clear. You can think such beautiful thoughts looking at the moon and stars. "Our" moon is just about gone. I saw "him" yesterday morning at reveille. We will have to get another one.

I was off yesterday afternoon and today. Sleepy and I went to town, had dinner and went to a show ("I Married An Angel"). It was a "screwball picture". Sleepy wanted to walk out on it. We walked around town for a while and came back to camp early. There is nothing to do but go to a show; the South doesn't have "much" in the way of entertainment. I was really "wishing for you" last night Honey. If I could have seen you for only five minutes, I would have been contented. So I got out a few of your letters and read them over. That helped a lot.

If I leave Wednesday I'll write before we "take off", if there is time.

Goodnight Angel,

Howard

P.S. No hugs and kisses in the last letter. I miss them.

August (I don't know)

[August 9, 1942]

Sunday —10:35 P.M.

Dearest,

This'll be short. I don't know about the sweet, but I'd like it to be. Tomorrow is wash-day and my wash takes all day to do ordinarily, but tomorrow I have to go to town so I am going to get up at six and try to get as much done as possible by nine. I am taking Delores to Annapolis. She is going to try to rent a house and then I can be one of her boarders, isn't that great? I'd feel so at home with her.

Darling, your Saturday letter was nice, but all your letters are perfect to me. I grin from ear to ear when I get them and I don't get rid of that pleased expression all day long.

So you liked my day-dream all except the foreign country part. I sort of liked that, but if you'd rather make it the U.S. I can change it. I've had many other day-dreams that I'll tell you about someday. I've had one a bit contrary to the one I described to you. I wouldn't meet you in a foreign country but you'd come home after the war and we'd be married here (with all the trimmings, on the lawn, or in the new church —me in organdy, you in "tails" or maybe your uniform —or even maybe you could bring enough of your pals home to make it a military wedding— reception afterwards —then we'll go to your post in the U.S. or otherwise.) Honey, just take your pick and perhaps we can make it come true.

Were you really sorry I took off my shoes? I thought you'd be glad. I didn't think you liked to carry me, you always called me "heavyweight" (sob!). I like for you to carry me and I also like to dance with you and I don't believe you like that either.

Howard, do you think down deep in your heart that if we got our "sailboat" we'd be good "shipmates"? I know I shouldn't ever doubt that we will, but sometimes I do. You doubt that we'll have our "sailboat" don't you?

We'll drop the "taking up time on your furlough". I am now convinced it was as you wanted it. It was heaven to me!

It's 11 o'clock.

Love always,

Your Glorious

P.S. I'll not write again until I hear from you concerning O.C.S. 'cause you may not get the letter. You'll get this Tuesday or Wednesday and you'll leave Thursday, won't you? So remember I'll be waiting to hear from you.

G.

P.S. I am in the attic and Herbert and Whitey have been here visiting Drilk's girlfriends. They were leaving and they looked up and saw me here. Whitey sang "Chattanooga Choo Choo" and stressed the S.C.

G.

My attic*

Monday, August 10, 1942

10:20 P.M.

Dearest Corporal Shenton,

I love you. How could I help it when you are so kind and gentle and sweet and thoughtful to me?

Your letter today was a total surprise and it made me so thrillingly happy. I've read it and reread it. Howard, I really believe you love me. If you remain the Howard I know now after I married you I know we would be happy.

I've had lovely day-dreams today and you were in every one.

Goodnight and all my love to my darling,

G.

* Glorious and her brother gave up their rooms in the hotel for the summer so more paying guests could sleep in them. They slept in the attic.

Annapolis

August 11, 1942

10 A.M.

Honey,

Here I sit in the car parked by the hospital, waiting for mother to come out. She has finished taking quinine and she is having another blood count or test to see if the malaria germ is gone. I think it has gone because it was a slight case to begin with. After she finishes we are going on to Baltimore to shop a bit.

Yesterday's letter was a total surprise and what a nice one! Darling, you say such wonderful things to me. Do you really love me that much? Yes, I believe you do.

The last letter I wrote I said would be the last before I heard about O.C.S. but since I am mailing this here I believe you'll get it before you leave. Now, remember if you go just drop me a card giving me your address 'cause I must write.

Mother has arrived —must be on my way.

Love always,

Glorious

Ordinance Officer Candidate School

Aberdeen, Maryland

"What's that loud boom, Daddy?"

"It's just Aberdeen, baby."

Conversation between the editor and her father, in the 1950s.

Aberdeen, Md

August 15, 1942

10:30 A.M.

Dearest Glorious,

I am writing this letter because I don't think there will be any week-end passes. I was "hoping" there would be a chance to see you before classes started. From the way things look now I don't think there will be any spare time, from now until the course is finished. It's tough being this close to home and yet can't get there. But that won't be the toughest part of this O.C.S. It has all the markings of a very rugged outfit.

I arrived here Thursday morning around 11:00. I called home from Washington, D.C. about 7:30 that morning. My idea was to call you then too, but I was afraid you wouldn't be up. I received your letter before I left Wednesday and it was swell. I do "love you" Buttercup, more than anything in the world. There is no use in my trying to see you while I'm here. (That is plan anything as to "when and where"). If I ever get a week-end off I'll see you. We have to be back at camp by 7:00P.M. Sunday when we go on "pass". This is for study period; we have two hours every evening but Saturday (7:00 to 9:00).

I wanted to call you last night but I couldn't get to a phone. I will try again tonight.

Honey, I may not be able to write much while I am here. Every minute of the day is scheduled, from 6:00A.M. to 9:00 P.M. If I don't answer your letters "please" don't stop writing. I'll try and get one in, once in a while.

Have to make a formation in about five minutes. Let me hear from you soon, I'm lonesome.

"Love with all my heart,"

Howard

P.S. Address

Mr. Howard C. Shenton (if you please) almost a civilian

Co. C, Ord. Off. Cand. School

Aberdeen Proving Grounds, Maryland

August 26, 1942

Dear Glorious,

I have a few minutes before we go to study hall, so consequently I'll try and answer your letter.

We had an exam on "organization of the Army" yesterday and we were informed today that one-third of the class failed. Of course no one knows whether they passed or not because it's a rule here that you never know the marks you get through the whole course. The tests aren't signed; even the instructors don't know whose paper they are marking. I've got an idea I passed this exam. I understood every question and all the material we had been given on them. There were quite a few true and false questions and they were very "trickly worded". All in all though it wasn't too bad.

This week the routine is becoming smoother. I can find time once in a while to smoke a cigarette.

August 27, 1942

The "time" for letter writing was cut short by the "fall out" whistle. We left for study hall early last night. I'll keep writing this evening until that whistle blows again.

So far this week I've four demerits against me. Some of the boys have as many as seven for one day. The officers that make these inspections for the demerit list never miss a thing. It must take five or six of them to make such an intensive inspection.

The last letter you mailed to Fort Jackson was forwarded here. It came in this noon. (Very nice letter, Buttercup.) I'd rather get a letter from you than eat good ole G.I. chow. They give me quite a pick-up; after reading them I could go through with any job.

Everybody was having a terrible time trying to keep awake in class this afternoon. It was rather stuffy in the rooms and we don't get over six hours sleep any night. (Four demerits for falling asleep in class.) All afternoon I was kicking the guy next to me, trying to keep him awake.

I would like to come home again this weekend if the demerits would let me. But I'd better stay here and catch up on a little sleep—and there are a few things on our Company Administrative course I have to catch up on. So I'd better stay in camp. (I still want to see you though.) Maybe I'll get a chance in a couple of weeks.

Wish I could have gone to church with you Sunday. I may be able to make Sunday School next time I come home.

That "whistle" is about to blow. I'll write again Sunday.

So long Darling, (The goodbye in Baltimore was much better than this.)

P.S. The demerit list just came in. I got one. The boy next door to me got five.

H.

Co.C, Aberdeen, Md
August 29, 1942

Dearest Glorious, (that "est" did want to go after the "Dear") I wanted it there too!

I wanted to come home this evening in the worst kind of way. My demerits would have allowed me this privilege, I got 5 this week. One more and I would have been restricted. There are so many things around here for me to do though; I thought it best to get caught-up before I got too far behind. We are having two "tests" Monday; one is an exam on ammunition supply and is going to be a humdinger.

I gave my lecture this morning and I was satisfied with the job I did. My subject drawn from the hat was, "What is the Cause of Lag in Defense Production?" I wasn't too much up on the subject as I haven't read a newspaper in two weeks. I boiled it down to labor and transportation in my walk from the rear to the front of the room. The constructive criticism was that I seemed to be a bit nervous at first but gained "poise" as I went along. I was complimented on my voice. With a little practice I believe I would like giving lectures.

What was wrong with the look on my face when you mentioned being good last Sunday? There isn't much chance of my kicking-the-gong around while here. In the first place there isn't time and besides you are too tired at the end of the week to indulge in any fast-moving

114

activities. The boys at Jackson can tell you though what a "good" boy Cpl.Shenton is or was. You were on my mind too much when I wasn't busy working and with you on my mind I could never do anything wild or bad. That's one of the many reason "I love you" Legna. I've seen so many girls that ran around with anybody and did "everything". They always left me with a rather cold feeling. (Far as love is concerned.) But I don't hold it against them, if they wanted to be that way that was their business, I could still be friends with them.

If the demerit system is still in my favor next week I may come. If it isn't I'll try the following week. Whenever I can make it I'll call you when I get in Baltimore, maybe you could meet me in Annapolis and we could go out somewhere. I'll write next Saturday or Sunday if I can't come home.

Goodbye Darling,

Howard

P.S. Do I love you? You can bet your life I do!

Howard

Aberdeen, Md.

September 2, 1942

Dearest Glorious,

Up to date I have 1 demerit and still have one more day to go. If I don't get over four between now & tomorrow I'm coming home this weekend. (To Annapolis at least.) There is another "if" connected with this weekend business. This is not my weekend off and I'll have to try and swap someone passes and this is very hard to do because when there's a

115

chance to get away from here, a fellow is a damn fool if he *doesn't* take it. If I can get away I'll call you from Baltimore and maybe you can meet me in Annapolis. I'll try to get the 5:05 train (B&O) out of Aberdeen and it will take me right to Camden Station and I can call you while waiting on the Toonerville trolley to Annapolis. Even if you can't meet me I'll get home some way but I thought perhaps we could go to a show or do "something". After that, I could even go back to Baltimore and stay Saturday night. I'll think about that when I get to Annapolis though.

The tension around here is getting very taut again. We are in our 3rd week and the first washouts are in the 5th. Everybody is really "bucking". (That's army term for trying to get an N.C.O. rating in the "ranks") Pvts buck for Cpl & Cpls buck for Sgts ratings.) We are bucking for a "little yellow bar", some say it's worth it and some say it isn't. That word "yellow" is never used in the army neither is retreat; the word for retreat around here is retrograde. The British brought this about!

Sorry to hear about you being sick. I started to come home last weekend. I should have, my pillroller experience might have helped you.

Hope I can see you this weekend, Buttercup! That would help me a lot. It's a relief to get away from here and seeing you makes it perfect.

Study hall period is blowing.

Love to *my* Darling,

Howard

Aberdeen Md.

September 9, 1942

Dearest Glorious,

Mother Nature stepped in this morning and gave us a break. It was raining so hard this morning we couldn't drill so we had an hour in which to browse around the barracks. It seems very unusual. Last night the lights went out during study period around 8:00 o'clock. We thought they would let us come home and take it easy until 9:00. "Time", the Nemesis of the Allied Nations and officer candidates.

September 13, 1942

Dearest,

I have a few minutes, so finishing this letter "seems in order". The bus left Baltimore at 2:45 and took us right into camp. So it was the best trip I've had yet, even had time to make "supper formation". From Shady Side to Baltimore was the best part of the day though. Saying good-bye wasn't so good, Glorious. I hate to say good-bye to you. Even though I know I'm not going very far, I feel like it's going to be an awful long time before I see you again. It will be a "great day" Legna, when we can hold hands and say goodbye to someone, instead of to each other. Anyway it was a swell weekend and "you" make that possible Buttercup. (Everything is perfect when I'm with you.) I didn't lose too much sleep either, at least I feel ready to tackle next week's work <u>with celerity</u>. (How did that get in here?)

There isn't a thing for us to study tonight unless we pick a few movements in drill and discuss them. This usually ends in an argument so that isn't so good. The platoon leader will be yelling every two minutes for us to keep quiet. But I can work on my ten minute lesson a little.

Got about 3 minutes left, so bye-bye, Darling and remember, I love you with all my heart.

Love,

Howard

My wee room

Annapolis

Tuesday, September 15—7:30 P.M.

Dearest,

When I entered the colonial door of 225 Gloucester Street this afternoon much to my surprise there was a letter on the hall table for me. It made me quite happy for it was from Officer Candidate Howard Shenton (pardon, Howard C. Shenton). I hurried up the steps to my room to read it and it was quite sweet. He says he loves me! That makes my heart go pitter pat. All joking aside, thanks darling, for saying that I made your weekend perfect. You made mine worthwhile too.

Derwill entered Annapolis Business School on Monday and he had to have his fountain pen back which I had borrowed for six months. Thus I am writing with a straight pen which I purchased at the 5 & 10 this P.M. At the same time I bought some ink, but I couldn't get the top off so now I am writing with borrowed ink. I just can't get away from that borrowing anyhow.

Tomorrow night I think I'll journey home 'cause I want to get some clothes to wear to P.T.A. on Thursday night. That seems silly to use gasoline just to get a dress, shoes, etc., but I really just want to go home anyhow.

Howard, as I pass the Ritchie Memorial and that gasoline station where we bought gas I feel as if they are sacred ground. Our happiness while being there has made them so. Surely Howard, after this mess is over and our love is still the same it alone will give us the right to marry even though there are obstacles to overcome.

Yes, it is difficult to say good-bye. As I ride out Camden Street down to Barrie and out Hanover I have a very empty feeling as if there is nothing to live for. As I ride farther that feeling begins to leave me as I think of your words, "Cheer up, Glorious, better days are coming." Oh darling, better days will come, I know it. And our days haven't been bad anyhow. We are lucky. I don't know why I deserve to be as fortunate as I have been.

You are quite good at handling the English language— "celerity"—I had to look that one up!

Now I must put on my little dress and take this over to the Post Office so it can go out in the 9:30 mail.

Hope I'll have time to write again this week so you'll get it on Saturday since you won't be coming home. However if I can't get to it you'll have to read this one over again. At least this last part anyhow 'cause what I say here is what I mean in every letter. I love you Howard, so very much —every minute I long to be with you.

Love always to my Sweetheart,

Your own Glorious

OOOOOOOO XXXXXXXXXX

I Love You

Barracks #7

September 16, 1942

7:20 P.M.

Dearest Glorious,

The atmosphere in this barrack is slightly electrified this evening. We are sitting around waiting to be called before the Company Board. Everybody thought only the boys washing-out would have to go before this Board but every man in the Company has to go. Why? No one knows. I think it is a procedure the Company officers use to get acquainted with the men and see what their general appearance is under the fire of a barrage of questions. It is rumored they throw questions at you and try to get you excited. This might have some bearing on the wash-out coming. (Aberdeen has very good launderers.)

So far I've collected "0 gigs" this week. (demerits). Wish I could get a "pass", I'd like to come home this weekend. There is something about Shady Side that really attracts me. Glorious, I miss you. Even as busy as we are I still think of you and wish I were with you. (Don't say I shouldn't do this, the next time I see you because it helps me a lot when I get a little tired & disgusted.) You can get disgusted around here sometimes too, even though you can't show it. The officers around here try to make you feel like a two year old kid at times but they can't get my "goat". I laugh at them (inwardly of course!) If one doesn't like the way you look at him, he'll pull his pen & little blue book out and give you a few demerits by finding something wrong with the way you part your hair.

To get back to Shady Side, I'll start a new paragraph. I wandered from the subject a bit in the last one. I want to tell you, Buttercup, I love you. (In case you didn't suspect it.) You are quite an attraction, "little lady". The trouble is, I don't see enough of you. But —there's a war going on and <u>that trouble</u> can't be helped now. Someday I'll give it a lot of time & thought to see if that trouble can't be remedied (pillroller).

9:00 P.M.

I had to stop & go before the Board about an hour ago. I think I did O.K., answered every question but don't know if all were correct.

I had better quit now before the lights go out. Will write again Sunday. Gosh, wish I could come home this weekend.

Goodnight "Darling",

Love, Howard

P.S. You are very lovely tonight Miss Andrews. I can picture you now. You probably have your hair up but you are still lovely. Howard.

Annapolis

My Room

Thursday, September 17, 1942 —5:15 P.M.

Dearest,

Thank goodness it is rainning (how many n's?) It may cool it off a bit which would be greatly appreciated by this infinitesimal bit of humanity existing on Earth in God's great Universe. Today has been terribly warm and being shut up with 40 kids doesn't make it any cooler. But I survived and they were good. My lessons were fairly interesting! Science slays them.

I came home on the train this afternoon and I thought about you. I came down with a couple of other teachers. The teacher we ride with went to Baltimore to do some shopping. There is a P.T.A. tonight so in a few minutes I have to go get the Wobble Bump and Ache and go back to Glen Burnie.

I refused an invitation to go on board a beautiful sailing yacht tonight. The Lieutenant who eats at our table was going to take another girl and me. He is an instructor at the Academy, a middle aged man. He seemed rather peeved that I couldn't go and he tried to persuade me to shirk my duty, but naturally I wouldn't. He wanted me to meet the Lieutenant who is on the boat now. Ha ha! He is 32. Too bad —isn't he missing a lot not meeting me? I am so sorry I couldn't go. No, Darling — only joking. I would like to have seen the boat, but as for the Lieutenant— he doesn't and wouldn't mean a thing. *You* are my Sweetheart and will soon be my Lieutenant too, I hope.

Be good darling, and remember I love you and am all for you.

Love always to my Sweetheart,

Your own Glorious

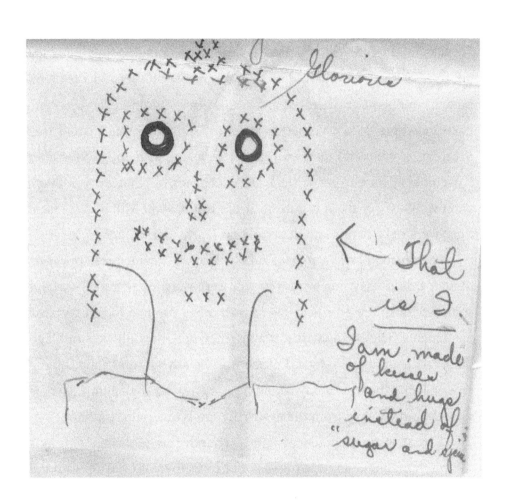

Shady Side, Md.

Sunday, September 20, 1942

5:30 P.M.

Dearest Howard,

Last night I missed you a great deal. It was tough going, but I got going on a cover for one of the living room sofa pillows and I felt a bit better. Your being at Aberdeen and coming home almost every weekend has spoiled me. When you were down in South Carolina I could take Saturday nights without a whimper. I was hardened to it. Now after November I'll have to get hardened all over again, but that is my problem and I won't worry about it now nor will I trouble you with it. At present I just want to be happy and thankful that I have you so near.

Thankyou (all one word) for calling, Honey. It made me happy even though I didn't say much. Just so you were satisfied with it, I was. Of course, with so few words to say to each other you had to bring up the Lieutenants. The sailing part was all right, you're the only person I'll go sailing with and you know it. I'm *sentimental* anyhow and about sailing especially. By the way, today would be a peachy day for sailing. There is a good wind blowing from the north, the sun is out, but it isn't hot.

I went to Sunday School and to church this morning. This was communion Sunday. I didn't take it, but I was there. Rev. Culp read the roll of men (boys) in the service. You were right there; or rather your name was on the roll.

Miss Grace called me this morning. She misplaced your address and she wanted to send your pants. Naturally I was the logical person to have your address. I was glad she called. I hope she has it right so you'll get them.

Yesterday I had my hair cut. You'll like it.

Six whole days before I see you, but it gives me something to look forward to. I wish I could find a nice formal dance to attend next week. You wouldn't like it. I love to dance with you.

Your letters last week were the sweetest ever. I know you love me and I promise not to tell you not to think of me. If I couldn't think of you I wouldn't like it at all. I guess "thinking" has been a great source of pleasure for both of us. Many are the nights that I have gone to sleep thinking of you and pleasant thoughts at that.

I am in the attic and Mother just came up to find some scrap metal. There is a drive on this week. She found a couple of pieces, an old pair of skates and a stove lifter.

Norman W. will not be called until November so he is going to teach till then up in Linthicum Heights. He was at church this A.M.. He has a terrific cold.

The atmosphere has completely changed in the past 3 hours from a hot sultry cloudy one to a completely clear, windy, chilly one. I am going to get a sweater to put on. I dug all my winter skirts out of the moth balls a few minutes ago so I'll be ready when it really gets cold. Can you wear a winter uniform before October 1st if it gets cold or does Order 387 (or something) mean that you absolutely must wear summer khaki until then? Gee, soon I can send your sweater, maybe! And you don't want it I know. We'll try it on this weekend. I've had it on lots. It'll be a piece of me when you get it.

I'll write again this week. Capt. Ennis Bast's wife died.

Mr. Frank Lee fell off a ladder and crushed his spine. He's in the hospital.

Thought I'd better tell you those bits of news.

125

Love, no I don't want to end yet. I want to tell you I'll be thinking of you tonight and I'll imagine you are very close to me.

Howard, if we ever do marry, you'll let me put my hair up, won't you? I'd look terrible if I didn't and I don't want to get a permanent! I guess if I must put my hair up we'll have to have twin beds! Now, I got you.

I love you, darling,

Yours,

Glorious

P.S. We'll compromise on 1 o'clock this Sunday morning and then we'll make Sunday school.

G

P.S.2 Darling, I almost forgot. We have the cutest kittens and there is a gray one like our other gray cat only this one has a tail. Please remember to see it this weekend. Also, we'll take some pictures. Now that makes three "musts".

1—Sweater

2—Kitten

3 —Picture

Always your Glorious

Aberdeen, Md.
September 20, 1942
8:30 A.M.

Dearest Glorious,

I feel a little out of place this morning. This is the second Sunday I've been in camp & I don't like it. Shady Side is where I should be on Sundays at least while I'm in Maryland. Honey, I missed you last night. There was a dance for the O.C.s at the gym last night. About ten of us went and we had a fairly good time but I kept thinking of you. I could have had a much better time dancing with you, Buttercup. The girls were from Baltimore and Wilmington and seemed to be quite a nice bunch of young "ladies'. The dance was very well chaperoned with Lts, M.Ps. & the dear old ladies who sit around the sidelines like statues. Anyway the fellows have something to talk about this morning.

As far as I know Legna, I've missed the first washout. I went before one Board but everybody did that. The following day though about eighty of the boys had to go before the "School Board". This is the Board the high officials of the O.C.S. "sit" on. There was a list on the bulletin board Friday of the boys deficient in academics & I wasn't in it. (I was rather surprised to think I passed Company Admini-stration.) Even though your name does appear on this deficient list, that doesn't mean you wash-out. It is a hint to buckle-down, you could be a little below passing grade and still continue the course. Of course there is a certain average to maintain. The academics count more in the second four weeks. This means I will have to get the Depot & Supply course under my thumb and believe me it's a tough one to "thumb under".

I didn't get any demerits last week and so far this week I haven't accumulated any. However there are four more days to go and it doesn't take long to get five "gigs". Keep your fingers crossed for me Legna; I want to see you next weekend. There isn't much studying going on around here on weekends. You try to study but there are so many boys around talking you can't really concentrate and the first thing you know you are engaged in a conversation that lasts for a couple of hours. Some of these guys sure like to talk.

Say, what was wrong with you Saturday evening when I called? Did I wake you out of a sound sleep or were you peeved about something? Maybe I got the wrong impression but you didn't seem to be enjoying yourself answering the phone. I still felt a lot better though after I talked with you.

Buster wrote me and said the Med. Det. of the 120th Inf. is broken up. There are only twenty fellows left. That is a darn shame, a swell outfit like that scattered to the four winds. That was an outfit which could have gone through hell & high water together. At least I wouldn't have minded going though it with them.

Legna, if you go sailing with those Lts, do me a favor. Take a life-belt along; I don't trust those guys under sail. They may know how to read a compass and steer a course but they don't know how to sail. Honey, I'm only kidding about the life-belt but they are still bum sailors.

So long, darling, I'll see you next weekend. (Provided I don't get six gigs.)

("There's *Love* in my heart")

Howard

225 Gloucester St

Annapolis

Monday, September 21, 1942

9:15 P.M.

Dear Totch,

Can't resist the urge to write a few words to you. Haven't anything to say, really, but I just feel nearer when I write and then I like to think you are hearing from me often.

Here I sit with a heating pad at my back. I've been freezing all day; the sudden drop in the temperature was too much for me. I hope I am not catching a cold 'cause they are such miserable things and I couldn't kiss you this weekend if I get one. Everyone around me has had or now has one. The other teachers in the car have them. The people I eat with have them so I've really been exposed.

Drilk left Ivan's ignition on all night last night and he wouldn't start this A.M.. Luckily Uncle John was at home and he helped to push and get him started. I was scared all the way to Annapolis for fear Ivan would stop because he is so susceptible to choking out. We got there though, and in plenty of time too. You see Drilk comes up with me on Monday A.M.s 'cause he goes to Business School. It is a relief to have him drive although I fuss with him constantly about the speed, etc.

The moon is almost full; it should be pretty on Saturday night.

I think about you often and wonder what problem you are tackling and whether or not you are happy. I try to picture you studying, drilling or sitting in class listening. My mind's eye always sees you intent on what you are doing, looking and being very intelligent, not smiling, but pleasant. I never see you in any mischief although Saturday night I had a tough time keeping myself free from a doubt about it.

Thought perhaps I'd receive a letter today, but I didn't. Tomorrow morning ought to see it appear on the hall table. I'll read it several times before I go down to meet Mrs. Elliot then I'll take it to school and read it at lunch, maybe. It'll boost me all day.

Must get some sleep, maybe I can stall the cold.

Love to my very own Darling,

Your Glorious

P.S. I'll save all kisses and hugs for this weekend.

G

Annapolis
Tuesday afternoon
5 P.M.
September 22, 1942

Hello,

Why do I want to write to you all the time? I know! So do you!

Your letter came this A.M., but it wasn't on the hall table for I received it myself from the postman on the steps. Ha ha! I was just coming back from breakfast as he came down the street.

Why did you write at 8:30 A.M.? Weren't you sleepy? Or were you up all night? I know you just wanted to get me out of the way for the day.

Golly, what I wouldn't have given to have been dancing with you on Saturday night. You didn't really miss me did you? Tell the truth. Those "ladies" from Baltimore and Wilmington must have been quite alluring, much more so than an ole staid schoolteacher who is quite a huzzy in private life. No, Howard all joking aside I guess you would rather have been with me (I hope).

Guess what? There is another "chaperonage" coming up for me. A dance! Saturday night October 3rd at Glen Burnie High. That is the week after this one coming. Dare I hope that you <u>could</u> and <u>would</u> make it? We could dance together at least, not so close as usual, but I'd be there. Do you think you could swap passes that weekend? I could meet you in Glen Burnie instead of Annapolis. I am going to have Ivan's lights fixed so I can use him. Dad has plenty of gas, but his tires aren't so good so I hate to use his car. Think this over and tell me this weekend how you feel about it. I know it depends on "gigs" and a pass. But your wanting to come or not wanting to come may have some bearing on it too. The question is, did you think you might be coming that weekend anyhow? I have to go and it would be marvelous to have you, if not I'll have to get Drilk to go with me.

10 P.M.

Honey, I'm cold, could you keep me warm if you were here? I haven't been warm since Sunday when that north wind blew in. Last night I went to bed with a heating pad. Oh well, I'm just one of those people who is always freezing.

Darling, I'm glad you weren't on the list of those deficient in Academics. Of course you shouldn't be 'cause I think you know what it's all about. Howard, you're a bright boy.

I'm sorry you thought I was peeved on Saturday evening. I wasn't peeved, but I was disappointed, very much so, that I wouldn't see you that night. You see, Howard, it's this way. Perhaps you wouldn't understand how I feel, but I love you.

In case you're worried, the dance isn't formal so there won't be that disturbing element.

I am reading a book. (Amazing). "The Raft" by Robert Trumball. The story of the three sailors who survived 34 days in a little rubber life raft when they were forced to land their plane on the water. Interesting, but gruesome!

If I'm troubling you with too much mail, just drop me a card and I'll keep on writing. Howard, I've got to write to you so I can be near to you. Do you mind my chatter so much?

I think I'll go to the movies tomorrow night. I'll see Clark Gable & Lana Turner in "something". Maybe I won't go, maybe I'd rather study.

Love to my sweetheart,

Always your Glorious

OX They are both mighty big and they are just for you.

Aberdeen, Md.

September 23, 1942

Dearest Glorious,

Honey, you are swell, I don't know what I would do if it weren't for you. Yesterday, I was really down in the dumps (so to speak). The big wash-out came and it took quite a few of the boys through the wringer. We lost 45 in the Company and 8 out of my platoon. It made all of us feel a little downhearted to see some of the boys go. Some were darn good fellows & seemed to be rather bright. In fact much more so than some of the guys still here. But that's the way things go in the army and there is nothing you can do about it. Anyway, I was feeling a little low about the whole thing and Honey, your letter put me on the beam again. I was a little surprised to get one today.

The gigs caught up with me today. I drew "one" for having dust on the rail of my bed. There is still a margin of four to catch one yet and one day left for the running.

September 24, 1942

Dearest,

That running was cut short last night by "lights out". I can't see how these letters can make sense. You don't have time to think about anything but O.C.S. around here.

I beat the gig list, none today, making me a grand total of 1 for the week. My bunkmate was going to Reading, Pa, this weekend to see his girl. He hasn't seen her for 14 months. (He won't see her this weekend). The gigs beat him; he got six & is confined until midnight Saturday. That's what makes you want to cuss O.C.S. & everything pertaining to it. But I can't cuss, I'll be home this weekend and Honey that makes me very happy.

It's almost time for study hall formation. I hope you get this Saturday. I'll call from Baltimore if there is time between connections. Will call from Annapolis anyway.

Love,

Howard

Aberdeen, Md.

September 27, 1942

5:20 P.M.

Dearest Glorious,

I just came back from chow and there is still plenty of time before study hall formation. So I thought I had better write now, when there is time.

I want to tell you about what a wonderful weekend I had in Shady Side this weekend. It all started in Annapolis & ended there too. But the best part of it happened in Shady Side. I was met at the train by a beautiful blue-eyed gal with a dark-colored bow in her hair. I never did find out just what color the bow was. First we went to a show & that was alright because she seemed to enjoy the picture. Personally, I thought the picture a bit on the silly side. There were too many love scenes and they weren't carried through with the right spirit. It was obvious the boy didn't love the girl & equally as obvious that the gal was crazy about the boy. But I don't think a girl in true life could throw herself at a guy who didn't love her. There would be no point to it. (Love is something which must be shared mutually.) So much for the show. Later we met her Mom, Dad & brother and went to Shady Side. It was swell sitting beside her in the car but she wouldn't play hands with me. When we got home & the folks went to bed, I kissed her oh! so many times. She wanted me to go home around 1:00 o'clock but that wouldn't work because I hadn't seen her for two weeks. Sleep doesn't mean anything when you "love" someone the way I love this little blue-eyed girl. She finally chased me home though but I saw her again this morning. Her hair was a little mussed but I loved it that way. We tried on a sweater she had knitted for me. It was a perfect fit but for some reason she didn't think I liked it. However, that's a mistake; I'd like to wear it under my blouse when I graduate from O.C.S., if I could. (It would make her much closer to me, if that's possible.) Next we took some pictures and then she "brought" me to Annapolis to catch the 1908 model of the Chattanooga Choo Choo for Baltimore. She said I was a bit indecent riding to Annapolis, but I just wanted to sit a little closer to her, besides I was afraid the door might fly open on a left hand turn. (The latter is a good excuse, No!) I kissed her goodbye and took-off. Gosh, I hate to leave her. She smiles when I say goodbye but it doesn't wrinkle her nose like the one she gives me when she is struck by a "spot of humor". I'm going to see her again, "as soon as possible". We still have a standing Sunday School date. I almost forgot, we like gray kittens but that's a very long story. I only see her on weekends but I think of her between these weekends. To her, "I give all my love"

So long Buttercup,

Howard

225 Gloucester St.

Annapolis, Md.

September 28, 1942

5:25 P.M.

Dearest,

I am cold and jittery this afternoon and your presence could remedy both, because if I weren't jittery I don't think I'd be cold. Yes, you could cure my jitters. Why? Well, you just can. I'm jittery because I've had a headache all day and I've relaxed since school was out and it has gone leaving me with a bad case of jitters. All I need to do is relax still more and away will go the jitters. You're the gentleman who can make me relax!

Honey, I loved being with you this weekend and I am hoping for many more just like it. Except that I don't like the 4 o'clock Sunday morning hours. Darling, I love to be with you, but we are being unfair to each other; such hours are bad for anyone and you have to work so hard. I just think you should get more sleep out of your 24 hours leave. By the way—I didn't sleep on Sunday afternoon, I painted. Yes, painted all the furniture in the bedroom which I am to have this winter (as yet I'm still in the attic). I painted it pure white with red tops. That is a red top to the bureau and washstand. Oh it's quite snazzy. I am having one completely red piece in it, a rocking chair. I can sit in my little red rocking chair and rock and rock. Uncle John didn't like the red chair. He said I should have put some white on it. I am going to have pure white frilly curtains and a white spread. I have to paint the floor too. No, it will be neither white nor red, but light gray! Honey, pardon me for troubling you with such domestic affairs but it's all I know.

This morning I woke up at six and wondered what you were doing and whether or not you were cold. Maybe two undershirts could have kept you warm.

Time for dinner. See you.

8:50 P.M.

Honey,

I'm down in the living room in front of the fire place. I'll not go up to get the rest of this letter 'cause the stairs are long and it's cold up there. I'll just say what I have to say then dash up, get the letter, address it, and take it over to the post office. I want to make the 9:30 mail.

I've had a fairly nice evening. Dinner was good, all the "Navy" was in blue, and looked quite nice. Everyone was gay! After returning to Mrs.Valk's (where I sleep) we lit a fire in the fireplace and Mrs. Taylor (an elderly lady who also lives here) sat down and played the piano. They were nice old songs that I knew. Stephen Foster's most of them, "Beautiful Dreamer", "Jeannie with the Light Brown Hair". The fire, sweet music, the old, old house made me feel as if I were living in a story book, but the papers which I had in front of me to be marked jerked me back to reality very suddenly.

My headache is still with me. I believe I've used my eyes a little too much. I painted until 8:30 last night and the light wasn't too good.

After I mail this I'm going to bed and really get warm. Huh! Here I am worrying about being a bit cold, when Gabriel Hester is talking about what's going on over in Europe. Golly, I guess it behooves us in America to be thankful for what we have and take the attitude that no sacrifice is too great. I have resolved long ago to be just as agreeable and "uncriticizing" as I know how to be, but I find myself forgetting often.

Love always to my very own Sweetheart,

From Your Glorious

XXXXXXXXXXXXXXXXXXXXXXXXXXXXXXXXXXXXXXXXXXX
OOOOOOOOOOOOOOOOOOOOOOOOOOO-
OOOOOOOOOOOOOOOOOOOOOOO

9:50

Didn't make the 9:30 mail so will mail in morning. Just thought I'd tell you I have plenty of cover and I am going to sleep nice and warm. I have a heating pad at my feet. See what a cold ole person you'll have to sleep with! You might have to say what the moron said, "What put that cold thing in bed with me!

Ha Ha. G.

Annapolis, Md.
September 29, 1942
4:50 P.M.

Darling,

Up to this point I've had a very hard day, but beyond this point I'm living on top of the world for at this point I received a letter from my own dearest sweetheart. And what a letter! I simply can't wipe the smile off my face. You see that's what he can do for me, just a piece of paper with a story on it and his name signed to it can take away all my burdens and I feel like a million dollars. What would happen if he were here to smile at me and talk to me and even maybe kiss me? Why I suppose I'd just be overcome with happiness.

Ivan has no lights and I walked down to the garage this afternoon to ask the mechanic to see if he could fix them. I may need to use Ivan at night and it would be bad if there were no lights. I saw about buying a new battery too.

I am going to get cleaned up for supper now. See you later.

G

9 P.M.

Are you cold? I am literally freezing! Do you have any heat in your barracks? I don't have any in mine yet, but I do have plenty of blankets. I thought about you this morning again and wondered if you were cold.

I had spaghetti and meat balls for supper tonight and I didn't like it. In the first place it is so hard to eat; by the time I get it in my mouth I don't feel it's worth the effort. There too, it's too filling.

Honey, I hope that you are succeeding in "thumbing under" that "Depot and Supply". You can, you know.

I am still hoping that you can make the dance, if you want to! Do you suppose you'd have time to drop me a line about the "demos"? So I'd get it Saturday. 'Course then would still be the uncertainty of the "pass". Never mind, don't bother. I'll just live in the dark till Saturday night and gosh, that would be a bright night if you would call and say, "Glorious, this is Ha'ard [the Shady Side colloquial way to pronounce Howard]. I'm in Baltimore". But, if you can't make it please don't worry and don't do anything that would put you in the wrong in any way. I understand everything or at least you once told me that I did. Drilk has consented to go with me if you can't come so I'll be escorted even if not by my <u>favorite</u> escort.

I am not going to take this over tonight, on second thought—I will.

Love to my darling,
Glorious

Aberdeen, Md.

September 29, 1942

5:25 P.M.

Dearest Glorious,

I feel a little let-down this evening. I thought sure there would be a letter from you today. But there wasn't so I feel better by writing to you.

The Depot & Supply class was a killer this afternoon. We had a four hour problem and I still can't account for about $9,000.00 in property. I filled out so many forms this afternoon, requisition, receipts, shipping tickets & stock record cards. (A very beautiful mess.) If I was Chief of Supply for the army, the troops would get their supplies but the records would certainly be shot to pieces.

This morning we had an exam on motor convoys, customs of the service & safeguarding military information. It was very simple. I can absorb "stuff" like that very easy. The exam was by far the easiest we had so far.

"Honey", I've really been thinking about the sweater you knitted. It would come in handy around here now. I've never known it to be so cold in Maryland this time of year. Maryland is still a great place though. I'll take it every time. (Maybe I had better say Shady Side.)

I've been inquiring around trying to get a pass for this weekend but so far it's no soap. These boys don't believe in hanging around camp when they can take off and another thing, pay day is sometime this week so lack of money won't stop them. But "Buttercup", if it's possible I will be at that dance Saturday night. At the present though, it looks rather hopeless.

You know I almost forgot about those pictures you took Sunday. If they turn out I want them. So when you have them developed get two prints. Will you?

"Legna", I have to go now. Remember what I told you in case you are asked, Do I love you? The answer is a big "YES", Honey.

Goodbye now,

Love,

Howard

Annapolis, Md.

October 1, 1942

5 P.M.

Darling,

This morning I was quite surprised to see another letter from you. When I opened it and found that you were disappointed at not hearing from me I was kind of hurt. You know by now that I didn't make that 9:30 mail on Monday night and that's why you didn't receive the letter. This one will make the 9:30 tonight so you'll get it tomorrow, and not only that, another will go off on Friday so you'll receive it on Saturday. I can't have you being disappointed 'cause when you're unhappy I'm unhappy. You see it's because I love you. You have never disappointed me after that first Saturday and I am aware of it. I think you must be a very sweet person, are you?

The lady who lives in the room right under mine is always asking the daughter of the lady who owns the house if she will have a highball. My, my, the girl doesn't refuse either, she merely says, "Mrs. Taylor, you're just leading me astray." And she goes on and drinks it. I'm just waiting for Mrs. Taylor to ask me. Boy oh boy! No, she wouldn't ask me, somehow or other just by looking at me people know I'm not the type. I'm really glad they can tell it because I wouldn't like to be pestered.

This week has simply flown on wings of I don't know what. I am still very optimistic about the weekend, but I noticed that you are not. I know, don't tell me again, you're just stating facts. Well, Honey, if the "facts" are stacked against us we can take it can't we, even though we don't want to. However I haven't given up yet!

141

This afternoon after school I had a terrific scare. As I was leaving my room to go up to a teacher's meeting I noticed a large crowd of children standing outside all looking in one direction so I looked too. In the center of the crowd there were two girls (big girls, too) having a tearing down fight, with fists, mind you. I was undecided as to what to do, but I finally made up my mind to push my way through the crowd and get one of the girls. I did that, even though my knees were shaking when I grabbed her and pulled her in the door. By that time one of the men teachers was on the scene. And the fight was over. My gosh, Howard, we certainly do have some tough customers at that school. Imagine, two grown up girls being undignified enough to have a fist fight right where everyone could see. Of course the other children (especially the boys) were sicking them on. I don't know whether I did the correct thing or not, I guess I should have sent them both up to the office, but I couldn't get hold of the other one through the crowd. Oh well, so much for my trials and tribulations, you aren't interested.

"Scoop" [Glorious's roommate at Hood College] wrote me yesterday and wants me to go back to Campus Day at Hood with her on October 10th. I believe I'll go. You won't be coming home and even if you were I'd get back Saturday night in time to meet you in Baltimore and we could go down together. I'd love to ride the Wobble Bump and Ache with you. But let's not discuss next weekend we'll get this one out of the way first. It's always best to concentrate on one thing at a time, you get along better.

So you lost track of $9,000. Not so much if you were dealing with a $1,000,000. Were you? That's all right, Honey, just keep plugging. Yes, I guess you're saying, "Uh! She can sit home and say that, but she doesn't know what it's like." You're right I don't anything about O.C.S., but I do know what "plugging" is like. It's tough, but it has its compensations and the harder the plug, the bigger and the more enjoyed are the rewards. If I could, you can bet I'd be right in there helping you for all I am worth. I love you, Darling.

Now that I have ranted my rant I guess I'll put this in an envelope and go to supper. On my way back, I'll mail it to the sweetest man I know.

Love, love, love, Your Glorious

Aberdeen, Md.
October 1, 1942

Dearest Legna,

I can't make the dance Saturday night. Sunday I am platoon guide & Monday platoon leader, so you see Buttercup I won't be able to leave even if I could get a pass. "I'll just have to dream a few dances with you."

Two of your letters came yesterday & Honey, they were alright. You could never write me too often, it gives me a swell feeling when I get one, but two makes my outlook on life shine better than an O.C.'s belt buckle.

Depot & Supply is still hitting me on the chin. I do believe though I'm beginning to understand it much better now. The four hour problem cleared up the situation a bit. The morning classes have been very easy. We've had Chemical Warfare and Bomb Disposal. The Chemical was easy for me; I had all the material covered, at Fort Jackson. First-aid figures in the subject a lot so that made it easy for me too.

Glorious, I'm sorry about the dance because I did want to come. I'd go anywhere to be with you. Let's go dancing somewhere next time I come home.

143

I said I wouldn't call you anymore: I retract that statement. I'll call Sunday around noon. I should be able to get a phone by that time. It usually takes two hours to get a call in so kind of expect it around 12.30 or 1:00.

Dance one dance with me anyway. Will you? I'll be thinking of you, Sweetheart.

Love,
Howard

My attic, in bed
Sunday, October 3, 8:50 P.M.

Darling,

You will not be disappointed this Tuesday. I'll see to that. This is going to be short and I hope sweet —at any rate, it's a word from me to you. I'll tell you I had a perfect weekend and of course, you know why. Howard, to hear your voice over that phone on Saturday evening was the most thrilling music I've ever heard. You can never have any idea how happy it made me. I appreciate your coming, for it must not have been easy. I hope it was worth it. I guess there is nothing we can do about losing sleep. As things stand we'll just have to lose it if we want to be together. I believe I'm used to it now, but I don't like for you not to get any rest. You look well though.

This afternoon I went over to the Episcopal Church to one of their anniversary services. It was rather inspiring, but the standing up and sitting down in the Episcopal ritual kind of got me. I sat and looked at my little "flaming bomb" and thought of you. (It was quite warm in the church so I had my coat on my lap.) After church the entire congregation went over to the hall and had a free supper. Really a celebration, I'd say!

144

Tonight I've pittled around, not doing much of anything. Took a bath, packed my suitcase, etc. I'm ready for another week's work and I'm looking forward to seeing you next weekend. Of course I know it's one chance in 100. At any rate it's nice to dream.

Honey, it's 9:10 and I want to get plenty of rest tonight, do you mind? I'd really get it if you were here.

Love, love, love always, my Darling,

Your Glorious

P.S. Mrs. Shea says if she were me and Howard asked her to marry him she'd say, "Yes".

Same day (October 3, 1942)
8:55 P.M.

Honey,

The first part of this letter will go off in about a half hour and you'll receive it in the morning, I hope. This continuation will be mailed in the morning and you'll receive it on Saturday, I presume.

Since I have talked to you this afternoon I've done quite a few things. I've eaten my supper, taken my walk to the post office, decided not to go to the movies and read the October Reader's Digest. Some very good articles in it, I believe, only I haven't read them yet. There is a condensation of the book, "See Here, Private Hargrove", that looks as if it might be pretty good. Here's one excerpt now, "He who can does; he who can't teaches". Ha ha! You ought to like that. Oh, there's lots more you'd enjoy too.

145

Howard, I've gone and done it, just what I didn't want to do. I've caught a peach of a cold and it's giving me heck and this is only the beginning. If you do come to that dance, I'd guess we'd better not dance, you might catch it and goodness, you can't kiss me. Maybe though, it'll be better by Saturday. I'll doctor myself up tomorrow night. Now, I guess you won't come if you could 'cause I won't be pretty to look at or nice to be around.

Yes, I know you could have used my sweater or rather your sweater. I've thought about you and knew you were cold, but hoped you weren't. Today you went into woolens though, so you shouldn't be cold anymore. However, just say the word and I'll mail the sweater.

Tomorrow will be an easy day, only two classes. How come? Well, there are only six periods in the day, one of them goes for lunch and five for class. It so happens I have a study period, a free period and three classes on a normal Friday. Tomorrow we are having an assembly which takes one period so I'll have only two classes. Long story to say so little isn't it, Honey?

This letter is punctuated by my stopping to blow my nose, it's very frequent, I assure you. I am glad it's loosening up though, for that makes me much more comfortable. Hope my Kleenex holds out.

Must go to bed, sleep is detrimental to the cold itself and I want it to scoot away fast. You'll let me go won't you?

Howard, I love you and I believe that you love me.

Hope to see you Saturday evening. You'll call by 8 if you're coming or rather by 7:45. If you can't come I can take it, but I sure do want to see you and dance with you in spite of my cold. Maybe if I'd not look up at you, you'd be above it.

146

Love always to my very own sweet sweetheart.

From,

Your Glorious

P.S. I am and will be thinking of you. G.

P.S. Be good, Darling. That means be better than when you are with me, 'cause when we are together, we're indecent.

Love, G.

Aberdeen, Md.

October 4, 1942

5:00 P.M.

Dearest,

Army camps are certainly desolate & forlorn looking places on Sunday afternoon. Kind of makes you feel that way too. I got to camp around 4:00 o'clock, made good connections in Baltimore and even had a seat. Met Sears & his Dad while walking to the Orderly Room to get rid of my pass. We "batted the breeze" for a while, then went to supper. I'm all set for study period now. This is our last week for Depot & Supply so I've really got to "buckle down" & get some good marks. Especially on the final exam.

I've talked with a few of the boys about being restricted next weekend. They all seemed to think we will be because the other O.C.S. Companies have been restricted the 9th weekend. But I'll let you know for sure about that Friday. If I can get off I'll call Friday evening. I'm still hoping the Baltimore plan materializes.

Honey, the sweater is swell. It's really warm and then it makes you much closer to me. That's the way I want you, very close.

Too bad we broke "Andrews General Order #6" by staying up so late Saturday night. However, I'm not sorry. <u>IT</u> was worth staying up for. Darling, I admit it isn't quite "up to snuff" but we are young & can take it. We'll set a deadline next time, if you want it that way.

Thanks for another lovely weekend Legna. I enjoyed the dance even though I couldn't hold you tight. Don't forget the pictures.

"To my very 'high particular'".

(Gosh, love is great)

Howard

P.S. I'll write again if I get a chance (this week). I'll still call Friday evening if we get the weekend off.

Goodbye, "Lovely"

H

Annapolis, Md.
October 6, 1942
9:20 P.M.

Honey,

Your letter was on the hall table when I entered this afternoon coming from school. I was happy to receive it. I came straight up to my room, sat in my little chair and read it. So you've finally gotten it down to "Dearest". Are you sure you love me enough for that? Sears' Dad must come up to see him often, does he help him study????

Now just how could your Company escape being restricted during the 9th week when all others have been? I know there is one very lucky man in that Company, but is every other man as lucky as he is? If they are then you have a chance not to be restricted.

I am so glad you like the sweater, and I really believe you like it! My work was not in vain. You know Honey, "every stitch is a stitch of love."

Maybe if we'd set a deadline for our getting to bed we could go to Sunday School. Oh, but, I guess we don't want to go to Sunday School, or that is I don't think I do. I haven't much use for Mrs. Culp's lessons. You wouldn't be in that class though. I guess you'd be in Mr. Thomas' class. We could go just to see the church though.

I'd like to see the Baltimore plan materialize too. But if it doesn't this week maybe it will another one. I am really going to Frederick if it doesn't rain. We are leaving Baltimore at 10:15 A.M. and returning on the 5:15 from Frederick. I am sort of wary about the 5:15; it is scheduled to arrive in Baltimore at 6:55. However if the bus is crowded and we have to wait until a later bus we may not get to Baltimore 'til very late. That would indeed break up our plans if you get off. Thus, if you do come and I do go to Frederick I should be at the bus terminal by seven, if I am not there by that time you'll just have to wait for me. If it is bad weather we are not going to Frederick, but I'll go to Baltimore to see Scoop anyhow so I'll be there.

I'll be waiting to get word from you on Friday. And in the meantime I'll write again.

Good luck on Depot and Supply! You know what I think you can do.

Must go to bed, it's late.

My room smells like moth balls, a winter rug was put down today and it must have been packed in them. At any rate it smells to high heaven. I am going to put my window up high and snuggle down under the covers.

Love to my sweet sweetheart,

Yours,

Glorious

P.S. So I'm "lovely", am I really?

G.

XXXXXXXXXXXXXXXXXXXXXXXXXXXOOOOOOOOOOOOOOOOOOOOOOOO
XXXXXXXXXXXXXXXXXXXXXXXXX

Aberdeen, Md.

October 7, 1942

5:30pm

Dearest,

The Company Commander came through with the announcement today; we are restricted for the weekend. The Company goes on guard Saturday & Sunday then again Wednesday & Thursday of next week. I was hoping Buttercup, that I could meet you in Baltimore this weekend. Maybe you can get to Baltimore the following week. As I understand it, the men that were to go on pass this Saturday will be allowed to go the following Saturday. So I'll see you Saturday 16th.

Honey, this has been the "day of days", nothing has gone right. The Depot & Supply instructor got all steamed up this afternoon and sounded off. I think the boys are kind of letting up a little. Then to top it off I came to the barracks this evening and found 5 gigs listed for R.J. Shenton. The clerk made an error; the name should have been R.J. Sheridan. His name follows mine on the Roster. Of course, I'll get clear of it but I'll have to see the Officer Candidate O.D., he'll refer me to the

1st sergeant and then I'll get to see the Company Commander and argue a bit. But he has no argument. Sheridan acknowledges the gigs belong to him so the C.O. can't have much of an argument. I'll get the thing straightened out though.

It was cold here this morning so I wore "your" sweater under my field jacket. Honey it's "alright". The boys commented on how nice a sweater it was. (<u>Nice</u> girl knitted it too.) I was very comfortable wearing it but had to take it off this afternoon. I like it too, because it brings you around me, so to speak. (Keeps me warm too.)

I'm sorry about this weekend, but it can't be helped. (No angles.) I'll see you the following Saturday though. Long as they give the gigs to R.J. Shenton, H.C. should get along alright. Will write when I get a chance.

Goodbye now,

"Honey I love you."

Howard

October 7, 1942
10 P.M.

Dear Totch,

Hooray! We go paid today and guess what? I got a raise. Not bad! I'll feel quite rich for a few days. I won't last long though.

The St. Anne's clock is striking ten and I must go to bed so this won't be long.

Tonight I went to see Mickey Rooney in "A Yankee at Eton". It was good. I enjoyed it a great deal. Lots of laughs!

I've thought about you this week and wondered if you were working hard. I've felt that you must be but I haven't been sure what kind of a humor you've been in. I was afraid there once that you may be in a bad humor, but then I thought, why I don't even remember seeing Howard in a bad humor so I just couldn't picture him that way. He must be his own jolly self, going about things philosophically and always seeing the humor when it's possible. He just couldn't be any other way.

Last night coming from dinner I walked up the street in back of a Marine and his girlfriend. They were looking at each other so endearingly and she had her hand in his. They were quite oblivious of anything going on around them. I thought of you and then I thought of how happy I would be if I had you to look up at and had your hand to put mine in.

Love to my Darling!

From His Glorious

P.S. Keep all those rafters clean in that corner, in other words "Brighten the Corner Where you Are". Do you know that song? It's a hymn. I'll sing it for you the next time you come home.

G.

Aberdeen, Md.
October 8, 1942
5:45 P.M.

Dear Darling Glorious, (How's that Buttercup?)

I was a bit surprised to get your letter today. I didn't get back from lunch in time to read it before class formation, so I read it during one of the ten minute breaks. These are swell, Legna, wish I could get two every day.

The weekend is still on my mind. Gosh, wish I could get a pass. But of course, it's an impossibility this time. We'll make it some other time. (The following weekend, providing the gigs stay away from my corner.) Speaking of gigs, the five listed for R.J. Shenton were rescinded today and given to R.J. Sheridan. I'll have to stay on the "beam" next week so I'll get a pass.

Tomorrow is going to be a tough day. We have two final exams, Military Law and Depot & Supply. Then tomorrow night we have another popularity contest. This is the beginning of the second wash-out and Honey there is going to be a good wash this time.

Next week we have guard duty & cook tours. We go on these tours to get a general idea of the courses to "specialize in", the last four weeks here.

I want to mention the gig sheet again. We read it this evening and one of the fellows was listed as having debris on his bed. He went to his bunk & after a five minute search found a piece of white thread 1/8 inch long on his blanket. Our Commander sure can "coin phrases" when it comes to gigs.

Yes Glorious, I love you enough to call you "Dearest". "I just love you," remember l-o-v-e covers a lot of territory.

Hope you have a good time Saturday. Let me know something about the following weekend. Maybe we can make up for this one we're missing.

I'm going to wear "our" sweater on guard Saturday.

Love,

Howard

P.S. You should get this Saturday or when you get home from Frederick.

Howard

Thursday, October 8, 1942
9:15 P.M.

Honey,

Just completed my lesson plans for tomorrow and also for Monday. That means I'll not have any work to do over the weekend and that is just as I want it to be. I am going to try to make it that way every weekend this year. If I attend ~~stricktly~~ (heck), I mean "strictly" to business during the week, I can see no reason why my weekends can't be totally free of work.

I have one very very slow math section this year. It's IX and is it awful. Golly, I really don't know what to do with them. The problem is aggravated by the fact that within the section there are about 4 degrees of dumbness. None of them can really do the math they are supposed to do yet some of them can take much harder work than the others. I hate to do what I really should do and that is to section within the section and let each group work at its own level. Of course that will mean four lessons to plan for one class. That's too much trouble, but my conscience says I ought to do it.

And that's not all my conscience has been telling me this week. It has been saying that you and I are wrong to do what we have been doing. Oh, Howard, I get so mixed up at times that I don't know just what to think. Oh well, 'nuff said!

154

I wish this were tomorrow night and I knew whether or not you were coming on Saturday. I am still very skeptical about the trip to Frederick, doggone it, I just don't want to be caught in Frederick 'till late Saturday night and then after I do get to Baltimore have to come to Annapolis all alone. Heck, I just think I'll call the trip to Frederick off and just go up to Baltimore and visit Scoop for a while and then return early. That is, if you aren't coming.

This letter must be terribly boring; all I've done is present my mental conflicts to you on paper. I'm sorry, Totch. I guess I am not leaving you with very pleasant thoughts of me for your "confined weekend". Anyhow I have very pleasant thoughts of you —if I could fully describe them to you, you would realize just what a wonderful person you are in my sight. Then too, you would realize that I love you dearly with a love that is beautiful and rather sacred to me. I know it is a true and good love because I feel it most when I hear inspiring music or see inspiring sights or think big thoughts.

If I do not see you I'll be thinking of you and picturing you as you go about your duties as an O.C.

Love, love, love, love (More than I could find paper enough to put it on and better than any paper I could put it one) to my very own Darling,

Yours,

Glorious

P.S. I'll get the pictures tomorrow.

G.

Saturday, October 10—8:10AM
On the Wobble, Bump & Ache

Honey,

Can't say much 'cause this train will wobble. Am enclosing the pictures. They are pretty good except for you and me taken on Sunday sitting on the chair. That one should be torn up. They made a mistake and didn't print the one of you at attention that Mother took. When I have my prints made I'll be sure they do two of that one. So I kept the extra one which they made of you in kakhi (How in the heck do you spell that?) It's good and I have it in my wallet.

I am sorry you couldn't make it this weekend, but it will make the next that much better. If it's possible I'll come up to Baltimore to meet you. Maybe I will whether it's possible or not.

I am on my way to Hood for the day. I'll meet Scoop in Baltimore and we'll go up together. Mother & Dad are coming up to Annapolis to meet me tonight.

I am thinking about you, Honey, and I will be all day. It's going to be a beautiful day. I think I'll enjoy that celebration at Hood.

You'll probably get this letter this afternoon, I hope. I have only one three cent stamp. Wonder if it'll take it??

Gosh, the country is getting beautiful. The trees are turning and the reds and golds are lovely.

This train is wobbling so I'll have to end it now.

I slept in my new room last night. It was quiet. I still have to get my rugs and curtains before it will be complete.

Love and thoughts galore to my very own Sweetheart.

156

Yours,

Glorious

XXXXXXXXXXXXXXXX OOOOOOOOOOOOOOOOO

Saturday Evening [Oct 10]
"Day Room"

Dearest "Angel", (I can't spell it backwards)

The week has finally come to an end and what a week. I haven't had time to get a haircut. (Even by missing a meal.) The Aviation Ordinance classroom is about a mile from the Company area & we spend most of our time walking back & forth. Saturday is the same as any other day in the Specialist Course. We have class the same as during the week, even the periods at night are used for instructing. Study hall is a thing of the past. Thursday we had an exam on the first phase of the course. (A Modification of the ole Depot & Supply.) Friday morning four boys were called out while class was in session. They had failed the exam & were told if they flunk the exam coming up Monday, they are "washed". The exam Monday will be on Explosives, Bombs & Fuses. It's just a general course in demolition bombs, their makeup & what causes them to tick. This morning we were given nine fuses to study & we must know them by Monday morning.

Say, you certainly wrote a nice long letter Wednesday night. I got it after lunch & finally finished reading it around 4:30 in the afternoon. I just read it over again to make sure I didn't miss anything. I didn't. Sorry you made such a mess with the ink, I would like to have seen it. You must have looked rather cute.

There was one thing I didn't like to hear about though. You said something about being scared of what happened the "last Saturday night". Glorious, please don't worry about that. I know nothing will happen from it. I don't want you to be scared, it worries me. Darling I love you too much to let anything like that happen. So please, don't let it scare you. However, you are right about the way we've been acting these past Saturday nights. I think we have been carrying things a little too far and that we should stop and "survey the situation" a little more closely. (But Honey, it's hard having to leave you.) From now on we'll cut it short & "sweet". Then again, there is another way to look at it. If & when I graduate from O.C.S. who knows where I will be sent. Maybe I wouldn't see you for a long time and we should take advantage of what time we can be together. It's a problem but we are big enough & old enough to work it out to be a "fine finish".

I'm going to the Guest House this evening & see about making reservations for you and Miss Ethel. Maybe I didn't seem so enthused about you all coming up to see me graduate last Sunday, at least I know Miss Ethel took it that way. But I can't get all hepped up over this graduating from O.C.S. There is too much uncertainty about making the grade for one thing and then again, Private, Corporal or Lieutenant; you are still a soldier in the good ole Army. But Honey, even if I can't get reservations at the Guest House you are still coming to Aberdeen on the 14th of November, I hope!

Next Saturday we go on pass at 12:30 that is, that order was put out last week. It could be rescinded by next Saturday but I hardly think so. If I don't get gigged-in which isn't likely as I have "0" amount to date, I'll probably shop around in Baltimore for three or four hours. I have to get

158

some shirts, ties and shoes to finish out my uniform for graduation. Wish I could meet you in Baltimore again, Buttercup. Your company is really appreciated by one Mr. Shenton. After I finish downtown I'll go to Harold or Myrtle's and come down to Shady Side in the evening with one of them. Although I'm not sure whether or not they still come home on Saturday. But I'll get to Shady Side if I have to thumb. (That's vital to "National Defense".)

It's pretty nice sitting here in the Day Room writing to you and listening to the phonograph. We have some very good recordings. "However", there is one thing lacking and that is you. If I could only glance across the room and see you once in a while I could be so contented. But what happens, I have to console Sears every now & then; he got his usual quota of gigs this week (6) and can't leave the Company area. How he always manages to get 6 gigs every week I don't know. (This is the 7th straight week.)

Had a letter from Jim Hale today, (he's in Australia). It was written August 19. It went to Fort Jackson, Camp Blanding, Fla. & finally caught me at Aberdeen. He seems to think Australia is quite the place. The army sure took a grip on him, he has been in about a year & nine months have been "foreign service".

Better go now; I have a few "fuses" to get straight for the exam Monday. (Concerning Dive Bombing).

Remember? I love you, Legna, I'll always love you. Thanks for the kisses. I appreciate them even if you say I don't appreciate your thoughts when they are pertinent to one O.C. [Officer Candidate].

Goodbye now, "Darling"

Howard

P.S. Will call tomorrow (Sunday)

Howard

October 11 —Sunday
9:10 P.M.

Sweetheart,

Mother put your letter on my dresser so I would get it when I came up to bed last night. It was to be a surprise, but Mrs. Shea told me about it so I came to bed a bit earlier than I would have. It was a sweet letter. Howard, I love you. I know I do because I get such a thrill from just a letter.

The trip on Saturday was grand. The day was perfect and so was everything else except the traveling conditions. They certainly are terrible! Honey, you must love me to make the trip from Aberdeen and back in 24 hours just to be with me for about 8 hours. But that's getting a bit off the subject. There were about ten of my classmates back. I met Ruth Duff (Scoop) in Baltimore and we went to Frederick together. We had seats both going and coming, but some people had to stand. The Campus Day activities were good, but the crowd there to see them was slim due to tires and gasoline and traveling conditions. I saw all my old profs and also Mrs. Parker, my "house mama". Scoop and I had dinner at the Francis Scott Key Hotel. Ham with raisin sauce —it was a good dinner. We got the 5:15 back to Baltimore and I got the 7:45 train back to Annapolis. It was packed and jammed. We had to wait so long before they let us through the gates to go out by the track. It was then that I realized that you must have had to wait at times too. I was very tired when I got home. Drilk came to meet me, but I came home with Gilbert and Esther.

Mother thinks it's a good idea for me to come to Baltimore to meet you next Saturday and of course I think it's great so I guess it's unanimous. If you can come, I'll be there.

Ellsworth has made Staff Sergeant and he's making enough for Evelyn to go out so she went two weeks ago. They have an apartment near Camp Crowder and Ells says he is so happy that he is afraid to breathe. Evelyn is making a perfect wife and she is a good cook, he says. Aunt Lill is very happy that Eve could go out and so am I. [Ellsworth Nowell, Glorious & Derwill's first cousin, the son of Miss Ethel's younger brother, Ellsworth Nowell, Sr]

Honey, I hope you did all right in those exams.

Must go to bed 'cause I have to get up early in the morning.

I missed you this weekend! And how.

I am getting a picture made that I think you might like, just maybe though, in fact on second thought I don't believe you will like it. It was one of the poses I had taken when I had my year book picture made in '40. We'll see!

We've had lots of company today. Kind of tiresome it is.

New developments in the church situation. I'll tell you what they were later when I have more time.

Will be looking forward to your letter and to seeing you next week.

Love to my Honey,

From your "Dearest Darling"

161

Aberdeen, Md.

October 12, 1942

5:05

Dear Buttercup,

I just got the letter you wrote on the Wobble. How about the pictures, they are awful. You look alright but they are terrible of me, especially the ones in which I'm wearing khaki. The shirt is a beaut, I'll do as you said, never wear it again. However the pictures did bring out that "beautiful smile" of yours and that's what I want to look at.

Honey don't get excited now but I may not be able to get a pass this weekend. I've had 3 gigs since last Friday. So far this week I haven't added to my collection but we have three days to go. As the O.C.s say, I'll be "sweating" the next three days. So don't plan to meet me in Baltimore until you hear from me. I should know by Thursday evening so I'll write you then and you'll get it Saturday. I would call Friday night but we are on a new schedule this week. We're having cook tours and no study periods in the evening. We eat supper at 5:30 and can't leave the Company area after 7:30. This wouldn't give me enough time to get to the Service Club and get my call in. So look for the letter Saturday. I want you to meet me in Baltimore if you possibly can. I'll meet you anywhere & at any time after 6:45 which is the quickest I can get in town. I'm trying my best to keep the gigs out of this corner.

The fifth platoon of Company C was certainly a sorry looking outfit today. We went on guard 12:30 yesterday and came off this morning at 6:30. I had three two hour tours, guard duty ranks next to K.P. in unwanted details. We go on again Thursday at 6:00 P.M. The worst of it

162

is the fact that we go to class the next day. Today we went to "Fire Control" classes to get a general idea of what that course was all about; tomorrow we take in the Automotive Section. Most of the boys went to sleep sitting in their chairs but the instructor was a pretty nice fellow. He knew we had been on guard. I wore our sweater while walking "post" and it certainly felt good around 3 o'clock this morning when the wind started blowing.

The "wash-out" takes place tomorrow or Wednesday. So far I think I'm safe. My name hasn't been posted for any deficiencies, so I must have beat Depot & Supply.

Let me know about Saturday. Try and make it Legna! I'll keep working on the "gig corner".

I thought about you Saturday night. I also wanted to call you Sunday but we had an inspection 10:00 o'clock Sunday morning.

See you Saturday Angel (I'd like to spell the middle name backwards.)

Howard

Aberdeen, Md
October 13, 1942
6:10 P.M.

Dearest,

The gigs missed me again today so with a little luck and some "bucking" thrown in, I might get a pass this week. The corner is certainly getting a work over this week. I've mopped & dusted in the morning, afternoon & night. If I don't get a pass this weekend I'll have to pull Miss

163

Ethel's letter out and read it again. (That's my morale booster.) Even then I wouldn't feel a lot better. I know it's only been two weeks since I saw you but that's a mighty long time where you're concerned. I've got two days to go and two gigs left, I should be able to make it.

I'm glad you got my letter Saturday night. I thought you would get home late Saturday night and wouldn't get to read it until Sunday. That letter was one of my Saturday letters. ("Fort Jackson Special", remember Wednesdays & Saturdays).

Things seemed slightly changed around here this week. We have no study periods at night and you find spare time on your hands. (We don't know how to use it.) Ammunition was our course today in the "cooks' tour". But the rub comes Thursday; we'll be in class all day & then go on guard at 6:00 P.M. til 6:00 Friday morning. Somebody is going to be awfully sleepy Friday in class. I had to keep digging my fingers in my eyes last Monday to keep awake. I caught up last night though, went to bed at 7:30 and felt swell this morning. (Then I received a very "nice" letter this afternoon which made me feel better.) It came right after lunch, I read it & then grabbed mop & dust rag. (My gig preventers.) This spare time won't last long though, next week we'll be rushing around again with fourteen things to do and only time to do ten. That's why I wanted to get a pass this weekend. The specialists' course requires a lot of study and maybe I won't be able to get home for the next four weeks.

Sure I'll like the picture you are having made. It's of you, isn't it? That's good enough for me.

Well Honey I'd better hang up now & rush over to gig corner and get some shut-eye. I'm writing this in the "Day Room", we've had it furnished with new furniture and I must say it's very comfortable.

Remember, let me know where to meet you Saturday and when. I think we said Camden Station but I'll meet you anywhere you say.

Goodnight "Darling",

Howard

Annapolis, Md.
October 13, l942
8:50 P.M.

Honey,

Tonight I don't believe I'll sleep very well because I haven't heard from you since last Thursday which is the date of your last letter. Of course, I received it Saturday. You were going into a very hard day and I've wondered how you got along and what is what. I expected a letter this morning; when it didn't come then I thought surely it would this p.m., but not then either. Well, at least I can hope for one in the morning. Don't let this worry you. I'm only telling you because I want you to know how much I think of you and how I want to know that things are going well with you. If I think you may be suffering then I suffer with you. If I know everything is all right then I can rest easy. So if you were busy and didn't have time to write why I can take it, but if there is something wrong, then I worry. Of course there is no way of knowing which is the cause, thus I worry. I am getting very much involved here. 'Nuff said!

I suppose you'll be disappointed at not hearing from me more often this week, but I've been rather busy and so far the rest of the week has all the earmarks of being still busier. Tomorrow we have an assembly with Dr. IQ. He is coming to sell bonds. That will be in the morning. In the afternoon, Mr. Fox will be observing classes and after school there will be a meeting to discuss Math and Science in Wartime. Of course those are my subjects and I'll have to show in my teaching that I've profited by the meeting. Thursday is P.T.A. and the parents are coming early to observe the classes, some fun! After school the meeting. Ah, Friday will appear on the horizon after all of that. Then Saturday will come in due time and I'll see my Darling whom I love so very much. I am going to get aboard the trolley and go to Baltimore to see him sooner. We'll have fun.

Where will I meet you, Howard? I think I might go in early to do a spot of shopping. You can't get there before 6:30 at the best can you? Perhaps I'd better meet you in the lobby of the Lord Baltimore Hotel 'cause the stores close at 5:30 and I'd have an hour to kill. Of course, maybe if I met you down at the bus terminal I'd see you sooner which would be fine, but I probably wouldn't even be able to get in the place. So unless I change it I'll meet you at the L.B.H. in the Lobby at 6:30 or 7. If you're late I'll understand.

There is no heat in this house yet and I am kind of cold so I guess I'd better get to bed. My bed is going to be very damp and cold, but I think I'll soon warm it.

Love to my Sweetheart!

Always your Glorious

P.S. I believe I'll sleep better now since I've talked to you.

P.S. They are little, but there are lots of them.

XXXXXXXXXXXXXXXXXXXXXXXXXXXXXXXXXXXXXXXXXXXXXXXXXXXXXXXXXXX
XXXXXXXXXXXXXXXXOOOOOOOOOOOOOOOOOOOOOOOOOOOOOOOOOOOOOOOOOOOO
OOOOOOOOOOOOOOOOOOOOOOOOOOOOOOOOOOOOOXXXXXXXXXXXXXXXXXXXXXXX
XXXXXXXXXXXXXXXXXXXXXXXXXXXXXXXXXXXXXXXXXXXXXXXXXXXXXOXO

xoxoxoxoxoxoxoxoxoxoxoxooxoxoxoxoxoxoxoxoxoxoxoxoxooxoxoxoxoxoxoxoxoxo
xoxoxoxoxoxooxoxox

My room—Annapolis
October 14, 1942
6:45 P.M.

Honey,

I am happy! I don't know exactly why and I don't want to analyze my emotion too closely 'cause I analyze too much anyhow. At any rate when I am happy I always think I should write and share it with you. Oh boy, could I be a devil tonight if I had a chance? Ha ha! I feel very mischievous indeed. Happy, devilish and mischievous all in one night — unusual for Andrews I'd say.

Today we had Dr. IQ at school. We sold $3000 worth of bonds in order to get him. He conducted a quiz program in assembly. It was pretty good. He is young and handsome and he didn't sound as he does on the radio. Honey, you're so smart, what is ½ of 2 and 2? If you get it right off the bat you're better than Miss Motley, she missed it.

Dinner tonight was good and I had to sit with the seven boys who go to the Cochran Bryan Prep—that made it even better. I like *boys*.

Your letter came this morning and I was very happy to get it. It was guard duty that kept you from writing. That is a legitimate excuse even though you didn't give it. I figured it out myself. What do you do while you are not on guard? You said you had "three two hour tours. What were you doing the rest of the time? I'm stupid, I know, but I like to know about such things.

Now Howard, if "our" sweater is going to be of so much use, maybe I'd better get busy on another one so it'll be ready when this one wears out. I feel quite elated that you are wearing it.

Last Saturday night while waiting for the train I bought a "Science Digest". Nice little magazine, it has some very good scientific articles in it. I believe you'd like them. Just wanted you to know I've been reading!

How did you get the three "gigs"? I would like to know what you did wrong. I do hope you haven't collected any more. By now you know just one more day to go.

You can't write me tomorrow night, you'll be on guard duty. How are you going to let me know? Well, I'll leave that up to you. Anyhow unless I hear from you to the contrary, or you hear from me, I'll meet you at the Lord Baltimore at 6:45 or after. From there on you make the plans.

I've looked in every encyclopedia to find the history of that "fire bomb", but so far I've been unsuccessful. I've had several people ask me who I know in chemical warfare and I say, "Ordnance" and proceed to tell them who I know. Is it the Ordnance insignia?

The pictures of the "shirt" were not so good, I agree. Of course I told you all along how it looked but you had to have a "photo finish" to convince you. Just listen to me on the clothes question and you'll never go astray. I have "glorious" taste when it comes to neatness of other people! Myself, I can't see so well.

Now look, Totch, I take back what I said about you make the plans. We'll try to get back to Annapolis by 11 and home by 12 and to bed by 12:30 or 1 at the latest and up by nine and to Sunday School by 10. Bud Rogers says he is going to teach a class and we can go in that. What we'll learn I don't know, but it might be something at that.

Isn't your new schedule better than the old one? No study period! Can you get more sleep? By the way! Won't you be very tired this weekend being on duty Thursday night?

I'll probably not write again this week. November is coming too fast to suit me.

Love, love, love,

Your Glorious

P.S. 9:40

A detachment or something of soldiers (probably Maryland Guard or something) just marched by the house. I put out the light and looked out at them. They were counting cadence like you said. I got a thrill out of it when I thought about you. There was an officer giving the commands. **P.S.** I am a silly girl.

GA loves HS

XOXOXOXXOXOXOXO

See you Saturday in Baltimore!

Aberdeen, Md.

October 14, 1942

7:40 P.M.

Dearest Glorious,

I didn't think I would write tonight but as usual my thoughts started running toward a blue-eyed girl that wears a ribbon in her hair, so I had to write. I've been taking a good reading on the pictures you sent me and honestly Legna, the pictures of me in khaki are sure "something". Looks as though I'd been on a four week drunk. The ones taken while I was wearing wool are pretty good.

Gig corner did alright today but there's still one more day to go. With all the rain the barracks are a mess. The boys really bring in the mud on the G.I. shoes. I wouldn't go near my corner lunchtime for fear of leaving some mud on the floor. The gig list was long today too. Sears got it on one side of me & Sheridan on the other. Some of the boys got five. I still have my margin of two, so I feel fairly safe, but not over-confidant. The mops will take a beating again in the morning.

We still can't get accustomed to the leisure in the evening. It just doesn't seem possible.

The boys on the "border' went before the School Board this afternoon. They took five out of our platoon. One of them is a swell fellow too; he messed up in the drill the second four weeks. I hope he did alright before the Board. His rating in academics is very high too.

Honey, I'm looking forward to Saturday, so don't disappoint me. I'll know for sure tomorrow evening about the gigs, so I'll take some paper & and envelope with me when I go on guard. I'll be able to write you in between tours, then I can mail it Friday morning. And you should get it Saturday. Wish I could call you Friday night, but I can't do it. (Regulation 32-4567, Paragraph 3, sub-paragraph b)

Well Buttercup, tomorrow night is going to be a little rough & rougher if it's raining. I have to take a shave & shine those G.I. slippers. "See you Saturday."

Goodbye now & I love you,

Howard

P.S. I didn't get a letter today. Remember what the radio announcer said. "Morale is important." Howard

Aberdeen, Md.

October 15, 1942

Guardhouse #2, 6:00 P.M.

Dearest Legna,

This has to be short & sweet, we go on guard 6:30 and I'm on the first relief. I'll walk until 9:00, then go on again at 1:00 A.M. What a night for guard duty. We are all wet now from walking to the guardhouse. Gosh knows, what we'll be before the night is over.

I just got your letter and I don't know but, we are likely to get screwed up on meeting in Baltimore. You said Lord Baltimore Hotel in your letter then you said something about the bus terminal. I'll go to the L.B.H. first and if you are not there I'll go to the bus terminal. We'll meet, if I have to keep running back & forth all night. I won't get in Baltimore before 6:30 at the earliest, so I should meet you around 7:00. Remember I'll go to the Lord Baltimore "first", and wait there until 7:30 that should give you enough time to get there if there's where we are going to meet. If you aren't there by 7:30 I'll dash over to the bus terminal. If there's still no sign of the girl with a "ribbon in her hair" I'll call Shady Side. (You can wear a hat; I don't need the ribbon for identification.) So try & make Baltimore Saturday, Buttercup.

Incidentally I held the 3 gigs to the minimum. I ended up today with the same three I got Saturday. I'd better go now or I'll get a few for next week.

So long, Darling, (See you Saturday)

Howard

My red and white room
Sunday, October 18, 1942 - 9:30 P.M.

Dearest,

My face is washed, my teeth are brushed, my hair is up, my pajamas are on, my window is up and my door is locked—in short—I'm ready for bed! So I can write to you.

By this time I hope you are coming from class and will get to bed as soon as possible. Darling, I've been thinking of you sitting in class. Go on and say it, "that didn't help me any". Well, whether it helps you or not, when I think you are suffering, I suffer too.

Mother and I think maybe we will drive to Aberdeen on Friday afternoon instead of taking a bus. I think we can manipulate the gasoline and if we drive slowly the tires can take it. So you make the reservations and let me know about whether or not we get them.

The weekend was perfect as usual and I love you more each time. My meeting you in Baltimore wasn't a bad idea. I enjoyed every minute of it. If I could only really make you know just how I feel when I am with you, you'd know that I love you with a love that can never be put out.

Iris told me that I looked better than she had seen me look for ages and that I had changed recently, that I was so happy all the time. She asked me if I loved you and I told her I did. She said then, that that accounted for the change in me. See! I've always told you that you are good for me. Except, I hope nothing comes of last night.

Norman Wilde was here when I returned and he told me I looked sleepy. Ha ha! So I guess I'd better turn in.

Honey, I had an awful empty feeling when I left you this afternoon. I think perhaps it was caused by the fact that you marched away across the street before I left and then when you waved from the corner you had a queer look on your face. It's getting tougher and tougher but we can take it.

I'll write again Sweetheart and in the meantime, I love you with every part of me, which means I am yours.

Love,

Glorious

XXXXXXXXXXXXXXXXXXXXXXXXXXXXXXXXXXXXXXXXXXXXX
XXXXXXXXXXXXXXXXXXXXXXXXXXXXXXXXXXXXXXXXXXXXX
XXXXXXXXXXXXXXXXXXXX

I felt every one of these as I made them because I remember our goodbye kisses this afternoon so very well.

G.

Aberdeen, Md.
October 19, 1942
6:40 P.M.

Dear Darling Legna,

I've got twenty minutes before study hall and I mean it's going to be a study period. The first day in Aviation Ordnance was a killer. We have about thirty mimeograph sheets to read and study tonight. They threw Organization of the Air Force at us today, most of the boys are still on a

Flight, they can't find a place to light. (There are three Flights in a Squadron).

I made good connections again yesterday. Caught the bus at 3:05 and got to camp in time for chow. Was lucky enough to get a seat, too. I had plenty of time to do my chores before study.

The gig system caught me again today. The list stated that my floor was dusty. That's a new one; the boys couldn't get over it. If it had been "debris on the floor" it would have seemed reasonable. To date, I have a total of three. I don't want to be restricted this weekend because I've got a phone call to put through to Shady Side Sunday.

Glorious, leaving you Sunday really hurt. I get a terrible empty feeling for a while after you're gone. But then I think of when I'll see you again and that snaps me out of it. Honey, I was tired Sunday but I'd lose twice that much sleep to be with you. I'm catching up on that lost sleep now by the middle of the week I'll be in fine shape. It's probably a good thing Miss Ethel didn't get a good look at her watch Sunday morning when she heard you coming upstairs. We would have been tried, convicted & sentenced had she known what time it was. We'll make it an hour earlier next time.

Have to go now. Will call you Sunday around 1:00 if I'm not "gigged in". I may not get a chance to write again until Sunday.

"I love you Legna, with all my heart," (Honest!)

Goodnight Buttercup,

Howard

Annapolis—my room

Tuesday, October 20, 1942 – 5 P.M.

Honey,

It's a beautiful afternoon, the sun is so nice and warm and everyone seems to be happy, at least everyone I met on the street smiled at me.

If I had been a person who acts on impulse I'd have handed my resignation to Miss Motley at 3:15 this afternoon. I had a very nice day teaching my own classes, every one ran very smoothly, but I had to take a class for an absent teacher the last period. They were holy terrors and I really took a beating. I was ready to quit, honest. That is how it goes though, some days I love it and wouldn't stop for the world and others I just want to give up. That's life I guess.

Last night the Shady Side delegation went before Mr. Cromer, the District Superintendent of our church. There were 14 of us who went to Washington. Bud was our leader, Mother and Dad, Tillie, Aunt Jennie, Evelyn Leatherbury, Norman, Buddy, etc., went too. We laid our problem before him and he reacted just as I expected him to and strange as it may seem he said we would have to do just what I thought we would have to do. That is, to go to church and try to be understanding. Of course that is the big or Christian way to act. Some weeks ago I made up my mind that I would get up in church and tell everyone that we must pull together and forget our differences of belief. I see the whole thing very clearly now, we do not understand these new converts and of course they do not understand us. It is difficult for people to work together who have lived such different lives. These new people have done such terrible things and are just now realizing how it feels to do right and naturally

175

they can't see why we don't get all elated like they are. We can't get excited over their new life because we've tried to be good all the time. Oh well, at any rate, the District Superintendent promised us he would look into it, but he couldn't promise us any action for some time yet. In the meantime we are to be Christians, forget our differences, keep our mouths shut and go to church. Thus when you come home again we are going to church. Not that you have anything to do about it, but I feel duty bound to go now.

I enjoyed our ride to Baltimore on Sunday. It was great to have you sleep in my lap, or rather —have your head in my lap. That first phrase sounded as if you were <u>all</u> in my lap. Goodness, you'd really be a "lap-full".

Tonight I am going to bed very early for I am very tired. Saturday night —little sleep —last night —little sleep —in the meantime two days of teaching, too much for a little girl like me.

In this paragraph I started to say I was thinking about you and how you were doing, but I don't believe I'll tell you that anymore, you evidently do not appreciate my thoughts.

Going home yesterday, Elliot talked about Officer Training School. He talked about Ronald washing the day before graduation and then he talked about some Siegert boy whom I didn't know. He said they were called before the board the day before they graduated and each one was asked one question. The Siegert boy's question was, "Do you want to be an officer?" He said, "That's what I am here for." So he graduated. Bud thinks if he'd said, "No" he'd have washed. What do you think, Totch?

Must wash my face and hands, powder my nose and walk to dinner.

See you —G.

7 P.M.

As I pulled down the shade I saw the man in the moon. He looks as if someone hit him on his right jaw and he stayed hit —his face is "indented".

9:20

Oh Howard, I'm in the doghouse around here. I just spilled about ¾ of a bottle of black ink on the rug and on my boudoir chair. Clumsy me! I called Mrs. Valk and she was very nice about it, but I still feel terrible about it. I was sitting in the chair with my notebook on my lap and the ink was on the corner of the desk nearby, my arm swept across it and the whole bottle went in my lap. I got it all over my bathrobe, my bedroom slippers (they were cute too, pink satin) and my pajamas. Such a mess. Mrs. Valk will send everything to the cleaners in the morning. Gosh I hope it comes out. I need you, Honey, 'cause I'm scared. Would you come and hug me tight and take all my "scared" away?

Now I am going to try to go to sleep. I doubt if I can now because I am too excited from my recent ink episode.

We do not have school on Friday. We are going to the State Teachers Meeting in Baltimore. I guess I'll go home Thursday night and go to Baltimore with Mother and Mrs. Shea on Friday.

Love to my very own Darling,
Your Glorious

P.S. Amy mailed my letter to you on Monday morning for she came up with me. I brought her up to the room and I hadn't put the letter in an envelope yet. She saw all the XXXs on it; I guess she thinks I'm crazy. Ha ha!

Love again, this time to my Sweetheart!

XXXXXXXXXXXXXXXXXXXXXXXXXXXXXXXXXXXXXXXXXXXXXX
XXXXXXXXXXXXXXXXXXXXXXXXXXXXXXXXXXXXXXXXXXXXXX
XX

These are all like the one you gave me at 5A.M. Sunday under the stars, I remember it well.

G.

October 21, 1942
7:15 A.M.

Dearest,

This is not a very appropriate time to be writing a letter but in O.C.S. you do things when there is time. We fell-out at 7:00 for drill and just as we started to move out for the drill field a very black cloud opened and poured rain upon us. The O.D. marched us back to the Company area and we fell-out. Class doesn't start until 8:10 so I have time to write my little—"Sweetheart".

I got your letter yesterday and you said something about me having a queer look on my face when I waved to you in Baltimore Sunday. I probably did because I hate to say goodbye. I always feel as though it's going to be an awful long time before I see you again. I think Aberdeen has made me realize more than ever how much I love you. Seeing you every, or every other, weekend has been wonderful. But it's going to hurt when I leave this place and won't see you so often. We can take it though, as you say. (We'll have to). However, we have been darn lucky or at least I have. Six months is a long time to go without seeing somebody you love. I'm thankful for the time we've had.

Haven't had a chance to make reservations at the Guest House but will take care of it. There should be some vacancies left.

Aviation Ordnance is going pretty good so far. We are studying the Supply set-up in the Air Force now. Thursday we have an exam on the first four days of the course. This is the administrative side of the course. Next week we start on the Technical side. That's what I'm waiting for, it should be very interesting.

If I don't get three more gigs by tomorrow and can get a pass Saturday I'm coming home. But that's just a thought. I imagine passes will be very hard to get this weekend. The boys want to get out and do some shopping. But I'll try and see if I can dig up one.

Have to meet a formation in 5 minutes.

Goodbye now,
"Love to my Darling",
Howard

Sitting up in bed
10 P.M. Wednesday
October 21. 1942

Honey,

Just a word or two before I turn in. Your Monday night letter was received with glad hands this morning. I've reread it again and again. You do love me, don't you?

So "they" are "gigging" you left and right eh? Stay with the mops and they'll carry you through.

Aviation Ordnance is not going to be a snap, huh? I'll make no comments 'cause I think you'd know just what they would be. I love you, Howard, and I want you to succeed.

So we'll make it *an* hour earlier next time. Nope! We'll make it *three* hours earlier and I mean it.

Howard, I didn't exactly like what went on, it gave me a good scare and I haven't recovered from it yet. We are going to have to stop it before something really happens, if it hasn't already. Please help me, I don't want to back down on this, we've got to quit here or else get married.

I went to the movies tonight and saw "My Sister Eileen." A silly picture and I laughed and laughed. The woman next to me was disgusted, but I had fun.

Tomorrow night I go home. I am going to wash clothes and clean up things a bit 'cause I'll be gone all day Friday, and Saturday is the football game. I'll get a good night's sleep Saturday night and I'll be all fresh for your phone call on Sunday. What are you going to say? I'll just wait and see. Don't tell me now.

The "inky" rug went off to the cleaners today and I am going to soak my pajamas and bathrobe in milk tomorrow. That won't be the end of it, 'cause about 150 test papers got splattered and that'll have to be explained to 150 quizzical freshmen.

On my way from the movies tonight I met our Maryland State Guardsmen or minute men or something. At any rate they were marching, "hut, two, three, four". Is that right? The officer had a loud voice, but kind of harsh, not nice like yours. I believe I could march if you counted for me.

To mention Sunday again, it was truly wonderful and I'll always remember it. I loved you as you slept with your head on my lap. I can't exactly describe the feeling it gave me, but it was pleasant. I've never seen you asleep and it was sort of a new experience.

It's late and I could keep on into the night, but morning will come and school bells will ring.

I'll write again.

Love always,
Your Glorious

x x x x x x x x x x

These are wee kisses like you'll give me some day when you are leaving for work in the morning or coming home in the afternoon. Just light ones but they mean a lot to me. I'll like them 'cause after you give me one you'll look at me and smile.

G.

In the car waiting for Mother
3:30 P.M. Sunday
October 25, 1942

Dearest Hunny Bunny,

After your call I felt very empty, nevertheless I was glad you called. Love is wonderful, there is no doubt about it, it gives one such a sense of belonging, a feeling that you can take most anything because there is someone who is all for you. I love you and I do believe that you love me. You are very sweet to me and I believe if we marry you will be the same as you are now.

Today is a dreary day, quiet, and quite conducive to loneliness. How wonderful would our little house on Rhode River with our fireplace and big chair would be this afternoon? We are going to enjoy this type of afternoon in our home so much more because we have had to be apart on days like this.

Daddy insists that he is coming so I guess you'd better make another reservation. If you've already reserved a double room then try to get a single one, also. I guess this might be difficult because you won't have time to do it and the time is getting shorter between now and then. Do it if you can and if you can't don't worry about it. They can have the room and I'll sleep over in the barracks with you. Ha ha! So remember, make a reservation if you possibly can. I am sorry I didn't say do it when you called today, but I really didn't think he meant he was going. We are going to drive up. So next weekend you can tell us just how to get there, how to <u>act</u> and how to get into the post, etc. Now Howard, if you really don't want us to come, say so. I don't want to do anything to make you unhappy.

8:10 P.M.

All my "chores" are done and I am ready for bed, in fact, I am propped up on a couple of pillows in bed right now. I haven't felt so well today, don't know just what is wrong, but I know what it should be.

Yesterday was a very strenuous day. I cleaned the living room thoroughly and put all the winter things in, rug, curtains, etc. That was a tough job and it took me until 12:30 to complete it. Then I rushed up stairs and dressed for the game. We journeyed to Annapolis and saw the game. It was good, lots of trick plays, but Howard, I just don't really enjoy anything anymore unless you are there. I don't know what I am going to do without you. Of course I had to imagine I saw you and to satisfy myself I went over close enough to the soldiers to find out. I found out, but I wasn't satisfied. I still wanted you. After the game I came home and had supper and at 8 o'clock we went back to town to see "Sergeant York". Dad was up there at a political meeting so we had to go anyhow. The picture was really good, but the theater was packed. I saw Mary Hartge with Elliot. She has joined the "Waves", I guess you knew. She leaves the last of next month she said. After the movie we came home and had something to eat in the kitchen. Thus it was 12:40 when we turned in — My, my, such late Saturday night hours.

Friday was not a good day at all. The teacher's meetings were long and very boring. I did go shopping though. I bought a pretty white spread for my room and three rugs —a red one and two white ones. Then I bought a bath robe to replace the one I ruined with ink. It's going to take me quite a while to recover from this buying spree, 'cause you see it's all bought on a "charge account".

I was glad to get your letter on Friday. It meant a lot to me.

Mother thinks I should come to Baltimore to meet you next Saturday and I want to come so I guess I will. The only hitch is that I may be sick. I'll just have to let you know about that. One more thing, I don't believe you ought to spend any money on me, 'cause you have so much to buy now. And I can't do much financing 'cause I'm broke. I don't know where my money goes, but it goes. We'll see! We can come home early and it won't cost us much. I got a hunch I might, or rather I will, be coming anyhow, in spite of the hitches. You brought it on yourself, remember? What are you going to buy? I'll meet you at Camden Station at 3 o'clock. I'll take the 1:15 if there is one. Just looked —it'll be the 1:05. That will get me in at 2:05 and I'll wait. You might get there early. Hey, wait a minute, maybe you'd planned to be all through your shopping when I got there, had you? You're just going to have to write and answer these questions, but if you can't, then we'll just leave it as it is, 2:05 at Camden Station and I'll wait 'till you come if it's all night.

I am looking forward to the weekend of the 14th. You know November 13th is Mother's birthday so when we go Friday we'll be celebrating her birthday. I hope we can see you Friday night, but if we can't, we can't. We'll expect you to come home with us on Saturday if the Army says you can.

My, this is a letter, filled with plans. Good ones, don't you think?

I love you Howard and I'll write again Tuesday or so. Getting sleepy now.

Always your Glorious

XXXXXXXXXXXXXXX

XXXXXXXXXXXXXXX

Nice little polite ones, just like I'd want tonight.

October 27, 1942
6:45 P.M.

Dearest Legna,

I only got a minute so here goes a brief answer to the letter I just received.

I'm glad you made up your mind about meeting me in Baltimore. That will be swell but if you change your mind and can't, let me know by mail, don't worry. If you're not there (Camden Station) I'll call Shady Side and find out whether or not you've left to meet me. But as it stands now, I'll meet you in Camden Station. Maybe I won't be there by 2:00

o'clock, we are supposed to get off at 12:30 but anything can happen to make it later. I kind of think the Company Commander will stick to his word this time though, too many boys are looking forward to this half a day off. So far I haven't gathered any gigs this week but there are still two days to go. (I'll make it.)

I'll try and get over to the Guest House tomorrow evening and see about another reservation for Mr. A. There's still time, I hope.

We are studying Fuses this week. (The mechanism which sets off the bomb.) They throw them at us so fast we can't keep up. A boy sneezed the other day and missed four of the darn things. The last two weeks won't be this tough, according to what one of our instructors said.

Honey I really enjoyed reading your letter this evening. It was nice and long, then again I like the polite little kisses at the end.

See you in Baltimore Saturday, I hope. Will be there soon as it's possible. If I'm a little late don't get impatient. I'll be there sooner as later.

Goodbye now, "Buttercup",

Howard

Annapolis, Md.
Wednesday, October 28, 1942
9:25 P.M.

Dearest,

Tonight I am very tired; I had a long, hard day. I had to get up early to come back to Annapolis and today all my classes required a lot of talking, that is extremely tiring for me. I had a nap when I came home this afternoon which made me feel a bit better. Listen to me talking about being tired and you are probably saying, "Huh, s'pose she really had something to do". Honey I know and I keep wishing that you were getting more rest. I do hope you'll get a furlough so you can sleep and sleep for a week.

Howard, I really don't know what to say about Saturday. I really believe we'd better leave it like this: if I am coming I'll come up on the train that leaves at 1:05 getting into Baltimore at 2:05. You'll just have to come to Camden Station and if I am not there then I am not coming. Of course if you can't get there 'till later I'll still be there waiting for you, if I am coming. That is the only way I know to leave it 'cause I don't know what Saturday may bring. I don't think I should come anyhow for several reasons, which I believe I explained before. Naturally I want to come if you want me to. I am still hoping to get a letter from you stating whether or not you want me. Will you do me one favor? If I can't come to Baltimore will you do your shopping and get to Shady Side as soon as you can? Huh, Honey, will you? I can't bear to think you are at leisure and I'm not near you. Is that asking too much?

Norman left Tuesday for Georgia to do some more training. It's a three month course and he doesn't think he'll be home before it's over. He is going to write to me!

Remember we are going to church this Sunday. Not to Sunday school, but to preaching, it will be preaching Sunday. Oh, no, maybe we can't, that might make you too late getting back. We'll see.

Two more days before I'll see you. It seems so long since I did see you.

We are going to be good this Saturday night????? I already feel a bit mischievous so, I really don't know about it.

Hope you can get around to making reservations for Dad, he really wants to come.

> Love, love, love to my Sweetheart.
>
> Your, Glorious

P.S. See you in Baltimore if I can make it.

> G.

Sunday, November 1, 1942
8:40 P.M.

Dearest Hunny Bunny,

The ride home was rather hectic, but I made it. I clung to the wheel for dear life and held her up to forty (in normal times that was slow, but it's fast now and especially for Ivan). I missed you. When I landed home I made a bee line for bed and there I stayed until 5:30. I was uncomfortable for only about a half hour after I got in bed, the rest of the time I slept and ate, yes ate. Mother brought my dinner up to me. Now, I am back in bed again, but I feel all right. It would be nice to have you here now. While I was in bed this afternoon, Mother put my new curtains up, they are very pretty and they dress my room up so nicely. Someday you'll have to see it even if you can't sleep in it with me now.

The weekend was wonderful as usual. It didn't seem real though, maybe it did at the time, but now it seems like a very pleasant dream. I think it must be because when I was in bed this afternoon I thought about you constantly and relived yesterday.

Bud Kline was in Shady Side today with a bunch of boys and girls. He must have come on his boat 'cause they came up from our wharf. I didn't speak to him 'cause he didn't see me.

I am glad I was able to come to Baltimore on Saturday. I enjoyed every minute of it. I sort of think you were glad I came, too.

Honey, I've got to cut this short because the ole cramps have hit me again so I'll just have to snuggle under the covers and try to go to sleep. Love to my Darling.

Your Glorious

November 2, 1942
5:45 P.M.

Dearest Darling,

I wanted to write last night but didn't get a chance. I'm being put through the paces, section leader for Aviation Ordnance and barracks inspector tomorrow. We all get a chance to gig one another before the course is over. But Figy is smart; he won't let us inspect our own barracks.

The first day in small arms wasn't too bad. We have a test tonight on the material we covered today. The hardest thing is remembering the names (nomenclature) of the different parts. It's easy enough to learn how the guns operate and what makes it "tick" but there are so darn many little parts with a ten syllable word for a name.

The boys are worrying more about their uniform and clothes than finishing the course. They are milling around the barracks examining and trying one another's hats and crats on, worse than a bunch of women at a bargain counter.

Honey, I had a wonderful time this past weekend. Meeting you in Baltimore is really swell. Say, you've caused quite a commotion in barracks #7 Co.C. The boys we met at the Hub can't quite figure how I could have such a nice girlfriend. They've even suggested I should get married just like the rumor I heard in Shady Side. (Two words) (The comment was, She's alright, Shenton) I agreed with them, of course! (About the comment.) Leaving you on Sunday is still a hardship though. I'll be glad when the one Sunday comes in a couple of weeks. I won't have to say goodbye. But it has been "great" being so close to you while I've been going to school and it would be "much greater" if I could be as close after I graduate. I have an idea though that isn't going to happen.

Have to shave and change uniform for 6:50 formation. Will write again during the week if I get a chance. I'll write Saturday night anyway. I'll also call you Sunday, around 12:30 or 1:00.

Goodnight Buttercup, or how about "Goodnight, My Love."

Howard

Annapolis
Tuesday, November 3, 1942

Honey,

It's very late and I must go to bed, but I can't bear to think that you may be disappointed at not hearing from me so I'll just write a line or so.

I came back tonight instead of in the morning (we had holiday today —election day) because Mrs. Elliot had invited me over to her house after church. I went to her church to hear a singer. He wasn't any good, but I enjoyed it all the same. Mrs. Hiatt and her husband went too. Mrs. Hiatt is one of the other teachers who rides with us. Her husband is an Ensign in the Navy, taking more courses at the Academy. We all went to church and then to Ellen's (Mrs. Elliot). She served us homemade ice cream and cake, it was delicious. Honey, I thought about you all the time. I went to Mr. & Mrs. Hiatt's apartment before we went to church and I thought how someday we will have a home or an apartment. Won't we be happy Darling? I will.

Ruby (Trott) and her husband sat right in back of us at church.

I don't know how the election is going yet.

Mother called Miss Grace today and asked her to come up to Aberdeen with us. She said she'd like to, but she can't leave Capt. Charlie alone and she can't depend on Mike to stay with him. She said she may be able to get someone to come in and stay, she's going to let us know. I hope she can come. Then she and I will take the reservations and Dad & Mother can go find another place, or if you get the other reservation then Mother, Miss Grace and I will take them and Dad can go find a place. In the meantime, don't you worry about it, we are coming —regardless. Honey, don't let any of this be a burden to you.

Love, love, love, love —more than I could ever tell you —to my dearest darling sweetheart.

Yours,
Glorious

P.S. I'll send my phone number in the next letter.

My room—Annapolis

Wednesday, November 4, 1942 —9:40 P.M.

Dearest,

Again, this can't be long 'cause I am tired and sleepy. Tonight I wrote to Roomie (College) and I planned quite a few lessons and the time slipped by.

My phone number here is Annapolis 4916. You'd better make it person to person just in case. I'll be here any time between 4:30 (approximately) and six o'clock. I don't usually leave for supper until the dot of six. The 4:30 is rather uncertain because often we are as late as 5 or 5:30 coming from school. Between 5:30 and six should get me though. Do you know why I am saying all this? You are to call me next week about the reservations if you can, remember?

Your letter came this A.M. and I was happy to get it. Honey, you're stringing me along about #7 saying I am nice and not understanding how you got me. What kind of impression do the boys of #7 have of you? So they think you ought to marry me. Not a bad idea at that! But times and things are so uncertain.

Hope you made out all right as section leader and barracks inspector. How many barracks did you have to inspect?

Dad lost the election, I sort of felt he would, but I would like to have seen him get it. He'd really be good in there I think. He'd say what he thought about things and best of all he would really do some thinking which is a heap more than most of them do.

Everyone likes my hair. I got the rest of it cut on Monday. It's not bad. One of the Lts at the house where I eat declared that I was a different teacher. Ha ha! I almost succumbed to a temptation to string him along and see what he'd say about the "other" teacher.

The inky rug came back from the cleaners today. They didn't get it all out, but it looks better anyhow. I haven't had a chance to talk to Mrs. Valk yet; she won't want me to buy her a new rug, I hope.

Sleepy —and I have to wash, put up my hair, etc.

Love, love, love, love, love, love, love, love, love to my Darlin'.

Me

P.S. I'll be waiting for your call at home on Sunday —12:30 or 1.

G.

November 8, 1942
8:45 A.M.

Dearest Legna,

It's a very dreary Sunday morning here at Aberdeen. A bunch of us are in the Day Room reading the paper & writing. Nobody is saying much, the "thought channels" are running many miles from Aberdeen. I for one have thoughts about a little town about 65 miles from here. This time next Sunday I'll be in that little town, I hope. It will be a lovely day after I make a phone call around noon; phone calls like this one are really a morale booster.

I stopped in the Guest House yesterday to find out about the "third reservation". The situation hasn't changed and I won't know for sure until Wednesday or Thursday. So I'll call you Thursday evening about 5:30.

We drew our assignments last Wednesday night. I got the one I wanted even though my drawing number was 47. My assignment is the 351st Fighter Squadron (Army Air Base), Richmond, Va. One of the boys in my platoon is also going to Richmond but to the 352nd Fighter Squadron. I could have taken any assignment from the West to the East Coast (even California) but Richmond was the closest to Shady Side so I of course grabbed it. This assignment is still not definite though. Maybe Figy's interview might change it; however there is a shortage of Aviation Ordnance officers so maybe Richmond will be the one. It doesn't make much difference to me, but the Air Force assignment seems the better. I like working with the guns used on the aircraft. There won't be much bomb handling in a Fighter Squadron. Sears is really happy. He was appointed to the Air Depot in California, about forty miles from L.A. His Dad, of course, got the assignment for him.

Last week was fairly interesting. We studied the different aircraft guns, tearing them down and trying to put them together again. One of the men in the class was a lawyer in civilian life. He tackles disassembly of a gun like a clerk unscrewing a fountain pen. We have a lot of fun with him. He's a good sport. During the breaks he rushes over to the Dispensary to get his bunged fingers wrapped. ("Dressed" in pillroller language.) Every night during study we have a test on the day's work, then when we finish a gun we get a final exam. I pulled a good one on Sears. We had a question on one test about the "charging lug on the breechblock slide." We handed our papers in and Sears saw my answer. He said, "Howard you have that one wrong." He was so sure of himself; he almost convinced me I was wrong. The instructor went over the exam and I was right. (Jerry will never live it down.) On one exam seven men out of 25 flunked and in another group (our class) 17 men flunked the same exam. So far I've passed them all. We have one on the .30 caliber tonight and it's going to be a toughie. I don't know too much about the darn gun. It's a complicated gun but a sweet firing piece of machinery. We fired it on the range yesterday.

I still don't know whether I can see you Friday night. If it's possible I'll dash over even if it's only for a few minutes. The graduation ceremonies start at 9:30 Saturday morning and only last about an hour so I should get away from here by 12:00 noon.

Jerry's Ole Man is coming up from Washington, DC this afternoon and he wants me to go to dinner. I have a very important call to make at 12:30 if I have to leave before making the "call" I won't go. I'll eat at the "Service Club".

So you had the rest of your noggin cut the other day. Well, if the Navy likes it, I guess the Army can "put up" with the change. Honey, I'd like your hair no matter what you did to it. I can still remember one Sunday morning while tearing through Shady Side in my "old egg beater", I saw you working on some flowers at the side of the Rural Home Hotel, your "bangs" (high explosive) were down and I had to look twice to make sure it was Glorious Andrews. Then, I saw her one evening with the "bangs" and hair wrapped around her head like a blanket. (She had just washed it.). I still liked what I saw, "a beautiful creature."

Goodbye now, Buttercup. I'll call you Thursday evening around 5:30 and will try to see you Friday night.

Love to my little demolition bomb,
Howard.

Sunday, November 8, 1942

Honey,

Here, I have messed around and let it get late again. I always do and then I have to rush through my letter to you, and I do so love to write lots and lots to you. If time is short I'd better get going!

Everything is ready for the trip Friday. You see this is the last time I'll be home before we leave 'cause I'll not come home Friday. They'll pick me up in Annapolis. Thus I had to get everything ready for Mother, getting the suitcase down, etc.

The three minutes today seemed so very short, it was strictly a business call, of course, I never do get up nerve enough to tell you I love you anyhow so I guess we might just as well talk business.

All the people I know who are interested in me have asked me when I was going to get married. Tillie asked me, Merle asked me and lo and behold tonight Mrs. Thomas asked me. I told them all that I wasn't going to —yet —! Mrs. Thomas was even more forward and offered some advice. She said she thought we should get married immediately —Ha ha! Mother made a very surprising statement. "Glorious, when you marry Howard, you'll live with us, won't you?" Gee, that almost floored me. I said, "No, indeed! I'll live with no one, but Howard." Now, Honey, don't take all this seriously. I'm not trying to propose to you nor am I encouraging you to propose. All of it just amuses me and I'm telling you 'cause I think it may amuse you also. I think we both know where we stand on the marriage question, or do we? All this discussion makes me feel like a bold huzzy again. Do you feel like a trapped animal in the clutches of this beguiling woman?

Howard, my love for you is so wonderful, so comforting, it has made me very happy. When I think of you I always think of you as the sweetest, kindest, gentlest person I know. I guess I've told you these same thoughts so much that you get tired of hearing them, but I just have to tell you 'cause I feel them so often.

It's ten and I just must go to bed. Tomorrow I have to teach and Monday presents a very full schedule for me.

I'll write tomorrow night, again.

I don't believe it'll be necessary for you to call me this week, unless of course, you just want to talk to me, or unless there is something which must be straightened out.

Love, love, love, love, love, love, love, to my sweet, sweet, sweet sweetheart.

Five whole days before I see you —

Love, and I'll dream about you,

Your Glorious

I fold letters the dumbest ways…

Annapolis
Monday, November 9, 1942
8:30 P.M.

Honey,

This morning Drilk and I were very late coming up; in fact so late that Mrs. Elliot was waiting when I arrived. I had your letter, or rather my letter to you propped up in the windshield for Drilk to mail, but I left in such a rush that I didn't tell him again and of course, for Drilk that means he would forget. I thought about it after I got to school and I thought he'd not remember so this p.m. I strolled past Ivan (parked on the street) and sure enough there was your letter in its same position. I got it in the 6:30 mail, so I hope you get it tomorrow afternoon. I'm sorry he forgot.

Today wasn't such a bad day. My classes were all fairly good, but they usually are sort of dopey or in a daze after the weekend. Monday is always a review day, 'cause they never remember anything taught last week. They look at you as if you're crazy if you start in without reviewing past material. I rather like to review 'cause I can see if I've really taught anything. If I have there'll be a few souls who can answer my questions in the review.

Speaking of tough days, Friday was a burner! It was a day of all days; it seemed to be about three days long for we had so many different activities. In the morning we had a concert pianist come and give a lecture-concert —that is, he lectured and then played. I enjoyed it except that the children did not keep quiet enough to suit me. At lunch there was a general discussion of the concert. There was a disagreement among the teachers as to whether or not it was good. Teachers can get pretty hot around the collar in arguments! Everything ran smoothly 'till 2:30 and then the bell rang for an evacuation drill. The children who were allowed to go home during an air raid got their coats and went outside as usual and we took the remaining people into the halls. In a few minutes in came all the children from outside saying that policemen and Miss Motley had sent them back that this was a real air raid. Well! Such a time. We were packed in the halls and to keep those kids still and quiet was an ordeal. We didn't get back to class 'till 3 o'clock when the all clear sounded. Of course, it was not "real", but it was a county wide practice. We had not gotten the 30 minute signal, thus the mix-up.

Homeroom teachers were instructed to get some data for the census in homeroom period in the afternoon. I got mine by the sweat of my brow and some yelling and pounding on the desk. When the kids finally left I was out cold, and I haven't fully recovered. So tonight I am going to bed early. Yes, all of that took place on Friday and even the weekend didn't get me back to normal.

Darling, I'm trying to hold myself in check and not get excited about the trip this weekend, but I am excited anyhow. I am happy about the fact that you are to be an officer, but I am happier about the fact that you can come home with us on Saturday and won't have to go back on Sunday. I am all ready to pin on the bars. I've taken them off the card and shined them and played with them and kissed them and looked at them hundreds of times. I'm a bit shy about what will happen after I do it though. I bet I'll blush!

You'd better write and tell me how to get to the building where you graduate in case you can't come over to see us on Friday night. I've forgotten since you told me. I think I told you on Sunday that we probably won't get to Aberdeen until 9 o'clock or so. We'll eat on the way up so don't miss your supper.

Hope I'll hear from you tomorrow.

Love to my Sweetheart

Your Glorious

xxxxxxxxxxxxxxxxxxxxxxxxxxxxxxxxxxxxxxxxx

These are very very polite 'cause I wouldn't want to do a lot of kissing tonight, I'd just want to sleep in your arms. G.

Annapolis, Md.

November 11, 1942

8:30 P.M.

Dearest Hunny Bunny,

Your letter was grabbed from the hall table this morning, by one eager Glorious Andrews and torn open, but not read for a few minutes 'cause Mrs. Elliot was waiting. Thus I read it in the car going up. When I read the "351st Fighter Squadron, Richmond, Va." I let out a whoop of joy and of course everyone wanted to know what went on. I told them and they understood on account of because they know all about you and what you are doing, etc. Mrs. Hiatt (the elementary teacher who rides with us and whose husband is an Ensign in the Reserves, you heard of her before) is quite sympathetic 'cause she's only been married since June and she knows what it really means to be separated from someone that you love, for her husband was in the service all last year before they were married. Mrs. Elliot is rather sympathetic too; at least she was this morning 'cause she had to sleep by herself last night. Her husband who works at the Experiment Station had to go to work at 12 midnight. Ha ha! She had a terrible time she missed him so! She has been married about five or six years. The other teacher who rides with us is Miss Moss. I don't believe she knows what love is and she wouldn't be sympathetic anyhow 'cause she's of real Navy stock and the officers in the real Navy have taken a beating so far in this war. She would naturally feel mean toward anyone who gets a break, but I understand.

I've tried to rest this week so I'd look my best this weekend but I haven't been able to sleep at all well. I guess I must be excited. Last night all I could think of was what would I do when I couldn't see you often. Darling, I love you so very much and I don't know what I'll do...

On top of sleepless nights, I believe I'm catching a cold so don't expect much on Friday or Saturday whenever it is I'll see you. Oh, yes, and my hair, I've had a terrific time with it. The "high explosives" have been a mess!

Saturday is drawing closer and closer, only two more days!!

After you get my letter maybe you'll decide not to call, there will really be no point in it, but of course I'd love to talk to you.

The girl next door came in to talk and interrupted my letter writing and spoiled my good intention to go to sleep early.

See you soon. I'll not write again 'till I see you.

Love to my very own dearest darling from

Your "<u>Demolition bomb</u>"

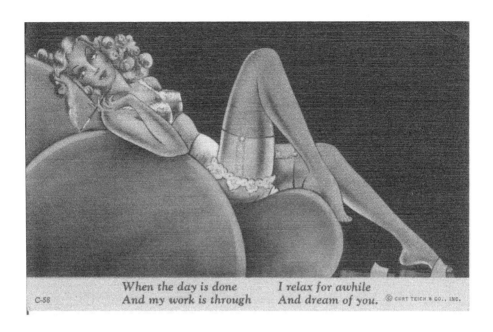

When the day is done | I relax for awhile
And my work is through | And dream of you.

C-56 · © CURT TEICH & CO., INC.

Newspaper clipping from the local newspaper:

HOWARD C. SHENTON GETS COMMISSION

Howard C. Shenton of Shady Side [Maryland] has been commissioned a second lieutenant after graduation from the Ordnance Officers Candidate School at the Aberdeen Proving Grounds.

For many years he has made his home with Captain Charles Hartge on West River. He is spending a period of leave there before reporting for duty at the Richmond Air Field.

Lieutenant Shenton attended the Shady Side public school and finished two years at Southern High School. Before entering the army he was employed in Washington [DC].

Monday, November 16, 1942

On bus duty down at the front door

Hello Mr. Shenton,

This note or notes will be difficult to read if you have to walk around while doing it 'cause you may lose a few paragraphs. That would be tragic! This however is the only paper ~~we~~ I have. Please pardon the "we" back there, I got excited 'cause Miss Motley just arrived. She is our principal who has been ill. This is her first day back. I shook her hand and told her I was glad to see her. Note: I didn't say "back". I could sincerely say I was glad to see her, but I couldn't add the "back" and be sincere. Things have run so smoothly without her. Of course I cannot deny that this smoothness may be due to Miss Motley's work in previous years. However it's just the tension in the atmosphere which was…

Homeroom study period

That last word should be "was"—that's right <u>was</u>—which was NOT here when Miss Motley was not here. Oh heck, what was I trying to say? At any rate there was no tension this year so far. The boys are giggling, I just told them they sounded like girls and they shut up for ½ second, now it has started again.

Mother was sick this morning, a cold. She says she has pneumonia, but I think she was exaggerating. I hope so. Darn it all she just can't seem to keep well. I don't know what to do about it. She just will not stop and rest, she seems to think she has to live up to so much. I guess the church business yesterday morning didn't help matters any. I am kind of worried about her.

My cold is much better; it's almost completely gone from my head. My throat is kind of scratchy and I cough once in a while, outside of that…

Just had to give a lecture to the Methodist minister's son, he's a noisy brat, he needs a good beating. He is quiet now…

My cold is all right. You can completely cure me of anything! Ha!Ha! The bell—My room, free period

Just walked though the hall and smiled at Mr. Henry. He was standing in his doorway as all good teachers should between classes to see how the traffic is going and keep down noise.

I have two more classes today. Math 1X which is such a dull class. They just can't see through even the simplest things. Then I have Science 1D. They aren't so bad. We probably will have a very good lesson today.

I hope you don't get my cold. Please get as much sleep as you possibly can. When I think about your saying you go around on nervous energy all the time I get worried about making you lose sleep. Honest, you shouldn't do it.

<u>2nd Floor Hall Duty</u>

[Purpose: to keep students from meandering through the halls.]

There isn't much to do on this duty, but I have to be here and I have to stand. On second thought, I don't believe I will.

<u>Sitting down</u>

I borrowed a chair from the library and now I'm taking it easy.

The bell will ring in about 2 minutes so I'll see you later, Honey. I love you.

<u>3:40 P.M. Detention Hall</u>

After the trials and tribulations of the day I land in detention hall. Place where all bad children are sent. This is just the place for me, no doubt. I don't mind staying after school and keeping the kids, but I had to make the other teachers who ride with me wait. I just have three boys left; three of them only had to stay for ½ hour. It's funny when you get them in detention hall it's hard to figure out just why they were bad, they seem meek enough just sitting here. But in different circumstances they are different.

I am tired. I believe I'll go home and take a nap before dinner. We should be home by 5 so that gives me an hour.

I'll bet my letters are boring to you.

You know I'm looking forward to Saturday. I hope you get off.

I wish I knew how Mother is.

Love to my darling,
From your Glorious

I don't like to put blank pages in letters to you. The weekend was grand, again. Thanks for coming. G.

Annapolis
Same date —8:30 P.M.

Don't read this until you read the wee papers.

Mr. Shenton, here I sit all wrapped up in my afghan. I have completed my work for tomorrow and I'm going to bed in ½ hour. In the meantime I'll say "Hello" to you.

I called home tonight and found Mother much better. I am quite glad about that.

I received a letter from Scoop. She wants to go to Frederick on Saturday if it isn't raining so I guess we'll go. And if we do not go I'll meet her in Baltimore and we'll just talk, shop, etc. If we do go, I believe there is a bus which leaves Frederick at 5 getting into Baltimore at 6:30. I am not sure of this yet, I have to go over to the bus terminal tomorrow to get a Frederick to Baltimore schedule. However if there is a bus at that time and you are coming the connections would be perfect.

Time to get ready for bed.

Love to my Sweetheart,

Me

Somewhere Near Norfolk

An officer without a squadron

Somewhere near Norfolk

November 21, 1942

Dearest Darling,

The army didn't do so well by me on this "first" assignment. In the first place the outfit wasn't in Richmond when I got there. It had moved out three weeks before and nobody at Richmond seemed to know where they had gone. I finally found Headquarters and received my bearings. The 351st was in some isolated spot near Norfolk. That meant I had to stay in Richmond for the night. So I called Sleepy's home and by gosh he was on furlough. Lucky me, I went to his house for dinner and stayed all night. We had a wonderful time talking about Fort Jackson and the 120th. I kept him up until 3:00 A.M. talking. It was swell talking to one of my "ole pillrollers" again.

This morning I "grabbed" the train for Norfolk, arrived here about 2:30 this afternoon. Glorious, I can't understand the set-up. There's an Ordnance Officer here and the question is will he or I stay here. (I hope it's him.) We are located about eight miles from Norfolk in the middle of a swamp. I've met most of the officers (pilots) and they certainly are a happy-go-lucky bunch of young fellows. Some look as though they are about 18 & 19 years old. They aren't far advanced in their training. Fact is, they've just started gunnery practice, which means work for the Ordnance Officer. There isn't much chance of them being sent overseas soon as it will take some time to finish the training program.

Legna, I think we had better cancel your trip for Thanksgiving. I was hoping you could make it but I may not be here next Thursday. Although I kind of doubt they will move me out so soon. It would be wonderful to see you for the three days though. I missed you last night, and again tonight. I'll keep on missing you until I see you again. Honey, the five day leave after O.C.S. was something I'll never forget. The last day was best though; I was with you all day which made it perfect. Your taking the day off was the best thing that ever happened to me. We'll have more just like it. Thanks for the whole week Darling, every minute of it.

Sorry about having to use this paper for letter writing but it's all I have until my locker gets here. I'll have to borrow an envelope from one of the fellows. I just had to write you tonight.

Love, (To the sweetest girl in the world)

Howard

My address is just, Box 1601 Norfolk, Virginia

Dispersed Airdrome
November 22, 1942

Dear Miss Ethel,

I think there should be an apology forthcoming from one of your pupils. (Howard C. Shenton.) You did so much for him when he graduated from Officer Candidate School and didn't receive any thanks. I hope this letter will take care of this short-coming.

Miss Ethel, you and Mr. Andrews were certainly wonderful to me last week. Graduating from O.C.S. would have been just another event in my life if it hadn't been for you two. You came to see me graduate and brought Miss Grace, which made it much more wonderful. You all made me feel proud, as though I had really accomplished something that really mattered. Then, bringing me home and treating me to a swell dinner in Baltimore. I'll never forget that weekend. (Even the papers floating through the air with the greatest of ease.) "Thanks for everything, you made the incident a very "memorable occasion".

Thanks too, for having a wonderful daughter. Miss Ethel, I love her.

Sincerely yours,

Howard

Dispersed Airdrome
November 22, 1942

Dearest,

Today is windy and damp, yes but I miss my "little vamp". Her blue eyes reflecting warmth and beauty, with her kissable lips parted in a smile. She's a beautiful creature, one I would love to see and talk to. But best of all I'd like to take her in my arms, hold her tight and kiss her. Then I wouldn't care about the rainy weather or being in an isolated spot with a bunch of strangers. I would feel at home with the world because she is "my world".

Glorious, I don't know exactly why I'm writing like this but I'm lonesome. It's a terrible day and there isn't much to do, so of course my thoughts are full of you. If last Thursday would be today, I'd say everything is lovely. I think Thursday kind of spoiled Lt Shenton; he hasn't quite gotten over it.

I went to Langley Field this morning with one of the officers. He had some business to take care of & I went for the ride. It took us about two hours to get there. You waste most of your traveling time waiting for ferries down here. We had lunch at the Officers Club and got back here about 3:00 o'clock this afternoon. I enjoyed the trip but not "too much".

Guess I'm a little homesick today. Can't seem to get enthused over anything. But I'll snap out of the rut, soon as I get my hands in some work. (Totch doesn't stay down very long; the "count" has never beat him yet.)

I took a look at the planes and the general set-up this morning. Sure wasn't much to look at but the outfit just moved in and things aren't too well organized yet. The other Ordnance Officer is on weekend leave so I didn't pick up too much information about the Ordnance in the squadron. I talked with one of the Ordnance sergeants for a few minutes. There are only six Ordnance enlisted men with the outfit now, which is kind of disconcerting too. There should be at least twenty-one men. The airplanes looked swell though. P40s primed and ready for action. (Kind of like sharks ready for the kill.)

I still don't know anything about whether or not I'll stay with the 351st. Probably won't know either for another week. (Remember the channels?) I should have picked the 352nd. They are in Baltimore. My buddy in O.C.S. ran into the same thing I did at Richmond. He had more worries though; he had his wife with him. They had to hop a train and dash to Baltimore. I would have enjoyed that though, it would have seemed like coming home. (Shady Side only forty-five miles away. Gosh! Right next door to heaven.) If I get sent out of here there's no telling where I'll be assigned.

Well Honey, I've run out so I'd better close. Wish I could get a one-way ticket for Shady Side.

See you in my dreams tonight.

Love,
Howard

210

Officers' Barracks

November 23, 1942

Dear Legna,

I got a letter from you today & it made me very happy. The letter was forwarded from Richmond. Nice work Honey, the morale is up to par. I couldn't believe it when one of the fellows said, "Shenton, there's a letter for you at the Orderly Room."

Well, I'm just loafing around doing nothing. We are waiting for orders to come through to see whether or not I'll stay here. I went down to the field this morning and helped the Ordnance and Air Corps men fix a .50 caliber machine gun. I also looked over the Ordnance set-up; it isn't what you would call an "ideal organization". But nothing is ideal during war, especially when you are in the combat zone. I want to start work though; this place is killing me with nothing but time on my hands. Gosh, I could have taken another five day leave for all the good I'm doing around here. Things will break soon and then I'll be yelling about having so much to do. From what I can see the Ordnance Officer takes care of transportation, ordnance, post exchange and anything else that happens to come along. Some of the pilots have extra duties such as supply officer and mess officer. It's a great life. (The Army). The Flight Surgeon (pillroller) received orders transferring him to an outfit in Connecticut. He just joined this squadron last week and I've never seen a man so happy about anything as he is about getting out of this neck of the woods. Maybe I'll be on "my way" in a few days. The trouble is I'll probably end up about a 1000 miles from home and as you know, "I'm dreaming of a white Christmas."

Talking about getting married, (I think you mentioned it in your letter) the pilots seem to have the same fever that O.C. boys contracted. Two were married last weekend and one is getting "tied" this Saturday. "Everybody's doing it!"

I wrote your Mom yesterday like I said I would. You'll probably hear about it though. She's a "grand gal" Legna, you're lucky to have her for a mother.

You know, I haven't fully recovered from last week. It seems like a dream, something that couldn't happen to a soldier. Wish I could go through another week just like it in the near future. (Very near.)

I had better close now and grab some sleep. Maybe I'll find something to do tomorrow. So long Buttercup.

Love,
Howard

Officers Barracks
November 25, 1942

Dearest Legna,

Is there something wrong with the mail service? Guess I'm just a bit impatient. I was expecting a letter from you today and of course I was disappointed when it didn't arrive. Maybe I'll get one tomorrow, I hope!

Still haven't received any orders for my transfer. Sure wish they would let me know something, this waiting around is kind of getting me down. Had a fairly interesting day yesterday. Went to Newport News. That killed most of the day; I was glad to get away from here for a short time. We were sending some men to Florida for schooling in radio. I had to get their transportation and food money, then put them on the train.

212

(Told you a Pvt never had to worry about anything.) Today I sat around all morning, after lunch I went down to the field and took athletics with the pilots. Also had a talk with the Ordnance Sgt. So it wasn't so bad this afternoon. (I'll live Honey.)

Glorious, I wish we could get together for Thanksgiving. It hurts to think you will be home for the holiday and here I am in Norfolk with nothing to do. Yet, I can't leave. Makes me want to throw up both hands and shout. (Can't tell what I would "shout".)

There's a beautiful moon tonight but I can't enjoy it. I'll just sit around the "Club" and swap stories with some of the boys. We usually turn in around 10:00 or 10:30. I'd like to go in town and see a show or do something, you kind of get tired hanging around the same place all the time. Wish I could get to Annapolis Saturday. You and I could see the football game. Even if we couldn't see the game I would still like to come.

I'd better hang up now, Buttercup.

Love,

Howard

Bolling Field, Washington, DC
311th Fighter Squadron

The Nearness of You
Music by Hoagie Carmichael
Words by Ned Washington

Bolling Field, D.C.

November 30, 1942

Dearest,

I don't feel much like writing tonight but I'll write "anyhow". One thing, I'm not blue and lonesome like I was in Norfolk. This place seems almost like home.

The bus made fairly good time last night. I was in bed by 1:00 o'clock and had a good night's sleep. We get up around 7:30 here and get to work about 8:00. (Nice hours.) I worked until about 4:30 or 5:00 this evening. It's going to take a little time to get things straightened out but I'll make the grade. The officers have been swell to me, so far. The pilots are the same here as in Virginia. (Full of fun & foolishness all the time.)

Say Legna, that "greeting" you gave me yesterday, I can't forget it. I'll have to hitch hike to Shady Side again. That kiss was and _is_ worth it. You were feeling alright, weren't you? I kind of thought maybe you didn't know what you were doing. Thanks Darling, I really appreciated that.

Hope Ivan didn't have too miserable a night. It seemed a shame to leave that "poor fellow", crippled like that. I guess you took care of him today, though.

Well Honey, I'd better turn in. Have to go to Baltimore tomorrow and see about some ammunition, probably take all day. Write me and don't be too surprised if I call you one evening this week.

"Goodnight my love,"

Howard

P.S. Bolling has two "l's" but the army spells it with one sometimes.

Howard

215

Bolling Field, D.C.

December 9, 1942

Dearest Legna,

Thought sure I was going to get a chance to write to you last night but "things" happened and I couldn't get to it. Business always picks up around 5:00 in the evening so the best thing to do is leave early and catch the work in the morning.

I certainly enjoyed my trip to Annapolis Monday night, Buttercup. In fact it was so pleasant that I can't quite get over it. I want to come over again this week but one night is enough, I guess. We'll make it a date for some evening "next" week. The movie we saw Monday night was pretty good; usually I don't enjoy a picture when I am with you. There's too little concentration on the show.

Far as I know, I'm coming home Saturday. If I don't have to make a Baltimore trip, I should get away from here early. That is my intention, but anything can happen. You'll hear from me even if I can't make it Saturday.

You were right about the letter. I liked it alright but the last paragraph kind of "beats me". We'll get that straightened out this weekend.

I'd like to take you dancing Saturday night, but you said something about shopping in Baltimore so maybe you won't feel like cutting-the-rug. But remember Honey, I'm willing.

Guess I better take a ten-minute break. See you Saturday.

Goodnight Buttercup,

Howard

Long break in the letters because Howard was stationed so close to home at Bolling Field he was able to see Glorious frequently.

311th Orderly Room

Bolling Field, D.C.

February 8, 1943

Dearest Legna,

I missed you yesterday evening; it brought back the departures we had while I was in O.C.S. and stationed at Fort Jackson. For 2¢ I would have called you last night but thought it best not to bother you. I'll do that little chore this evening though.

Believe it or not Honey, but I came home and went to bed at 9:00 o'clock. (After three hands of poker.) Felt pretty good this morning, "eager as a beaver damming a stream."

Legna, I don't know how you feel about yesterday. Maybe it wasn't what you would call right but it will be my <u>best</u> and <u>longest</u> memory. You really convinced me that married life is going to be alright. Honey, I can't say I love you anymore for yesterday because you've had all my love for a long time and Legna, you will always have it. Nothing could happen that would change this feeling. When you left me yesterday I really had that "lonesome blues". I felt like I had lost everything that really matters to me, but I'll get it back, soon I hope.

I'm going to try and make Annapolis one night this week for dinner but don't be disappointed if I can't make it.

Goodbye now Darling, keep your nose clean and throat gargled.

Love (to my little angel)

Howard

V.O.Q. Annex

February 25, 1943

Dearest Legna,

Your "nice little letter" came in this morning's mail. I like it very much; in fact it made me feel a little bad about not getting you on the phone last night. I called about 10:00 and the operator tried to get 4916 for twenty minutes, so I gave up. There were about six fellows waiting to use the phone by that time. But I'll call tonight.

Honey, I don't know exactly what the score is now but we definitely are on the move. However, it won't be an overseas move. We are going to another field and train for about six months. (New England, I think.) So don't get excited if you don't hear from me for a few days. I think we will be here for the weekend so more than likely I can get home. According to your schedule it looks as though I could meet you in Annapolis Saturday evening.

What's this about my being stubborn? Now Legna, you know it isn't so. That's a slight misinterpretation of something. But it's alright Honey, maybe I am.

My throat is much better today. Doc gave me some sulfathiazole pills and they did the trick. Now I have to see the dentist, a filling came loose and has to be fixed. Looks like I need a lot of attention. Believe I'm falling apart.

Darling I love you! (See you Saturday, I hope)

Bye now,

Howard

219

On the Move

"We are going to have peace even if we have to fight for it."
General Dwight D. Eisenhower

Bradley Field, Connecticut
March 7, 1943

Dearest Legna,

I've tried to send you a wire six times at least since we arrived but couldn't get to a phone to get it in. When I would get close to a phone there would be two or three fellows waiting for long distance calls. I'm still trying though, should contact you this evening sometime.

Well Honey, from the looks of Bradley Field, this little soldier isn't going to like the place. We are located about sixteen miles from Hartford which is the only town close by of any size. Windsor Locks is about six miles but it's a sort of Shady Side "Metropolis". Haven't had a chance to buzz the place yet but expect to before long. We halfway decided to go in last night but it was snowing, sleeting and raining and the roads were foul. Like all camps you move into nowadays nothing is completed. In the process of course, but you have to carry on as though it was the ideal set-up. We have no place to store our equipment and no buildings from which we can operate. At the present we are operating from boxes as though we were on a tactical mission in the field. Then there's another problem. All three squadrons are together here and there is quite a bit of rivalry among us. Mostly the enlisted men; our boys don't want any part of the other outfits.

Gosh, it's beautiful up here today. The sun is shining and the trees and hills look beautiful covered with snow and ice. Wish you were here, we could take a run around the country, have dinner together, then everything would be lovely. I miss you, Legna and I want to be with you very much. I don't know how you can plan to make a weekend trip. It will take at least eight hours to get here but try and plan one pretty soon Legna. I want to see you. Don't worry about the cost, I'll pay for it —be darned glad to. You would have to stay in Hartford, I guess. Let me know a little ahead of time so I can make arrangements to get off.

The trip up was a slow one but I enjoyed the ride. We came through the mountains and the scenery was exceptionally good. Arrived here about 5 o'clock Friday evening and expected to take a bath and turn in. Instead we fell-out and unloaded box cars until midnight. The freight just had to be unloaded immediately upon arrival.

Goodbye now Legna and you can make that a "one way ticket" to Hartford.

Love, (with all my heart darling!)

Howard

P.S. I'm trying to get you on the phone now. The operator just had Annapolis West River is coming up.

Howard

Orderly Room, 311ᵗʰ
March 11, 1943

Dearest Legna,

From your last letter I gathered Lt. Shenton is a bit tardy with his correspondence. He shall be reprimanded immediately and necessary disciplinary action will be taken. (He will be confined to his quarters until he has completed and brought up to date his correspondence with one Glorious Legna Andrews who resides part-time in Annapolis and the rest of her waking and sleeping hours in the flat lowlands of southern Anne

Arundel County.) Sorry Honey, guess I could have written a few more times but we have been pretty busy. I went to Hartford last night with some of the boys. We really buzzed the town, everybody had a good time. I met a very "cute little blond Dutch girl" from Pennsylvania, very nice Legna but my heart belongs to "my" schoolteacher".

Say, that's really a drawing of the train meeting. It had better happen or take place soon. (The Rebel is going Yankee.) Yes, Hartford is a very interesting place, think we'll all go back Friday night and "buzz" again. When we got back the other day we found out most the places we had visited were listed as "undesirable" for officers & men of Bradley Field. One of them happened to be the best, most popular place in town. (Nice dance floor, large bar and plenty of pretty girls.) I almost learned how to do the rhumba —that seems to be the dance up here.

Legna, I don't like to tell you when to come up for a weekend. If you come I'll make the best arrangements possible to see and be with you. But I want to see you. I'm looking forward to Easter. Please don't disappoint me on that. Come when you can "Honey". I'll do my darndest to meet the train.

I've been working pretty hard lately. This base is much more formal than Bolling and it's a tough job to get supplies.

Goodbye now Darling, I love you with all my heart, I love you with everything that's in me.

Love,

Howard

P.S. If your letters go out in Annapolis morning mail I get them the following day around noon.

Bradley Field, Connecticut

March 13, 1943

My Dear Miss Andrews,

Do you and I have a problem to settle with Uncle's Post Office? I kind of expected a letter today from you but, no letter. There definitely was a mistake in delivery, yes! I don't know Legna but there's a suspicious arising in my mind to the fact that you are a little mad about something. That's not hearsay either. What's wrong Legna? I know I haven't written but two letters, I couldn't. We've been so darn busy getting set up that I haven't had time to get a haircut. Believe me? (No) After all Honey, I am in the army and there is work to be done. Right now I'm pulling three departments, Ordnance, Transportation and Armament and I've got my hands full. I'm not apologizing, just stating facts.

The weather up here is certainly in cadence with the way I feel. (Mighty bad.) Rain & fog yesterday, snow today and I still feel pretty mean. Another day like today and I'll go completely batty. For 2¢ I'd put on a "Jag" tonight. If we had only gone overseas I could stand it but the longer I stay in this country the more I feel like somebody who is not doing what he could do. Maybe I'm wrong but you kind of get fed-up on things once in a while. Allen and I had a little scrap yesterday, I was about to mistake him for "Tojo". However, we are on the beam again.

This Base is sure a humdinger; there isn't one thing I like about the way it operates. Then again the squadrons being close together and group H.Q. next door is rather trying. I want that deserted island tacked on my itinerary somewhere. Could stand a little isolation about now; guess I have to develop a case of measles or something. Oh! I want that isolation to be with a little gal I know too. Right now, she would be hard to get along with but she'd get over her peeve or whatever it is. (I think.)

How about writing me and let me know what's on your mind. Your last letter wasn't a great morale builder Buttercup. But remember, in case that guy drives up, I still <u>LOVE</u> you and I want very much to see and talk to you.

Goodbye now Legna,

Howard

P.S. If you expect me to answer every one of your letters, don't write so many.

Howard

B.O.Q. #145
Bradley Field, Connecticut
9:30 P.M. March 21, 1943

Dearest Legna,

I really thought about you on that train trip to New York. Hope you made it alright Darling. It's tough enough to be sick much less be sick along and among strangers. Honest Legna, I wanted to go with you to New York but the army makes things like that impossible. I felt much better after 10:35 this morning because I know you would be with Margaret.

Legna, I'm really glad you came up even though I don't feel you had a good time. But you did me a lot of good, I have a new lease on Bradley Field and everything is going to be "O.K." (No blondes and no drinks.)

My "leave" date has been changed. Group wants all leaves to be over with by the 1ˢᵗ or middle of May. So that knocks June right off the calendar. Could sure stand a ten day leave about now.

I'll bet within two weeks we have quite an epidemic of the measles in the squadron. I went to see and take some cigarettes to Lt. Fricker this afternoon. He sure hates that hospital; they keep you in the darn place taking your temperature until old age catches up with you.

Well Honey I'd better dash off now. I love you sweetheart. Thanks for coming to see me. You're a real shipmate. We'll take that world cruise someday.

Good night now. I'll be thinking of you.

Love,

Howard

311ᵗʰ Orderly Room

March 22, 1943

3:40 P.M.

Dearest Legna,

I told you Shenton was really running wild, even gained a reputation. A slot-machine was busted at the officers' club last night. This morning Lts. Bennert, Herbst and Shenton were put on the carpet for said offense. But I was dismissed. Last night Shenton was at the B.O.Q. #145 writing a letter to a little gal down in Annapolis. Bennert and Herbst were guilty. The Colonel dismissed me with an apology when he found out I was in my quarters. He knew I "poled" around with Herbst and Bennert so therefore thought I was in on the busting of slot-machines. But I turned over a new leaf since a visit from a very charming young lady who wields a heavy club when it comes to influencing a 2nd Lt. in the Ordnance Dept. See Honey, your visit paid-off already. If I hadn't seen and talked with you this weekend chances are nine out of ten that I would have been at the club drinking and playing slot-machines.

Honey I've really thought about you today. How we could make a "go" of it together and how much I'd like to be with you all the time. I really miss you, just like I knew I would when you left Sunday or "yesterday". We wear well together, and go and look well together. Bradley Field made the colors clash but that's over with; we are back in the scheme again.

Haven't done much today. Went to a two-hour meeting at Base Ordnance with the Ordnance Officers of the other squadrons. We are still in the same status —meeting accomplished exactly nothing. Too much of this New York Broker attitude prevailing among the officers. They try to sell something that isn't for sale. It belongs to all of us but you'd think it was personal property. However we'll make the grade.

The radio is playing "for me and my gal". How about me and my gal? The bells aren't ringing but that's included in things to come.

Legna, please take care of yourself. A little less worrying will do the trick.

So long, (for now) Love! All my love!

Howard

B.O.Q. #145
Bradley Field, Connecticut
March 23, 1943
9:30 P.M.

Dearest Legna,

Received your letter this morning and believe me I was waiting for it. Sure glad you made it back without getting sick or should I say "sicker". Honey I wasn't disgusted with you for the way you were feeling Sunday morning. I was very much concerned. That's the first time I've seen your blue eyes bloodshot and I was plenty worried. (Couldn't have been caused by drinking intoxicants, I hope.) Maybe they were sunburned like you said mine were the Sunday we turned over in the speedboat. Remember?

Had two meetings to attend today. If we would cut out these gatherings maybe we'd get some work done around this place. Every other hour there's a meeting of staff officers.

Legna, I haven't much more to say except "I love you", if you still want to hear that phrase.

Goodnight now, Darling,

Love,

Howard

B.O.Q. #145

March 25, 1943

Hello Honey,

You wrote a very nice letter today, I really appreciate such correspondence. One thing, Shenton doesn't have to answer by indorsement for not writing to "one Glorious Legna". I think I've "out-done" myself this week.

Lt. Baxter, (he's the pillroller) wanted me to go to Boston with him today. His wife had a little girl last night and he wanted to go in and see the noble pair. But Capt. Tuman wouldn't say, "Yes, Shenton, go ahead". He said, "Shenton I'd rather you wouldn't", and so I stayed at Bradley Field. That Capt. sure hates to see me take off. Doc will have to go by himself.

Well Legna, "my leave" starts May 1st and ends May 10th. So maybe it wouldn't pay for you to come up Easter. But Honey, you come if you want to, and I want you to.

You kind of put me "on the spot" about the middle aisling in June. Legna, I don't know what to say. I know I want to marry you but I don't think it's the thing to do yet. Legna, I don't know. I know you're not going to like the indefinite answers and I don't blame you. I'd rather hear a yes or no but Honey I'm not sure, after all it's a big step. I'd rather talk about it person to person; I can't put in writing what I think anyway.

Today was really ideal. We should have been together. Nice day for sailing, too. I had a little fun shooting tin cans and bottles with shotguns. The Doc and "the Wasp" participating. We threw our hats in the air and then the fun begun. The Capt. didn't like it because I didn't tell him about the shooting. He wanted to join us.

The boys are playing poker upstairs and want another player. I'm going to fool them and not play. I want to write Miss Grace.

Goodbye Honey.

Love,
Howard

B.O.Q. #145
March 26, 1943

Dearest Angel, (how about me not spelling it backwards)

I wrote to you and Miss Grace last night but left in such a hurry this morning I forgot to pick them up and get them in the mail. I'll put last night's letters in the envelope as I had addressed it for Shady Side.

The only thing I like about this place is the letters I receive from you. Honest Legna, I'll go nuts if I stay here for the duration. I'd like to get overseas where I could forget all about reports and paperwork. If there is a shortage of paper the army certainly doesn't know about it. Every time you breathe it's drying ink on some damn report or letter explaining why you eat three meals a day and should have a minimum of eight hours sleep. That leave can't come any too soon.

I went reminiscent tonight. Looked at some old pictures and papers, left-overs from the infantry days. Gosh, it would have been great if I could have stayed in the 120th and we had gone over together.

Remember the Lt. who was with me at the station when you come in? The poor boy is off the beam, he's getting married Easter and it's really working on him. He can't wait till the rabbit gets around.

Legna, I'd really like to see you tonight, more than anything I know. I'd like to talk and whisper "sweet-nothings" in your ear but no you can't do anything you really want to. Someday I will but till then this will have to do.

Too bad about Joe washing in O.C. S. Hope it doesn't change Judy's mind about him. It won't if she loves him.

Well Andrews I'd better say goodnight. We are having a big inspection tomorrow. 1st Air Force officials.

Good night Honey,

Love,

Howard

B.O.Q. #145

March 30, 1943

9:15 P.M.

Dearest Legna,

I'm trying to get you on the phone so until I do I'll keep writing.

Everything is in a mess again. I'm going to Florida for a month. This is a funny set-up. All the officers in the 58th Group except six are going to take a course of some sort in Florida. There won't be an officer left in the 311th and in addition the leading non-coms of the different departments are going too. I don't know who is going to run the squadron while we are gone, guess Group HQ will arrange for that.

So Honey, that upsets all plans for my leave. Gosh knows when I'll get a leave now, when this course is over we'll probably be tied-up with squadron work for a long time to come. Legna, I'm sorry this had to happen because I was really counting on that May 1st to the 10th proposition. That's what I love about this army life, plan on something and you are sure to be messed up somewhere on the deal. Honey, I'm disgusted. In the first place, I feel that this course isn't going to be of much benefit to us and certainly detrimental to the squadron while we are away.

Say, you certainly wrote a letter today. I felt it way down in my toes, if you know what I mean. TELEPHONE: _____

Nice chat, Legna but don't use that word "never"; I don't like it where you and I are concerned. It may be sometime but I wouldn't say never.

Honey, I'd better close now. Next time I'll write from Florida.

Love,

Howard

Orlando, Florida

Army Air Force School of Applied Tactics

A.A.F.S.A.T.

Orlando, Florida

April 4, 1943

Dearest Legna,

Arrived in this "Wonderland" at approximately 3:00 P.M. yesterday and at 4:00 o'clock I had made up my mind that this was no place for me. It is very much like Wheeler & Jackson. Hope we get back to Bradley in time to catch the bluebird. Legna, I'll say right here and now, don't come down. The train ride would be an ordeal in itself and I wouldn't be able to see you except on Saturday and Sunday. According to the schedule we are going to be very busy for 30 days.

Looks like this course is a refresher of what we had in O.C.S. — makes me feel like a raw recruit. The last week will be devoted to field activities so maybe I won't get an opportunity to write you but I'll try.

The whole Group made this trip in coaches and it was pretty bad. Took us about 48 hours. A bed felt mighty good last night and we slept late this morning. The boys are thinking of going horseback riding this afternoon. Transportation is in sad shape at this base.

Legna, I love you. I'll close with that little sentence.

Good bye now,

Love,

Howard

P.S. Had to write this in pencil; my pen ran dry.

Howard

B.O.Q. #2646

April 5, 1943

Dear Darling Legna,

The School of Applied Tactics really got under way this morning at 8:00 o'clock. We had organization of the Army Air Forces, the same course I had in O.C.S. Tomorrow we have practically the same thing on schedule. I am being bored and unless something pops soon I will become very disgusted, which doesn't matter to anyone but me, of course, but I can still gripe.

Orlando is very much like the towns of South Carolina and Georgia —nothing doing but the place is always jammed with people. There are two theatres and always a line of people about a block long waiting to get in.

We had one very interesting hour today. Three captains formerly of the famous 19th Bombardment Group (Queens Die Proudly, Readers Digest, latest edition) gave a talk on their experiences in the war and it was really great. All three are very young officers.

Honey, it still goes about my not wanting you to come down. Honest you wouldn't like any part of the trip. I can't wait until the 30 days are up and we can go north. Don't know whether our leaves will be cancelled or just postponed.

I guess we'll know when we get back to Bradley. I could sure use 10 days at home.

Well Legna, I'd better hang-up, it's getting late.

Goodnight Honey,

Love, Howard

Air Defense Auditorium

April 7, 1943

Dearest Legna,

We are about to engage in a two hour lecture on Airdrome Security. I would rather engage the enemy at this point. The first period after lunch is a tough one. At the present I feel pretty secure, Allen is on one side of me and Fischer on the other.

One nice feature of this school is that we have two hours for lunch. Thus we eat, get a sun bath, short nap and shower. Very nice but it can't last. I expect tomorrow to be the last day for bankers' hours.

Lately I have been taking to writing poetry. All about hairless noggins. Lt. Burns doesn't have much hair so I wrote a few poems about the fact. He got sore after reading the second one so I stopped writing poetry. Maybe I'll write one about you but you might get mad. How about that?

Ordnance put on a swell demonstration for the students this morning. It was held outdoors and everybody enjoyed it. All classes should be held in the open, the weather here is beautiful.

It is impossible to see a show in town. There is always a line two blocks long waiting to get in. We have discontinued shows from our entertainment list. Maybe I'll get in some tennis while down here. Also swimming.

Legna, I really miss you, no doubt about it. Bolling Field spoiled me. I'd give anything to have a dinner with you and then maybe do a little dancing. Hope I get that leave when we go north. The Group Adjutant seems to think we will but I'm not counting on it too much. I don't want to be disappointed with a big let-down.

236

We are located just a little too far from Camp Blanding for me to dash over and see the boys in the 120th. Sure would like to take a gander at all the "old" fellows.

I am expecting a letter from you this afternoon.

So long for now, Buttercup.

Love,

Howard

AAFSAT

April 10, 1943

Dearest Legna,

I don't know but can't help think there is something wrong with the mail service here. I have only received one letter from you and Legna that's not enough. A minimum of one a day is a very nice supply but just a little too much to expect. I'll settle for two or three a week.

Things are tightening up a bit down here. We finished the orientation course and took an exam on the material covered. Now we go to school eight hours a day with one hour for lunch. So far the subjects have been very dry but next week we go into Ordnance exclusively and should be a bit more interesting. (Sort of specializing course for Ordnance officers only.)

Honey, I wrote a poem about "Legna" but I'm afraid there's one line you wouldn't approve of. I've got a good mind to send it to you anyway. I think it's kind of cute. The boys wrote a poem about me —my long legs and infantry stride. We are always arguing about the Infantry & Air Corps.

Honey, I'd like for you to do me a favor. We've had quite a few expenses since arriving at this place and I am about out of cash. How about drawing that $75.00 out of the bank and send it to me? Probably your only chance would be to get it on Saturday if you're in Annapolis. I think the best thing would be to wire it. The mail situation is very bad. Now don't you pay for the wire. Take the charge out of the $75.00. If it will make things inconvenient for you or something, don't bother. I'll borrow from the boys.

Legna, if I stay here much longer I'm going to be absolutely good for nothing. This climate makes a man so darn lazy it's pitiful. The classes really take all the pep out of a fellow.

I just can't wait until we leave Florida and head north. I don't know for sure about my leave but I wish you would plan on coming to Hartford around the 1st part of May. Start thinking about it, will you Honey? I want to see you as soon as possible. There's no use of you coming to Florida for Easter because I'll be out in the field that week.

I love you Legna! (Just like that)

Love,

Howard

B.O.Q. #2646

AAFSAT

April 13, 1943

Dearest Legna,

Say you really knocked out a letter over the weekend. It came in this morning's mail along with one you mailed on the 9th. Nice work Honey, but I'll never be able to match it. But I'll try and not make my letters precise. Guess though I can't write them oushy-goushy, as you call it. Your weekend letter was wonderful, made me feel like a million.

I can't wait until this blasted course is over; even if I don't get a leave I'll be able to see you. We could even meet in New York if you say so. I really want to see you Legna, more than anything I know. Rumor has it that we leave here the 1st of May. That sure suits me.

Classes are getting a little tougher now. We can't cut class; attendance records are kept for everyone. The Ordnance has taken over, the Ordnance officers get nothing but Ordnance work from here on out. A bit more interesting too. The Ordnance officer in charge here is a pretty swell fellow. (A West Pointer!)

Doc Baxter has an elderly sister living in Orlando. The home is on a lake and it's beautiful. Four of us went out with Doc Sunday and spent the day. I got, or absorbed, a severe case of sunburn, but am about over it now. We had a good time, swimming and a swell chicken dinner. First time I'd done anything like that since our excursion last summer. It sure brought back that day we went sailing.

Sounds like you had a swell weekend at R.H.H.. Too bad I couldn't be there Honey. I would have loved it. (There will be days like that!)

Darling I have to go now, so long Honey.

Love,

Howard

P.S. That poem is enclosed. Don't let it make you angry.

H.

Quite a Name (Legna)

"L is for love, of which I first think

For I love this gal with a love distinct

Other girls I like and hand a line

But Legna, my heart is all thine

"E" is for excellent and tastes she does have

Because where else could she pick a guy who isn't a cad

Of bad habits she has none

Except for a little smooching when day is done

"G" is for the goodness, I like in her best

Although sometimes she thinks I am a pest

With her wrinkled nose and smile so wide

She has something that money can't buy

"N" is for never and she said

No, not till after we have wed

"A" is for all, you can think or say

Angel spelled backwards; our love is here to stay.

H.S

B.O.Q. #2646
April 18, 1943

Dearest Darling Legna, (and I mean that!)

Your last letter made me feel like a traitor. Honey I wrote you twice last week, kind of thought that would be enough. (I started to wire you and let you know I am still alive.) Even though I only wrote twice, your three letters were appreciated. Sometimes I get spells and can't write letters, you know that??

Florida still isn't any better than it was when we first arrived. School is more of a problem now. "Roll is taken quite often." I don't believe any of us are learning anything. Tomorrow should be a pretty good day, we get a chance to fire all the weapons pertaining to the Air Force and I'll like that. This sitting in class all day listening to dry lectures is a pain in the neck. I want some active duty. (Action)

Saw a good show this noon, The Moon is Down. Very good but just a trifle over acted, also a bit too much like propaganda. Gosh Legna, wish you and I could be together. Seems we are losing or wasting an awful lot of valuable time, but that's the way it has to be, I reckon. I thought about you quite a bit last night. The weather was nice with a full moon silhouetting the palm trees. Would have been a good night to get a sail boat and take a whirl or even dance to a swell orchestra out in the open. We'll make up for all this when I get my leave.

Hope Buddy W got a good send-off. It's pretty tough leaving home for the first time.

Wish I could be your Easter Rabbit. I'd bring you an egg weighing 500,000 lbs.

Legna, I love you!

Goodnight now,

Love,

Shenton (remember him?)

He used to write you letters ... and still does!

Sun Bath Room

April 20, 1943

Dearest Legna,

Received your air mail letter and wire yesterday. Mighty glad to get them, "Honey". I'm glad you finally got a letter from me, must have been quite a surprise. Thanks very much for the wire, I've paid all my debts and it's clear sailing from here on out, I hope.

School is pretty good. Can't cut more than two classes a day now. We are learning an awful lot. All of us will be military experts when the course is finished. That is, far as tactics go, "military and otherwise."

Legna, I hope your plans for the trip to Hartford aren't messed up. I want to see you just about as bad as I ever wanted anything in my life. If you would rather have me meet you in New York I think it could be arranged. Can't say for sure though because there's no telling what we'll run into back at Bradley. We'll be busy as an old hen with 45 chicks for a while, I guess. The most important thing though is my leave. Gosh I hope it goes through. Ten days could be spent with the utmost of pleasure in Maryland.

Someone said this Sunday is Easter. In the army you don't know one day from another. If you want to know what day of the week it is you have to stop and think for a while. "Greetings and Salutations" for a Happy Easter, Legna. I still would like to be that "rabbit".

Buster and I have written a few letters since I've been here and he thought Major Sebastian and some of the boys would come to Orlando to see me last Sunday but they didn't show up. I was a little disappointed. Sure would like to have seen some of the ole bunch. We are only about 100 miles apart and the Major has a car. Maybe they will come next weekend.

Darling, I love you with all my heart; always intend to love you no matter what, why or when. Goodbye now.

Love,

Howard

P.S. How did you like the poem?

H.

B.O.Q. #251
Orlando Air Base
April 25, 1943

Dearest Legna,

I have moved from AAFSAT and am now living at the main Base. Tomorrow we'll go out with the 81st Squadron. From what I hear this field work is going to be a cinch. Honestly Legna, I haven't learned a darn thing since I've been here but maybe this squadron detail will give me some ideas. Had a big exam last Thursday on two weeks work and I think I came out alright. Every time I get disgusted in a set-up such as this I wish with all my might I was overseas. It seems like such a waste of time to be sitting in on classes from which you don't gain anything except a groggy mind.

The fellows are all going swimming this afternoon out at Rollins College. Doc's sister is turning over her house to the boys. We should have a good time. A bunch of us went swimming yesterday for a few hours and it was alright. About the only thing we're getting out of this course is a sunburn and a few swimming lessons.

Just think, one more week of this and it's back to Connecticut. Will I be glad? I'm really looking forward to your trip to Hartford. Seems like six months since I've seen you.

Sure would like to be in Shady Side today. The weather here is lovely but I'll still take Shady Side even in a storm. I'm just a country boy at heart.

Had a letter from Whitey last week. He's a pretty good Joe.

Legna, I have to go now. Write me at the same address. We should be leaving here next Saturday or Sunday.

Love,

Howard

WESTERN UNION

1201 (47)

A. N. WILLIAMS
PRESIDENT

NEWCOMB CARLTON
CHAIRMAN OF THE BOARD

J. C. WILLEVER
FIRST VICE-PRESIDENT

The filing time shown in the date line on telegrams and day letters is STANDARD TIME at point of origin. Time of receipt is STANDARD TIME at point of destination

BRA167 14 TOUR=FN FLORENCE SOCAR 28 5557P

MISS GLORIOUS ANDREWS=

225 GLOUCESTER ST

1943 APR 27 PM 6 40

ON WAY BACK TO CONN WILL CALL FROM WASHINGTON IF THERES A CHANGE

WESTERN UNION
TELEGRAM

Apr. 27

245

Providence, Rhode Island
Greenfield Air Base
And other bases around New England

E'verytime We Say Goodbye

By Cole Porter

B.O.Q. 202

Greenfield Air Base

Providence, Rhode Island

April 30, 1943

Dear Legna,

I've just received the two letters you mailed to Bradley Field. (I'll get the ones you sent to Florida when the other officers come back.) We arrived at Bradley Tuesday afternoon about 1:00 and right away we started packing and hauling our equipment up here. After riding a darn train for about 36 hours, I had to bring a convoy of trucks up here Tuesday evening and go back soon as they were unloaded. I got to bed Wednesday morning at 5:15, got up at 7:00 and did the same thing over again. (Hold tight Legna, I'm a day behind. We didn't get back until Wednesday afternoon and finished moving yesterday, so I'm wrong about the days in the first part of this paragraph.) Anyway, I haven't had time to shave hardly. Only two officers of the 311th came back, Lt. Bennert and I. The rest are going to finish the course. They'll be back around the 2nd or 3rd of May. Bennert & I were just starting to have a good time in Florida, too.

Just when everything was set-up and functioning smoothly at Bradley we moved out. This Air Corps beats the hell out of me. I'm just about sick of this moving business. Guess I was meant to be a permanent fixture. When the war is over I'll find me a spot and just camp there for one week anyway. Somehow I have a feeling we won't be here long enough to get a shave and a shower. I kind of hope not, this is not much of an air base. We also have Group HQ's tagging along and Buttercup, the less I have to do with Group the better I like it. We had a cinch being on our own at Bolling. Capt. Hykes (Group S-4) is enough to put any man down on the army. I'll be glad when Capt. Tuman our C.O. [Commanding Officer] gets back so we can have somebody to back us up.

The camp or field is located about four miles out of Providence. So, Honey, if you'll grab a choo choo and come on up here I would be tickled blue & pink. No fooling Legna, I want you to come soon as you can but you'd better bring some money with you. I haven't been paid and don't know when that event will take place. Don't worry about the money though. I'll borrow a 100, 000 if you will just dash up to Providence this coming weekend. (May 7th). If anything happens between now and then to change my/our plans I'll wire you.

I love you, Legna!

Love,
Howard

BRA240 22=PROVIDENCE RI 5 958P

MISS GLORIOUS ANREWS=

225 GLOUCESTER ST NS=

1943 MAY 5 PM 10 05

POSTPONE TRIP UNTIL NEXT WEEK CANT GET A DAY OFF AND HAVE
TO BE IN BY MIDNIGHT WILL WRITE AND EXPLAIN LOVE=

HOWARD.

249

B.O.Q.

May 9, 1943

6:00 P.M.

Dearest Darling,

I guess you are pretty sore because I haven't written for so long. But Legna, I haven't had time to even get my laundry and cleaning out of the shop. We have really been busy and that's no alibi. I was a bit peeved because the Captain wouldn't give me yesterday off but he of course was taking orders from Group HQs. The days off for the officers begin today and I've already put in my 2¢ worth for next Saturday, unless something drastic happens I will see you then.

Gosh, Legna, I want to see you so bad it hurts. Honey, if ever you feel I don't care or think about you, please expel those thoughts from your mind. I know now and have known for a long time that you are the only gal for me. I want to hold you tight and kiss you till it hurts. I also want to have a long talk with you. Don't know if we'll be able to do any dancing when you come up. Most of the places are a bit wild. The Navy makes up ¾ of this town. It's dirty and I might say a very nice place not to be. (Even worse than Hartford.) So please, if it's possible come this weekend. I'll have a room reserved for you at one of the hotels.

What do you think of this 12:00 o'clock curfew we are undergoing? From now on we are known as Boy Scouts of the AAF [Army Air Force]. The Colonel will probably be dashing around tucking us in bed at night.

Honey, if anything comes up and I think you shouldn't make the trip, I'll wire you. I'll try everything possible to meet you when the train comes in.

Goodbye now, Legna. I love you and want you.

Howard

Base Headquarters

May 16, 1943

Dearest Legna,

Right now I am in a position from which your presence could make quite delightful. I'm sitting at the Base Commander's desk in Hangar No. 1 and what could be more lovely than to have you sitting on my knee. (Taking dictation. I don't know?) The view from this office is quite panoramic. The sun has set and the field lights are on with the New England hills making quite a background. The A.A. Sky-rider just came in, stayed for ten minutes and took-off again. I've just inspected the guard and have nothing more to do until midnight. The 311th men are downstairs in the hangar checking over the planes which came in a few minutes ago from the last flight for today. The boys start flying again at 5:00 A.M. tomorrow morning.

Legna, I didn't quite gather what you meant about my being (ice-berger) this trip. I know I acted a little cold and detached in the station when I was about to leave, but there is a reason. Sitting in the Savarin, eating dinner and listening to the music with you and knowing I had to leave within a few minutes kind of hit me pretty hard. You looked as though you were going to start a little private, or should I say public, shower of your own and I was feeling just as bad. So I acted tough or whatever you want to call it. But forgive me Honey, I didn't mean it. I was so damn miserable, sitting at the table across from you and hearing that beautiful music, well I was cussing the Army and everything that had anything to do with our parting. There are no doubts in my mind about loving you, I know that I do and always will. I hated to leave you more

251

than anything in the world but what else could there be? I had to be in camp by midnight —and I was (arrived at 11:50).

Another A.A. plane is taking off.

Had a nice day today. Capt. Tuman and the pilots shot skeet this afternoon. So I had a lot of fun shooting with them. They all wanted to know when I was going to get married. (Must be in the air.) That incidentally was the first question asked me this morning in the mess-shack. I didn't answer. But, guess there was some reason for their asking. Maybe I had a more serious look on my face this morning than usual.

Well Honey, thanks for coming up, even if I did see you for only twenty-five hours. It was great and I loved it. Hope my leave goes through so I can be with you again pretty soon. I love you!

Goodnight Darling,
Howard

B.O.Q. "B"
May 19, 1943

Dearest Legna,

Received your letter this A.M., read it at lunch time in the mess-shack. Wish I could be in Shady Side with you. Maryland is really the place to be in the spring.

There's been quite a bit of activity around here this week. I've been rather busy. The pilots are getting in a lot of skeet-shooting and that means work for me. All the officers have been attending meetings setting up a training program for all personnel. I'll be glad when it's finished so we can settle down and start work. I'm all slated for the range work and qualification in weapons.

Had two visitors to my Transportation Section this week —a civilian inspector from 1st Air Force and a Capt. from our Ordnance 3rd echelon shop. The Capt. stayed with me the whole afternoon and we had some chat. He gave me some very good points on how to operate my section.

My leave has been approved by the Group Commander. It begins June 18 and lasts for six whole days. But I'm not holding my breath; anything can happen between now and then to cancel it. Maybe another AAFSAT deal. (pessimist)

Friday is my day off this week but I don't think I'll take it. There's much too much to be done and besides I have no place to go or anything to do. I might take off early and see a show in town.

I'm still trying to get a plane ride but not having much success. Guess I'll fly me a kite.

Legna, I miss you an awful lot. Wish I could see you every weekend. When I come home let's go somewhere and get a big steak. (I'm hungry.) Goodnight little gal.

Love,

Howard

Tomorrow you are 23, right?!

B.O.Q. "B"

May 23, 1943

Dearest Darling Legna,

I didn't get in your quota of letters last week but it was close. (Two letters & a wire). Glad you like the roses, you almost didn't get them. I gave Lt. Reikseit the money to send them as he was going to Boston for his day off. The sunfish left the message and your address in camp and had to wire me for it. I, of course, wired the info right back with a few additional phrases that the telegram gal didn't want to let go over the wire. But you got them and (the roses) that was the point. Too bad I couldn't get a taste of the birthday cake.

Maxwell and I had a pleasant afternoon. I managed to get the afternoon off; the Capt. was pretty hard to win over. Max and I went to see a double-header in Boston. The Chicago Cubs were playing. The Cubs took both games 2-1 & 1-0. The Capt. doesn't want me to ask for anymore afternoons either.

Say, about that Ensign's car. How about petrol? I'm not crazy about driving it down for him but will gladly do him a favor. The gas situation is getting serious. If he can swing the gas deal, it can be accomplished. I'll bring it down.

Legna, there's a terrible argument going on. The boys are arguing supply; we'll win the war right here, tonight. If the supply lines hold up?? (The boys are doing pretty good.)

Honey, I'd better shove-off for bed. I love you and hope the leave actually happens this time so I can come home, even if it's only five days.

Goodnight Honey,

Howard

Tillie's Shop

Sat. May 29, 1943

Darling,

I just have to write to you now, for I am feeling very sentimental and quite happy this morning. It is such a beautiful morning, cool, but not too cool. I've had so many errands to run for Mother and I've been dashing up and down the street smiling at everyone. I would much rather be in Shady Side, but things must be done. Mother had to get a permanent, there was no gasoline so we had to come up with Tillie. I've been to all the banks, I had the May allotment put on our book, now we have $150. Or was that April? The May one will come in June, won't it? I've bought flowers for a basket to be put on the altar at church tomorrow in memory of Grandmother, Aunt Minnie and Aunt Erispe. I had a terrific time getting them; the flower shops get only two shipments of flowers a week now, thus the flowers are old and there isn't the variety. I had to go to several shops before I got enough for the bouquet. I am going to arrange them myself in the morning before church.

Honey, guess what? Do you like to go to a circus? I know it's childish, but I love it. I've never really been to a great big one. Well Barnum & Bailey is in Baltimore the week you are home, can we go? I think we'd have fun.

Last night we went out to school to a defense meeting. Movies were shown of how to prepare an air raid shelter that is a room in your own home. One on war gases and how to treat yourself for them, or rather against them when you have been exposed to them. Then one on the new incendiary bomb that explodes. They were interesting, but horrible too.

255

Tillie has all kinds of customers while I've been writing this letter she has had a little bride come and get her whole trousseau which Tillie has altered (including a night gown). She is a cute kid, she was so happy her eyes were sparkling, her husband is in the Navy and he will be stationed in Florida for three months, she is going down there. Next, Tillie had an old woman come in, she was the most persistent woman, she wanted Tillie to fix her dress today and Tillie never stays here after noon on Saturday. Tillie could handle her! The public is difficult to deal with.

I know it's wrong, but I am just building and planning so much for your leave. All the time I am trying to realize that there are ifs and buts in all my plans. I am living for the day though, when this mess is over and you and I can settle down to a life of our own. When I can brush your hair for you and you can rub my back for me. By the way have you bought a brush yet? You ought to, get a good one.

Now I must go over to see how Mother is getting along.

Hope there is a letter for me from you when I get home.

Love to my very own dearest Darling Sweetheart,

Your Legna

B.O.Q. "B"
June 6, 1943

Darling,

The boys are getting cleaned up to go in town and see Capt. Tuman at the hospital. He had a crack-up last Thursday while taking off. The plane was a total wash-out but Tuman walked away from it with a few cuts and a broken arm. He was really lucky. We are all going in tonight to see him and also to present the bomb I dreamed up. First though we must get some long-stemmed flowers to put in it before the presentation.

Honey, I wish you had come back with me, I thought about you all the way up. Legna, we don't want to get married though. Everything is so uncertain and in a state of more or less confusion. I love you more than anything in the world but we mustn't rush into marriage and make a mess of it.

I got back last night around 7:00 o'clock and it's a good thing. The Colonel got a wild-hair and had a work call at the "line" last night. He wanted to find out how many men were failing the curfew. We had 23 E.M. and 13 officers absent. I worked until 2:00 A.M. and decided to go home and hit the ole sack. Consequently, Shenton overslept this morning but it wasn't too bad.

Legna, I have to go now. Goodnight Darling. I'll write again soon, 100,000 letters.

Love to my sweet Legna,

Howard

B.O.Q. "B"
June 8, 1943
10:20 P.M.

Dearest Darling Legna,

Don't you know, I've lost my fountain pen so this will have to be in pencil. I'll borrow Maxwell's pen to address the envelope.

Had a rugged day Honey but outside of being a little tired I feel swell. Took the boys on the rifle range and we had quite a session. Of course, I had to fire a few rounds but my score was so lousy I quit.

Orderly Room 311th
June 9, 1943

Dearest Darling Legna,

I'm taking a few minutes out to write this missile, the Capt. doesn't mind. Things are really shaping up around here. I've been going so strong with all the work that accumulated while I was away till a spare moment this afternoon seems quite a shock.

Had some of the boys on the rifle range yesterday and I enjoyed it. Shot a few courses myself but didn't get such a good score. Tomorrow I'll be out all day again. Saturday the same. Then I'll be out again three days next week. This training program is an awful lot of work and Shenton will be glad when it's over so things can go back to normal. I don't expect to get a day off for some time. Which reminds me, I told the C.O. what you said about getting two days off and he said, no Shenton, I can't let you stick your neck out like that. How about it, Honey. Would you cut me off at the neck?

No kidding though Legna. I want to get married just as much as you do but I just can't see it now. There are reasons why we should and reasons why we shouldn't. I frankly don't know which is the better to take into consideration. Maybe I lack the nerve or whatever it takes to say, "I do." But regardless Honey, I love you and want you for my own. I know you are the only gal I would ever marry. Better change the subject.

The Group has me scheduled as Duty Officer tonight. On duty from six this evening till eight tomorrow morning. If they keep on we won't have a darn minute to ourselves. It's either Base O.D, squadron O.D. and now Group D.O. Those boys that sit behind desks can sure think or dream some beautiful ideas.

Goodbye now Legna. Wish you were here darn it.

Love,
Howard

58th Group Headquarters
"Lt Sagen-bomb's office"
(the Group D.O. uses it at night)
June 9, 1943
9:40 P.M. [2140 Army time]
(The phone is ext. 125, give me a buzz next time I'm D.O.)

Hello Legna Darling,

I've been setting here waiting for action but nothing has happened as yet. It would be worth a month's pay to get away from Group H.Qs. so they couldn't heckle us all the time. In just about twenty minutes Shenton is going to hit the "ole sack" and get some sleep.

Legna, did I tell you how much I love you? This afternoon I mean. Gosh, I want to see you and kiss you one time, then I could go to sleep so comfortably. (Sagen-bomb's pen doesn't write so well. His real name is Sagendorph.)

I've been drinking cokes and eating candy all night also reading the Digest and paper. If it hadn't been for this detail this evening I could have played ball with the enlisted men. Schwen and Maxwell played.

As I was waxing romantically a moment ago, think I'll go back to the subject. According or in accordance with Army Regulations an officer mustn't let his personal life interfere with his duties. (Think that's AR 715-10 dated March 15, 1943). You're really not interfering with my duties but I've been thinking about you all day. Saw that almost a new moon this evening and wished for Shady Side and you very much. Course, I'll still take you without the moon, but it's quite a reminder. (Full moon, coming up around 10:00 "northeast of R.H.H. I've seen it there many times.)

Honey, I'd better go to bed and get some sleep. Range work coming up at 6:30 in the morning.

I love you!

Howard

P.S. This is Sagen-bomb's stationery too. I don't like it either. Fact is I don't like anything about Group.

H.

Goodnight blue-grey eyes . . .

June 14, 1943
8:00 P.M.

Dearest Legna,

I've started to write you almost 100,000 times and haven't been able to make it until now. It's 11:00 P.M. June 14, 1943. I'm going to finish this if I have to stay up until reveille tomorrow morning.

Your letters have been coming in everyday and Shenton feels guilty because he hasn't answered. But Legna don't stop writing, please! I love you, your letters and everything about you. I'm sorry about my letters, but I just couldn't get around to it.

Things are still happening pretty fast. The ground school is going strong, range work three days a week. The range work is getting monotonous and very trying. The men aren't qualifying and I tramp up and down the firing line sounding off like a siren. But I'll get them qualified.

Honey, what about this not seeing you until the war is over and I come home? Aren't you and Elsie coming to Boston in July? I'll be O.C. sometime that week (1st of July) but come anyway if you can. This business of not seeing you for the duration plus six months I can't relish. Are we at war? If we are, let's call a truce. After all Legna, I only love you, if that makes any difference. Even though you are hurt and just about through, how about looking upon my (smirking or beautiful) countenance sometime in the near future? I'll even kiss you when I meet the train. Honey, I'm kidding now but in all seriousness, you'd better come and see me pretty soon.

Legna, I'd better hang-up. The C.O. is calling me at 5:30 in the morning. There's a beautiful moon tonight and no beautiful girl to hold in my arms. How about giving me an opportunity to do that?

Goodnight Darling,

Howard

B.O.Q."B"

June 17, 1943

Dearest Legna,

Two days now and no letter from you. How about that? You must be giving me "tit for tat". It's alright though, Honey, I don't expect you to write any more than I do.

Had a pretty nice day, no range work and things were running smoothly. Some civilian inspector came in from 1st Service Command to look over my Transportation and he didn't find too much wrong. I have a new sergeant in Transportation, the old one stayed out after midnight so Group busted him to a buck private. (This is what happens to little boys who don't recognize a curfew when it's put into effect by Group H.Q.) Shenton has beat every curfew so far.

Legna, I wanted to write you last night so you get my letter Saturday but I didn't get off the rifle range until late and Group was giving a party which I had to attend. So there was hardly time to get cleaned up and dressed for it. There were lots of girls at the party but I didn't dance once. Just wasn't in the mood for it. The moon and sky were beautiful coming home and I was thinking of you, Legna, but it didn't help much. I wanted to see and talk with you —thinking wasn't enough.

Tomorrow I take all the pilots and ground officers on the range. That should be a "good deal". There are only 44 all told.

Legna, I've a suspicion I'm going to run out of money before this month is over. So if you happen to be in Annapolis one day, maybe you'd better send me about twenty. "All donations appreciated."

I love you, Legna! Just in case you're interested.

Goodnight Honey,

Howard

P.S. How about that week in July? I'm weakening, make it two weeks.

H.C.S.

311ᵗʰ Orderly Room

June 19, 1943

4:40 P.M.

Dearest Legna,

I have nothing to do for a moment so I'll write to you. How about that, a fine thing, when there is nothing else to do I write to you. Rather considerate, I call it. No Honey, I think about you all the time and wish there was more chance to write.

Say, about the delivery of that hair and clothes brush. You know, I haven't much hair and am not in great need of a hair brush. I'd like very much for you to deliver it in person, but what about the statement you made when I left Baltimore that Saturday morning. Honey, I can't get enough time off to get married or even get a license. However, if you don't hurry and come up here to see me, I'm going to be a sad, disappointed, disillusioned man. Legna, I want to see you and soon. Can't you deliver the brushes without changing the "Marital Status" of two people who are very much in love? Yes one of them doesn't think it's just the thing to do. Please, Legna, come to see me.

Oh! There's another item which I might mention. Shenton is now a 1ˢᵗ Lt. and had to buy a box of cigars today. I've been a 1ˢᵗ since the 17ᵗʰ which practically makes me eligible for longevity pay, of course. Too bad we couldn't celebrate the occasion together. There are still possibilities of that happening, I hope. Coming up for that event next month?

Think I'll go to Westover Field, Massachusetts Monday. I've only been off this Base one day officially since arriving in May. There are a few Ordnance things to pick up.

Tuesday and Wednesday I have to start instructions in the "firing of the rifle". Our men really did miserable on the range. But 50% have to qualify so that's what it will be before I'm through.

Good evening Darling. In case you want to be reminded, "I love you."

Love,
Howard C.

B.O.Q. "B"
June 23, 1943

Dearest Legna,

Received the money and a letter from you today. Thanks for both, Buttercup.

So you think maybe you'll be coming up sometime in July. I'm glad because I really want to see you. Can't say as yet where you will stay because I haven't looked for a place. Bob Schwen brought his wife and kid back from Toledo and they are trying to find a house. Bob and I looked for a place yesterday afternoon and again this noon. Gosh, Honey, after those two excursions I'm kind of glad we aren't married. It's so much trouble and bother along with worry when you've got to have something and that something is hard to get. Schwen said you could stay with him and Gloria when you come up, but I thought maybe you wouldn't like the idea and maybe Gloria wouldn't think so much of the idea. We'll find a place for you to stay so don't worry.

The days are hot and the nights are cool. Don't think you'll need an evening dress but you can bring one if you like.

Tomorrow is my day on the range again. Damn I'll sure be glad when that little chore is over. Then I can sleep a little later in the mornings.

I had quite a time at Westover Field the other day. The Base Ordnance didn't want to give me any supplies. Tried to give me the "ole run-around". After six phone calls I got what I wanted.

Goodnight, Honey. See you in my dreams.

Love,
Howard

B.O.Q."B"
June or July <u>something</u>

Dearest Darling Legna,

I just bought a new pen so this is a very appropriate time to break it in. Never could locate the other one, darn it.

I know I'm a little tardy with this letter, but excuse it, please Legna. For the past five days I've been so busy and had so many things go wrong till I'm about to shout over the terrain. Sometimes I wish I was a buck private again. Life was so peaceful then.

Capt. Tuman came back off his leave today and found out that he was transferred into an outfit at Westover Field. That burns me up. I would like very much to go with him. He's a little angry at the idea of transferring him and I don't blame him. Gosh, I wish he could stay with us. He is about the best C.O. we've had and the damn fools in higher headquarters are making a mistake. Sometimes I wonder what this Army is all about.

Honey, if anything comes up and I think you shouldn't make the trip here, I'll phone or wire you. But please come if nothing turns up. I haven't found a place for you to stay but we'll manage that somehow.

The boys in the barracks get a kick out of me talking to your picture. They think it's a joke but I'm very serious about the conversations I have with your picture. You should really be here to sit in on some of them. I love you, Legna.

I'll write later and let you know about meeting the train and so forth. So goodnight Honey.

Love,
Howard

Base Commandant's Office
July 3, 1943

Dearest Darling Legna,

I'm sitting up here with that wonderful view again. But there are other things I'd rather sit with. Taylor and Collins, two of our pilots just made a very poor landing. I'll take it up with them in the morning. Honest Honey, this place really looks good from this position. It's very interesting to watch the crew chiefs and mechanics swarm over the planes when they come in. The A.A. plane is checking his mags preparing for a take-off. It sure has been a wonderful day for flying. I was tempted to take a hop in the B.T. Trainer.

Haven't had a chance to look for a place where you can stay when you come up. But don't let that worry you. We'll manage somehow. Sure will be glad to see you, Honey. It seems like months since I've seen those blue eyes and little "serious look" of yours. Schwen still wants you to stay with him and Gloria but I don't know so much about that. You didn't state how long you were going to stay???

Tomorrow night I'm Group "Slop Officer". One good thing I won't have these details to bother with after you arrive. Sure wish I was coming home instead of you coming here. Group Slop Officer is a good name. We go on Duty at 6:00 P.M., take incoming telephone calls, empty all waste paper containers and burn the contents.

Honey, far as I know, Shenton will be at the station to greet you when you arrive. If I can't meet you I'll notify you to that effect.

Goodnight Legna.

Love,

Howard

A break in letters during the time Glorious came to visit Howard

B.O.Q. "B"

July 19, 1943

Dearest Darling,

It seems kind of new living in the B.O.Q. again. The boys all said, "Welcome back Totch", and honestly it seems like I've been away a long time.

I miss you very much tonight, Honey. In fact I've felt pretty bad about your leaving all day. Legna, I felt like you and I should be married and together. Honey, if I never marry you, I'll never marry anyone, that's definite in my mind. You would sure make a swell wife and I'm more in love with you now than ever. Please, don't think I wanted you to go home just to get rid of you. I love you with all my heart and everything there is in me. I really felt bad this morning seeing you sitting on the train. Looked like you had a nice companion though, even if he was Navy. I was glad you got a seat. Sure sweated that one out.

Your package and some letters came today. I mailed your package back this afternoon and am enclosing the letters. Also a few pictures I picked up in the Orderly Room this afternoon that were taken at Bolling Field.

I played volley ball with the officers this evening, until 9 o'clock. My team won by many games.

Honey, I'd better scratch off. Goodnight sweetheart.

Love,

Shenton

Orderly Room

July 22, 1943

Dearest Legna,

Just received your letter and decided to answer right away. I came in from the range at 10:30, this rain drove us in. I'm going out again this afternoon if the weather clears up.

Honey, I returned your letters and package. Of course I didn't think to open the darn thing because I figured it was your clothes. You should have all the things by this time.

The boys have sure been kidding me about living off the Base while you were here. They insisted that I was on detached service and asked me if I reported to the C.O. for duty when you went home.

Legna, that New York deal seems to really have possibilities. Rumor hath it, that in a few weeks we are going to a field on Long Island Sound for two weeks of aerial gunnery. Don't know for sure but there should be a chance for me to go to New York once in a while. I'm still going to C.W.School in New Hampshire. So I'll let you know how we make out on Long Island Sound and maybe you can see me then.

I'm glad you had a nice trip back. The Navy man looked like a pretty nice chap. Guess the sailor was a bit amazed at the weight of your suitcase. [As the story goes, Glorious took a load of used shells back home with her in her suitcase. When the sailor picked up her suitcase to carry it on the train, he said, "What have you got in here, lead?"]

Well Honey, I have to get ready for the range now. Will write again soon.

Love, to (Legna-Annie)

Shenton

B.O.Q. # 205 R. #12
Grenier Field, N.H
July 27, 1943

Dear Legna Darling,

I left Rhode Island late Sunday evening and arrived here late in the night. Signed in, found a room, went to bed and reported for duty 8 o'clock Monday morning. This course is pretty good but I've had the darn stuff half a dozen times. One thing they do here and that is trick you. At any time you can expect gas thrown around and unless you put on your mask pronto, it leaves you crying your heart out or should I say profusely.

Grenier is a fairly nice field, not very large but compact. It's been activated for about 2 years. Lots of planes here, bombers and fighters. I feel a little lonesome without the old bunch around but I can stand it for a few days. I shouldn't have had to come here though, haven't learned a thing new. Just a waste of time, which could be put to more advantage back in R.I.

I'm still planning on seeing you in New York. I think we'll leave R.I. around the 5th, 6th or 7th of August for Long Island. I know I'll be busy then with aerial and ground gunnery for the pilots and more training in weapons for the enlisted men. But I'll keep you informed as to whether or not I can get a day off to spend in New York.

Saw Bob Sunday noon before leaving and I think he's going to send Gloria home while we are in New York. See what a mess it is to be married to a wife and the army. He also told me about receiving the things you sent Gloria. Legna, you're some gal and I love you.

I'll write again before leaving this place. Goodnight Honey!

Love,
Howard

B.O.Q. #205
July 28, 1943

Dearest Legna,

Thought I'd drop a little note before turning in. This C.W. school is very trying and wears me out. If the material was new I'd be interested. But it's not so Shenton spends his time trying to keep awake. Honest Honey it's pretty awful.

One of the students and I went swimming this evening after the last class. Some place called Crystal Lake, about 5 miles from Camp. I enjoyed it very much. Swam for about an hour, came back to Camp and had chow. Very nice evening. One thing lacking though, I miss you. When I'm busy I don't think about us so much. But when I'm not busy that's what I think about. Gosh it seems like two months since you were here. I'm going to call you Sunday or Monday night.

I expect to leave here Friday evening right after the last class which is 5 o'clock. Don't know whether I'll even stop for supper.

Odren said he might pick me up in the B.T. but I doubt that.

Goodnight Honey.

Love, Howard

B.O.Q. "B"

August 3, 1943

11:00 P.M.

Dearest Legna Darling,

I just came in from Bradley Field about an hour ago. Picked up your letter at the Orderly Room, read it, took a shave and a shower and am now indulging in a little scratching. All Transportation Officers had to attend a meeting at Bradley. The fellows from this Base (yours truly included) left this morning at 5:00 A.M. and what a day it was. No wonder I don't write more than I do.

Bob wanted me to go out with him (he?) and Gloria tonight but I didn't get back in time. Gloria is leaving tomorrow morning. She seems pretty much broken up about it. I think she and the baby are going to fly home on the A.A. ship.

How about that phone call! Honey I can't be serious all the time. I'm that way too much of the time anyhow. Too bad about your jump upsetting the ink.

I don't think we are leaving here as scheduled but continue to write me here until notified otherwise. The mail will be forwarded. It may (might?) be next week before we pull out, somebody should make up their mind.

I miss you tonight very much, Honey, for some reason or the other. Goodnight and I love you.

Howard C.

(as the Wasp says!)

V···— MAIL

Miss H Louise Andrew
N by side, B.Q.
Maryland

V-Mail Service provides the most expeditious dispatch and reduces the weight of mail to and from personnel of our Armed Forces outside the continental United States. When addressed to points where micro-film equipment is operated, a miniature photographic negative of the message will be made and sent by the most expeditious transportation available for reproduction and delivery. The original message will be destroyed after the reproduction has been delivered. Messages addressed to or from points where micro-film equipment is not operated will be transmitted in their original form by the most expeditious means available.

INSTRUCTIONS

(1) Write the entire message plainly on the other side within marginal lines.
(2) PRINT the name and address in the two panels provided. Addresses to members of the Armed Forces should include rank or rating of the addressee, unit to which attached, and APO or Naval address.
(3) Fold, seal, and deposit in any post office letter drop or street letter box.
(4) Enclosures must not be placed in this envelope and a separate V-Mail letter must be sent if you desire to write more than one sheet.
(5) V-Mail letters may be sent free of postage by members of the Armed Forces. When sent by others postage must be prepaid at domestic rates (3c ordinary mail, 6c if air mail is desired).

274

Lt. Howard C. Shenton

311th Fitr Sqdn

Green Field, A.A.B.

Providence, R.I.

Dearest Legna Darling,

I'm sitting on the carbine range and found this V Mail stationery, so decided to write. The boys are blazing away and I have nothing to do for a few moments. This will be my last detail for the carbine range, I hope.

Sure was nice up here this morning. The air was cool and crisp, made you kind of feel like doing a good days work. Really, I'd like to be stationed here for the rest of the summer.

Honey, I'm sorry you felt so bad the other night about my leaving. But don't worry; we'll be here for some two months yet. (In the States.) Honestly Legna, I want to go so bad because I feel as though I've been practically useless so far in this war. Please don't worry about me when I go. You should have enough confidence in me to know that I can take care of myself and a few others if necessary.

Gosh I'm glad you could see Scoop, while I'm stationed on Long Island. Things have certainly worked out good for us. We've been together quite a bit. In fact, I believe more than any time or period since the night of August 29, 1940. How about that Buttercup?!

Legna, I love you for all I'm worth and why you keep asking me if I do, I can't figure out. We'll build a home for two or three or four some of these days. I'll like that, because when this war is over, Shenton wants to settle down. Don't know if Rhode River will be the site or not but it will be a very close comparison. So long for now Darling.

Love,

Howard

Suffolk Airdrome

August 22, 1943

Dearest Darling Legna,

The latest story is that the squadron will be here longer than expected. I don't think we will leave until Friday which is four days longer than the original time. But it suits me; I like it here very much. But it's a killer around here in the winter though. Three miles from the ocean is a mighty cold place to be in the winter.

Honey, I've thought about our parting the other night in New York. That was once when I felt like we should be married and damn sorry we weren't. Too bad it had to be like that, Legna (parting I mean). We'll get together someday and there won't be any more goodbyes. I love you, Legna and that's all.

You know the summer of 43 is just about on its way out. The nights are really getting cool and the days are just right. Too bad we didn't have this kind of weather for those twenty mile hikes in South Carolina. I've always hated to see summer leave for some reason or another.

The pilots are doing a nice job at aerial gunnery now. The Base C.O. is very well pleased and so is the Squadron C.O. even though he hasn't been on but about two missions.

Honey, I'd better wrap this thing up and get some shut-eye.

Goodnight Darling,

Howard

Suffolk Airdrome

August 25, 1943

Dearest Darling Legna,

I wanted to write you last night but just couldn't get around to it. We are pretty busy getting ready to move out. We leave Friday morning early. I kind of hate to leave this place. It sure is a great spot for summer, just about the best I've hit since being in the army.

Took my first plane ride the other day. One of our pilots took me up and we had a lot of fun. We went all up and down the beach for a hundred or so miles, stayed up for one hour and a half. I enjoyed it immensely. In fact, I've been worrying him to take me up again but he hasn't had a chance. They all want to take me up and give me a real ride. I don't think I'm quite ready for that yet though.

The pilots are going to get leaves soon as we arrive at Bedford. There hasn't been anything said about ground officers but we are hoping.

Took some of the officers to the pistol range today and shot a sharpshooter for myself. Kind of amazed me.

Well Honey, I'd better hit the ole straw. Next time I write it will probably be from Bedford, Massachusetts. Goodnight now.

Love to my Darling,

Howard

B.O.Q. Bedford, A.A.B.

August the last day, 43

Dearest Legna,

I received a brace of letters from you today. First time in a long while. But it's just as well, for I haven't had a moment to write since last Wednesday. This moving around sure keeps a fellow busy. There are so many small details that have to be taken care of.

We left Suffolk Friday morning and arrived here 9:30 that night. What a ride, 250 miles by convoy. The trucks had to be unloaded soon as possible. That was a little rough. All of the men were tired and gosh, I know, I was. I finally got to bed around 2:00 A.M. Every night I've just come in my room and fell right in bed. Had to make a 300 mile trip yesterday to Groton, Connecticut. One of our vehicles was disabled during the convoy and fell out. I had to pick up some parts at Bradley Field, take them to Groton and repair the darn thing. I tumbled in bed at 12:30 last night. I'm going to do exactly that when I finish writing this letter.

Honey, I was a little perturbed about your last letter but I feel that you don't have a thing to worry about. My God, I hope not. You had better let me know as soon as possible.

Bedford isn't such a nice place. It's more like a farm than an airdrome. We are only 21 miles from Boston which makes it nice for the boys who like to kick the gong around.

Legna, I don't know for sure but somehow I don't believe that ground officers are going to get a leave. The leave we had in June seems to have made a difference, but don't get excited, please. We'll be here for a couple of months yet, at least.

Honey, I'd better hit the linen now. Goodnight and remember I love you, one time ("All the time").

Love,

Howard

311th Operations Officer
September 6, 1943

Dearest Legna Darling,

If you're cussing me for not writing, I'm sorry but Legna, I just haven't had time to write. Everything is going full blast with the 311th Fighter. At this rate we'll be in aggie-sackie in no time at all. Sure wish we could speed it up a little more; I'm in a hurry.

So all the girls in Shady Side are getting hitched. Too bad Honey, I feel sorry for them. Especially Betty Lou. She's too young for that wedlock business. Bennert is getting hitched today. None of us could get away to attend. I'd like to have made the Reception though.

Gloria is here. She just sent Bob a wire saying, "here I come". Don't think she will be here very long though. All the boys have to send their wives home by the 7th. Bennert is getting married just in time to send his little pigeon home.

Honey, you misunderstood about that "leave". I said it was likely we wouldn't get one. Sure wish it wasn't so though.

We lost another pilot the other day. He got lost on a late mission and cracked up about 80 miles from the Base. I took-off with Capt. Odren the next morning at 6:00 A.M. to see if we could locate the pilot. The ship was found but no body. The search is beginning to be somewhat of a mystery. Odren and I got about 30 miles from the Base and had to come back because the weather was so bad. The airplane was dropping 20 & 30 feet when we hit a rain squall. My second plane ride and with the maneuvers of the plane Shenton's stomach wasn't feeling so good. But I like to fly; it's a lot of fun.

Legna, if I don't get a leave please don't mind. I'll write to you at least once a week. Don't worry about me, I'll be alright.

Save all your love for me, Honey. So long, Shorty.

Love,

Howard

B.O.Q. # 207

September 10, 1943

Dearest Darling,

I received the money order yesterday and thanks Honey. I've never spent so darn much money in my life. My shaving equipment alone cost me over ten bucks. This trip abroad is sure costing something.

Legna, I might send my short overcoat and leather jacket to you for safekeeping. There's talk of taking the leather jackets away from us at the P.O.E. and I don't think we will need an overcoat where we are going.

I finally kept a promise. Yesterday Wood and I had our pictures taken. Everything is all paid for and you will get the pictures in about 2 ½ weeks. There will be three of them, keep all of them if you like, but how about giving Miss Grace one and if you don't want two, give the other to

Miss Mary with "my compliments". I'm going to send you the receipt so if you don't get the pictures in about three weeks you'd better start a little five column work. The worst part of this deal is that I won't see the proofs because I'll probably be on my way by Thursday, but the lady at the studio is going to pick the best one and have it printed to send you. The entire operation takes over two weeks as everything has to be sent to New York. Hope you like the pictures, Honey.

I was thinking of church this morning and all the "amens" the congregation at Centenary answers the prayer with at Sunday School.

Legna, I love you Honey and don't tell anyone but I'm beginning to feel you and I should have been married some time ago, but that's up for argument, of course. PRO & CON.

I'm going to call you this evening.

Goodbye now,

Howard

Operations Officer
Bedford, A.A.B., Mass.
September 11, 1943

Dearest Darling Legna, (I love you one time…that's all the time)

I was just disappointed. Erzen was going to take me for a ride in the AT-6. We were going to test-hop the egg-beater, but the radio was <u>out</u> so we couldn't take-off. I'll catch it tomorrow morning at 8:00 o'clock. I've only been up in the AT-6 once and it was so foggy and rainy I couldn't see what was going on. We'll get the sun when she comes up in the morning.

281

Everything is kind of on edge around here. The pilots have finished their overseas training program. The stage is just about set for the "third act". Sure hope it turns out to be natural. I'm fed-up with this old routine. Nothing definite has been said but if I have a change of address sometime next week, then we are on our way.

Legna, I sure wish I could see you again before we go. It's not entirely impossible either. There's a rumor floating that the ground officers may get a leave if we pass thru the staging area without any trouble. Maybe we'll get five or six days, how about that! Won't be bad if the staging area is somewhere on the East Coast.

The squadron received a couple of 50 calibre machine guns mounted on trucks. For the past few days I've been teaching and instructing the boys how to shoot them. Seems like this squadron has shot enough ammunition in the past six months to supply an Army. Well, our training is just about at the end and believe me "Buttercup", I'm glad.

I've been to Boston once and that was enough. I don't think much of either Boston or Bedford. Maybe I'm just fed-up with everything in general.

Legna, I haven't written Miss Grace in a quite some time. Give her a light check for me, will you. I'll try and write her tomorrow.

Well "Buttercup", as usual I haven't said much but that's just like me so you shouldn't be disappointed. I still love you though, in case you'd like to know.

Goodnight Darling.

Love,
Howard

B.O.Q. # 207

Grenier Field, N.H.

September 16, 1943

Dearest Legna Darling,

We left Bedford yesterday morning and it was one time no one knew where we were going. I was here a week in July and knew what the place was like. We come here for reconditioning prior to overseas shipment. It might take a week, month or six months, you can't tell. But it sure looks like the real McCoy this time. All I hope is that we won't stay here very long. I want to get out of here and see what's doing around the other side of the globe. Frankly though, I don't think the outfit is ready for combat service. But we are as ready as we will ever be, even six months from now. The 311th is what it's cracked-up to be according to my opinion, but that's no good. We'll know for sure when the chips are down.

Legna, I wish to hell I could see you one more time anyway before we go. However, I think that's out, because I can't make it home. If there's a chance I'll take it but it's a very slim one. So don't worry about me calling for Miss Andrews at Southern High. Sure would like to though and have Anthony answer the phone, er-er.

Goodnight Honey, I love you.

Love,

Howard

311th Operations

Grenier Field

September 20, 1943

Dearest Darling Legna,

Thought sure I was going to get a chance to write before now. Every evening it's something to be done which must be finished before morning. We are being inspected by every command from a squadron to the War Dept. and Honey, it's rough. This will go on between now and the time we leave the States.

No one has any idea when we will leave here but I sure wish they would "get the show on the road". But somehow I'm not eager or enthused about going overseas like I was before. After so many turn backs it's hard to get hepped-up about leaving. Course again, I won't be too disappointed if we don't go, like I was at Bolling last winter.

I received your wire and money-order. Thanks Honey. I've spent an awful lot of money for clothes and equipment for this trip and still have a lot to go.

The 58th Group and all squadrons have been restricted since arrival at this wonderful field. The men are a little sore about it and of course you know the officers <u>aren't</u>. When the restriction is lifted some town nearby is sure in for a beating.

Still don't know about a short leave. I'm beginning to doubt the possibilities of it taking place. It would be nice to come home for a few days though. I'd love it. One of the pilots got a six day leave while we were at Bedford and went to Cambridge, Maryland. He said it was swell down there.

Anyway Legna, I love you. Surprised? With all my heart, Honey.

Goodbye now,

Howard

Group Headquarters
September 27, 1943

Dearest Darling Legna,

I know you are kind of worried and maybe a little sore because of "no letters". (Hold tight, I'm offering my apologies.) Somehow when I started to write or thought of writing, something always happened. But I'm not doing so bad, you received one or two letters from me last week.

Looks like our time in the States is drawing to a close. We should be pulling out any day now, but then it might be two weeks yet. Anyway, I wish they would get this show on the road. We are losing too much time doing unimportant things.

Boxes are being packed and all equipment crated. Every other day we have to change marking on the boxes and revise our packing lists. We are about to give up in disgust.

Honey, I don't think Shenton will get that leave. Seems as though we are going on a long train ride before we go "abroad". I'm so damn tired of moving around from base to base. This is supposed to be the real McCoy though.

Speaking of writing, you know I don't believe you've written me for five or six days. How about that? You must be trying to match my letters. That's alright Honey "tit for tat" is pretty good philosophy. I never have anything new to say in my letters so I think they'd be a little boring.

Went for another plane ride yesterday. Evans and I buzzed around the White Mountains. We'd shave the tops about 250 miles per hour, then dip down in the valleys and buzz a few houses. Some fun, but I'm still not accustomed to flying upside down. It's quite a sensation. I'm beginning to enjoy my rides now (ain't so scared).

Legna, how about writing and telling me you love me one time. Honey, I must go now. Goodnight.

Love,
Howard

Grenier Field, N. H.
October 2, 1943

Dearest Darling Legna,

Just received a very nice letter from a little gal down in Shady Side so thought I'd retaliate with a missile quite as imposing. I love to get mail from that little wench but I don't answer as often as I should.

Honey, right now we are sitting around waiting for the "go signal". No one knows when it will be given but we are ready, almost eager, I'd say. This place is getting monotonous like all the other Fields we've been to. I would like to be on my merry way. Haven't been doing much hacking around lately. Been busy packing equipment—squadron and personal. Managed to slip off yesterday and go to the races at Rockingham. Seven of us went and we sure had a good time. I ended three bucks winner, which was very good as I bet every race and lost on two pretty heavily. We brought about $100 away with us. Some of the boys were really lucky. I was thinking of you and how much I would like to have had you with me. We could have had a lot of fun. I get spells like that Legna, sometimes I want and wish for you so much, it's kind of like an obsession. We were going to the races "one time", remember? That's alright though. We'll get there, you and I.

The weather is sure sloppy. The boys haven't flown for three days. I miss my rides in the AT-6. Sure wish I could fly that egg-beater, maybe I will be able to if I get a few more rides. Course I couldn't land and take-off, but in the air straight and level flying is fairly simple.

We are supposed to get some squadron insignia's soon and when we do I'm going to send you one. Wear it on your trench-coat or something.

Got to go now, Honey. Bye.

Love and no fooling,

Howard

B.O.Q. # 207

October 9, 1943

Dearest Darling,

I feel that you think the squadron has gone over but nope, we are still at Grenier packing and marking boxes. The advance detail has gone and we should be leaving in four or five days. I have been appointed Billeting Officer and might leave a few days in advance of the squadron to make arrangements for quarters and bedding and food for the men. I almost believe I will be leaving about tomorrow. Capt. Tuman will be in charge of the billeting group and that is fine, we should have a lot of fun. Legna, I kind of think we will be in the U.S. at Christmas, but I'll probably be so far from home it won't do any good.

Say Buttercup, I haven't had a letter from you for so long. What's the trouble? I think you are exasperated. Honey, I've been so busy I just haven't had time to write.

I wish you could come to Manchester to see me before I leave but you can't make any arrangements. We were supposed to leave here any time after the 1st of October, so if I suggested you come we'd probably pull out about the time you arrived. That's the way it goes in the Army, but I like it.

New England is sure beautiful in the fall. I've been wanting to take a plane ride but can't get one in. This is the most beautiful country from the air I've ever seen.

Legna, I've got to rush off. Do you still love me? How about a letter one time?

Love, (real honest to goodness)

Howard

P.S. Couldn't get any Squadron Insignias.

Headed Overseas

I'll Be Seeing You

Music by Sammy Fain

Lyrics by Irving Kahal

Published in 1938 by Marlo Music Corporation

California, U.S.A.

October 24, 1943

Dearest Darling Legna,

I've been wanting to write since arriving here but just couldn't find the time or even the paper to write with. We've been here three days now and I wish we were leaving tomorrow. I want to get out of this damn camp.

The trip out was a long drawn out ride. It took us five days. We had a ten hour lay-over in Chicago and spent six hours of that trying to get Pullman reservations on the train to California. We managed to eat dinner, get a room and take a bath. I picked up the money without any trouble at all. Thanks Honey, you're a top-notcher. There were some of the strangest characters on the train I ever met in my life. I had a lower berth and didn't sleep in it. Some elderly couple had the upper so I gave them my lower and took their upper. We had to stand in line for an hour waiting to get fed in the diner.

Don't know how long I'll be here. Couldn't say if I knew but I sure hope not long. This is really a beautiful state. You and I should drive out here on our honeymoon. I know you would like it. But we'll still live in Maryland, that's good enough for me. Legna, when I come back from this trip let's get married even if the war is still on. I want you so bad at times till I feel miserable. Maybe, though it would be worse if we were married. I don't know. It's a jumbled up affair, no matter how you look at it. People's lives are sure messed up by this war. I know I love you though, Legna, and also, you are the only gal I will ever love no matter what happens. But Honey, just because I say that, I don't mean for you to just sit and wait for me. If you want to date, go on ahead and have a good time. But save that real spark in your heart for me.

I won't get a chance to see Dot and Miss Grace even if she was out here. The restrictions are pretty strict even for officers.

You can write to me by my A.P.O #4927. That's permanent now. Don't know if I'll get another chance to write. So bye Honey.

I love you sweetheart!

Love,
Howard

B.O.Q. # 2
October 28, 1943

Dearest Darling Legna,

I just received about three letters from you and Honey, you've certainly had a time with "one-time Lt. Shenton". Legna, I'm sorry about the trouble and inconvenience I caused you about the money. I don't care what Miss Mary or anyone else thinks about our joint-account, we have it and as far as I'm concerned it's going to stay that way. Look Honey, don't worry about what other people think. If you need any dough get it out of the bank. I don't care if there isn't a red-cent in that account when I come back. So to hell with all those "scandalizers". If you want to buy a hat with that money, buy it. I don't care. I wish you would get a Christmas present for yourself. Legna, I trust you with my life. The hell with them anyway.

What's this about my getting brave as the distance between us grows? Honey, you don't think I'm a very gentlemanly sort of person nor do you place much confidence in me. It still goes Legna, you're the one and only gal for me. The only gal I'll ever marry. If you meet someone you like or think more of than me why go ahead, Honey, and take him. It would hurt but I've been hurt so damn many times, till I can take it, I guess. My feelings for you will never change, Legna. I know that for sure.

I haven't much to say about anything. I've been in a kind of daze during the past few weeks. Sure would like to see you Honey, just one more time. Wish I could whisper a few sweet nothings in your ear. I'm kind of lonesome. Anyway, we've been pretty lucky considering. I still make a mistake even with all the distance. Does that sound brave? You hit a vulnerable spot and drew blood when you said, "I don't think you'll ever marry me." Honey, that wasn't fair. You are the practical one!

If I don't get a chance to write Gilbert, thank him for me. He's sure alright. I'll bring him a prize for that deed. (One chopstick).

Goodbye now, Darling and please trust me where you & I are concerned.

Love,

Howard

P.S. I couldn't see Dot or Miss Grace. Let me know about the pictures.

H

Written in transit to overseas destination via troop ship

Lt. Howard C. Shenton

311th Fitr Sqrn

APO 4927

% P.M. San Francisco, Calif.

November 19, 1943

Dearest Darling Legna,

It's been so darn long since I've written till I've about forgot how to begin a letter. There isn't much I can say except everything is going fairly well though a bit rapid. We've had a very nice trip but it was sure a long one. Life on the boat was calm, routine and highlighted once in a while by a game of skill involving cards. I was almost seasick a couple times but managed to pull out of it alright. The food was good and served in an excellent manner, in fact better than most restaurants. But oh, I got awful sick of the sea.

I wired some money home from California. Wonder if you received it? I'd like to send some home now but have no way to do it. I probably won't be able to write again for some time, we are moving and shipping around so much. However you can keep writing. My mail will be forwarded.

Legna, in case the fellow in the jeep still wants to know, I love you. So long for now.

Love,

Howard

Lt. Howard C. Shenton

311th Fitr Sqrn

V-MAIL

APO 4927

℅ P.M. San Francisco, Calif.

November 26, 1943

Dearest Darling Legna

I've been waiting to hear from you for two weeks now and haven't received a scratch. I've only received two letters since arriving in this country (Australia). Your last letter came when I was in California. What's the matter, Buttercup?

There isn't much to say about the country. It doesn't differ from the U.S. greatly. The season here is summer and it rains every day. The sun is very hot when it <u>shines</u>. The people appear to be nice but there are more Yanks than natives. Had a little trouble with the monetary system at first but it's relatively simple. You can get beautiful steaks here but the people sure don't know how to cook them. Nothing much to do in the evenings except go to a show and they are almost a year old.

All in all it's a pretty good set-up here. You begin to realize a bit that there is a war going on. Haven't the slightest idea when we'll hit the combat zone but it shouldn't be too long. I still love you, Legna. How much? You'll find out when I get back.

Love,

Howard

Lt. Howard C. Shenton

311th Fitr Sqrn

APO 4927

℅ P.M. San Francisco, Calif.

November 28, 1943

Dearest Legna,

I still haven't heard from you since leaving the States. Frankly, I'm beginning to get a little worried. There's no inflation of postage stamps, is there?

Sure would like to be in Shady Side about this time. If you all had our Australia climate it would be nice, but that's all we've got, climate. I suppose you are completing your Christmas shopping and are all set for the big event. Old Nick must have a heck of a time in this country; there are no chimneys for the ole boy to clamber down. Some of the boys are wearing sickly expressions on their mugs this morning. I think they underrated the alcohol content of the local wine last night in town. I'm going to start washing them out of the tent in a few minutes.

Legna, I didn't get a chance to write Gilbert and thank him for the favor. Take care of that, will you, please?

If I don't get a letter from you soon I'm going to be in excellent fighting shape when I meet the Japs. Goodbye now.

Love, Howard

V-MAIL

Lt. Howard C. Shenton

311th Fitr Sqrn

APO 4927

℅ P.M. San Francisco, Calif.

December 3, 1943

Dearest Legna,

I'm still waiting to hear from you. It's been just slightly over a month since I've received one of your letters and Buttercup, that's a long time. I'm about to call it quits in hope of ever getting a letter. Guess I'll get one some of these blooming days.

Haven't been doing much lately, putting in a lot of time but getting very little accomplished. I was in town yesterday and finally got two little items chalked off my list.

Legna, I didn't have time to increase my allotment before I left the States. Consequently, I'll be drawing more money than I can spend so I'm going to wire money home from time to time. Throw it in the bank for me. I'll buy you a paper doll when I come home. There is a 10% increase in pay for foreign service, you know.

How about letting me know if you got those pictures from Manchester and whether or not they were any good. Sure would like to see one.

Honey, I'd better turn this off now. I still love you if anyone wants to know.

Love, Howard

Australia

December 5, 1943

Dearest Legna,

I'm still "sweating out" a letter from you. Really, I can't figure it out. Maybe you didn't get the right A.P.O. #. (4927) This will be changed before long but don't let that stop you from writing. All mail will be forwarded. I've gotten some mail from the States dated as late as November 20. That's why I can't figure out not hearing from you.

Lt. Wood and I are going to shuffle in town for a little chow this afternoon and maybe stop at the club for a short beer. After that we will probably see a show —the usual procedure.

A few of the officers have been mighty busy getting supplies and equipment since arriving here. I was on the go all day yesterday, not even stopping for breakfast and lunch. I'll be glad when we settle down to a regular "wartime" routine.

I've been trying to get to the races here but just haven't had time. There's a track a little way from camp where they run some darn nice horses. The Aussies sure like to bet and watch the nags run.

To think that it is almost Christmas is quite an amazement. Here it is summer and not the slightest indication that there is going to be a Santa Claus. Sorry I can't help you decorate the tree this year but will catch that up next year maybe. I suppose Derwill will be home and will probably go ducking. Hope he can get some gun-shells. By that time, I will be shooting ducks that shoot back, I hope.

Legna, I'm enclosing a money-order for $125.00. How about buying yourself a Christmas present and throw what's left in the bank. I'll buy you a yacht when I come home. Don't mind buying yourself a good present, I want you to have "something nice".

Give my "Greetings" to the folks. Sure wish I could help you celebrate.

Goodbye now Honey! For morale sake, write, one time.

Love,
Howard

Lt. Howard C. Shenton

311th Fitr Sqrn

APO 4927

% P.M. San Francisco, Calif.

December 7, 1943

Dearest Legna,

There isn't a damn thing to write about but I'm trying to keep a correspondence going. It certainly has died though on one end. When the mailman says he has a letter for me from Shady Side, I'm going right to the pill-rollers for shock treatment.

Honey, we are back in the old slot again, same routine. But it's really nice; we've been on the go so darn much. For the last few days I've been helping the mailman with the outgoing mail. There hasn't been much incoming.

Lt. Wood is still trying to get command of an Australian Waac detachment. Can't find anyone who would like to serve under him. He did a good job of commanding the Waacs back in the States.

Well Fuzz, I've got to check my vehicle-roster. Will write at every opportunity. Save "my" love. It's really worth saving.

Goodbye now,

Howard

New Guinea

Embarking on a trail of adventure
Lt Howard C. Shenton quoting someone from the States

V-MAIL

Lt. Howard C. Shenton

311th Fitr Sqrn

APO 503

% P.M. San Francisco, Calif.

December 29, 1943

Dearest Darling Legna,

At last I have the opportunity to write you for the first time in three weeks. I am now in New Guinea, fancy that! Seems to be a fairly nice place except for the heat. (Not like Shady Side though, that's the best place in the world).

Someone mentioned in the States that we were embarking on a trail of adventure. I am beginning to accept those words as "wisdom". So far we have found excitement. What's to follow may be more than exciting, I hope.

Legna, today was a big moment in my life. I received eight letters from you —the first since I left the States. It was certainly wonderful to read them. I thought perhaps you had merged with the Navy and forgot about the Army. That's kidding, Honey. I know there was a slight delay in the mail; we've moved around so much lately.

You mentioned in your letter about Gilbert admiring my picture, so I know you've received them now anyway. I wrote Gilbert a letter some time ago, no doubt you know about it. I thanked him for the wonderful favor. (He was swell.)

[Here I am again]

Didn't have much of a Christmas. Spent it on the high seas. The Chaplain had a program and short service. Ended in a kind of community sing. Oh! The Red Cross took a very important part. Each man received a gift, candy, cigarettes, etc. We have a very capable representative with our outfit. I think the Red Cross is doing a splendid job overseas and deserves a lot of credit.

I can't think of anything I'd like for you to send me. A box of good chocolate candy would be nice but I don't know if it would be accepted by the mail department.

Honey, I still love you and it's going to be a great day when we get together again. That's a fact.

I thought of you and me and trimming a Christmas tree when we were on the boats (no middies though) Christmas Eve. I love to think about us doing that kind of special event, I guess.

Will write again soon.

Love—all of it,
Howard

V-MAIL

Lt. Howard C. Shenton

311th Fitr Sqrn

APO 503

% P.M. San Francisco, Calif.

December 31, 1943

Darling Legna,

I think all your mail has finally caught up with me. Two V-mail letters arrived today, one the 16th & 20th (postmarks). This is New Year's Eve and there isn't any celebrating but everybody's happy. Remember alley-29 on New Year's Eve just before I came in the army? Some fun and I'll have it again soon, I hope. Baltimore is a swell place to be on the turn of the year. The people really go in for fun there in a big way.

Legna, we have a wonderful camp-site. It's in the jungle but we have about as nice a set-up as you could find anywhere. Running water, electric lights, a running stream to swim in, good food and plenty of work to keep our minds occupied. It will be better yet when we start operating. We still have the Headquarters Group with us and we don't like it but there is nothing we can do about that.

The mosquitoes aren't so bad here as they are back home. Lots of ants and bugs though.

Say Buttercup, if you don't buy a present with that money at least buy an Easter bonnet, will you? I'll be sending some more money home pretty soon. I didn't make my allotment to the bank large enough and money is useless here. Unless you want to gamble. Even that gets tiresome. To increase an allotment over here it takes a long time to get through and isn't worth the bother. So I'll use money-orders so long as I can get to a post-office.

Legna, I think of you an awful lot especially when there isn't much work to be done. Gosh, it will be great when this war is over and the men can get home. That is really something to look forward to. I still can't make up my mind about whether I was right or wrong about not getting married. We are losing a lot of money which helps to make it wrong.
[Third Act] Real Play Though
It's a problem we can discuss at some future date.

From your letters it sounds as though you are a very busy little woman. Until two days ago it was just the reverse for me. Don't work too hard, Honey, and pick up about ten pounds in weight. I'm glad to hear the teachers praised you for your latest accomplishments. That helps a lot when you know you are doing a good job.

You mentioned my pictures again but I still haven't got a letter saying you received them. I know I was grinning like a jackass chewing briars on a barbed wire fence when it was taken. Lt. Wood was talking and that always brings a laugh.

Buttercup, I'd better close before I get too close to the bottom. Best wishes to Mr. & Mrs. "A". If you see Henry and Peadie say Hello from me. I'm going to write Gilbert again.

I sure do love you, Legna.

Bye now, Howard

V-MAIL

Lt. Howard C. Shenton

311th Fitr Sqrn

APO 503

% P.M. San Francisco, Calif.

January 1, 1944

Darling Legna,

Just have a minute to drop a line. There's a show tonight across the road from camp. Can't miss it!

Today was more or less a holiday for us, swimming, volleyball and a day of rest. We'll catch it tomorrow though. I worked on my shack again. It will be in A-1 shape soon. All we need is a little furniture and we send out invitations for a housewarming.

You mentioned buying some clothes. You look better in light and bright colors than you do in dark. Guess it's because you are so small. I'd like to pass in review with you at the Easter Parade.

Honey, I've just about a minute to tell you I think you are a great little lady and that I love you very much. Goodnight Buttercup.

Love,

Howard

V-MAIL

Lt. Howard C. Shenton

311th Fitr Sqrn

APO 503

% P.M. San Francisco, Calif.

January 3, 1944

Dearest Legna,

I think there are still four letters in the mail from the original 18 you sent. The mail service is pretty good though, no griping there.

<u>Buttercup, if you can get them, how about sending me a box of cigars.</u> Any brand will do. I have a yearning for a good smoke. It is so damp here you can hardly draw on a pipe or cigarette, the tobacco gets stinking wet. I'll reimburse you pay-day.

There is no reason why you can't save money here. You can't spend a cent; there is nothing to buy. I wish my allotment was $100 more than it is, but I can mail or cablegram any amount whenever I want, so it shouldn't make much difference.

Our camp-site is really a swell place. We've had 600 men working on it since the outfit arrived. Mother Nature sure smiled on us when she ran the river through our camp.

BYE NOW

[Part II of basic communication]

At least we can keep clean and wash our clothes regularly.

The natives had a large gathering about three miles from here, to celebrate something? They had various contests conducted by the Aussies and then a large tribal dance. Sure would like to have a camera.

The natives were almost hideous in their costumes. No one seems to know what the dances signified. One would dance in the center alone brandishing a knife, then one by one the others would dance up to him. He would chant a few words then touch them with the knife as though it were a fairy's wand. Gosh, you wonder what their people get out of life, though. They seem quite happy. We will all probably go native after 6 or 8 months in this country.

Legna, always address my letters to the latest APO # on my return address. I'm likely to have a few more. Every time we move we get a new number.

Goodbye now. I think of you.

All my love,
Howard

New Guinea
January 8, 1944

Dearest Legna, (Darling)

I happened to get a few air-mail envelopes today so it's time Shenton wrote you a nice <u>long</u> letter. Honestly though, there isn't much to say.

Today was pay-day. After paying my debts and civilian insurance for this year and next I still have about fifty bucks left over. Am enclosing a money-order for that amount. Put it in the bank for me, will you "Fuzzy"?

Our camp is really something to see now. Hard work sure pays dividends in this country. We have running water in the mess hall, frigidaires and a swell officers' mess. Transportation has a nice shack for maintaining vehicles, believe me we need it, too. The outfit has received quite a few vehicles fresh from the assembly line. They must have been put together by a bunch of "basic" mechanics. We have to go over them from top to bottom and really you might say practically assemble the darn things ourselves. The roads are very dusty and rough so transportation is going to catch hell and the section will have a real job to keep up the maintenance. (Getting back to the camp.) Our individual tents are shaping up in a good fashion. We manage to take three steps now before falling through the floor. Before we were allowed one and one only. One of the best laughs we've had was New Year's Eve. Lt. Smith, one of the Group officers is a kind of nervous and scared type. At midnight he heard some shots and thinking it was an air-raid he donned steel-helmet, gas mask and came rushing out of his house headed for a fox-hole when all at once in his running both feet went thru the floor and he was stuck. The shots were fired by some of the boys welcoming in the New Year. What a sight. He was the only man in the camp who interpreted the shots as an air raid warning. The running stream is still doing an excellent job of keeping us clean and is a means of escaping the heat.

There was a big show in camp last night. One of the Engineer outfits has a swell band. They came over accompanied by some magician who performed like a professional and it was great entertainment.

Capt. Tuman has one Zero to his credit already. He's going to have a good record before leaving this area. One of the pilots in the squadron also got one. Nice work, but we have far to go to equal some of the other outfit's records. The flyers are doing a great job over here and our planes are sure superior.

Our communications officer has installed a radio in the mess-hall. Now we eat and listen to the news flashes. Once in a while a re-broadcast from the U.S. of some big name band.

Someone said there is a show around camp. Think I'll take it in. Haven't seen one for a long time. Went out in the field to see a show two nights in succession and both times the show was called off due to projector trouble. Hope there's no trouble tonight. Maybe there won't even be a projector.

Legna, I hope you can get those cigars for me. I could sure stand the fragrant aroma of an El-Ropa.

Guess I'd better go now. The boys are waiting for me. Honey, I love you. A guy can't be unfaithful here unless he wants to go native. After seeing the natives, that's impossible.

All my love,
Howard

New Guinea
January 9, 1944

Dearest Legna,

Your 22nd letter just arrived, but I still haven't received all of them. In fact, I'm about six short.

Today is supposed to be a day-off for everyone in camp. I worked harder this morning than any time since being here, washing clothes, doing a little carpentry on my tent and expect to have a good volleyball game in about five minutes. If I can get off this box. This climate makes a man lazy. I won't be worth two cents after a few years in this jungle. I think I'm putting on a little weight now. The heat doesn't stop me from eating. Also the best tan I've ever had. The only way we can keep track of the days is by way of Atabrine. We take it six days a week, Sunday being the off-day, hence we know when it's Sunday.

As of tomorrow I am being relieved as Transportation Officer of the squadron. What a break. They figure I won't have time for it when we start operating on the line. That department is one big headache. Everybody in the air force seems to think they should be issued, one each, a jeep for their own personal use. Consequently you have a minimum of 12 men around heckling you for a vehicle. Of course, I suggested the change and after a good stiff argument the weather officer was appointed my successor, poor guy. He doesn't have to work at weather anyway, just an addition to the T/O for some unknown reason. Beginning tomorrow we set-up the line and I'll be glad when we really start operating. Working labor details is monotonous and boring.

Had a letter from Miss Grace. She has my picture that you sent her and says it's alright. She wants me to look like that when I come home, even though I'll probably have grey hair by that time. No reason why I shouldn't though if the "going" all the way stays as it is now. She also said California was beautiful but she's homesick for Maryland and expects to return next spring.

Shady Side must really be quite a place now. Are there any of the young boys left? Guess Bud Rogers is still around. Sure could use a guy like him around a camp. Could build a lot of furniture for the C.O. and come out with a darn good rating, maybe.

The war is really going good for the Allies. Russia is doing a great job. If we could defeat Germany in six months this war would be over very soon. Those are our sentiments, anyway.

Glad to hear Derwill is batting a 100%. I hope he doesn't have to go in the Army though. Course the training he's getting now would help an awful lot.

Fuzz, I'd better get to that volleyball game. I was injured temporarily yesterday by a swift kick with the hard toe of a G.I. shoe. Rough game when we play it.

Will be glad to get some snapshots of you.

Love,
Howard

New Guinea
January 18, 1944

Dearest Legna "Darling",

This is the first opportunity I've had to write for almost a week. I might also add that it's been a week since I received any mail. Got your 22nd letter three days later than the 16th arrived, there are still some missing, 15 to 21 inclusive. Nothing much to say Honey, we are just working and doing it for all we are worth.

We have movies three times a week now and it's certainly a diversion. Tonight Casablanca is the feature attraction. There is the great game of volleyball in which to participate, every evening right after chow. I accumulate more abrasions, misplaced finger joints and also collect a few sharp kicks from G.I. shoes. We make it a rough game, so many of us play on the net and slug it out.

Sorry to hear you've been the third and fifth party to congenial and friendly gatherings of people enjoying themselves and all the intimacies of life. I know how you feel Buttercup and it's no fun. Why not make a twosome or foursome sometime? I wouldn't mind so long as it's in the right company, which of course would only suit you. This will change when the war is over. The three and five set-up, I mean. Life is so much fun Legna, if one accepts it as it comes along. Have you ever heard the proverb, "Life is like a spear which some seek to escape: I would prefer impalement on the shaft." I heard or read that somewhere a long time ago, just happened to remember it. We have tough times here but then again it's all new and you learn something even if it takes the hard way.

Schwen is back with us now and he told me you and Gloria had been corresponding. Good ole Bob, always a laugh and doing a good job. I have a lot of fun with him.

Honey, your air mail letters get here faster. I intend to use this system as long as envelopes are available.

About to run out of paper. Keep writing even if you don't hear from me for as much as a month. There will be times when I just can't write, so follow thru. I'm still in love with you, do you mind? I like loving you!

Goodbye Darling,
Howard

New Guinea

January 24, 1944

Dearest Legna, (Darling too, of course.)

Same old story, haven't had a chance lately to write. Believe it, Buttercup? I've been mighty busy for the past few days and it's so hot, we are exhausted when day is thru. We crawl in our sacks to rest and hit the mill, fresh, in the morning. Around midnight it cools off enough to use a blanket. The mornings are fairly nice so tis then we do our hard work.

You mentioned Massanutten in one of your letters. I've been talking to our Red Cross representative and he tells me he was football coach there for years. He name is Glunt and a pretty swell fellow except for one thing. He likes alcohol immensely. So you can tell, I've been hearing what a wonderful place it is.

Sunday is really our big day here. We wash clothes in the afternoon and have a nice bath in the river. Another big event, we don't have to take Atabrine. Some of the boys are taking on a beautiful yellow tan as the result of the sweet tasting medicine. I'm getting a slight tinge but it doesn't show too much as I have a good tan. The men make faces like children taking castor oil when they swallow the little yellow pill.

Went for a short ride yesterday. This is sure rugged country. Beautiful though in a wild sort of a way. Especially when you are on the beach and can see the jungle with the mountains as a background, just like in movies.

The Group now has a band, about seven instruments. They aren't bad, but you can't go to sleep for the horns blarin'. Another thing, there isn't anyone to dance with so they are not boosting our morale too much.

I wish you would buy a $100 & $25 bond with the money I'm going to send home this month. If there is any left over put it in the bank or buy yourself something. Make the bonds payable to you and me. I think there can be co-owners. I want you to do this for me every month for about 6 or 8 months.

Honey, I must go. Say "Hello" to everybody for me. (I'm really sweating.)

Love, (all mine)
Howard

New Guinea, U.S.A.
January 28, 1944

Dearest Legna,

I was going to write you last night, but some of the fellows came in going to a show and asked me to accompany them. I, of course, complied so no letter yesterday. How about my getting a letter from you, Miss Ethel and Derwill, all in one day? Wonderful! Too bad it doesn't happen more often.

Nothing exciting has happened lately, usual routine. No mishaps, drinking, and no gals. You might say we are in training like a football team. We don't have a beefsteak diet though.

The Ordnance Section has a nice set-up on the flight line. My boys have really put their all into the building of our shack. We have electricity derived from a gasoline generator, level and sturdy work bench with a few power driven tools and a <u>floor</u>. Floors are unheard of in New Guinea, lumber is very scarce. We dug-up some odds & ends and finally accumulated enough to cover our shack. I'm waiting for some Major from Group to come along and <u>try</u> and make me take it up, so he can use the lumber for his own benefit. The squadron has all new trucks, it's a continuous job keeping them greased and in shape. The roads are rough and dusty. A ten mile trip and you are black with dust and dirt. Vehicles aren't as hard to locate here like they were back in the States. The boys have no place to go when there's a slack period during the day, or night either for that matter.

Schwen is back and carrying on as usual. I see him every day and we always pass on few smart words. He still mentions Legna-Annie; in fact he's predicted my life ten years from now. Not such a swell future the way he tells it but I tell him he has a warped mind. I'll tell you about it when I see you in person. Lt. Wood was helping Schwen put it over, but they didn't get the best of me.

Legna, I'm sending you a bracelet made from Australian coins. One of the boys in an Ordnance Supply and Maintenance Company up the road makes them so I bought one for you. It's handmade and a nice job. My boys are going to try and make some like it, when we get the tools and time. If it starts to tarnish, use a soft rag and tooth powder to shine it. This will be your birthday present even though I'm premature. By May 20th the war <u>should</u> be over. I'll enclose a card explaining the monetary value of the coins (American).

Saw a pretty good show last night, Meet John Doe. I sort of appreciated the point even though it was a bit fantastic. We do have some good pictures even though they are a bit old.

Say, don't forget about those War Bonds. We'll be co-owners. It's about time I was buying a few. Money certainly is no good over here—

the roots of evil have been washed-up. But wait until we get a leave and hit Sydney. That town must be taking a terrific beating from the boys who have been in the jungle for six and eight months. I intend to be good; Australia doesn't excite me one way or another. I'd almost rather be here than in some towns we passed thru.

I'm waiting for those snapshots. Better send me at least one every six months. I want to know you when I came home. I don't think either of us will change much in that length of time, except maybe I'll be grown up.

Honey, I'd better rush off. I send all my love. What a volume! Take it please; don't let it get away, not even for an instant! I'd better rush!

Love,
Howard

New Guinea
January 31, 1944

Dearest Legna,

Received letter #32 today, that is the 32nd you have written but about the 20th I've received so far. Kind of difficult to understand; you must have used some of my old APO numbers and the mail is coming by the same route the outfit took, instead of coming direct. It will get here, eventually.

Thought I'd be sending home about a hundred and fifty bucks this month. I took inventory and found a hundred would have to suffice. The pilots have been borrowing to gamble. Their pay is always held-up because of flying pay. I'll collect some of these days. Buy that "bond"

Buttercup; I want to do my part for the "war effort". Sure would like to win some money gambling but my luck hasn't been so good lately. I don't play very often. We played so much on the boat it got monotonous.

I had quite a job fixing up my tent today. One of my roommates broke the stairway last night. He was coming down and on the first step the stairs just crumbled. We are about ten feet off the ground. He escaped without injury but he sure sweated helping me build a new one. This climate rots wood in a very short time and I'm beginning to think, <u>men also</u>. But I like it fairly well. Would still rather be here than in some parts of Australia.

Lt. Wood & I were invited down to the 69th tonight for cocktails and dinner. He had to work late on the line and I had to finish my stairway, so we turned down the invitation. But, took a rain check!

Sure was a nice letter today, Honey. So we are going to get married when we are within "discussing distance" of each other and "no maybes". How about that? Don't suppose there is a chance of you changing your mind? You know Honey, I might be here for four or five years and that's a long time. We certainly are losing the best years of our life now. I hope within two years I'll be on U.S. soil again. That wouldn't be bad. Any time after that is going to find me expectant and ready to take the boat home. I imagine Shady Side is going to be a little strange for me when I get back. Everything changes so in a few years. You can see changes in men, even in our outfit, and we've only been here a short while. The best thing is to keep busy so you can't meditate. I never could do much thinking so don't suffer too much.

Think I'll take in a show tonight. Haven't seen one in three or four days. They can't show them on rainy evenings and it rains just about every other one. Very few days go by without rain. It's a blessing though. The dust is awful after a day without a shower.

Legna, I was kidding about changing your mind. I don't intend to change mine or expect you to change yours.

Keep Anthony's bald head up.

I love you!

Goodbye now,

Howard

Dearest Legna,

This is an added note. I received your letter mentioning my income tax return form. Tear it open to make sure it's just a form. I paid my income tax for 1942 which I shouldn't have done, so maybe they are refunding the money. If it is just a form, throw it away. I won't be paying any income tax for some time. Thanks Buttercup.

Love,

Howard

New Guinea

February 3, 1944

Darling Legna,

Received three of your letters today, postmarked November 26, January 3 and January 22. As soon as I use a new APO#, use that Honey, then my mail has more chance of coming direct. One of them told me you had the pictures. I've been hearing about them but didn't know when you got them. I'm still missing quite a few of your letters.

I've been working very steadily this week, never had so many small jobs to take care of. Getting rid of Transportation was sure a break for me. I spend all my time in the Ordnance shop and keep things right at my finger-tips. Everything is going pretty swell. Only I still do my own laundry and it's quite a job.

Up until a few days ago we could wear shorts and T shirts on the line. Now we must wear long pants and shirts with the sleeves rolled down. Can't appreciate that. It is so much more comfortable wearing shorts. You sweat thru a uniform in a few hours during the day.

You mentioned the fact of sending me some candy and are obtaining cigars. Thanks honey, they will certainly come in handy, it being so damp makes cigarettes and a pipe hard to smoke. (Cigars should do the trick.) What I wouldn't give for a glass of cold milk. (5 bucks, right now) Those pictures too. Hope they turn out alright and I get them. Soon as some of the boys get their cameras I might have a few pictures taken.

Honey, haven't any more to say for now. I love you very much.

Goodbye,
Howard

Ordnance Shop
February 10, 1944

Dearest Legna,

I haven't written for quite a long time. There are a few reasons I guess, but no excuses. I haven't received any mail for a week and then there isn't much to write about.

Had a little fun this morning. Took a machine gun and some ammo, went out to the butts and fired for an hour or so. The boys get a kick out of shooting. It's alright providing there's no one shooting back.

The C.O. pulled a raw deal on me. I am now (again or yet) transportation officer for the squadron. Just when I thought I was so darn lucky to get rid of the job, the Major slaps it right back at me. Oh well, such is life in the Army. I'll be glad though when I can do what I want, when and how I want to do it. Can't for the life of me figure out why in the hell the Major wanted me to have the job again.

We have many more officers in the outfit over here. The number of pilots has increased. There is hardly room in the mess-shack for us all. Guess we'll be eating in shifts before long.

Legna, it sure is hot in this country. I really feel for the infantry boys who are fighting in this area. The temperature isn't so high but the humidity just about smothers you. Some days are reasonably nice though. The nights are the best. What beautiful moons there are, almost like South Carolina.

Honey, I haven't any more news to tell you. Damn, but it's hard to write a letter.

My foot-locker came in the other day. In it was the picture you gave me last winter. I have it mounted in the tent. (Quite appreciative.)

All my love, (Got plenty of it)

Howard

New Guinea

February 14, 1944

Dearest Darling,

Don't know what is wrong, but haven't received a letter for over a week. Nor have the same fifteen letters you wrote in November & December arrived yet.

It is getting hotter every day —sure can't go much in this weather. What a life-saver our stream is on days like this. It is the only way you can get cool.

We've had another change in the officer personnel. Major Carter, our C.O., has been relieved and Capt. Odren is now the man who hangs the ring in our nose. He's a darn good man, Odren, one something like Tuman. We should have a very good outfit now; I was glad of the change. (Should have happened long ago.)

Legna, I'm sending most of my winter clothing home. These are clothes that were packed in my foot-locker and I couldn't store in Australia. It will probably be six months or more before you get them. Pack them away for me, will you? They might come in handy when I hit a cold climate, which incidentally will be when I get back to the States. (What an incident.)

Life is rather monotonous now, but it won't last too long. The monotony, I mean. You don't know or care what day or month it is. Atabrine is our best calendar. Time passes rather swiftly, especially when you're busy. I stay busy.

Honey, remember what I told you about periods when you won't hear from me. Don't worry; there will be times when I can't write, maybe for two or three weeks. It's just something that can't be helped, so don't worry.

Miss Grace writes about every week or so. Seems she's getting to like California. She will be back in Maryland next spring. I'd bet a £ on that (LB.)

She mentions the pictures you sent in just about every letter. It was swell of you to do that, in fact, you're a pretty swell gal. Look out for that build-up; I'm serious though.

Honey, if there is any way possible, wish you would send me some tooth-powder. (In cans). Calox preferably, but any kind will do. Your teeth stain easily here and tooth-paste isn't so good.

Buttercup I'd better go now. How about sending you a 100,000 kisses. Can you handle that many? I could long about now. (No receipt needed.)

All my love,
Howard

New Guinea
February (about 17th) I think,
(took atabrine today)

Dearest Darling,

Ole Shenton got eight letters today, all from S. S. Six were from you, nice shot! Maybe I'll get a few of those letters you wrote a long time ago. Two or three of these were written in November & December, one January 12. Also got a couple of Christmas cards. Legna, I hate to get cards, seems like there is nothing to them, almost like getting a typewritten letter. But oh, those letters in longhand! How I love you & them!

I'm slightly handicapped writing now, cut my thumb darn near off yesterday. It's wrapped or I should say padded with bandages. Always my right hand that gets in trouble.

Everything is going along smoothly now. Sure am proud of my Ordnance men. They might not be professors but how they can turn out the work. We are having a terrific heat wave now, it hasn't rained for three or four days and dust is ankle deep. Makes working rougher and dirtier but guess it's still better than mud.

I've been working in Transportation steadily for the past few days. We have quite a few vehicles just shipped in crated. I'm supervising and helping the boys assemble them. It's a lot of fun. I like tinkering once in a while. Running two departments isn't so hot, you can't be both places and just when you aren't there seems to be the time something goes wrong. But I'm-a-shuttling back and forth, Legna. Don't know what's going to happen when I go on leave. Guess I'll have to train one of the old pilots to fill in for me. They are hard on ammo though, sort of like a kid when it comes to weapons.

Say Buttercup, how about that "warm letter from the tropics"? Honey I can't write mush and you know it. I always feel silly for some reason, course I act silly at times, but that's because I never grew up. Legna, I love you more than anything in the world and it will be a great day when we "middle aisle" to become united, should we say. Doesn't quite seem like the right word. You know what I mean.

Goodnight Honey.

Love,

Howard

New Guinea

February 27, 1944

Dearest Darling Legna,

The mail man knocked-out about four letters from you yesterday. First time I've had any though for about a week. Even had one from Mr. A, that was a surprise. The reason I haven't been writing lately is because I haven't received any mail. It is discouraging as the deuce when you write expecting mail, then get disappointed. I blame the mail service, it hasn't been very good lately.

Say, how about this amazing revelation I'm going to find in you. Sounds good. I like to hear you talk like that. But don't let things like that bother you, we'll get along. I arrived at that conclusion some time ago. Legna, sometimes I wish so hard for you it actually hurts. I admit that it isn't often because we don't have much time for thinking. In fact we try not to take time, because it's a bit detrimental to your well-being. As we were told in Australia, when you get to New Guinea turn in your ammo, 'cause your best friend might shoot you, after six months in the jungle. 'Course that's exaggerated but a fellow feels that way once in a while. So far, I haven't. I'm contented as an "ole cow" chewing her cud. Still laugh as much as ever. My roommates and I pull jokes on one another before we get out of bed in the morning. I walked in the mess-hall half asleep this morning and four boys were giving me the raspberry treatment. I immediately woke up and imparted a little sharp repartee. Ah; we do have fun.

Fischer has a radio from his department installed in our jeep to check planes. We ride around in the darn thing at night listening to broadcasts from the States and programs from Australia. You know, over here we drive on the left side of the road as they do in England. A bit confusing at first but it comes natural after a while. We will have to start all over again when we get home. Newcomers have a little trouble but seeing an accident really puts you straight.

Honey, I'm about run out. Glad you got the coin bracelet. It's handmade. Maybe you can have it cut down to your size. Be on the lookout for the clothes I sent but don't worry about them. It may take six or seven months.

Goodbye Darling.

All my love,
Howard

New Guinea
March 1, 1944

Dearest Legna,

It is raining again. Torrents of water are hitting the tent and cascading off the roof in sheets. Going to be a good night for sleeping. I would like to have a good book to read on a night like this. Better still, you and I sitting by the open fireplace, swapping stories. Gosh, that would be heaven. I'll have to suffice with teasing Bruce, I guess. He's one of my roommates —hails from Washington State. The poor fellow leads a wretched life. We all make life miserable for him but he takes it in grand style. Once in a while I bear the brunt of sharp repartee. I like it though.

Things haven't been so easy this week. I'm having vehicle trouble. We have all new vehicles and we must take care of them. There won't be any exchange when these egg beaters wear out. At the rate we've been going this week we'll be fresh out in six months. I try to instill all of this in the enlisted men's mind but the officers in charge of the departments will not give me their cooperation. I had a long talk with the C.O. He's the boy who can really straighten the situation to its normal channels. I get so tired of hearing fellows talk and gripe about the conditions. Really, so far it has been a picnic and I have a few minor gripes but that's a usual occurrence. There is always something a fellow can moan about but not about our set-up and conditions of living. I'm looking forward to some new excitement. It's a lot of fun to work and realize you are doing a job. Accomplishments, that's what I mean.

Legna, I'm sending some more dough home. About 50£ (pounds)/ 160 dollars. Buy a $100 War Bond and stow the rest for me. I'll be sending at least a hundred home every month. Keep buying a $100 Bond each month until we get a $1,000 worth, then we'll put it all in the bank. I want those ten though. Sure irks me sometimes to think of all the money I'm losing by not being married. It amounts to considerable but Shenton is to blame. You know though, money doesn't mean a thing here. Sometimes I wonder if there is any meaning to it. The States will answer that one when I get back.

Haven't received the candy yet. Not much mail has come thru the last few days.

I hope you thanked Mr. A. for me. I'll write him soon as I get an opportunity. Somehow I don't feel much like writing —must be the climate.

Say we had real live honest-to-goodness eggs for breakfast this morning. What a treat! That powdered stuff hasn't much flavor. I was on hand for the meal very early —the mess officer lives in my tent. I was warned of the occasion.

Three more months Fuzz and I'll be drawing fogey (longevity pay for three years in service.) I feel like a veteran. Had some swell times though, quite a revelation being in the army. I'll be ready to come out though when the war is over.

I'm still thinking of the fireplace and you. Just a sentimental reaction, I guess, no. I love you Honey, that's what makes it so.

Goodnight,

Love,
Howard

New Guinea
March 4, 1944

Dearest Legna,

The mail situation is really rough. No letters have come through for five days. It doesn't give you much inspiration for writing. This is the first letter I've written in about two days.

Nothing very exciting has happened lately. We are still nosing along the usual routine. The higher echelons demand a report once in a while on different items. You rush your head off getting it in, then it sets in someone's office for a week. I thought red tape and paperwork would cease once we were overseas, but there is as much if not more required here. Typewriters really catch hell in the army.

Today has really been swell. The sun hasn't shone at all. We can work without sweating too much on cloudy days. It's not so sharp for flying though. Still haven't had my airplane ride. The C.O. said he might take me for a piggy-back ride in a fighter plane. That would be swell, those babies really are fast. Schwen has been up and really enjoyed it.

I'm enclosing a few pictures some of the boys took at one of the native villages. Notice the little kids with their fat tummies. The condition is caused by an enlarged spleen. (Result of malaria, I believe.). These natives are really getting smart. They even charge the boys a shilling or florin, just to pose. The Aussies are disgusted with us for being so free and easy with the natives. The poor people certainly don't have much to live for. They seem happy though.

I had a Christmas card from Marguerite and Dick, Virginia Linton and Darnell and also Amy. Pretty nice, I guess, but damn I hate cards. Don't mind them too much if there is a short note inside.

Legna, I've got to go now. I'm still thinking of the "you, chair and fireplace arrangement". Sure is a long way off, but I don't mind.

All my love,
Howard

New Guinea
March 9, 1944

Dearest Darling Legna,

Sorry about not writing Honey but for the past few days I've been working. I worked for sixty hours without rest but I did have time to eat. It will take me about three days to recuperate from this one. The army is that way though —do nothing for weeks then, wham, you're so busy you don't know what day it is. But I like it, very much.

329

Three more pictures from you arrived yesterday. They are swell. Legna, I'm still missing a lot of your letters. They must be ones sent regular mail. Air mail is the best, even better than V-Mail. I'm looking for that candy any day now. One of the boys got a letter from his wife saying she was convalescing from an operation. (Home) A few days later he got a letter saying she was in the hospital and a week later one saying she was going to the hospital. Hence, our mail service.

Bud Kline sent me a Christmas card so I'm going to drop him a line. Was wondering if he and Mrs K ever took that long jump. If I know Bud, he hasn't.

The past few days have been rainy and damp. Clothes are almost wet in the morning when you get up. I've had clothing hanging on the line for a week and they're still wet. I have my washing done on the outside now for a small fee. It is much better than doing it myself but the job isn't being done too well. Even the beds are damp at night when you crawl in.

Honey, don't tell me you are thinking of joining the WACs. If you feel you must do something of the sort, make it the Waves or Marines, I don't think too much of the WACs from past experiences. I think you'd do better by forgetting the whole thing, but do as you like. I think a person should be content. I am now even though not too happy. Being in the service might be good for you though. You get around, see and learn a lot. Do what you like, Buttercup.

Soon as you see a new APO# on my return address use that immediately and forget all others. I love you Honey.

Goodbye now,

Love,
Howard

New Guinea

March 12, 1944

Dearest Legna,

Sure don't have much to write about but will make a stab at it. A bunch of fellows are right in the midst of a terrific argument. The air is crammed with verbal denunciations.

I've been working very steady all week, in fact night and day. But it's alright, I like it. Have felt the monotony for a long time and that suits me.

Still a lot of your letters missing, receiving about one every other day now. The candy hasn't shown up, maybe someone intercepted the package. A piece of chocolate would be good, very good.

So Mrs. Shea is giving Capt. Ennis the business. Well, he's probably having a good time. I don't think he will get hurt. I understand a lot of Australian gals who have married U.S. boys are being sent back to the States. (Must be a rumor.) I do know a lot of our boys have married over here. The 311th didn't spend enough time there to make an impression with the gals. We've done everything, so I wouldn't be surprised if some of our men do it when they get a furlough. Personally, I haven't seen a gal in Australia that even appeals to me.

The argument has ceased but I'm going to start another. Lt. Wood is having his hair cut by one of the enlisted men. Think I'll supervise the job. We do have a lot of fun!

The weather has been very nice this week, lots of rain. The moonlight at night is beautiful and it's so cool you really enjoy them. There are about a 100 nurses around here and "ole Shenton" can't get a date. There isn't much you can do if you get a date, talk and drink coffee.

Guess Miss Grace will be coming home soon. She wouldn't be happy living with Dot. She's too independent, "besides having a very uneven temper". (Nice shot, Shenton, you say some awful things.) I could always get along with her though, guess I got to know her after 5 years.

Seems like everybody is getting married in S.S. Must be a fever. Some couples get hitched after knowing each other for about five hours. They can't or probably don't intend to make it a life-time job.

I think we are going to have a great time living together. The idea appeals to me.

Goodbye Darling.

Love, Howard

New Guinea
March 17, 1944

Dearest Darling Legna,

It has been a long time since I last wrote you. Haven't had the time or facilities for writing. I swiped this piece of paper and will try and borrow an envelope.

Things are certainly progressing in this theatre. We are making knots. Remember what I said about this country being hard on men and equipment, well it just about had this man. Guess I can take it though, I love it when the fur flies.

Went on an airplane trip the other day. This land is certainly beautiful from the air, but that's as far as it goes. I'm getting flying in my blood. Sure is a swell way to travel. It's tough when you land and walk around in mud up to your thighs. There is a question in my mind as to whether or not New Guinea will be developed after the war. It will be a tough job taming this wild country.

The cigars came today and were accepted with pleasure and enthusiasm. The boys and I really appreciate them. Guess the candy was waylaid. Thanks Honey!

Got a letter from Miss Ethel too, pretty nice. Sure is great to get mail over here.

I understand we can mention cities in Australia, the ones we came thru and visited. Here goes: I've been to Sydney, Brisbane, Townsville and Cairns. All very nice towns. I want to see more of Sydney. Understand it's quite a place, for a good time. Anything would seem nice after six months up here though.

How about one of those mood-moods you gather once in a while, when I get home. I can take them. I still like to tease and horse around. Right now I'd like to have someone untie my shoes and rough me up a bit. Would be rather relaxing.

Honey there isn't any more to write about except my love for you. What an incindiation —would kind of set the world on fire. Guess I'm putting it too strong so had better shut-up.

Another 100,000 kisses.

Love,
Howard

New Guinea

March 22, 1944

Dearest Darling Legna,

Bit by bit your letters are coming in, one dated January came in today. In it you mentioned weight. Gosh Honey I'm glad to hear that you weigh 112 lbs. I hope you reach the objective (115). What are you doing, taking vitamin pills? I take one every day along with my atabrine. Can't say that it's done me any good though. Boy, what I wouldn't give for a glass of cold milk each morning. (Either that or a kiss from you each evening.) Imagine the reactions would be quite different.

I wrote Jackie L. a letter today. Guess I'll have to knock-out one to Mrs A. pretty soon. My writing isn't any too good right now, the right thumb is out of commission again. This time for blisters —axe disease — I've been in the jungle with a detail cutting timber. Just an old softie I guess, maybe I'm getting old.

Legna, did you get it straight about those bonds? I want you to buy a $100 each month with the money I send by money-order. There may be a month or two when I won't send money home. Sometimes, now for instance, I may not see the outfit for 6 or 7 weeks and can't get in a pay-voucher. But I can draw it after two or even three months in a lump. If that happens, skip a month and buy two when I send the money. I want to have a 1,000 dollars' worth by the time I get home. When you reach that point sock the stuff away (money I mean). Gosh, we are losing money by not being married.

You'd better meet me in Frisco when I come back, otherwise I might get lost crossing the country! How about that? No, I'll be taking the straightest route for S.S.

I got a real sunburn today. My body is generating more heat than a furnace. No matter how burned you get, you always get red after a few hours exposure. The tropics are not for me. Yesterday in the jungle I was walking in my own sweat, squashing along like I had fallen overboard. There are only a million other fellows going thru the same thing though.

There is one thing I wish for more than anything in the world. That is, for you to be in Australia when I get a leave. Kind of like reaching for the moon, but the fact remains. It would be wonderful. I'll have to dream about it.

You know I'm about out of paper and my blisters are aching. Legna, I like loving you, it does me an awful lot of good.

Goodbye now. Love (all my)

Howard

Legna, I just thought of something. What was Roomy's name? Lt. Hopkins, one of the boys, was formerly a school teacher in Scranton, Pennsylvania. He knows a lot of gals who went to Hood. Send me her name.

As ever, all my Love,

Howard

New Guinea

March 24, 1944

Dearest Legna,

Don't know what I'm going to say tonight, material is scarce. Got your fifty-eighth letter yesterday, I see you have it straight about the bonds. "Nice work, Legna."

Been building on the camp today. I'll be a contractor when the war is over. It's very interesting to start from scratch and see what you can make from nothing. Everything is going fine. The place will be fit for a General before long. It would be nice to be a pilot; they have no other duties than flying, whereas we catch everything that comes along, from building camps to playing head stevedore on ships. "Quite versatile this army life." I just hope I can get rid of the Transportation Section in the Squadron. What a headache and constant worry. Vehicles take a severe beating in this neck of the woods.

Too bad about Francis Proctor. I know what it means. I thought an oysterman could stand anything.

Legna, when you and I are married, promise me you won't ever have corn-beef for any meal. I've had it in every form and it's turning against me. In civilian life I liked it, but that's all, sweetheart. I'd like to have a porterhouse steak three times a day for my board, with a gallon of fresh milk. Nice eating, huh?

Talking of marriage, I was just thinking, people like Jean H. and Winnie C. married and about to have children. Why they seem like children in my mind. I must be 100,000 years old. Can you picture me on a bended knee Honey? What a sight! To top it off being a father, the responsibility of that chore makes my army work seem minor. We'll do it though, Legna. I'll probably be more nervous then than I would in an air-raid. Seems like only today though that we took that boat ride, on a rainy Saturday night. Almost four years ago, wasn't it? What a cold-fish you were, but I love you. Just a young college squirt who was going to take the world by the tail and sling it in any desired direction. You were even going to revolutionize teaching or something, I believe. Well, you might yet, that's what I'm afraid of.

Honey, I'd better go now. Don't take the last paragraph seriously. I'm teasing.

How about 100,000 kisses, one for each year of my age. (From me to you.)

Love,

Howard

New Guinea
~~March 28~~, 1944
April 4 (slight mistake)

Dearest Legna-Darling,

I know I'm a little tardy writing but I've been so busy lately, there hasn't been time nor have conditions been favorable for letter writing.

Yes, old Shenton has been working again, but I've really enjoyed the job, especially with the boys I've worked with (officers). There has been wonderful cooperation all the time with the exception of a little occasion which didn't amount to much. Then again, the results have been satisfactory, believe me that helps. Time means nothing when you are busy, the days fly, I honestly think a man would go crazy in this country if he had nothing to do. (Very few people go crazy.)

The only way I'd like to come back to New Guinea is in a palatial yacht, anchor off the beach, come ashore and stay for 15 minutes. Our present locale is alright, much better than the last. Maybe I'm becoming acclimatized, not going native though.

That operetta of yours should be about over by now. I know you have had quite a time. Guess it wouldn't do for me to be handling children —my army vocabulary would be a bit drastic. You know, I hope to forget it in a hurry when I come home. Guess the speech gets a little rough when you are around a bunch of men all the time, but it's a habit that can be broken.

In just about another month or so I might be going on leave to Australia. How about that? Sounds good. I didn't draw my pay for last month, maybe I'll let it ride and collect two pays, so as to be well fortified when I hit the mainland. Can't tell for sure though, it might be six months before the leave actually goes thru. I'm sweating it out. Still think the most wonderful thing in the world would be for you to be waiting there when I land. "Just another dream, which will change to reality someday."

Hope Mr. & Mrs. A. don't feel too bad about my not answering their letters. I'm sorry Honey, just extenuating circumstances. Oh! I had a swell letter from Bob Wilde —seems as though he's doing fine and is getting quite a kick out of life. I'll have to answer that one too.

Legna, the time has come to say good-night. I think of you in pleasant dreams.

Goodbye Honey,

Love (all my), Howard

New Guinea

April 9, 1944

Easter Sunday

Dearest Legna Darling,

Can't remember exactly when I wrote you last but it couldn't have been too long. Your mail is coming thru alright now. Haven't received the candy yet, it should be along any day now. Sure wish it would get here, a little chocolate candy would go good.

My new home is much better than the last but it should be, I built this one. If it would only stop raining long enough for the roads to dry. Honey, when it rains, you think the bottom has dropped out of the sky. You haven't seen anything that can quite compare with it.

I took time out this morning and went to church. The service was very good. I can say I felt a lot better after going. (The chaplain congratulated me on coming.) Think it was the first time I had been to one of our services. The Group Chaplain is Methodist but his sermon and the services were both Methodist and Episcopal. Memories struck again for a short while. Yes, I was back in our church singing with women and men. I could hear Miss Ethel's voice above the rest, especially when the singing lagged and she would pep it up. Could hear you chime in lustily at intervals. Even Mrs. Phipps and Josh H. were in the picture. I could even imagine how the weather would be, the sun shining but a very sharp wind blowing making a top-coat comfortable. (Just a trifle too cold for those new spring suits that gals all buy and wear to church on Easter Sunday.)

We are having an egg-hunt but we are hunting for a place to hide them. The place isn't so hard to find but the accessibility is slightly hazardous. Also we have a few eggs hunting us every so often but we don't make such good hunting. Anyway Honey, I enjoyed going to church very much this morning.

Went to see a show the other night but just when the show gets going we have an alert, so it's never completed. I understand Madam Curie was showing at the last base but I wasn't there. Will see it when it catches up.

Fischer is living with me now. He has a radio mounted in the tent. We are listening to a command performance right now and I like it. A U.S. broadcast is great to hear. Fischer just surrounds himself with radios and telephones. I'd like to call-up and have a case of "beer" delivered to the tent. No, I'd rather have a quart of ice cream. (Or pick up the phone and say, "How about a date, Legna?) We have one, don't we?

Goodbye now,

Love, Howard

New Guinea
April 14, 1944

Dearest Legna Darling,

A few letters came in today, the past couple haven't been so good for the mail man, but we have no kick coming on that score. I couldn't possibly give you the numbers of the letters I have received. I destroy most of them right after reading. You can't afford to keep them. Today for instance three of your letters came in, one dated March 20, 21st and 1st of April. That's the way we get them. No sequence at all.

So, you bought a what-not. Well how about that? Never heard of one, but Bennert has, he told me all about what they were. We can go off in the forest somewhere and set-up housekeeping. Shenton is getting pretty good at building homes in far flung remote places. No, wouldn't want that, we want to be close to everything. Have to make up for all the time I'm spending in New Guinea. (Could stand New York for just about two days right now.) In two years that will be up to eight days.

Guess you will feel kind of lost now that your operetta is gone. Well it won't be too long now before school will be over, then you can take a long rest. That will be swell. You can gain about 20 lbs, brush up on tennis, swimming and maybe a speedboat ride. Kind of reminds me, wrote Bud K. a letter but no answer yet. Their Kline days in S.S. are probably o'er, although Mrs. Thomas said she heard from them frequently. Say, what did Mrs. Thomas think my name was? She had my letter addressed to Lt. H.C. Shenkan. Well, I've been called much worse by scores of people.

Legna, there's been quite a few changes in some of the boys since we hit New Guinea. I just hope I'm not following suit. The men are touchy, irritable and pretty hard to get along with. My training in the infantry is standing me in good stead. I've expected everything we've encountered and a little more. The going hasn't even been bad so far. I get sore because some of the guys lose their sense of humor. Better not say too much, I might lose mine. I think I can take a year and a half or two over here right in my stride though. Course you can't predict in the army.

I see you finally got it straight about the war bonds. I didn't get paid last month, so will draw two checks this month. If I don't get my leave in

May I'll be able to send quite a bit home. It's really amazing how worthless money is up here. 'Course in Australia it has a value.

Give my regards to ole Anthony Bischoff sometime, the old bald-headed so and so.

So long, Legna.

All my love,
Howard

P.S. Keep using air-mail.

New Guinea
Sunday, April 16, 1944

Dearest Darling Legna,

What a miserable day it is, the rain is pouring, but I feel secure and dry sitting in my tent writing this letter. It's a darn good thing the floor is three feet off the ground. Think I'll flag a streetcar and take a ride to the mess-hall. Honest, it's raining so hard you can just see the next tent 20 feet away. Doubt if I'll even stir out of my hole for the rest of the day. My vehicles are going to take a terrible beating tomorrow. This deep mud is hard on the wheel-bearings.

I've enjoyed today a lot. Been sitting and laying around, talking and reading. Even brewed a little coffee and had a few of the boys in. (Quite the host!) This is the first day I've taken off. Intended to take just the morning but the downpour changed my mind. Work is easing up a bit, the camp is about complete. Here we sit in a dry tent having a good time and not so many miles away are a bunch of men fighting for everything in the world. Those infantry boys deserve all the credit you could possibly give them. The Air Corps does its share in the battle but we live and work under such wonderful conditions in comparison to some of the other branches. We are very fortunate.

Of course, I've been thinking about us a little, while moping around today. Legna, must we have a big wedding. I'd just like to go off somewhere and tie the knot. I don't like being fussed over nor do I like a big fuss made about anything I'm about to do or taking part in. If you say so, we'll have a big wedding but I just want you to know it won't make much difference, just so long as we do it. I realize it's quite an event in anyone's life, getting married. It's probably something you will always think of as long as you live. But just as soon say, "I do" with only you and the preacher present. Whether it's big or small doesn't matter but I thought I'd tell you how I felt about it. Don't mind my sounding off, do you Honey? The whole thing is too far away to do much talking about it or to make any decisions. We will be married and that is what interests me.

The box of candy has still not arrived. Maybe we've been hi-jacked. The cigars came almost a month ago and I understand you sent the candy first. Did you say you could send me another box of cigars? I sure would like a box. It's wonderful the way the boys appreciate them, not to mention one-time Lt. Shenton. I asked Miss Grace to send some but it seems they were unobtainable or something.

I'm having a little trouble with my teeth. All the old fillings seem to be loosening. I'll get Doc. Shapiro on the ball first thing tomorrow morning. Just so I don't lose those choppers I'll be satisfied. There's no immediate danger of that.

Legna, today would be a great one for you and me to sit before that fireplace. We could talk and grab a cat nap every so often. Either that or go up to Woody's to shoot pool and drink beer. Which would you prefer, my dear? (Answer known, it didn't take algebra to solve that question.) It would also be a good day for ducking —nasty weather is good weather for ducks.

For supper tonight I'd like to start off with an enormous shrimp cocktail then an oyster stew followed by a steak an inch and half thick with French fried potatoes and two cups of coffee. That's a pre-war meal, isn't it? I have to leave for a short while.

Here I come again. Had supper and it was almost as good as the one mentioned above.

Speaking of our being married again. You meet me in Frisco, we'll get married and honeymoon across country. That would do it, Legna! Another dream though. I'll still be in the army and probably in charge of an "advanced echelon". I'm beginning to feel like a "pioneer", in addition to my other duties, of course. I've been everything in this squadron, including being the "Ordnance officer".

Legna, I miss you and I love you with all my heart. I've got an athlete's heart, too!

Goodbye now, Darling,
Howard

New Guinea (Land o' milk & honey)
April 21, 1944

Dearest Darling Legna,

Can't for the life of me think of what to write about. Letter writing is getting to be quite a chore. Just about getting ready to hit the ole routine again. There's plenty going on, but it's all "old stuff". Maybe I'll be getting another APO pretty soon. That's what I like, in that way, time doesn't drag.

My tent-mates and I are fairly comfortable now. The tent is quite a home. We have a radio (Fischer), telephone and electricity (sometimes). We've even erected a tank and made a wash basin so we can have running water for drinking and washing. Of course, we match coins every three days to see who fills the tank, but that isn't such a bad job. The squadron has a water trailer equipped with a pump. The tent has shelves above the beds. Over my bed I place your picture. The boys walk by, look at it and say, "Poor fool". (Maybe you'd better straighten these fellows out, Honey.) There is also an addition to our happy home—a fox-hole, something that no house is complete without. Sometimes I think it's an absorbing ditch—how that hole accumulates water. Dig a fox-hole here and you have a "Leatherbury well."

The best, or maybe it's the worst, part of the day is in the evening. Then we have our arguments. I get exasperated, throw my hat on the floor and yell. It's terrific! Think I'd better take up all the ammunition. We certainly enjoy our arguments. The boys say I never think so and so about something, they say, "I always know". Once in a while we take in a show, but the sound hasn't been too good lately. Right now, I'm contemplating throwing Fischer out of the house; he's walking around and the floor isn't so solid. Soon as the ground gets dry, I'm going to reinforce it from underneath.

Haven't had much mail for a week. Expect a thousand later this evening. Can't for the life of me think what happened to the candy.

Say, you should hear the roar of those U.S. planes overhead. It's really wonderful to see them flying formation, in wave after wave. (I like Wacs) and Spars too. The Air Corps is doing alright!

Summer is about over now, we can settle back for a hard winter. I'd like to be home, for at least three weeks right now. The weather doesn't vary much here. It's hot and hotter.

Just about off the page, so remember I love you.

Good day Darling,
Howard C.

New Guinea
April 25, 1944

Dearest Darling Legna,

A missile arrived by mail today and it traveled with such speed and force, it took my breath away. Kind of swept me off the old terra-firma. I'm talking about your letter dated April 2nd #70 in the filing cabinet. What in the world made you write a letter like that? I was shocked, amazed, in fact, I didn't believe it. Sure you were feeling alright and normal when you penned that "interlude of stupefying and incoherent mess of phrases"? Gosh, Legna, I can't quite fathom the damn thing. I don't know what I said, but you know me well enough by now to realize that I don't deserve that sort of treatment. I have never read a more disgusting or humiliating letter in my life. It's worse than the one you wrote while I was on maneuvers in S and N. Where in the hell is your sense of humor and I might say "common sense"? Legna, this does it. If you can't trust me and have faith in me now, what would marriage be like? I hate to think of it! Maybe I did say something about Yanks and Australians and Nurses, but what has that to do with Shenton and Andrews? So you cried yourself to sleep one night and maybe you'd do it another night. Well how about that, there's a lot of fellows who won't sleep for week maybe around this part of the world and it's not because someone mentioned something in a letter. I'm afraid your practical and analytical mind is playing you false, my dear. Can't you get it through your mind that you have to have <u>faith</u> and trust in people? Maybe you'd better go to summer school and brush up on "Understanding of People". This is a rough letter Legna, but honestly, I get more exasperated as I write. I love you gal, doesn't that make sense nor strike some chord in the nutshell we call a brain. Don't be so suspicious and imaginative, come down to earth and make a few simple deductions with a broadminded view. You are a woman, not a sixteen year old lovesick kid. If you only knew how a fellow thinks and feels about coming home to see, meet and live with the people and habits he had before this mess. That's what drives some of them off the well-beaten path (Mentally). I forgive you, Honey, but "please" and I repeat "please" don't do that again.

Now that I have that out of my corn and bully beef system, let's talk about things practical. Schwen, Bennert and I built a shower for the squadron officers today. It's a hum-dinger, very convenient and cleaning installation. I'll even be able to do plumbing work, "after". There's a military band playing "Tea for Two" in the Rec. Hall across the way. Sounds good. Try and fathom the words sometime when you aren't busy. (That's the thing I want from life.) Nice band. They are from an infantry outfit on the "base".

We seem to have the mud situation under control. Roads are taking shape: it's good for the vehicles. Amazing to note how dusty it gets a few hours after the rain has ceased. But it rains most of the time.

Extra work is slacking off now, so I'm almost back to the usual routine. That routine doesn't seem to last long around here, thank goodness.

Three of your letters came today, 70, 71, and 75. Guess the intermittent ones were delayed. No candy and no wallet with the loose buffalo. I'm not worried though, it will arrive sometime. You just have to sit back, relax and things come along.

Wouldn't be a bit surprised if Norman W. were around these parts. I was talking to a few of his colleagues the other day. Pretty nice bunch of chaps, good flyers, too.

Legna, don't let this letter keep you awake or upset you. It's not meant that way. Read and grin —even sigh if you want to —but don't worry about the situation, it's well in hand.

Got to go now.

Love,
Howard

New Guinea

April 29, 1944

Dearest Legna,

Been getting quite a bit of mail from S.S. lately. You must be drumming up a few letter-writers in your spare time. It's nice to get mail, but what a job to answer! I'm going nuts, trying to think of things to write. Things are moving slow with us, sometimes I wish I was an O.C.S man again. That would do the trick.

We haven't had much rain lately. The dry season is in. But my, how it does get warm. You get a peculiar reaction to the sun here. You can work in the sun, get a real brown burn, stay out of the sun for few day and sweat, you're a paleface again. It's really strange!

Legna, you mentioned something about censorship of your letters. Incoming mail isn't censored. The army doesn't give a hoot what is said in the mail coming in, it's just the outgoing and all of those aren't given the third degree.

Had a letter from Gilbert L. and he mentioned horses. We have quite a few race track fans among the officers. I'm still taking a ribbing from them, because I bet on a horse named "Maryland Morn" at Rockingham Track. The betting was purely sentimental, in fact when I was in line getting my ticket, some stranger behind me asked what I had. My reply, "Maryland Morn", I'm from Maryland, he came back, you'd better pay your respects to Maryland down in the "Show" line. Sure enough, the nag ran third. I'll still bet on Maryland!

I'm reading "Merchant of Venice". Really good. I was surprised. Most of the books we get are either mysteries or Tom Swift jobs and they are all alike. Also read a book titled "Elmer Gantry" by Sinclair Lewis. I recommend it highly to Rev. Culp. I think every young preacher should read it. Some story!

Honey, how about taking a few snapshots and send them over. I have quite an album now and besides pictures are swell to get. Ray Woods' wife sent him some and the boy became alarmed. Said she looked terrible, lost weight and all that. Maybe he won't get anymore.

Won't be long now before Bennert will be a father. It's kind of tough, your wife having a kid with you not around. (On the father, too.) You are fortunate, my dear, guess we are both lucky. (Are we??) Say, my thoughts are wandering, guess I'd better call off this blooming fountain pen.

Legna, I still love you —tell anybody that's interested.

Goodbye now,

Love, Howard

New Guinea
April 30, 1944

Dearest Darling Legna,

Been pretty busy for the last few days. The outfit is bombing now and that means more work for my Ordnance department. My boys didn't know too much about the handling but they are ole hands after a few days coaching. The work is hard though and the hours long. Sometimes we work half the night. The pilots are getting quite a kick out of the deal, gives them a chance to do a little aerobatics.

Honey, your candy came yesterday and darn it, I had to throw the whole thing away. One corner of the box had gotten wet and the whole interior was mildewed. Some of the boys have received candy in good shape. Guess I wasn't lucky. You certainly had it packed nicely. Can't figure how the wetness seeped thru, but that's New Guinea.

Bob got a real break. The lucky sunfish has been sent to the mainland, pursuing a six weeks engineering course. Just think of how interesting the homework will be at night. The work will consist of "Interior Decorating of a Night Club". After this school he'll come back and after a short interval go again on leave. Six weeks in civilization, how about that! Sounds like a life time.

I've been appointed to another job. This time I'm the assistant prosecuting attorney in our "Court Martial". This climate is not fit for a trial proceeding, every point and argument gets a thorough shake-down.

We took some pictures the other day, they should be developed in a few days. In fact, about the next letter you get from me will probably contain the cartoons. No natives this time, strictly G.I.

The mail service is getting pretty good again. Got three letters from you yesterday. Also one from Mrs. Harold Hartge and a short note from little Harold. Not doing bad at all.

Gosh, it would be great to roam around S.S. now. Guess the locust trees are about in bloom and soft crabs should be coming in. I could murder a soft crab on a homemade roll. (Could eat 1,000)

Honey, that's about all for now. Got to check my bombs.

Love,

Howard

New Guinea

May 2, 1944

Dearest Darling,

Thought I'd better write a short note and tell you how much I love you. Lt. Wood doesn't approve of this, he says, keep 'em guessin' Shenton, they like it that way. But me, I'm frank and very serious minded. I say, Legna, I love you Honey, more than a G.I. loves a 15 day furlough in Australia. That's really a lot, ole dear. Much more than I could ever make you believe. (About the G.I.s or Yanks, I mean.) I have a date with you every night — the pace is kinda hard to keep with all this defense work going on but we'll outlast the war. (Junglistis is a hard job to beat though.) Certainly am spoutin' off, aren't I?

Sorry I can't send you something for your birthday. There isn't a darn thing I could send except maybe some unique insects or jungle foliage. You wouldn't like it. Gosh Legna, you're almost an old maid—24 is quite an age nowadays. You don't feel that way, Honey, 'cause if you do, then I won't feel so good about the whole thing. I don't feel like an old bachelor, in fact I'm suffering from adolescent complex. Act like a twelve year old at times. My tent mates will vouch for that. Every night they put me out so they can have peace.

Been busy for the past few days. Our boys are running up the missions. Pass the ammo, Shenton, we have an engagement. That's all I hear and, of course, comply with alacrity. Sometimes even frivolously. We are using lots of bombs and that's hard work. Ask any Ordnance man.

I'm enclosing a few pictures. Any resemblance between me, the picture and anything living or in the process of elimination is purely and 100% coincidental. Must resemble a lower form of life, inorganic. Hope you enjoy them.

Saw a good show last night, Standing Room Only. We really enjoy them —Paulette G. and them, I mean. Was good, so don't miss it. Guess it's in the movie album by now. Annapolis gets them pretty early.

Did I tell you how much I love you in this letter? Answer: No Shenton, you never say what I want to hear! Maybe I'll call you on the phone and say it with my own lips. I love you, Legna—more than ____ _____ _____. I don't know what, but it's immensely.

All my love,

Howard

New Guinea

May 3, 1944

Dearest Darling Legna,

Our mail system is going "screwie" again. No mail to amount to much for a week now. It's damn hard to write when you don't get letters. Honestly, it's awful, there's nothing to write about —a fellow doesn't even know how to start.

I've had to shave all the hair from under my arms for treatment. Picked-up a jungle rash and my arm-pits are pretty sore. Can't relax my arms at my side. Nothing to worry about but darn uncomfortable. We had quite a few cases in the Group. Wherever you perspire you are bound to pick up a rash sooner or late. The infantry boys suffer more than anyone else. (In more ways than one.)

So Bischoff remembers me. I don't believe it. Any memories he retains of me would have to be unpleasant. Seems all of our contact ran on that line. He's a good math teacher. Never will forget the days he made me be the last one on the bus because of pushing to get on. Those were good old days, can still remember Townsend making eyes at Iva Fern over a Bunsen burner.

Schwen just came back from school at Sydney. Guess he had a good time, the lucky bugger. I'm thinking our leaves to the mainland are never coming thru. The way work is coming to us now, half the outfit could take two or three weeks off and the difference would never be noticed. I will be mighty glad when we move out again. We should move at least every two months, then everybody would be busy all the time. I'm bored.

Got to go Legna. Buy a couple of bonds with the enclosed money-order. Also those size 36 T-shirts and cigars.

Oh, but I love you.

Goodbye Honey,
Howard

New Guinea
May 6, 1944

Dearest Legna-Darling,

I came to life this evening and discovered I hadn't written you for a couple of days. There isn't a darn thing to write that's new, same old stuff. (Nothing ever happens.) Work is going fairly steady. We've had "not so good" weather lately, but it didn't slow us down too much. This war is a bit boring at times but if there was a lot of excitement, I'd still be complaining so that's the way it goes. Wish I could get a leave pretty soon, no kick coming there though. So far we've been very fortunate in not having things too rough. Quite a few of the fellows have been up here much longer than we have, and see "no leaves" even in the near future.

Haven't had a letter for five days from anyone. Guess something has slowed down the delivery. One of these days I'll knock down about ten. Great day!

Thinking about your birthday this month, I sort of took inventory on the ages of the fellows around me. You know, with the exception of about one man, I'm the youngest screw-ball in this outfit by a few years. Would like to be with you on the 20th. We could celebrate the occasion quietly, sober—and have a lot of fun. What's the meaning of that word fun? I'll learn when I get home. Shouldn't be too much of a job. Maybe I'll learn before then! What could we do on the 20th to have a good time? Take a drive, have dinner, a show and maybe a dance later. Oh, we could go for a speedboat ride, if there was one available. Water is kind of cold yet for swimming but we wouldn't necessarily have to take a dip. We could have fun though, Legna! Right now I could have fun sitting around the house drinking milk all day. I'm going to cherish a "cow" when I get home. How I miss that vitamin.

Got paid this month so am enclosing a money-order for $200. Don't forget the bonds. Wish I could buy a thousand.

Guess the juke box at Miss Mary's will be making its "yearly porch debut" pretty soon. If I lived at R.H.H. I'd know all the latest tunes.

Honey, I'd better turn this off; it's getting rutty. I'll drink a toast to you on the 20th.

All my love,
Howard

New Guinea

May 10, 1944

Dearest Darling Legna,

Had quite a thrill today —got a letter from you. How about that? First one in about ten or twelve days. The war has sure been holding up delivery. That's the reason I haven't written much lately. It takes a letter to make a letter, if you know what I mean.

Glad to hear you had a swell trip to New York. I'd so much rather hear about someone having a good time than the usual everyday routine. Honey, I think you should take more trips like that. It's good for you. If I had known back in the states what I know now, Shenton would have had a few more good times than what he did. Of course, I wasn't suffering from boredom at any time, but I let a lot of opportunities go by. We are going to have some good times together when I hit the states. Prepare yourself for it, my Dear.

No unusual events taking place —same old stuff. I'm ready for new doings again. It's surprising how quickly you tire of one spot. Moving around makes the time fly and that's good enough for me.

My "one hitch" in the army is drawing to a close, three years the 30th of this month. Seems like 23. Looking back it's kind of startling, almost a jumble, but I don't think it has changed me in any way. I still think the same about life, wonder if my perspective will change? The whole thing has been a great experience.

Had a letter from Bob Wilde and also one from Miss Grace. The wallet with your picture and Peadie's buffalo came yesterday. Honey, you look wonderful in the picture. Look as though you've gained quite a few pounds. (Healthy as a G.I.) The boys kidded me about the wallet. That's just about the most useless thing a man can have in N.G. but I'll sport it, if and when I get a leave. Expect to carry quite a few pounds in it, ($3.22 to a pound), that's on the trip down. You always come back light.

Legna, I miss you an awful lot when I'm not real busy. I'd give anything to see you, even if it was for just a couple of days. Rough, isn't it?

About run out Honey, guess I'll have to write Roomy, if she writes me that letter. (Will comply!)

Love,

Howard

New Guinea
May 14, 1944

Dearest Legna Darling,

Looks as though I'm slipping on my writing detail again —a letter every three days isn't bad though. (Will suffice?) The mail situation here has been terrible of late. I did get the wallet and tooth powder this week. Legna, you are taking a beating and don't realize it. When the boys saw there were no edibles in those packages, they started raising hell. Things like, What are you going to do with a wallet? Why she sent you enough tooth powder to last 5 years. Just like a woman to do something like that. It's all in fun though. We have to do something of the sort or else we would go crazy.

Today is "Mother's Day" and what a beautiful one, hot but really pretty. Things are sure quiet now, the war has left us behind a bit again.

We'll probably catch it again in the near future. I hate sitting around taking it easy, very monotonous! The pilots have it nice though. All of them have had a leave and will start on their second in just a little while. The ground officers are sweating theirs' out. I don't think we will get one for some time. One day a leave looks forthcoming, the next, it seems like you'll never get one. So that's the way it is.

Had another letter from Bob Wilde. We have an engagement when the war is over. We are going out and celebrate. He said he was over this way a short while ago. I think Norman must be in the Admiralty's. We see quite a bit of the Navy. I anticipate going on a PT boat mission. I've always wanted to, maybe now I'll get the chance. Have to do something for a little excitement. Sure wish you could take that mission with me, something would be bound to happen then. Wish we were transferred to another theatre. (Not movies my dear.)

Legna, would you buy me about a dozen T shirts the next time you see a sale or go to town? They are short-sleeved undershirts. In about six months I'm going to be completely out and they wear nice over here. Pay for them with some of my money. (Don't want anything but T's.)

Honey, I miss you aplenty now. Oh my!

Goodbye now,

All my love,

Howard

P.S. I'll have to listen to that wallet and Calox deal for another week at least. But that's all I wanted. H.

New Guinea

May 16, 1944

Dearest Darling Legna,

There isn't a thing to write, nothing much happening, back on that endless chain. I took the afternoon off and went swimming with Fischer. We took a pilots life raft along to paddle around on. Enjoyed the water and picked up a little sun-tan. Came back to camp, had chow and went to a show. The show was held-up for an hour —the sound wouldn't work. The show always has its technical difficulties but it's not too bad. We do see some of the later shows, six months later than the states!

Haven't had a letter for about three days now. Most of the Christmas packages are coming in now. Mail even gets hauled around here in fighter planes. Yes, we even carry the mail.

Understand there's construction underway for a post-war policy. Some people sure are optimists and believe in being prepared. Makes you think the end of this struggle is near. Sure hope so, along with three or four hundred million people. But it won't be real soon. It's going to be a long winter here.

Guess you will be whipping up a few stiff exams pretty soon. Hard work for you, but oh, how some of the kids sweat those babies out. The worst I ever saw was in OCS. Thank goodness I never studied for one in my life. The kids will really feel great though after it's all over. No stern and strict personality to tell them what and how to do. It's a break for the teachers too, then they too can act and be natural like ordinary humans. What am I doing Legna? Those remarks are classified as secret and confidential and should be confined within the realm of those who inject (like getting a tetanus shot), beat, well, impart knowledge. Gosh I hope you don't take this serious. I'm only fooling. Sounds cynical doesn't it? Well a fellow has to write something.

After reading what you've seen on paper so far in the missile I want to tell you I love you, Honey. If you were here with me Legna, we could really do a lot for <u>forward</u> progress of this battle. But they say, a woman's place is in the home and this ain't nobody's home. So that lets you out but it was a great thought. Damn Legna, it's going to seem like a century before we get together.

All my love (ship wouldn't hold it),
Howard

"Rough isn't it". That should be figured in the P.W.P. (Crazy letter!) Is it worth an air mail stamp? H.

New Guinea
May 20, 1944

Dearest Legna Darling,

This is the day you gain a full year. Guess you will celebrate tonight. I would, and I mean celebrate! Dinner out, night club with music, dancing and lots of scotch and sodies. I wouldn't want to do that here though. Too hot for that sort of thing. Very few things are celebrated around here, but we have fun sometimes. At the last post we had a few dances for the nurses of surrounding hospitals but those are gone with the wind. No nurses, no dances and no nothing. Gosh Legna, I haven't seen a woman for four months, but we don't miss them too much. I'm hoping that you and I will be together on your next birthday. It's possible, I guess!

Haven't had any mail for a week now and don't expect any for three or four more days. I'm getting one of those non-writing spells. Haven't written much lately. We have been told air-mail envelopes will not be available anymore. Guess everybody was using air mail instead of V-Mail, which results in a transportation problem. I hate to get V-Mail letters but they are better than nothing. Don't be surprised if suddenly you don't get any air-mail letters from me.

Wish we would move again. I'm getting tired of this one spot. Haven't been here very long but activities are slowing down.

Think the ground officers' leaves have been suspended for an indefinite period. Wouldn't surprise me if we didn't get one in the next six months. Well, we'll save our money —whatever that is. That stuff seems so unimportant in this place.

You know, I forgot to tell you what size T-shirts to get for me. (SIZE 36 or medium, if the size isn't listed.) We like them to fit tight. Try to get them for me, will you, Legna? About a dozen should do the trick.

Thought I was going to have some fun today. A PT boat skipper promised me a ride when he went on a mission but our Colonel wouldn't allow it. Sometimes I think we'd make a good "Boy Scout" outfit. I would really enjoy a trip like that. Seems there is something like insurance involved. I didn't bother to find out after we were told we couldn't go. (One of the boys was going with me.) "POUTIN."

Life has certainly been uneventful and dull lately. Poor Fischer sure takes a beating when we are sitting around doing nothing. We razz the poor fellow unmercifully about his accent and Brooklyn in general. He's about to go mad.

Legna, I really mean that about being together this time next year. If I knew it to be a fact I could lick my weight in wildcats. In the meantime, don't get too old. I'm only sixteen! (M & P)

Love and goodnight,
Howard

New Guinea
May 24, 1944

Dearest Darling,

It's raining this afternoon so we all wandered back to the tent. Most of the boys are in the sack and a few are writing. You can't sleep during the day when the sun is shining. The perspiration will down you.

I had to laugh when you mentioned the grand opening of that clothing box. I thought about you opening it when I packed that darn thing. How about those long screws in the lid? Kind of a surprise to learn the stuff got to S.S. so quick. The postage was only one £, 14 shillings. Not bad at all. The sun glasses are for you if you want them. If not, keep 'em. Guess you'd better give Jim Nick those long-handles (underwear). I never expect to use them. The rest of my clothes are in Brisbane. Don't know if I'll get a chance to pick them up before I come home but the storage company will ship them for me, upon notification.

Honey, the only reason you haven't had a letter from me in two weeks is because of the mail service. I never write less than one letter a week and usually every other day. (Ahem.) Sometimes the transport facilities get tied-up and only essential and critical items are moved. It won't be long now before you will only get V-Mail letters, I've got about three air-mail left.

Something tells me I'm never saying the right things in my letters to you. Like love, dove, moon and June. I'm sorry, Legna but there's a good excuse. It's the environment more than anything else, living like we do you never mention or think of things pertaining to romance and etc. We get a little rough and don't think of things on the, should I say, velvet side of life. But anyway, you know what I think of you and that will never change. (Unless a miracle takes place and I don't like miracles.)

Had a letter from Bud Kline the other day. Seems to be the usual man-about-town. He and I are going to get drunk when I get back. (Double scotch and sodies.) Told me all the current events of S.S. and Gals. [Galesville], also mentioned spending week-ends at Rough Point as a member of the "Exclusive Club". Too bad they sold that place. Bud should have married and settled there. (How's that for a word of advice?)

Still in that usual rut, can't for the life of me see why the Colonel doesn't give all the ground officers a 21 day leave in Australia. I could stay away that long now, nobody would miss me. Guess I'll have to come back to S.S. to get out of this arroyo.

Legna, sure hope you can send me another box of cigars. Pay for them with my money. The boys and I consider them quite a treat.

Better shove-off now Honey. Remember what to tell that fellow in the Jeep.

All my love, (It's increasing)

Howard

New Guinea

June ? 1944

Dearest Legna,

I hit jackpot luck yesterday; five letters from you, one from Mrs. A. and a copy of the Galesville News. First time we have had any mail for over a week. (Good shot Mr. Postman, keep-a-shooting.) Miss Ethel's' letter was "great", about the best I've received from anyone.

Say, I'd have given (five pounds) to have seen the fire at your house. Must have been really exciting. We had an ammo dump catch fire the other day and it was "very exciting". Bullets were flying all around the place and bombs exploding, seemed almost like a Jap raid. Didn't do too much damage. Too bad you haven't a movie camera, so you could have recorded the highlights of your battle with the flames.

Legna, I sent $200 home around May 5th. Didn't you get it? I have the receipts so if you haven't received it, let me know. I also sent $180 yesterday or the day before. Keep an eye peeled for it. Whenever I ask you to send me something, pay for it with my dough and wrap the packages securely. They take a terrific beating. If they ever break open, that's the end! You never recover the articles.

I'm sorry the married boys are being drafted. Should think it wouldn't be necessary. A lot of replacements are needed here though; some of the boys have been here over two years. Just being in this theatre for that length of time, without ever contacting the enemy is good enough for me. Those boys deserve to go home, but quick! I don't expect to get out under two years, that's the minimum. You wouldn't mind it too much, if only you could see and become part of civilization once in a while. Some of these boys haven't had a leave since arriving. I should think there were still enough single men to fill all quotas. Gad, they'll be drafting women before long.

Legna, I'm glad you didn't join the Wacs —that's a sorry outfit. You can do more good and render better service to the country right where you are. Stay there "Buttercup". (EXPERIENCE!)

We've got a full moon on down here. Nice for pitching woo. The nights are sure beautiful, enough to change any man's fancy. But that's all (!) it can't go any further. War is hell! Well I'd better leave the sublime; I should say ridiculous because that's what it is and say bye.

All my love,
Howard

June 9, 1944

Dearest Darling Legna,

Got your 110th letter today, quite a sum. I'm sure you've put it on me, if I keep on as I've been doing lately, you won't get a 100 in two years.

How about those big doings in Europe? Wouldn't mind being in on that, history is in the making. We get the latest news over Fischer's short-wave set, then rebroadcast over the P.A. system in the area. Guess everyone thinks the war is in its final stages after this latest move. You know me; I'm not too optimistic —going to be a long time yet. A longer one in this theatre, but we're making rapid progress. Our outfit has been too long in the one spot to suit me, I'm getting restless.

How about that dance at Southern? You can get a date and I know it. Chaperone's row is a tough position when there's fun going on. You should get some of those blooming Navy men at Annapolis to drag you. I wish I could be there —had fun the last time I went. Been a long time since I've danced. Don't know if I could do the ole two-step again or not. (Be a lot of fun trying.) There are lots of things I'll have to learn over.

The cigars were passed around again today. One of the pilots became pappy to a boy. He's been saving the smokes for two weeks, waiting until he got word of the event. Two in one week. Going pretty strong, eh! I've been trying to imagine myself a father; doesn't seem to fit. (Imagination isn't strong enough, I guess.)

Was wounded today, took my usual beating in volley-ball. Came out with a black-eye this time. The games are too rough for me, I guess. War is child's play compared to our volley-ball games. I get in some good blows though —knocked Bennert out one day.

Legna, I don't think I can make another page. I love you honey. (Never diminishes, that!)

Love,
Howard

New Guinea
June 14, 1944

Dearest Legna,

Feeling kind of sharp today even though I do have a light cold. (Getting a little mail now.) Been carrying on a little repartee with some of the boys next door. My tent mates are going crazy. Seems they are trying to listen to the radio. My fellow contestants have retired in disgust, but warned to watch out because they would be back. I might come out of it with another black-eye, like that volley-ball game. We have fun, sometimes.

Sure not doing much work these days, Legna —beginning to believe I've been pensioned instead of on active duty. If it weren't for kidding Fischer, life would be very dull.

Finally knocked-out a letter to Aunt Jenny L. Writing letters is getting to be my toughest job now. (Some days I can't make a scratch.) Still owe Miss Ethel one. Got another copy of the Galesville News. You better donate $5.00 for me, to cover their postage expenses. I enjoy the publication very much. Have recommended that Gilbert submit subjects to the feeble-minded section. (Flattery!)

I haven't the slighted idea how much money I've sent. Doesn't make any difference, except I've been holding the money-order receipts, even those are mixed up. So just let me know if you get the money so I can tear up the receipts. I think there are possibilities of letters being lost. Shouldn't be any doubt about my trusting you, (dig) even though I don't believe it's mutual all the time. Anyway my C.O. trusts me!

Gosh, I'm glad you got those T-shirts. Thought maybe you would have trouble. In Australia you have to use coupons entirely. The shirts will be swell. Size 38 and medium should do the trick. Thanks Honey, I might send you a grass skirt for that. (Censor won't let them go through now.)

Enclosed are a few pictures. Hope you like them. I'm trying to get a few scenic ones to send you. This country makes beautiful pictures. Don't remember the bags in the background of those I sent you. I'm sure there weren't any "nurses" wandering around that day, though.

Marriage in 1945! By that time I probably have to get an O.K. from the C.O. and his staff to take such a step. Hope it happens, Honey. (You are very optimistic.)

Say, tell me something about Miss Grace. I haven't heard from her for over a month. Guess air-mail stamps are <u>too much</u> for the ole gal. Someone said, she was back in S.S. (Send out your secret operations.)

Legna, I've got to rush off somewhere.

Love,

Howard

New Guinea
June 19, 1944

Dearest Darling Legna,

Been getting quite a bit of mail from you lately. You are right, I haven't been writing much lately. Once or twice a week should be enough, don't you think? Everything is so damn dull a fellow can't think of anything to write about. Speaking of writing, I haven't heard from Miss Grace for a month and a half. The old gal has deserted me, I guess, not that I mind it too much.

In accordance with the latest news, our boys are going great-guns in the European theatre. Kind of wish I were there. The war here is getting monotonous. (A man is never satisfied though, must be his nature.). Volley-ball is our biggest battle right now. My eye has healed, so I'm back in the line-up. Why in the hell we don't get leaves while we do nothing, I can't understand. It would be pretty nice to get back in a town and make the rounds. I like it here, but sometimes it backs-up in your throat.

I see by the Galesville news that the sailing season is underway. I'd give anything to have a boat on this island. You could really have fun fishing and visiting other small islands. Seems as though Bud K. has become an honorary member. He likes that sort of thing. I had a lot of fun sailing with Bud in the old days. (My eyes were always getting sunburned though.)

We just got in a couple of new officers right from the States. (The most surprising event to them is the fact we have no black-outs. The lights go out at a signal from the AA Batteries about 15 or 20 minutes before a raid. They also wonder why there was such a rush to get them over, when everything is normal routine. But they are administrative officers, so it wouldn't make much difference to them if thing were hot. We are running a few bombing missions ourselves. But they don't amount to much.

Legna, I'm beginning to believe I'll be glad to settle down when I come home. Had a little time to exercise my imagination lately. You and I were the focus point. Looked pretty good too. Are you going to keep a few bottles of beer in the ice box for me? Gosh, but a cold bottle of that slops would be so good. The pilots have lots of liquor but I haven't had over three drinks since N.G. I could go for that beer though. There isn't a drop on the island! Yes Honey, I'm sure we can make a go of married life. There might be a few differences but that's natural. The only thing I can't imagine is my being a father. For some unknown reason I can't conceive of that. (Funny, that's natural too.)

I'd better shift gears and get out of here. Will try to write before another week.

All my Love,
Howard

New Guinea

June 22, 1944

Dearest Darling Legna,

Wanted to write you last night but startling events happened so fast and furious I didn't have time to take care of that matter. I managed to obtain a leave, but there was and still are complications. You can have a leave, but must get your own transportation. ("The transportation" is hard to crack.) I bummed a ride on a bomber for a short hop, now I'm sweating out another ride. Just like hitch hiking, I had the whole trip set-up but as usual things didn't fit the slot so good. But we'll make it. Fischer is with me and that's a help. He can talk his way into anything. So next time I write it will be from the mainland, I hope.

Of course, this means I won't get any of your letters until I get back to the outfit. (But keep writing, to the same APO #321). I'll try and write you at least twice a week (three is my goal.)

I've borrowed so darn much money it will take a couple of months' pay to get me out of debt. It's going to seem funny spending money again. I'll try to buy you something. I understand Fischer has a checking account so we shouldn't run short on money.

If only you were waiting for me down on the mainland. Might not be good though, I'm sweatin' it out too much now. Think of what it would be if I knew you were there. Gosh Legna, wouldn't it be super-something if you were waiting for me? Seems like I've been in the wilds for years.

Of course, I expect to consume large quantities of milk and fresh vegetables, not to mention a "bloody steak" every other meal. Schwen was down not so long ago, you know. After talking to him for half an hour when I found out I was leaving, I feel like I'm going to my home town. No orientation course needed.

Legna, I've to go see a fellow about a plane ride. Keep on writing same as always. I want a thousand to accumulate.

All my love,
Howard

Auntie Glorious 1940-1942

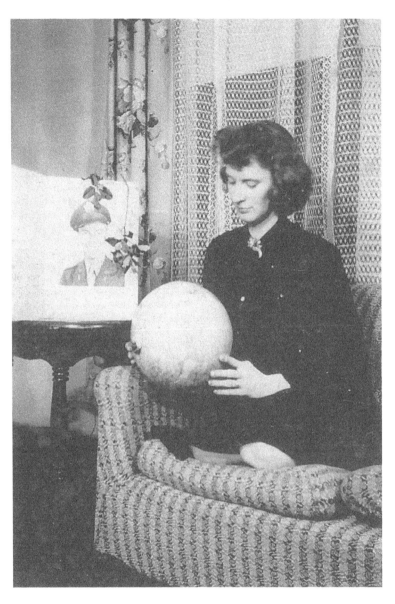

Glorious searching for Howard's whereabouts on her globe.
Christmas 1944

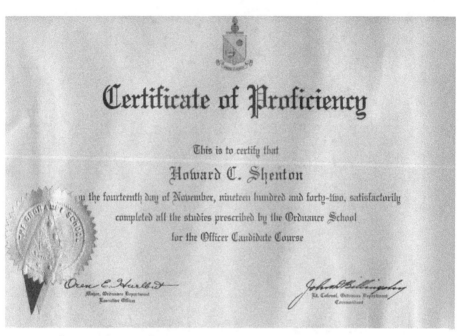

Howard's Diploma from OCS

Howard on an island in the Pacific

Derwill (Drilk) and Glorious in front of the Rural Home Hotel in Shady Side, Maryland

Glorious with her younger brother, Derwill Fraser Andrews [Drilk]
wearing his Massanutten Military Academy uniform. Taken around
1943 in front of the Rural Home Hotel, Shady Side, Maryland

Glorious in front of the Rural Home Hotel during WWII

Glorious posing in front of the Rural Home Hotel during WWII

*Derwill (Drilk) in Navy uniform. He was stationed at Pearl Harbor
and manned the fireboats. He was too young at the start of the war so
was not there during the attack on Pearl.*

Glorious & Howard in Baltimore, Maryland

"Chez Shenton"

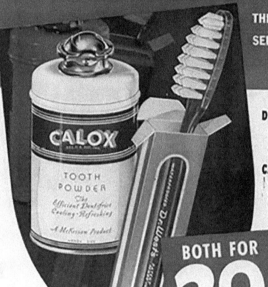

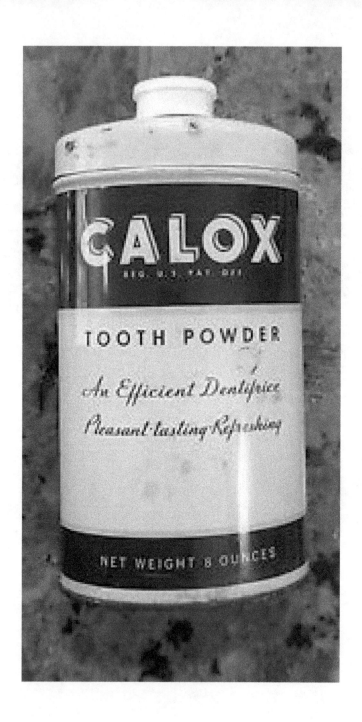

Glorious and Ivan, her old Model A Ford

On Leave in Australia

Waltzing Matilda

June 25, 1944

Dearest Darling Legna,

Taking time out between steaks and beer to do this. Boy, have I been cramming the good chow. Honestly, I didn't know food could be so good. Can't get all the milk I want, but manage at least two glasses a day.

Flew down and what a trip. We covered in a day and a half, the same trip it took twenty some days to make going up. You've never seen such beautiful scenery in your life. We traveled above the clouds part of the time and even they were pretty with the sun reflecting from them.

Seems awful cold here, but the natives think it's fairly warm. Guess I won't ever be able to stand cold weather again. (Willing to try it though.) It never snows here. People have never seen the white stuff.

Don't believe I'm going to send you anything. Everything is rationed here. There isn't anything you can buy without the ole coupons. I'm going to try though, Legna. I'd like to get something real nice.

It's going to take me a few days to adapt myself to this new mode of living. Certainly surprising how a person can lose his metropolitan air. Almost like coming into a new world. Won't take Fischer long to "hit the groove". He's off to a running start anyway. The place is crowded with service men on leave from the combat areas and you know what that means. Hell-raising good times, but I'm going to be good boy, Legna, just for you. (Won't be a sacrifice considering it's for you.)

I'm going to a football game this afternoon. Might be interesting to see how the Aussies play the game. You and I never made a football game. That's one of the things to come.

Legna, if you were here we could have two wonderful weeks. You'd like the Australian life. Keep that fire burning for me Darling.

All my love,
Howard

Australia
June 30, 1944

Dearest Darling Legna,

Still on vacation and is it wonderful. Eating fresh food, plenty of vegetables and best of all, milk. The waitress here at the Red Cross, where we most always eat, knows about our wanting milk —lots of it —so she just keeps bringing us more. The food is the best part of this leave.

Saw a few stage shows and I was surprised that Aussies can put on a good comedy. 'Course everything seems better than it actually is after six months up-north. I'll be ready to go back when the time comes.

Fischer is doing his usual wolfing. Seems to be doing alright too. The gals here are quite eager and they've seen so many flushed Yanks on leave till they can really show you how to spend the money. I'm being true to you, Legna. It may sound hard to believe but tis the truth. I think some of the gals find this pretty hard to understand and probably think there is something radically wrong with me but I just can't give-them-a-go (Aussie slang). I'm spending most of my time drinking beer and eating. They have excellent beer here.

Haven't found anything to send you yet but Fischer and I are going searching one day. We'll find something, I'm sure.

I'm still wishing you were here with me, Honey. WE could have such a wonderful time, seeing all the sights and being together. I'm more lonesome for you here than I ever was in N.G. (This is what we call hardships but it won't be for much longer I hope.)

Got to go Darling. Remember I love you, will you? That's vital!

All my love,

Howard

Australia

July 5, 1944

Dearest Darling,

Celebrated our independence last night and don't want to be "independent" any longer. Damn it Legna, I can't have any fun here without you. The parties we've had have been a total loss for me because of that reason. I just can't accept any other companionship or whatever you want to call it.

I had some pictures taken and you should get them in a month or so. These are serious pictures. The photographer insisted I should give my toothsome grin, so I frowned up him. They are pretty good though. There are two poses. I want you to keep the large picture of each pose and give the smaller ones to Miss Grace. Keep what you want though.

Went to a barber shop yesterday for a haircut and noticed some water colors decorated the wall. Decided to send you one —scene of Sydney and I think it's pretty good. Can't find a darn thing to send you. Tried to get some woolen cloth for you but they won't allow the stuff to be shipped. Saw a dress I know you would like but couldn't buy it; just wouldn't sell the dress to me.

I'm eating my head-off, wallowing in milk like a newborn calf. (A few beers in between of course.) Really going to miss this chow when I go north.

Fischer tells me he's in love. Met some gal who is gorgeous and he must see her every minute for the rest of his leave. (They all look gorgeous to that guy.)

> *Don't believe everything you read—and I am having an awful time trying to make Andy darling remember his true love—he is so forgetful!*
>
> *—Bud*

Honey, I have to go to the dentist this morning. Will write again. So long Darling.

Love,
Howard

Australia
July 13, 1944

Darling Legna,

I'm still down south, my leave was up on the 10th but transportation facilities aren't so good. Kind of hope to get out tomorrow. I've been ready to go back for over a week now. You get too much of this life in a short time. If you had been here, I would have enjoyed myself. But I got kind of lonesome, most of the fellows run around with high-flying daisy-cutters (a high explosive bomb) a little bit of that goes a long way with me. Guess I'm all yours, Legna. Can't stand much of the other women, they bore me terrifically. You and I could have had a wonderful time here, just think, two weeks of being together. (That's better than a milk diet after 7 months in New Guinea.) Gosh, but I've been storing away the solid liquid, must of gained a few lbs. Been an expensive trip though — really went thru the money.

I mailed the pictures I had taken. Hope you get them soon. Wrapped them myself, so can't vouch for the shape in which you'll receive the package. Made a deal with the photographer for the negatives and enclosed same. In case you want any more prints, you can have them made. Do what you want with the pictures. Honey, I had them taken especially for you. If you want to give Miss Grace one of the small ones, do so, but do what you want with them, they are yours.

Hope you like the water-color of Sydney. You should get that in a few weeks. Sorry, there wasn't more I could send you, but there's so little a fellow can buy. You can get a lot of trinkets, but it's all junk. I know you wouldn't like the stuff.

I miss your letters more than anything Honey, must have quite a stack waiting for me. Haven't had a letter for almost three weeks now. I'll probably have to take an afternoon off when I get back to catch-up. Lt. Wood has them in a safe place for me. Wouldn't be surprised if he had them tied with a ribbon.

The war news sure sounds great. Looks like we'll all be home before we know it. Won't be too soon though. I'll be ready to take off soon as the last shot is fired.

Well, guess Shenton had better be pushing along. Keep writing to APO 321 until you see a new one on my return address, then use that.

I've missed you more these past weeks than any time since being overseas. Guess "I just love you, Honey." I love loving you Legna.

So long Sweetheart,

Howard

Back in the Harness Again

Carry me back to old New Guinea

New Guinea

July 16, 1944

Darling Legna,

I'm back in the harness again, got back last night. Made a record trip, two days flying. I was never so tired of an airplane in my life, but can you cover territory in those eggbeaters. One day I was freezing to death, the next heat prostration had me. Great life though, Legna, wouldn't have missed being born for anything.

Went thru a pile of dough down in Sydney but the good time was worth it. My only regret is, not being able to find you something. I tried, but nothing available. Sure caught up on my milk drinking, also had a few beers. The Australian beer beats anything we have in the States. I errored Honey. I have another regret —you weren't there. That was something beyond our control. (Way past.)

The place here is still the same, nothing new. The boys are suffering from boredom. My leave came at a very good time; I didn't miss a thing. Sorry Ray Wood couldn't go with me instead of Fischer. Ray and I, as the Aussies say, could really "give it a go". Our tastes would have been more alike. Fischer's too much "Wolf".

Had a stack of mail waiting for me. Saved yours until last and took my time reading them. Must have been at least twenty from you alone. School quit early this year, didn't it? Those school days in June were awfully long when I went to school. Could stand a few of those long days now, with you as the teacher. Honey, I never missed you so much in my life as I did on my leave. (Quit wandering Shenton.) Seems as though you are worried about not having enough work to keep you busy this summer. Take it easy Legna and gain about 1,000 lbs. don't worry about me, just think of me as being on a traveling trip. (I've done that the past few weeks.) Maybe we will have next summer together.

Had a letter from Bob W. He told me about Buddy. Too bad, but that's the service for you. Some fellows get great disappointments. Guess I've been lucky. So you love Buddy. Darn Legna, I thought you were "all out for Shenton"! Well, I can say, Buddy is very fortunate. Don't think he would marry you, do you? Love is a wonderful thing, Legna, you taught me that. Guess I'll never get over you Honey. (Even if I go on oxygen at 50,000 ft.) Don't let those air corps terms confuse you.

Let me know soon as possible what you think of the pictures I had taken down south. (Darn good photography, I'd say!)

With all my heart, LOVE!

Be gentle and take care of that heart. It's got to last you a long time.

Love,

Howard

V-MAIL

July 18, 1944

Dearest Legna,

I've got a little job for you. The allotment bureau has messed up on my allotment payments. Claim they've paid me $75.00 too much. I want you to check with the bank and find out how much money was deposited to my account from March 1943 to April 1944. That's a total of 14 months, the first fourteen payments. The total for that period should be $725.00. The bureau claims they paid $800.00. Find out what they deposited and let me know soon as possible. I might owe the government $75.00. Don't you try to do anything about the payments, I'll take care of that on this end. Just get the information and send me a V-mail letter. Thanks, "Lovely"!

Bye, you gorgeous little wench. I love you.

Howard

New Guinea
July 19, 1944

Dearest Darling,

I wrote you a V-mail yesterday. I think that's a bit quicker than air-mail. Answer that one by V-mail but that's all. I hate them. Get that information for me soon as you can. But don't worry about the darn thing, it's only a small matter.

The boys are sure disgusted with nothing to do. We sit around talking and reading most of the day. Hope we get out of this slump soon; I'm getting lazy. Won't be worth my salt soon. Could have stayed in Sydney for a long time at this rate.

Wrote Miss Grace a letter. She finally wrote me one. The old gal finally came thru. I was really surprised. Understand she and Cap'n Mike are holding the fort on the river. Would like to have listened in on your conversation about me. (Did I get to be a four-star general?)

You know Honey, I was under the impression that I answered Mrs. Thomas's letter. Maybe I didn't. I'll try and knock one out to her. I write to quite a few people at times and it's hard to remember who and when.

Legna, I don't care what you take out of the bank, buy anything you want or need. I want you to take $100 out and get yourself a Christmas present. I'm serious about this, buy yourself anything you like. I'll like it, I know.

The snapshots I sent you previously were taken in New Zealand on the way over. The ones enclosed are of N.G. —the one with the airplane wing taken in flight. How about getting some of you over to me? I want to see what you look like with the added ten pounds.

So Derwill is going in the Navy. At least he will have a clean place to live and good food. That's all I love about the Navy. Tell him the "best of luck" from me and beware of foreign ports when on shore leave. He'll do alright though, probably come back a beer-drinker, but that won't hurt him.

So you can't dance without paying a tax. Going to make it tough on the jitterbugs. Guess there will be plenty of fishing parties this year. Legna, what is Jack Nieman doing now? Isn't it about time the service took him or does he have a few kids?

Honey, I'm still lonesome for you. I'd better find some hard work to do or else you'll be reading "mush" before long. I'm a poor hand at writing that stuff, too. Gosh, I love you, Darling.

All my love,
Howard

New Guinea

July 24, 1944

Darling Legna,

Life is certainly drab and uneventful around these parts. Every day is the same. At the present we are spending most of our time just existing. The serenity is broken every so often by an explosive argument. We have some beauts. They are a lot of fun, no one gets sore. Wouldn't make any difference if they did. Sure would like to get busy again.

Got your letter of July 8th today. The last one was July 1st. That's how the mail comes in, probably the same on your end. I'm glad I mailed those pictures in Sydney —you should be getting them before long. How about giving Miss Grace a couple of small ones. I want her to give Miss Myrtle one.

Something new has been added. Beginning August 1st, we are going to be issued beer, about a case a month. That's going to be nice. We already have a nice cool stream picked out in which to chill the beverage. The men are all for it and I believe it will go swell. You can't drink liquor here; the climate won't allow it. The Aussies always have issued grog to their men. (Grog? Anything with alcoholic content.)

The weather has sure changed here. Haven't had any rain for a long time. We are having a little trouble with our water supply. No more mud but the dust is terrific. Wouldn't be surprised if we had a monsoon soon.

The boys are playing volley-ball again. Two ended up with patches over their eyes. Seems like every one gets it in the eye. It's rough on the pilots; they can't fly for a few days. I'm learning to duck fast. Once in a while we play softball. No casualties in that game. Most of the fellows play cards a lot, but I haven't had a card in my hand for six months. I've just lost all interest in the pasteboards.

Your vacation is about half over. The summer months sure go by fast. (Seems that way to me.) The U.S. is having lots of trouble with teachers. What is the difficulty Legna, aren't you getting a square deal? Now is the time where we should have good teachers. I think war has played havoc with children and they really need guidance.

Will take a few lessons myself, Honey, so keep in form!

All my love,
Howard

New Guinea
July 29, 1944

Dearest Darling,

There isn't a darn thing to write about, I hate to even start a letter. We aren't doing a thing now. The boys are fighting for the little bit of work there is to be done. If I had a boat, life would be fairly enjoyable. Fish are plentiful and the sea is beautiful. But we just sit in camp and get in one another's hair. I managed to get in a couple of airplane rides around to different bases. Sorry I didn't stay in Sydney for a few more weeks.

Schwen is on leave. He just came back from Australia a short while ago. Was supposed to be attending school the previous time but it was a vacation, I'm sure. Bob's changed a lot since coming overseas. He's pretty hard to get along with at times. Of course, I never let things like that bother me one way or the other. It's all the same far as I'm concerned. The climate affects most of these fellows.

Time is going by fast. We've been gone nine months now. Be about another year before we start sweatin' out going home. If we keep traveling at our present rate, I'll be ready to make that trip long before a year is out.

Haven't had any mail at all for a week. The mail service isn't what the magazines and papers say it is back home. But we can't kick too much; we do get it sooner or later. Mail and fresh food are our hardships these days. Had fresh eggs this morning. First time for about six weeks. Sure tasted good.

Legna, can't think of another thing to say. I could say, "I love you", but you know that for sure.

Big volley-ball game in the making for this afternoon.

All my love,
Howard

New Guinea

August 1, 1944

Dearest Darling,

The mail-man kicked thru with three of your letters yesterday. About time, I thought we were never going to get any mail.

Our area is rapidly turning into a rest camp. The sacks (beds) are getting a real work-out. Darn good thing we were issued air mattresses. Makes living much more comfortable. Hope our next move is a long trip; I'm getting a bit tired of N.G.

The beer ration starts today. Every man gets a case a month. First thing you know someone will be opening a drive-in restaurant. Now everybody will be "gathering at the river" to take a swim and cool their beer.

So our honeymoon is going to be a long, drawn-out affair. Six months is kind of long, isn't it Honey? Have you decided where we are going to spend this pleasant six months? I'm willing and ready for it, Legna. South America sounds like a good place to me. I always wanted to see Rio de Janeiro. Talked with a few transport pilots that have been there and they say it's a wonderful place. I don't care where we go. We will be together and that is "good enough for me".

Finally, came the rain. Last night we were just about washed out of the tent. Never saw it rain so hard in my life. Nice out today though. Almost like a spring day back home.

Too bad about the roll of film. Darn it Legna, where would you have put it? I might have some more pictures for you pretty soon. Nice ones, too.

Be careful what you say to Miss Grace. She cries at the slightest provocation. Give her my love when you see her and tell her to start writing some letters.

Love,
Howard

P.S. Thought you had gotten over the habit of wasting writing paper.

New Guinea

1944

Dearest Darling,

Here I go again —letter writing is the toughest job I have. Got two letters from you yesterday. One containing the snapshots. Darn good pictures. Can't believe you weigh 110 lbs though; you look the same to me. The new hair-do makes you look like a siren. Do you know what I mean? (A little hussy) I like it very much, considering I wouldn't take a gal to a formal dance one night because she had her hair piled on the noggin. Don't know whether or not I told you about that. It happened in Baltimore before "our" time. Pictures are nice to get Honey. So send them whenever you can. I'll have a few more for you soon, but I'm not in any of them.

What's this about you and babies? I wouldn't even want you to have one by "proxy" while I'm gone. Looks like everybody is having them, doesn't it? Wonder what part the so-called war-hysteria plays in that construction job. Our boys' wives can't have any more babies until they return. We've "been-out" for the full time limit (so the "Flight Surgeon" says).

The volley-ball teams are attaining a real competitive spirit. Getting lots of outside games. The enlisted men want me to play on their first-team. We play according to the rules now, no more bruised shins and stitched eyes. Before it was just a rough and tumble wrestling match — brute strength winning out.

I have a new theme song now. It's titled, "Long Ago and Faraway". Taken from the picture "Cover Girl". Describes us (you and I) exactly.

Wish someone would write a song entitled "Together" and let us live up to it.

I've got to go now Legna, guess my letter average isn't so high. But I'm not doing too bad.

Love,
Howard

New Guinea
August 6, 1944

Dearest Darling,

The rest of your snapshots came yesterday. They were pretty good. I like the one of Miss Grace very much. Isn't that dark dress the one you were wearing in New York the last time I saw you? Seems to me you had some white collar or something around the neck then. I don't like the dress at all —stick to lighter shades, Legna.

Had another letter from Aunt Jenny. She also enclosed a letter Livingston wrote her. I see he's in the Marine Corps. Must have just gotten in, if he's only completed boot-training. From the information I gather in the Galesville News, looks like all the Galesville boys are stationed around home. It's just as well, 'cause we certainly aren't doing much here right now. I'm about fed-up, might just as well send us all home.

Schwen and our Flight Surgeon are still on leave. We are beginning to wonder if something has happened. Guess the life in Sydney was too much for them. They are probably convalescing along the way. I'm almost ready to go back — have to collect some money though. It goes like a wild horse down there.

Say, you shouldn't have aroused my curiosity on that problem of yours. Wish I could discuss it now. I've plenty of time to think. Wouldn't go so good by mail, I guess. And about your political problems. I'm not allowed to argue politics; tis one of the nonprivileges of an officer. But I think you are all wet, "maybe prejudiced". Sounds like it! I love you regardless, little Republican.

I'd like to know what was "surprising" in the letters I wrote from Australia. Seems like to me they are all the same. I did miss you more while I was there than any time since the fatal rainy Saturday night long ago.

Honey, goodnight!

All my love,
Howard

"Same ole place"
August 9, 1944

Dearest Legna,

Your mail has been coming thru pretty regular. That's good. Got the first shipment of T-shirts. They are exactly what I want. Just the right size. I've already been propositioned for a couple. No sale. I'll need them.

What's this about me slipping? I've told you before in letters that I loved you. Guess the letters from Sydney were a bit stronger. Maybe it was because of the prevalent romantic atmosphere around that little town. Fischer says he had several romances. I didn't look for it. Don't think I would have found it anyways. My definition of the word "romance" differs greatly from Fischer's.

Legna, you should have the pictures and the water color by now. The post office wouldn't insure the photos but the Aussie gave me a receipt for the water color, so keep me informed.

Schwen came back yesterday. He sure took a long leave. He's getting awfully fat. Must be the Aussie beer.

I'm finding a little work now and then. Been doing a few jobs lately and it sure helps. I'd rather be real busy and get something accomplished. Sort of gives a man some "satisfaction" and that's what I like.

Still got "Guinea crud" beneath "me" arms. Thought I had it licked but the darn stuff popped up on me again. Isn't serious this time though. A little treatment should set it right.

The "special service" has been putting on some good movies. That's the height of entertainment. We get a lot out of them, too. The "big star" stage shows have all by-passed us. Haven't had a one at our base. Of course, once in a while I put on a show for the boys. Our best shows are arguments —so far friendly.

I'm glad Derwill made the Navy. They have good food. Guess they don't take atabrine either.

All yours (Love—better put it in)

Howard

New Guinea

August 11, 1944

Dearest Legna,

I'm sitting around "Group Supply" this morning doing nothing, batting the breeze, of course. We've certainly been exercising our vocal chords, worse than a bunch of old women. The Group Supply officer and I are settling a few problems. He insists I'm always trying to hook him. Maybe I do, but at least it's in the open and he doesn't mind too much.

The squadron volley-ball team is really doing the business. We've had some good games and I came out on top mostly. Gosh, we even argue when we play that game.

Legna, what in the world do you want to see Texas for? There are lots better places we could go. I'd like northwestern U.S. if we made it in the summer. Would still like to give Rio "a go". Maybe though it's not for honeymooners. I don't really care where we go, I like S.S. too, you know.

Seems like Bob & Gloria had a slight mix up over those pictures you sent. Bob caught hell because he didn't send Gloria any, and Bob gave me hell because I didn't give him some copies to send home. It's O.K. though, everything is smooth as glass. Damn, wives are a bit peculiar and don't hesitate to chew a guy out. Sometimes I think the husband should wield the rolling pin.

Honey, I'm going to cut this short. There's some Capt. from higher HQs prowling around. He wants to inspect my transportation department.

Just remember Shenton still loves you Honey.

All my Love,

Howard

New Guinea

August 13, 1944

Dearest Darling,

Just got back from a show and what a show! I've never in all me blooming life seen one as terrible. Saw Christmas Holiday. How it ever got on the screen is beyond me. I'd rather see our group show and that's pretty bad, too. We are always griping, even about the shows now.

Say Legna, what's behind the living in S.S. question? Haven't quite figured it out yet, but what difference does it make whether it's S.S. or Kalamazoo? What bearing will this have on us making marriage a success? Right now, I could live anywhere but New Guinea and love it. You have some funny ideas <u>sometimes</u>. Enlighten me a little more on this subject, will you Honey? Of course, I have no post-war plans at the present time. I figure plans at present should involve finishing off this mess. (A 1ˢᵗ Lt. doesn't do much figuring one way or the other, at present anyway.)

Haven't had any mail at all for the past few days. The squadron has had some V-mail but thank goodness, I never get V-mail letters. They are almost as bad as cards. It must be true about Gloria getting so much mail from Bob. He told me he wrote her three letters in one day. How in the dickens can anybody do that and make sense, it beats me.

I'm still taking life easy. Would sure be a wonderful life if we had some good chow. We eat it but it's not because we like it. Something tells me there are a few things I'm not going to eat at all when I get home.

Guess you've heard enough of my bitching Legna. Don't pay much attention to it. We are fairly well off and life could be much worse. (I like it all the way.)

Goodnight Darling,

All my love,

Howard

New Guinea

August 17 or 18, 1944

Dearest Darling,

Long time, I don't write, please don't get angry Legna, there just isn't a damn thing to say. Haven't had any mail for some time now. Your V-mail came in yesterday. Only letter I've had for nigh on to 12 days. Thanks for the information Honey. I'll need the 'statement" from the bank, of course. When it arrives I'll send it with a letter to the allotment bureau and get the situation straightened out. Won't be much trouble.

Wood and Bennert left for Sydney this morning. Fifteen days leave. For all the work we are doing at the present time everybody could take 15 days. I'd like to go back myself for a week or so just to get some good chow and a drop of Australian beer. I think even you would like the Aussie beer. "Fine nectar." Those two married boys are going to find a tough go of it down south. It's no place for married men.

The cigars came day before yesterday and they are good ones. Now we can enjoy a good smoke while watching the movies. Thanks Honey, your generosity is exceeded only by "my love for you". Guess I'll be a little short-winded until the cigars are gone but they won't last very long with five men in one tent.

Saw a good show the other night, titled "Gaslight". It was very good even though it did start quite a few arguments. It's about psychology. Three of the boys in our tent think they know psychology (Fischer, Bennert and Oche). Of course, I was in the midst of it, even though I don't know much about this particular subject. "Common sense" is another word for psychology in my book, though I'm pretty sure "you think" differently. These boys were so wrapped-up they missed the points of the show. I even went and got the Surgeon to settle one of my points in the argument. The fellows all had a different view on the climax of the show. I put them straight on that. Some fun.

Darling, I've run out unless you want to hear about the weather. I love you Legna, and "I mean constantly."

All my love,

Howard

New Guinea
August 20, 1944

Dearest Darling,

The snapshots of you in the canoe and on the lawn came yesterday. They are pretty good. I like the one of you in the bathing suit very much. Sort of like a pin-up picture. Thought sure you would have received the pictures from Australia by the time you sent these latest shots. Hope my wrapping job withstands the journey. Never was much at "bundling" (Packages, I mean).

Those last cigars are really tops Legna. The boys and I sure like them. First time I ever smoked Muriel's. They are quite mild. I expend them when we have beer and movies.

Honey, we are still "hacking" around doing nothing. We manage to fill in the day with swimming, fishing and a few "Goldberg inventions." The fishing and swimming are out for me now. The darn sharks are so bad now. A couple of the boys and I with a native had quite a run-in with the beggars the other day. We were diving for fish that we had blasted. They were in water about twenty feet deep. The native yelled shark! When I heard that, the water just opened before me and I was perched on a boat we made about twenty yards away before he finished saying the word. Nice one too, about eight feet long. We lost about 10 good fish, too. That's what hurt. I tried to blast the shark but couldn't do him any damage. The coral reefs are certainly beautiful beneath the water. All sorts of life and I've even seen so many different colors. Wearing goggles you can see bottom in 50 feet of water. We did get about three dozen fish and had a lot of fun.

Looks like I might be going back to Australia for a week pretty soon. Someone has to attend a C.W.S. there. I'll probably be elected. It will only be for a week or so —guess I can stand it.

The war in Europe appears to be going good. Shouldn't last too long at the rate the Allies are going. I think it's going to be a long haul out here though. Most everybody is optimistic with their predictions though. That helps too!

Reckon I'd better shove-off.

Love,
Howard

P.S. Thanks for the tip on Capt. Venis. I've written to him. H.

New Guinea

August 25, 1944

Darling Legna,

I'm almost happy again. Been busy for the past few days. A little work sure helps out. I really feel like a new man. This work should last a little while, but it won't be long, I know.

Just got your letter of August 9, the pictures were pretty good. Nice looking boat you were sitting on! Why don't you just get a G.I. haircut instead of piling all that fuzz on top of your head? Would be comfortable to "say the least". I like it like that though, Legna —kind of makes you look like a "siren". I shouldn't be talking about one's head. I haven't had over an inch of hair on my head for a long time. It is the correct fashion for N.G. at that. Just about the only way you can keep your head clean and it's so cool.

I can't understand how you got the water color before the pictures. They were mailed at the same time. Sure hope my wrapping didn't come loose. Can't say I'm so good at that particular chore. Guess I could do a pretty good job on a nice little package like you though. (How about that?)

Still don't know anything definite on my proposed trip to the mainland. Everybody but the right people say I'm going. These everybodies seem to know more about the set-up than I do. But that's the way of the army.

The Galesville Home News has certainly been coming in regularly, even better than air-mail. Not a bad paper, except for the accounting of so and so was home for the week-end from Camp…… Doesn't bother me much though. At present I'd rather be where I am.

Legna, I've got to rush-off now. Someone is paging me. Will write at next opportunity. Might be awhile. Keep my love locked up tight Honey. It's worth it!

Love,

Howard

S.W.P.A.
(South West Pacific Area)

Praise the Lord, and Pass the Ammunition

Written by Frank Loesser

1942

By Famous Music Corp

S.W.P. Area

August 31, 1944

Dearest Darling,

Been a little while since I've written, but you should have expected it. I mentioned in my last letter that I would write at the first opportunity. This is it, Honey!

As you notice I have a new APO#. Yes, we've moved, but I can't tell you a thing about it. Glad to say though, we are busy again and it sure helps a fellow along. We go for months doing nothing then WHAM, you don't even get a chance to sleep for a couple of days. The men like it, too. We've been together so long, we work like a clock. Our men can really put-out when there's a job to be done. You get tired but there is so much excitement and things to do, you don't even think about being tired. Anyway, I'm happy as a lark and I'm serious.

Don't know whether or not this move will affect my prospective trip to the mainland. Can't say that I care much one way or the other. I'm still paying for the last trip. (Financially)

Legna, I hope you got those pictures, because if you haven't, they are possibly lost and there isn't a darn thing you or I can do about it.

I've been eating some good food lately and believe me that is enough to make a man happy. Feel like I've gained a few lbs, needed a little bit of weight. I was falling off a bit.

We haven't had any mail for some time but it should catch up with us in a few days. Bennert got a box of fruit cake, but it came while he was on leave. Poor fellow, I doubt if he gets a crumb, however he brought it on himself. Told us to go right ahead. I never cared much for the stuff before but it tasted pretty good.

Sure wish I could put a "little mushie" note in this letter. I feel that way tonight but can't put it in writing. Kind of wish you were around. I know loving you makes me happy, too.

All my love,
Howard

New APO # 704

S.W.P.A.

September 1, 1944

Dearest Legna,

What a wonderful day! Some of our pilots paid us a visit today. They brought lots of mail. I had four of the "bestest letters" from you. They were written quite recently, too. Really wonderful, Honey. My day was perfect —the letters "highlighting", of course.

Glad to hear you got the pictures. I was beginning to get worried. The one with my hat off was strictly my idea. The short haircut making me all the more determined. The photographer didn't want to take it that way, but I insisted. My hairline is receding a bit but it was cut awfully short. (It was the "rage" of Sydney.) I wear the stuff short but just before my leave I went beyond the usual, simply because I didn't expect to get a leave for some time. Higher HQs changed the set-up so often a fellow didn't know just what to do. (The same applies to my expectant trip south at this present.)

About the Christmas problem. I'll take care of Miss Grace. But how about you? I want you to take a $100.00 and get yourself a present. If you don't like to draw it from the bank, I'll send you a $100 money order and you can take it from there. As for me, "from you to me", I mean, see if you can't get some canned shrimp, crab-meat, seedless olives, maybe some oysters, too. The boys would like those. Anything like that will do the trick. That's about all I can think of that would do me any good. One other thing, forget about that wallet, It was a lot of fun. Remarks are still passed around about it and I like it. (I get my share of ribbing and we really dish it out.)

Put in a good day. Things are taking shape. Guess I really needed a good work-out.

How about the summer-school business? Maybe I'll be able to enroll with you. Remote possibility, but a pleasant thought.

Thanks for the letters, Honey and I don't think our times together did us any harm. Horrible writing isn't it? Guess my knee isn't much of a table.

Love,

Howard

S.W.P.A.

~~August~~ September 3, 1944

Darling Legna,

Didn't get a chance to write to you last night. The C.O. flew in for a surprise visit and we had quite a few details to take care of. Guess he wanted to check and see how we were making out. The work is still going strong, but it's worth the work. We have a very nice camp in progress. It will be a honey when we finish.

Fischer and I put the final touches on our home today. Wish you could see it. Little knick-knacks here and there. Already electric lights have been installed. Expect running water any day now. The floor is clean white coral sand. It means a very neat tent. Bennert and Wood being on leave left Bert and I all the work to do, but our efforts have make a pretty good showing.

This is really the tropics. It rains every day, sometimes twice. Things are a bit damp but not too bad. Our food is very good, almost like in the states. If we eat like this all the time, I should put on some weight —my frame can stand it. It's just a bit too hot for hard work but right now, the working day is short. Doesn't pay to work under forced draft in this climate.

Got two letters from you yesterday. You mentioned the pictures again. Glad you like them. I thought the one without a hat was the best, even though it was taken thru a bit of fun. Bob had some taken while on leave but there was a mix-up somewhere. He hasn't received them.

I understand there are some beautiful shells hereabouts. When I have time I'm going to try and round-up a few, maybe I'll be allowed to send them home. Possibly it's just a rumor but I'll look into the matter.

Hope you got my present straight in my last letter. That's the only thing I can think of which could "give the mostest". How about that "correspondence love-affair" involving Goose H? Things like that amaze me. Seems like the most unnatural thing a person could do. Think I remember his brother Freddie doing something of the sort a long time ago. The old man's laugh would make an asylum out of any sane dwelling; maybe the gals get scared.

Looks like my war bond really has lost its momentum. I'll speed it up again. About next month I guess.

The outfit got its beer ration again today. Sure is fine nectar. Gives a fellow quite a pleasure to sit back and sip (you'd probably call is swilling) the ole brew.

Honey, I've run out, nothing more to say except "I love you" and that's the most serious saying I ever speak!

Love,

Howard

S.W.P.A.

September 7, 1944

Darling Legna,

All of the outfit is together again. The occasion was like a family reunion. Everybody is busy putting the finishing touches on their shacks. Of course, mine is all set. Fischer put in the radio today and that completed our house. Guess though we'll have a phone in before long.

It really gets hot here and we have lots of rain. The air gets very cool when it rains, making a raincoat quite comfortable. Much damper here than it was at the last base. Your clothes are almost wet in the morning.

Bennert & Wood are still on leave. They sure went at a good time. Missed all the fun though, even a little work. There won't be any cake left for Bennert if he doesn't get back soon.

We've been listening to the demobilization plan. Sounds alright — makes the close of the war seem very near. Somehow or another we can't see it so near. I say a year or eighteen months yet. The Japs are persistent sun fishes. Haven't heard anything about officers. Guess we'll get out, some of us before we realize it.

Hope there's mail tomorrow. Could do with a letter from you. The mail should be catching up with us any day now. With our pilots running back and forth we've kept up with the mail from our last base.

My transportation section is set up and operating. Vehicles can to go pieces in less than a week. The road conditions are rough and the mud & dust play havoc. Everyone but me thinks a Jeep is a marvelous vehicle; I hate the darn things. They aren't worth a darn in this country. Takes a lot of maintenance to keep them going.

The pictures were taken at the last base.

I've been thinking of you in the ole school room again. I'm still willing to be taught!

All my love,
Howard

S.W.P.A.
September 11, 1944

Darling Legna,

Everything is just about set now. Won't be long before we are in the ole-slot again. Well, it was fun for a while anyway. A fellow can't stand much hard work in this climate though; it shows on a man. There will be a convalescent period —probably last a month or so. I'd like to spend that time in Brisbane but don't think I'll make it.

Got three letters from you today, written around 24 August. Pretty good service. Our mail should be coming thru regularly now. Bob got some mail too. You'd better write and tell Gloria. You made a mistake in reading my letter about him being back from leave. Damn women are something, aren't they? No wonder I didn't get married. Can't understand the creatures most of the time. I'm kidding Legna, but I do believe some of that is true.

Gosh, I'm glad to hear Bob is home again. Is he on leave or discharged from the service? He's probably seen quite a bit of action. All the Navy in this theatre have —those boys have done a darn good job. Their living facilities are certainly better than ours though. They have good food and a dry, clean place to sleep. I had ice cream in the middle of the ocean out here, on a Navy boat. In fact, we had apple pie "a la mode". Can't beat that anywhere! Sorry to hear Bob had been drinking. You know Honey, you are prejudiced about this drinking business. I would like to see you looped just "one time". What a sight that would be. A few drinks or a couple of beers doesn't hurt anyone. Some people can make a nuisance of drinking though, I'll have to admit. But when they do that, I lose all patience and walk away.

Our pilots are really getting a work-out and they seem to like it. Plenty of flying, that's what they like. Sure weren't doing much at our last station.

Guess I'd better rush-off now. How about forgetting the Dearest Legna? Darling is good enough for me.

All my love,
Howard

418

S.W.P.A.

September 14, 1944

Darling Legna,

It's raining something furious this morning, so operations have been discontinued till the let-up. Looks like the closer you get to the equator the more rain you get. There isn't too much to do anyway. I had an appointment with the dentist this morning but he doesn't have his drill press set-up yet. Teeth taking a beating over here. Must be the diet. Haven't lost any yet though, thank goodness.

We sent a plane to our last base yesterday. Should come in today with some mail. The outfit managed to get a C-47 for a while. They sent it to Australia last week. It came back loaded with eggs, fresh fruit and vegetables. The lettuce and tomatoes were really good.

I have my departments all set for operations now and we are getting good missions. Mostly bombing, but the pilots like it. My boys like it too, keeps them busy.

The war news certainly sounds great. We get the latest from other fronts. Lucky we have the facilities —lots of outfits don't.

We have a very nice open air theatre now. The Special Service officer got some natives to erect the stage and projector room. The natives up here are quite different from the Southern boys —cleaner, healthy and intelligent. They even wear clothes. The movies aren't too new though. We saw most of them down south.

Say Legna, I wasn't peeved at you in my letter. Can't recall having been since "that one", maybe you misinterpreted the letters. Bob says Gloria got on him about the leave so you'd better get it straightened out.

Guess the best thing is don't tell her anything I say about Bob. These young married gals have quite an imagination and never fail to exercise it.

How about this drinking proposition Honey? Aren't you going to keep a half a dozen "lagers" on ice for me? Will be a disappointment if you don't. There isn't anything wrong with a fellow drinking or drink. I know you've been taught different, but try a bottle of good "ole Budweiser" when you are hot and thirsty. (I could drink a thousand!)

I've been dreaming of you. Last dream I had we were off in a boat somewhere. Seems to me there was romance involved too. That's natural, I presume. Your picture is mounted on a shelf over my bed now. Don't think you'd better send anymore big ones. The climate tears them to pieces, especially if they get wet. So far, I've managed to keep these dry.

Legna, don't have any qualms about my using "Dearest Legna" in my letters. I couldn't love you more or less than I do, no matter what was used.

So long for now, Honey,

Love, Howard

S.W.P.A.

September 17, 1944

Dearest Darling,

Today is Sunday and for some unknown reason you can always tell when that day comes around. There's a let-up on the work, far as the ground personnel are concerned. Of course, the pilots fly their usual missions. But everything is quiet and you see the boys gathering to go to chapel. Kind of ashamed about this guy Shenton. He hasn't been to church since Easter. I like Sundays. We have a pretty good meal. The only thing we need is a feeble-minded section of the newspaper and we would be all set.

Haven't had any mail for a week now. Should have some tomorrow. Jander the Operations officer, flew a P-70 down to our last Base. He should be back tomorrow with lots of mail. We have received word that there's plenty of the stuff piling up for us. I could stand about an even dozen from you right now. Everyone but you must have forgotten me. I get very few letters from my old friends. Doesn't bother me though — just so I hear from you. The fewer letters I get from other people, the fewer letters I have to have to write and I like that. Say, how about sending "Galesville News" my latest address/ They are still using APO 503 Unit #1.

Just finished a pretty good book entitled "Crescent Carnival", all about the loves and lives of the Creoles in New Orleans. After reading it, I'm convinced they played a big part in building and regulating the so called "Society". They sure had traditions even more than the army, and what a gay, playful life they lived. A bit too confined and restricted far as the women were concerned, but the men certainly knew no bounds.

The Yanks are certainly carrying the war to the Japs now. Honey, it's wonderful, the strategy used in war. The taking of this and that island, cutting the Japs off from their supplies and the coordination of all the Forces, air, sea and land, when a landing is in progress. Everything is timed right to the minute and it sure pays dividends. I'd like to view a landing from the air. Must be a wonderful sight. Yes, we are doing alright now. (Sure are a lot of Japs starving in this part of the world.) There are a lot of interesting things I'd like to tell you about our present base but censorship forbids. You will probably hear about it all though when I come home. We have the most beautiful sunsets here. I've never seen anything that would compare with them. The nights are pretty too, a star-filled sky with a deep blue background. Cones of light reflecting on this, guiding some plane in for a safe landing. Then everything dark and silent when we are alerted for an air-raid. (So far no planes have come, but we've been alerted several times.) Coral makes hard-digging for a foxhole. I feel pretty confident we won't have any raids now. Our planes keep the Japs out of the sky.

I don't envy you being cooped-up in that school room —don't think I could stand it, not in this climate anyway. Guess I'll never enjoy working indoors again —the army has spoiled me. (In more ways than one, probably.) Don't think it will affect us though, we just won't let it, regardless. I'll be glad to get out when the war is over, gets a bit tiresome at times. Wish I could come back and see "old Totch", he was quite a guy. Shady Side won't be the same for me without him. Guess he was the best pal I ever had. You realize those things more than ever when you are off on your own for a long time. Sort of like you and I only "ours" is much deeper and has a different meaning. Surprising how my love for you has helped me when the going got tough. I'd better get going before this philosophy throws me.

All my love,

Howard

S.W.P.A.

September 22, 1944

Hello Honey,

Considering the mail situation, I'm doing pretty good, writing you every other day or so. Doesn't seem like the Post-Office has been notified of our new APO. All the mail we get comes from our last base, if and when we can send one of our ships after it. The pilots are very busy flying combat so we can't send for the mail often. The C.O. flew a transport down today. We should have some mail tomorrow.

Sure wish I could have gone with the Major on this trip with the transport but he couldn't take me. Promised me a trip at a later date though. I'll have plenty of time then; work is hitting the routine stride again. (As usual we are ready to move again —sure don't like staying in one place very long.)

Talked with a Capt. this morning. He's been in the S.W.P. for 31 months. He had an opportunity to go home and refused. Can you beat that? He had several silly reasons, but no real ones. I think he's crazy! (Must be sweating out a Majority.) Hope I never have to see 31 months here, but by that time I'd be more than ready to see the States.

It's raining blue blazes again, but the planes still fly. Takes nasty weather to keep our boys on the ground. Sometimes I wish I were a pilot. They have all the excitement in an Air Corps outfit. We are getting in a few new pilots, fresh from the States. Getting younger all the time —some of them look and act like high school kids.

I don't think I'll be able to get any sea-shells for you. I understand they are underwater on the coral reefs. You have to dive for them and the sharks don't like such goings-on.

Hope to get some mail soon.

Love,
Howard

S.W.P.A.
September 19, 1944

Dear Legna Darling,

The Operations Officer came back yesterday in the P-70 and he brought lots of mail. I had two letters from you, 29th and 30th. Sure was glad he went on that trip. We hadn't had mail for over a week. Shouldn't be long before our letters with the new APO catches us. It usually takes three weeks.

The weather is bad this morning, raining like the dickens. Surprising how cold it is here during the rain, just like a rainy April day at home. You could even wear a jacket and be comfortable. Seems so strange when the temperature hits 130° on a sunny day. The humidity is high, too.

Legna, I know I don't elaborate in my letters. Seems to me a letter should be written without elaboration. Sounds too much like a descriptive narrative then. I like them brief and to the point. The Army's correspondence is that way; guess it's getting to be a habit with me. I write very few letters.

So Mervin Hardesty has a medical discharge. Mervin and I came in the army together and separated about two weeks after. Last I heard he was an instructor at Army Air Force O.C.S. in Miami. Guess he never got overseas. Those teaching jobs are rough in the army. Sure glad I was never ordered to one. He should have three years and that is enough for anyone, considering we came in for just one year. I still don't want out though until it's all over —no doubt but what "I will have my way."

Now to tell you about those two pictures I didn't elaborate on. "Christmas Holiday" was terribly miscast. Deanna Durbin looks and can act like a "tart" about as much as one of the native boys here could act like a New York broker, in New York. Gene Kelly is a wonderful dancer but he carries his lines like an overloaded truck on a muddy road.

Then we have "Gaslight". I liked it simply from the psychology study view point. It caused quite an argument. Fischer, Bennert and Ochs claim to be masters of the study. I claim to be nothing. (No claim there.) I said the picture was pure fiction and that any average or normal person would not become a slave of such diabolic and crazy psychology. They said, yes, a person would and could be susceptible to such a deranging of the mind. We even had the pillrollers in on it. So then, I popped up and asked which scene was the climax of the show. They all had different answers. Mine was different, too. They finally agreed I was right. (1 point) About the only thing they did agree with me on was one of the masters even had in mind to experiment on me. Of course he said it with that fine air of supremacy that a lot of <u>teachers have</u>. He was told to go ahead. So far he's had no success. These guys probably studied Freud and a few others, but I think the sexual angle interested them the most. T'was a lot of fun anyway. I just wanted to argue. I hardly know the meaning of the word "psychology". Know "common sense" though.

How about this "forgetting". What made you ask that? No Honey, I'm not forgetting you. Afraid it's quite the other way around. I think of you constantly, more as time goes by. You know though, we are going to find a few changes in each other. Haven't seen you for over a year now and it will be at least two maybe three by the time we get together. That's a long time, Honey. We are bound to change in that length of time. I'm speaking of small changes —things like figure [manner] of speech, habits, likes and dislikes. I'm confident it won't make any difference. We can take a short orientation course. That should put us straight. But I'm not forgetting you Legna. You are the only love I have in this world. (All definitions of that word, too.)

Guess elaboration better shove-off.

All my love,
Howard

S.W.P.A.

September 26, 1944

Legna Darling,

Six days past and you didn't write me. My, my, seems you could have done better than that. "Retribution", that's what is. I don't mind though, if you don't write I know there is a reason. Had a letter from Miss Ethel yesterday, otherwise all my mail has been from you. I never hear from the Hartge family anymore. Guess Miss Grace has deserted me. Having been deserted before, I don't mind this one. Maybe though she is using regular mail.

Life is about the same with us here as it was before. The pilots are getting lots more flying though. We see a movie three times a week. That covers the entertainment. I might take a trip tomorrow on our transport. One of the pilots wants me to check-out in it. Frankly, I couldn't fly a kite. The trip will be a diversion and maybe I can pick-up some supplies & equipment.

Wood & Bennert finally got back from leave. Both shadows of their former self. Guess they worked too hard at playing. The furious pace set by Australia is hard to keep up with. They were bringing back food and liquors but someone broke into their bags at Moresby and took everything. They evidently had a good time. Took them 40 days to make the trip.

Understand from all the reports that the Home Front isn't what it's cracked-up to be. Returning soldiers from overseas are a bit disappointed, mostly with their women. Too bad, the boys should have something nice to come home to. Seems to us though, most of the fellows want to get back in the fight. I think a lot of this was caused by hasty marriages and "good times" as people call it. People aren't happy nowadays unless they are always doing something wild. After what I saw in Sydney, I'm convinced most people don't know how to have a good time. A good time to them is comprised of drinking and sex, and the emphasis is on the latter. All of this looks and seems wonderful for a few days, especially after having been in some remote spot for few months. But after a few days it becomes nauseating and you feel like running away from it all. Well, the adjustments will be made I suppose, but some people are sure going to suffer from them.

Still raining out here. This must be the monsoon period. Been raining now for five days, always in the day time, too. Our camp is complete now. We have a swimming pool right in the middle of it. You can stand outside the tent and take a shower anytime.

Honey, I'd better go now. Would like to say more about the readjustment of peoples' lives (post-war) but we'll talk about it when we get together.

Love, Howard

S.W.P.A.

September 29, 1944

Darling Legna,

Had two nice letters from you yesterday. The mail set-up is certainly no good at this place. I wrote your Mom the other day —did pretty good on that one. Wrote it about two days after having received her letter. There sure isn't much a fellow can write about, I'm getting to hate letter writing.

So Mr. Bischoff thinks he remembers me from my high school days. I doubt very much that he does. Any memories he has of me must certainly be unpleasant. We were hardly anything but that in those days. (Would like to do it over though.) I still don't recollect us being "so fresh" in my freshman years. (Exaggerated)

Saw the picture "Jane Eyre" last night. Wasn't so good. I'm glad now I didn't attempt to read the book. We are getting fairly new shows here these days. Seems like they are all pretty much the same (Flag wavers).

The picture of you and Miss Ethel taken on the street in Baltimore was pretty. As usual you had that "yap" of yours open. Wonder whom you were frying then. You looked kind of sharp though. I see you are still wearing hats camouflaged on the back of your head.

Legna, I'd be glad to write Howard Hartge but I don't know his address. Last time I saw him he was living somewhere on South River. Send me his address and I'll drop him a line. You know, Miss Grace can say I put it on thick when she doesn't write but I haven't heard from her for at least two months. Maybe she doesn't love me anymore!

Wood & Bennert brought back lots of candy and other food. We have a party about every night. They also brought back some beer but that didn't get this far north. They were hijacked enroute. Too bad, we would rather have had the beer than anything.

We are still having lots of rain. Clothes won't dry and cigarettes are so damp you can't keep them burning. Roads are getting in bad shape. The vehicles are taking a terrific beating. The wet season shouldn't last much longer. This is supposed to be the monsoon period.

The natives here are quite intelligent. They speak fairly good English. They tell us all about the bombing raids the Americans put on when this territory was held by the Japs. They have a hatred for the Japs unequaled by white men. Guess the yellows treated them rough, worked them and gave them little food and no pay.

I'd like to talk about you and me this evening. But I can't put anything definite. We'll have plenty of time for discussions in person. That's better anyway.

Guess I've run-out.

All my love,
Howard

429

S.W.P.A.

October 3, 1944

Dearest Legna,

Got a couple of letters today, fairly recent at that, September 19 & 21st. Not bad considering it went to our last base. One of the pilots brought it up from there. We still haven't received mail at our present base, though the mail is addressed to our present base.

There isn't much to write about, we haven't done much work for the past few days. At least it has stopped raining and that's something. We're having high winds and it really blows at times. Almost took away our mess-hall yesterday. If the rations don't get any better, the place might just as well blow away.

Fischer isn't with us anymore. He was transferred to a Fighter Control Squadron. He wanted the job and has been trying to get it for some time. It's a job calling for more rank and that's what he wanted. If I know Berte he'll get it, too. Too bad we lost him. He's a good man — knows how to get a job done. He fumed and sweated for the transfer and when it came through he felt like he didn't want to go. Guess he hated to leave the outfit. He and I were the oldest officers of the squadron, almost two years together, so now I've been in the outfit longer than any of the officers, including pilots. The only way I could be promoted would be by transferring to another outfit with a higher T.O. (Table of Organization.). I would kind of hate to leave this crew, but there isn't much chance of that happening. I'll be in this outfit when the war is over.

The beer ration went the way of all Japs —it just died! We only got twelve bottles last month and doubt very much we get any this one.

Transportation is quite a problem here. The lines are getting longer and right now they are plenty long. Guess we can do without the "ole slops" though. Sure helped our morale when we were getting it.

So Bobby Wilde has gone back. Wonder how he felt? I guess he didn't care too much about going. I'd sure hate to get a leave to U.S. then have to come back to this. Would much rather stay here until it's over and then go home for "keeps".

Legna, what's all this chatter about "you wanting children of your own"? What's the matter Honey? Are you fed-up with teaching already? The year has just started. Were you in New Guinea people would call that "hardships". You have my sympathy. I don't envy any teacher that has 30 or 40 kids to put up with. It's bad enough to instruct and teach grown men. You wanting children of your own sounds like a pretty good idea, but don't do anything rash until you see me!

Someone is blasting a hole near our tent. Every blast brings a rain of coral on the ole shack. I'd better discontinue operations for a while.

Love,
Howard

S.W.P.A.

October 6, 1944

Darling Legna,

Just got your letter saying you and Miss Grace had a long chat. Honestly, I don't think I've had a letter from her for three months. Glad to hear she's alive and still in Shady Side. Don't say anything to her about not writing, she might cry! Guess I'm not popular anymore.

Word came this morning that I'm to attend a C.W.S., the one I was talking about some time ago. At the time it was in Australia, hence I would get to go to the mainland. But they put one over on me, the school has moved to New Guinea so now I don't want to go. However, I don't have much to say "in the matter". It will do me good though to get away from the outfit for a short while. I'm going to look-up Carroll Smith. Understand he is stationed down there. That would be nice. I haven't run into anyone from home yet.

Legna, don't you send me any tuna fish in that food package. I'd never forgive you for that. Tuna and salmon I can't eat. We used to get it every other day. Sardines are O.K. but I was thinking of shrimp and crabmeat —stuff like that.

Enclosed you will find a hundred bucks. That's your Christmas present if you don't want to draw the money from the bank. I'll take care of Miss Grace's present, even though she never writes. Couldn't get a money order.

Honey, you won't see me by the end of next summer. Of that, I'm pretty sure. I'll be here until it's over and then some. It would be swell to get home but I feel somehow I wouldn't be quite contented to leave here before the war is over. We read and hear a lot about fellows that have gone home. They don't seem to be too happy about the situation and want to get back in the fight. (Maybe yes and maybe no, with me). Could tell more definite after being home for a while.
Goodbye Honey.

All my love,
Howard

S.W.P.A.

October 9, 1944

Darling Legna,

I'm slipping. Haven't written for three days. The incoming mail is still just about nil. (No incoming; no outgoing.)

One of my boys had an accident this morning. He was hurt pretty bad. It happened while operating the bomb hoist on our bomb truck. I feel pretty bad about it. I hate to see anyone get hurt accidentally. The poor kid's jaw was broken in three places and will be a long time knitting. Good man too. One of the best in my section. Guess we have to expect those things.

We finished putting up a volley-ball court yesterday. Today we tried it for size by whipping the officers from another squadron. Little too hot here for a good fast game, but it's a lot of fun.

Thanks for sending the package. The food will sure come in good. Gee, but I'd like to have a steak covered with eggs about now. We did have fresh meat last night for a change. About the only fresh foods we get are meat & eggs, very little of either. Some of the American canned meats are pretty good, but the Aussie stuff is no damn good at all. I wish all our rations were American.

We are having a dry spell, hasn't rained for three days. The roads are so dusty you almost have to wear a respirator. The laundry system is much better. Before you couldn't get clothes dry no matter what was tried.

Honey, I'm impatient for the things we use to do, too. Another year should take care of that though. The next one will be the longest, I guess.

Seems like the first six months went by fast but the last slowed up a bit. Maybe my next leave will speed the time along. Should be getting it around Christmas. I spent the last one on the Coral Sea. Hope the one of '45 finds me home. Yes, Legna, I miss you more than I can say or put in writing. (Guess it's hard, but fair!) We will make up for it, of that I'm certain!

All my love,

Howard

Back to School Again
New Guinea

Two things greater than all things are
The first is Love, and the second War,
And since we know not how War may prove,
Heart of my heart, let us talk of Love!
—Rudyard Kipling
"The Ballad of the King's Jest"

S.W.P.A.

October 13, 1944

Dearest Legna Darling,

I'm off to school again; how about that, teacher? Having a little trouble with transportation but I'll get there. (Maybe a little late though.) Too bad I'm not going all the way to the mainland. I'll probably learn just as much up here. Course parts of N.G. are civilized these days. The Wacs have landed if that means anything! Have to stop for a while now.

October 15, 1944

Quite a stop, wasn't it?

I have arrived and what a place. I was stationed here about ten months ago. It's altogether different, hardly any activity. Sort of like a camp in the woods back home. Guess I'll be around for a couple of weeks. School doesn't start for a few days yet.

Spent half a day yesterday looking for Carroll Smith. He has evidently moved out. Couldn't find a trace of him. Too bad, I was looking forward to meeting someone from home. The Galesville News gave his address as APO 503, that's what I was going by, but it was about two months ago that I read it. You can cover a lot of ground in two months over here. Well, maybe I'll catch him some other time.

I've been staying in a transient camp waiting for school to start. There are lots of men here waiting to go home. (Been over for thirty months or more.) When I moved in they asked me if I was going home. Guess I have quite a tropical sun-tan! In a way I envy these boys, but I'm

436

not sure I want to join them. None of them seem very enthusiastic about it. You have to leave the old outfit. I hope the 311ᵗʰ goes back intact.

Then we also have in camp fellows that just came over. They've been here for a week or so waiting assignments. Course, they are getting their fill of wild stories from the old timers. You can spot a newcomer right away by the look on their face (which is one of do or die for the ole college) and their general appearance. This tropic climate does things to men's skins and manners. (Blame it on the climate.) Most of the men coming over now are young and quite new to the army. They will lose that eager look and calm down after a few months up-north. Not that things are exceptionally rough up-north but a lot of fellows come in with the idea of coming in bodily contact with the Jap and pinning him to the mat right there, so ending the war. I used to entertain some such thoughts but found it wasn't much different from working back home in the army. The usual routine with food not so good at times and a bombing raid once in a while at night. (Oh, foxhole, l love thee!)

Legna, I sent you $100.00 in cash money, USA from APO 704. Let me know if and when you get it. I tried for two weeks to get a money order but couldn't. So I sent it with a letter. Maybe I was foolish but I think you will get it alright. There isn't anything I can do if you don't get the money but maybe I can send you some more. I want you to have this for a Christmas present. Sure wish I could have gotten a money order though.

So you are making "fresh remarks" about my taking a picture without wearing a shirt. I was on my way from the dispensary when the picture was taken. Had been taking treatment for the Guinea krud beneath me arms. I admit there isn't much there for show, but we can't

437

all be "muscles". Don't be surprised if I make a few fresh remarks about you some day. I haven't forgotten "Hector & Oscar". Seen lots of those on the natives but I only love yours, Honey. (How about that; fresh!) Did you ever hear or read these lines?

Then, come kiss me, sweet and twenty
"Youth's a stuff, will not endure."
So gather your rosebuds, while ye may
And while you may, go marry.
For having lost but once your prime.
Ye may forever tarry.

Naughty poems, aren't they? (You'd say nasty!) I know quite a few like that.

Legna, I'm going to enjoy the food you are sending. The sardines will be alright. They go good with beer. I think the seafood is fairly expensive, pay for it with my money. I don't care what it cost just so I get the goods.

Today is Sunday and for some unknown reason I want to go to church. Don't go very often but today I'd like it. Have to see if I can't find one around here. Like to pick you up and have you go with me. Maybe I can find a Wac. Might be pretty hard though —the Wacs are kept under constant guard, almost like prisoners.

Honey, I'd better stop this letter. It's kind of long for me. Don't know if I'll get a chance to write at the school. Understand they have a tough schedule.

Oh! I haven't forgotten you at all Honey! In fact, I remember you quite well. The re-acquaintance period for us shouldn't be difficult. (I make friends pretty easy, read a book once on How to Influence People, too. Now I'm getting smart!)

I'll write if I have an opportunity.

All my love, Angel!

Howard

New Guinea
October 17, 1944

Dearest Legna Darling,

School is about to begin, starts tomorrow. It is located about five miles from any camp at the Base. It's situated up in the foot-hills, elevation about 1,000 ft. We have a beautiful view, can see for miles around. Also have a nice view of the harbor and ocean. The mosquitoes are bad at night, worse than any place I've been yet but it's cool during the day and at night, that's what really counts.

Yes, tis a swell camp. We have cots with springs & mattresses, certainly a luxury for N.G. There is also an officer's mess and the food is prepared fairly well. I think I'm going to like it here. Won't be able to leave the camp because of transportation but there's no place to go. There is a movie here three nights a week, so we have nothing but school and entertainment, which isn't a bad set-up. The school lasts for ten days. Sure hope I don't have to wait for transportation back north. The transient camps aren't so nice. Then again, I want to stop on the way back and see if I can't pick up some supplies.

Some of the fellows have been trying to make contact with the Wacs. Don't think they will do any good. The deadlier sex are almost prisoners and can't get around much. I get sore every time I think of Wacs over here. It's bad enough that nurses have to put up with this climate. There is no job for the Wacs —we have enough limited service men to do any work the Wacs might do. If they wanted to send them overseas, why not wait until we hit civilization, the Philippines for example. Legna, don't you ever even contemplate joining any of the services. I couldn't quite go with that.

Haven't heard the news lately. Mighty curious about the war in Europe. Hope it ends before Christmas. It will certainly be a great encouragement to us when it's over. Although we are doing alright too, I give it another year here. That should do it. We traveled a long way in the year I've been here, but it's still a long road.

Honey, I've about run out again. Wish I could write about Love, our love, but can't find words fine enough. Anyway, I'd rather whisper sweet-nothings in your ear. I'm still a-loving you!

Love,

Howard

New Guinea
October 20, 1944

Dear Darling Legna,

Still can't find anything to write about. Guess life is just a bit uninteresting for a soldier. Even going to school is getting a bit boring. Was alright for a few days but it's all old stuff. I've had it many times before, hope I never have to put in practice though, what I've learned. Convinced now that this course would be more interesting were it pursued on the mainland. I've only been away from the outfit about a week and it seems like a month. Expect to be here another week anyway. Will probably get another diploma for proficiency and no doubt diligence. Can't see how that latter could come about. (We are slow-motioning thru this one.) Sometimes I wish I were a little more diligent in one phase of my life that has nothing to do with this course, so I shouldn't even be mentioning it in this paragraph.

In that last sentence I was referring to you (Us!). When I get to thinking about us, damn it all, Legna, I think I was a complete ass. We had everything any two could ask for or would want. By that I mean you. You are everything I want. 'Course there are other wants but they are definitely secondary. That I have learned this past year. (Looks like this school has brought the word "learned" to the head of my vocabulary. The school has nothing to do with us!) We should have married, Legna, you were right. I'm sure now that it would have been the thing to do. (The 10,000 miles doesn't have anything to do with this. Remember you once mentioned my bravery when we were miles apart?) I just feel it down in my heart. But why didn't I? That's the real question. Not sure I can answer it. Perhaps it was because of my early life, the way I grew up. I always got along, but never asserted myself. Really though I wasn't in a position to assert myself or anything. Had a few disappointments and as they came, accepted them and let it go at that. I fought at first but that didn't help. I was licked almost before I started. I wonder about that though! Your Dad was right about me. He said I was a "bit reticent" and I think he was hitting the nail on the head. He doesn't know, probably, that I know he said that. When I heard it, the meaning didn't sink in, just bounded off that invisible suit of armor I used to wear. It was like that

441

when I knew I loved you. Maybe I said I did once or twice, and maybe conveyed it as much with a look or action but I really didn't commit myself and I know it. It wasn't because I wasn't sure. I knew you were the only gal I ever loved and was certain the feeling was mutual. That should have been enough to set me straight, so I blame it on the "reticence" of one Lt. Shenton! (I repeat, what an ass!) On the occasion when presented, I'll follow thru. So there you are Honey, we'll get right into the "Caper"!

I'll send this with a verse from one of Kipling's ballads:

Quote: *Two things greater than all things are*

The first is Love, and the second War,

And since we know not how War may prove,

Heart of my heart, let us talk of Love. Unquote!

All my love,

Howard

P.S. Quite a missile, eh? But I'm sincere. OX

New Guinea
October 22, 1944

Darling Legna,

Another Sunday has come to New Guinea and here it is a day of rest. No school today. Everybody is taking it easy, reading, writing letters and sleeping. I've been doing a lot of the latter, go to bed around 8:30 and get up at six. Still I feel tired and lazy. Won't be worth a damn by the time I leave this island. It's a nice day here, cloudy with a fairly strong breeze. Certainly a lot cooler here than up-north.

Wish I could get some mail. Mail-call makes a day complete. I'll have a stack waiting for me when I get back, I hope. Haven't been getting much mail the past few months. Guess my friends ran out of stationery. Doesn't matter much, just so I keep getting your letters. They are the ones that count, "mathematically and otherwise".

I'm not learning too much at this school. Sort of repetition of what I've learned in the past. Quite a few of the instructors here were school teachers in civilian life. They do a good job but the subject is sure a dry one. We have quite a few good arguments whenever a point is brought up; the instructor says it should be this way. Well, the boys who have been in the field know that "this-way" is the way it's done. Because out there you never have an ideal situation, so it doesn't work. But the instructors can't understand that, unless, of course, they've been there. Frankly, instructing in the army is a job I would not want. There are a few hard and fast rules in the combat zone.

I'm a little homesick for the outfit. Will be glad to get back. Kind of like being away from the family when you're a kid. Miss the sound of airplane engines and the bustle when the boys are going out on a mission. Guess they were kind of glad to get rid of me for a while. At least there will be peace and quiet in the officers' area, while I'm away.

Get homesick for home occasionally, right now for instance. I could be up at Woody's having a few beers and shooting some pool. Then dash out and see you this afternoon, play tennis or something. Those are the things I'm homesick for (Mostly you!). I still remember the night Miss Aggie hit the old Ford with her brand new Buick. Sure had a lot of excitement that summer.

Honey, I'd better get ready for dinner.

All my love,
Howard

443

New Guinea

October 24, 1944

Dearest Darling Legna,

Just got rained-out of a movie. Every night we have a show it rains. We've seen all the shows here, guess they hit the north first. But we go anyway; there isn't anything else to do. Tonight was a pretty good show. I could have enjoyed seeing it again. We might see it yet, if it stops raining within the next hour.

Gosh, but I've been getting plenty of sleep at this school. Go to bed every night around 8:30 and manage to get in an hour at lunch time. The fellows in my shack get worried when they see me walking around. They insist that I'd better lie down and rest. Usually though, I don't give them the chance to get perturbed as I'm right in the ole-sack.

All of us are getting a little fed-up with the course. Repetition is getting the better of me. Not a bad life though, certainly an easy one. Get our first exam tomorrow. If you don't pass, they send you home. (Just like a private school.) I'm not worried; I've had most of this stuff many times before. I deserve this though. The C.O. and I thought the school was in Australia and he was giving me a break. Hereafter, I don't want any breaks, except the one to get me back to the States.

The war news is sure good. Looks like we've taken the spotlight from Europe for the time being. Was hoping we'd get in on this latest deal but don't stand a chance. Will probably get our share a little later though. We are making rapid progress—can't go too fast for us. (We are eager enough to get this thing over in a hurry.) At the present rate, it shouldn't take very long.

We are having a merry time in our shack. The tent is leaking all over the place and the fellows are playing checkers with the beds. I managed to pick a dry corner; this time! Couldn't stand it if my sack got wet. But we do have a good time. (Sometimes.)

Well, Honey, there isn't anything more I can think to write about. I can tell you though that every time I get away from the outfit my thoughts run to you more than ever. Guess I'm in love with the outfit also. I'd chuck it for you though, after duty performance, of course. (Ahem!). Guess I'd better trot along now before I get involved. I do love you Legna. Constantly!

Love,
Howard

New Guinea
October 28, 1944

Darling Legna,

I have graduated and school is over today. We took our finals and received a diploma. Only got a very satisfactory rating out of this one. You know I usually pull down an "excellent". Guess I'm not as sharp as I used to be. But if we ever have to use what we've learned here, I'll do a good job, regardless of the "rating". I didn't concentrate or over-indulge in study but I didn't miss much of importance. Glad the course is over, now I can go north and get my mail —also go back to work. Haven't worked for a long time now. Expect things along that line to pick-up pretty soon. Hope I don't have to wait around here for transportation, not more than two days anyway.

Certainly haven't been doing much socially around this place. There's nothing to do except go to a show. Some of the boys have been trying to make contact at the Wac encampment. Don't think they are doing so well. Those Wacs should never have been sent here. This climate is tough on gals —course some of the gals are <u>tough</u>.

Most of the fellows here at school are new overseas, 4-6 months. They have hot and lengthy discussions on "time" in N.G. They all want to get back to the States in a hurry. Of course, you can't blame them for that. However, it will do a few of them some good, pulling time in the island. They are mostly men who had more or less permanent base jobs and lived on the fat of the land. Thank goodness I've always been in a tactical outfit. You don't get promotions so easily but there is a certain satisfaction "that you are doing a job".

See by the magazines that we are going to have turkey for Thanksgiving. That will be swell. Bully beef is in our blood and how we do hate the stuff. I'd settle for two fried eggs. We might get turkey but I have my doubts.

Guess I'll be sweating-out a leave pretty soon. Hope we can go to Sydney again. Probably won't let us go that far south though. Maybe we won't get a leave at all. Either way it doesn't make much difference.

You and I were in a dream the other night. Hector and Oscar were involved too, nasty isn't it? But oh, how I wish it were true, Honey. I've to go now.

All my love,
Howard

Back to the S.W.P.A.

I was glad to get back.

Guess I'm just one of the family where the 311th is concerned.

—Lt Howard C. Shenton

S.W.P.A.

November 3, 1944

Darling Legna,

I finally hitched a ride out of APO 503, sweated it out for five days. Got a ride right thru to my base, which was lucky, since there is such little air traffic that far south. Rode all day long and I was really tired when we landed. Military planes are not built for comfort. I was glad to get back. Guess I'm just one of the family where the 311th is concerned. Things are kind of quiet up here now, though the boys are getting in a lot of missions. Anyway I'm glad to be back.

Some of our boys will soon be eligible to go home —the pilots, I mean. Honey, I don't stand a chance of coming home with them. The ground crews will be here for a long time. Guess I should have been a pilot. They are fortunate in getting leaves every three months and not having to spend two or three years in the combat zone. They deserve all of that and a little more, I guess. Piloting is an exciting life, especially in fighters.

Had a lot of mail from you waiting for me —about 15 letters. Dated from the 1st of October to the 19th. Not bad, Honey. Also have a letter from Aunt Jennie. Still haven't heard from Miss Grace. Must be close to three months now since she's written. Doesn't make much difference; I've about given up of hearing from the "ole girl". Long as I get your letters everything will be O.K.

Legna, about that si-kad [cycad] tree. There are palm trees over here that have cones similar to our pine cones. But there are several that have cones and no one has ever heard of a tree called a cycad. I'll investigate a little further and will tell you if I learn anything.

What in the world ever made you suggest my going to a "Chapel" when I come home? No Legna, I don't know what I'm going to do exactly but whatever it is, I won't be studying to be a preacher. I think religion is a mighty fine thing, but it's not for me. I don't want something to think about, will probably have plenty of thinking to do otherwise, but I won't go into that now.

I've been thinking of taking advantage of Uncle's post war educational plan for boys who came in the army under 23 years of age. You get four years of college providing you maintain a fairly high grade. Uncle bears most of the expenses. Think I'll try that if the opportunity is presented. I could stand a little education, other than military, when this "thing" is over. Maybe we can get married and I'll still be able to go to school. That's one we will have to decide on when the time comes. Be nice for a student to be married to a teacher. Doesn't sound right, does it?

It's nice that you are sending me that food, Honey. Ours is getting a little rough now. It will be a real treat anyway; our diet rarely changes.

Legna, I have a new method of sending money home now. I send it through the Army Finance Department. They cable Frisco where checks are made up and sent to the payee. I'm sending a $100 today by this system. Let me know what kind of service you get. They say it takes about three weeks. It is the safest way to send money back to the States. (Hope you got those 5 twenty dollar bills I mailed in a letter, like a damn fool!) Don't forget my war bonds. I should say "our bonds". Get a thousand bucks worth then put the rest in the bank. Don't forget, that $100 in cash is your Christmas present and I want you to buy something for yourself with it.

I received the statement from the bank, the one you sent. Wrote a letter and enclosed said statement to the allotment bureau. Haven't heard from them yet, but they will notify me one way or the other.

Darling, I have to get this in the mail now. Will write again tomorrow.

All my love,
Howard

S.W.P.A.
November 5, 1944

Dearest Darling,

Seems as though I got back just in time. Think I'm going to be awfully busy again. Should have taken another week to get out of some heavy work but I like to work, so guess I won't suffer. A little labor does a fellow some good once in a while. Outside of volley-ball, my exertions "physically" have been nil for the past month.

Gosh, but I'm glad to get back. I was only gone a little over two weeks and it seemed like months. Think boats are the best method of travel — air transports are so darn uncomfortable. But when you can travel 1500 miles in eight or so hours, airplanes count.

Had a letter from you yesterday. Looks like your quota for the month of October is going to be below the standard you set. Honey, I'm afraid it's going to be a long time before I see any of those packages you sent. Hope I get one of them by Christmas anyway. (Wood & Bennert still insist they will contain nothing but Calox tooth powder.) Our mail is coming thru very slowly now. Sometimes we go for a week without a letter. Finally heard from Miss Grace. She wrote me on the 21st of September. The letter came yesterday. Damn it, I told her to use air-mail but she insists on the 3¢ rate. (Thrifty Hartges)

So you told Miss Grace not to send me a gill-net because of the sharks. Legna, that's the reason I wanted a net. Then I could set it in an inlet or river and work it from a boat. We were blasting with TNT and diving for them, while they lay unconscious on the bottom. However, 'tis probably just as well. Don't think I'll have an opportunity to use a net anyway. But nevertheless little lady, don't be perturbed about sharks; we have worse things than that in these parts.

Bob Schwen is a changed man, Legna. Can't understand the boy. Maybe it's because he hasn't been promoted. His job calls for a captaincy. He's been put in three times and turned down each time. Don't know why it hasn't gone thru. The squadron C.O. has O.K.ed it every time but it was stopped in higher Hqs. Hope you got Gloria straightened out, but don't worry about the darn thing, 'twas nothing.

Can't find out any more about your palm tree, they are a bit scarce where we are <u>now</u>. Maybe something will pop-up later.

I'll try to write you again tomorrow, if I get a chance. So for now, goodnight Fuzz. I love you fiercely.

All my love,
Howard

S.W.P.A.

November 11, 1944

Dearest Darling,

I had three letters from you yesterday. Nice going! In one you stated that you had received the $100.00 I sent in an envelope. That was a good shot too. The last money I sent is traveling by cable, handled by the Finance Office. I think this is the best system. (Intend to use the "cable system" often as possible.)

Honey, I'll forgive you for sending me salmon and tuna in the packages but tis a promise that I won't eat the stuff. Maybe the natives will get it. Somehow I think it is going to be a long time before I see any of the packages. Whenever they arrive, I'll be glad to get them.

I've been eating with the Navy for a while. What food! They live like sultans, just like being in a hotel at home. Why, oh why, didn't I join the "bloody Navy"? Had another one of my sleepless sessions but after so much idleness, I sort of enjoyed the work. Getting no sleep is rough on me though. Tis one of my requirements for "personal well-being". Working at night in this climate is much better than the days. (Must be at least 30° cooler.) I'll have a week or so to recuperate, so won't be so bad.

You say the same things about my going on leave as the other boys' wives. The wives grow frantic though because their hubbies don't write. Guess it is startling, especially when they are accustomed to a letter every day. Legna, I drank quite a bit and had some fun but I saved the kisses and "one other thing" for you. I'm not very loose with kisses and as for the other, it's all yours. (Saving myself for you, Honey.) ("For all that one should care to fathom, I was never deep in anything but, Wine!")

The poetry I wrote is pretty well known literature "O Mistress Mine". "To the Virgin" One by Shakespeare, the other by R. Herrick. Besides, you aren't so innocent that you can't understand those lines. I read a lot of poetry but can't retain like I did when going to school. Gosh, but I use to eat that stuff up when I was young-er.

Think I'm going to hit a cooler climate. Sure hope so; this heat is rough on a person. Doubt if I'll be able to stand a winter in Maryland anymore. Oh, I forgot though, love is warming isn't it?

Legna, I'd better shove-off. Will write at next or first opportunity.

All my love,

Howard

V-MAIL
APO 704
November 13, 1944

Darling Legna,

I have some air-mail envelopes but can't get to them, so I'm falling back on the V-mail forms. There really isn't much to write about but I might not have a chance to write for some time.

Right now I'm about as well fed as anybody would care to be. The food is wonderful —prepared like home meals and served as though we were in a high class restaurant. Right now, Honey, I'm as close to "having a wonderful time, wish you were here" as I'll have ever been, or almost anyway. Wish this would last for a month or so. I like it.

Haven't received any packages yet and I think it will be some time before I do. Don't need them now but they will come in handy later, of that I'm positive.

About my wanting to come home. You are the only reason that makes me want to come back. That goes for now and always. You know Legna; I don't believe I even have a home now. That's what you and me are going to make at the first opportunity.

All my love,

Howard

Philippines

I shall return.

Words of General Douglas MacArthur in 1942 as he left the
Philippine Islands

Phillippines*

November 20, 1944

*Howard spelled Philippines incorrectly with 2 "ll's" until his January 2, 1945 letter. He comments about it in his January 26th letter.

Dearest Darling Legna,

This is the first chance I've had to write for five or six days. We really had a wonderful trip up here. The Navy treated us as honored guests. They gave us ice cream every day. Imagine that, right in the middle of the ocean. It was certainly a treat for the army, but those nice things are gone now, for a short while anyway.

Legna, we've made great progress in this theatre of war. In one year, we've come thousands of miles and I think we are going to keep right on traveling. The "business" seems to be a little rougher up here, but we can stand that too. Something tells me that our outfit is going to see a lot of "action" from here on out. That's what we've been crying for and now we need cry no more. (We are sitting right in the middle of it.)

The country here doesn't differ greatly from that we passed thru south of the equator. Here it's a bit cooler, but just a few degrees. Every day it rains, sometimes without a let-up. There isn't a need of setting up showers, we just stand out in the rain and whip up a lather. Mosquitoes are bad though. I've seen and felt more of the pests in the short time we've been here than I saw in a year down south. (Something like Maryland.)

Just in case you would like to know, for the past few months we were in Dutch East Indies or Guinea. Kind of glad to get out of there, it was too hot —we were almost on the equator. I'm enclosing some Dutch money "guilders", one guilder is worth 53¢ Americano. We've certainly learned a few monetary systems, first Aussie then Dutch and now it will probably be Philippine (pesos). I'm also putting in some Jap invasion money, it

456

has no value. We went back to American money while traveling with the Navy, that's what they always use.

You might send me Norman Wilde's address. I've run across a few navy pilots, sometimes they operate from shore and tis possible I might run into him or contact him. We usually know what outfit these boys are from.

Honey, don't be confused by my APO#. It is 321. That's one we had in New Guinea and we've picked it up again, so use 321 now. Guess we won't get any mail for a long time (month or so anyway). Maybe though, we will get our packages by Christmas. Some people think so, I hope they are right.

Say, I never thought of blackmailing until you mentioned it in one of your letters. That's an idea. Perhaps I'd better be careful. But "Heart of my Heart", we'll still speak of Love.

All my love,
Howard

Phillippines
November 21, 1944

Darling Legna,

Don't have much to write but thought I'd better try and get a letter out. We are fairly certain that no incoming mail will be "forthcoming" until a month or more has past. That's no-good Legna, I need my mail! If we get it for Christmas or by that time, I will be very happy.

Wood, Bennert and I went for a dip in the ocean this afternoon. Our camp is right on the beach and that makes it nice. Must have been a few thousand boys in the water. Too bad Fischer isn't around; we could kid him about "Coney Island". Someone saw Fischer since we arrived and he's coming over for a visit in a few days. (We'll get him then.) Right now we are having a real vacation and it's a wonderful place for one. The Nips pay us a call every so often but it isn't too bad. I do love me fox hole though. We had rain for 20-30 hours but being on a sandy beach it doesn't bother us much. Today has been lovely. There has been a nice off-shore breeze all day and it's been fairly cool. The climate is something like that of Florida.

Honey, I wish you could see and talk with the natives here. They are quite intelligent and very nice to the Americans. The Japs evidently treated then rough, took their food, clothing and made them work. Money doesn't mean much to these people. They would rather have food and clothing for any work they do. One ole fellow comes by and picks up our laundry. The first time he took it he brought his family with him when he returned—one boy and three girls. Told me how he helped his wife do the work, because she wasn't so strong. What a contrast between these people and the natives of New Guinea. These people are civilized. They have really felt the Japs' cruel hand and now they have freedom and really seemed to be happy. When I asked this boy what he wanted for doing my laundry he said, "I set no price, pay what you want. Me friend of Americano and I'm happy." So I gave him a mattress cover and a dollar, then we gave him a stack of canned food. After this transaction he started a speech. I listened closely and said, "Yes, that's right." Did I take a ribbing from the boys on that. Now they are running around squealing double talk, then very solemnly saying, "Yes, that's right." (They do darn good laundry.) Some of them pull K.P. to get food.

Legna, don't trim the Christmas tree with anyone "but me". I still recollect pitching-woo around the tree with you. Even enjoyed it the Eve you were out with the midshipman. You almost didn't get a present that year. Maybe I'll be there in "45".

Goodbye now, Honey,
Howard

Phillippines
November 25, 1944

Darling Legna,

I don't know if today is "Thanksgiving" but we are having turkey. Pretty nice, for being in the Philippines —I was surprised. We had fresh eggs for breakfast too. All we need now is some plum pudding with rum sauce and we'll be all-set. The food hasn't been bad here. Looks like it is going to pick up. Guess the Army will never compete with the Navy on that score.

Fischer came over to see us the other day. He came in D+4 and told us startling stories of his experiences. Things were pretty hot around here then, I guess. Said he had seen enough of the war and was willing to get back where the Jap bombers couldn't range. Seems to think he would get to go back to the States for a month or so pretty soon. It has something to do with going to school. After the school is over he will get a short leave and come back here. If it's any way possible, Fischer will do just that. Great guy on working deals. He's a good man and I wish he had stayed in our outfit.

Don't guess we will ever get to Australia again. The pilots won't like that either. They are going to miss Sydney. My clothes are still in storage at Brisbane. Think I'll write the storage company and have them sent home. So don't be surprised if in 3 or 4 months you see them coming in. I'll have no use for winter uniforms up here. Will have to write and get the cost of sending, then send the money before the clothes will be shipped.

Wrote Whitey Wilde yesterday. He's somewhere out here. I'm also looking for Kenneth & Carroll Smith. Damn I'd like to meet someone from home.

The war news sounded good last night. Looks like the boys are loose again in Europe. We aren't doing so bad out here. Sure wish it would hurry up and get over. The Nips are putting up some stiff resistance now, with them it's do and <u>die</u>.

The sun is shining today for a change. Think I'll whip out to the beach this afternoon. We told Fischer to come down. I've already named the beach "Coney Island" and he should be right at home. This place would be nice for a vacation, if there weren't any Nips.

Legna, I've about run out again. I don't know how I'm going to keep on writing without getting some mail. I'll do my darndest and get thru somehow but it makes for "sorry reading".

Still love you Honey!

All my Love,
Howard

Phillippines

November 28, 1944

Darling Legna,

It is kind of tough, not getting any mail. Especially so, when you have to keep writing. If we were getting mail, life would really be pleasant here. The food is good. So far there hasn't been much work and we are having a lovely time at the beach. I don't think though, that we will remain in this status very long. We definitely didn't come up here for a vacation; so far that's what we've had.

Quite a few of the boys have visited some of the small surrounding towns. But from the stories they bring back, there isn't much to see and do. I haven't been out of camp and the only time I intend to go out, is on business. The boys are buying native souvenirs, but there isn't much use in buying the stuff. You can't send it thru the mail and it isn't so nice lugging it around from place to place with your baggage. I've seen some pretty nice handwoven straw mats but you can't mail those either, so I'm not buying any right now.

I have to attend a Courts-Martial this afternoon. Got roped in on this one as assistant defense counsel. There won't be much for me to do and I'm glad. I don't like to have anything to do with them. Guess a lot of officers feel the same way but we have to do the job.

Our native boy comes around every day to pick-up laundry and to see if he can do anything for us. He speaks pretty good English and tells us some very interesting stories about the Japs. He wants money now for his services. Says he has plenty of food. He wants to buy clothing for his family. What these people won't do for a shirt. Every time you see one he wants to buy a shirt. In peace time, the number of shirts a man has establishes his financial status. The natives say, "Americano rich, he got many shirts." One good thing, they never set a price. You give them what you think is enough for whatever they do, or sell you.

Looks like Tokyo is going to take a heavy pounding from here on out. The B-29s are starting mass raids and quite frequent too. Hope they keep it up —it will help the boys fighting in the lines considerably. If the Japs can't get war materials they can't put up a good fight.

Legna, how about that house on Rhode River? Does it seem as far away now as it ever did? I think about it a lot. Maybe it won't be on Rhode River but 'twill be some place. I'm getting a little impatient. Hope it won't be too long.

Bye Honey,

Howard

P.S. Sorry if my letters sound like a travelogue circular, but there is little to write.

H.

Phillippines

December 1, 1944

Darling Legna,

What in the world am I going to write about? My letters are beginning to read like a travelogue magazine. I don't recommend the places I've been though. This is probably the best of them all.

Our planes haven't caught up yet, so consequently there's no work. We are taking life very easy, just like a summer at the beach. We are eating good but I still can't put on weight. Think I weigh about the same as when I came in the army. No one has gained though; most of the boys have lost from 10 to 20 lbs. We have miles of beach right at our front door and we take advantage of it —sun baths, volley-ball, softball and swimming. It's wonderful.

The Japs aren't hitting us from the air much now but they were persistent at first. We've had red alerts all night, from six to six. The ack-ack is beautiful, just like fireworks on the Fourth, but you certainly don't get any pleasure from watching it. When they fire you know there is a bomber setting up there waiting to find a nest for his eggs. They've dedicated to me a song, describing my feelings for the fox-hole. It's entitled "Cuddle a Little Closer". Very appropriate, that's exactly how I feel about it. Wish you could have seen four of us diving into that hole one night. Some were farther away than others when we started the run but all of us hit the bottom at the same time.

Honey, I've just been thinking or reminiscing. It's been two years since I came from Bolling Field to take you to dinner in Annapolis. That's a long time. Gosh, I hope it won't be that long from now before we are able to do the same. Those were the happiest days of my army life, almost like being right at home. Remember the President's birthday ball that you were going to walk out-on because I had a scotch and soda with the Shady Side gang? (Darn, a scotch would sure go good now!). We don't even get a beer ration anymore.

I'd rather have a dance with you than to have a "scotch" though, Legna. In fact I'll take you every time.

All my love,
Howard

463

Phillippines

December 3, 1944

Darling Legna,

We are still "hacking around" doing nothing. I'm beginning to get tired of this life of leisure. Hope we get started at something pretty soon. The good chow sort of compensates for a lot. We've had fresh eggs two mornings in a row. There will be plenty to do, once we get started and I'm all for starting. (Want to be "right in the caper"). The weather hasn't helped matters either. It's rained every day for the past week. No need to install showers, just stand outside and lather up.

Haven't had any shows since we arrived here. They are really missed, too. There are too many alerts to enjoy a show though. One night they started the show at six-thirty o'clock and it ended at one-thirty in the morning. Japs were pretty active then. Maybe we'll be able to have them again shortly. I'd like to see a good show.

I'll be damned if our APO hasn't been changed again. This time we come up with 72. Tell Miss Grace about the change, will you? In my last letter I was quite emphatic about the 321. At this rate we won't get any mail for another month.

Sent you $150 today by way of the Finance Office. Never did hear if you got the other check I sent but of course it's been almost a month now since I've had a letter. Let me know if this system works alright for you. It's the best yet on this end. Looks like I can't win at gambling anymore. I win a couple hundred pesos one day and lose it the next. Think I'll give it up as a bad job.

Picked up a darn head-cold in the last two days. They are kind of uncomfortable in this warm climate. My noggin is as tight as a newly caulked seam on a boat bottom. The pillrollers have been dishing out the pills. Every time I look at my watch it's time to take another one. Well, guess I won't get a "homer" out of it. Understand you have to be mighty ill before you are evacuated. We sent quite a few men home since we've been overseas. Had a complete turnover in flight surgeons. Guess the docs can't take the grind.

Honey, that's about all I have for now. I'd better get some letters soon!

Wish I could be with you for Christmas!

All my love,

Howard

Phillippines
December 9, 1944

Darling Legna,

This is the first attempt I've made to write for some five or six days. Doubt if it will be much of a "success". I think everybody is experiencing the same thing. One of the officers went to the post office to check the incoming mail. There isn't much hope for the near future. That is the only trouble we have. Guess we move around too much.

The outfit is still taking it easy. Honestly I won't be worth a damn when I get home. After doing nothing for so long it sort of becomes a bad habit. I'm not the most eager man in the army but I hope something "pops-up" for us pretty soon. Had a cold about a week ago and wasn't feeling so good but I'm hale and hearty again. The boys have threatened to throw me out of the tent for making so many disturbances. (Think they're wishing me another cold so I'll calm down.)

We are still pretty active in sports. Lucky we are right on the ocean. The beach is like a big playground. My volley-ball game is slowing down. Guess I'm getting a little stale. Once in a while we play for money—that kind of steps the game to a faster level. Most of the day we spend in the sack, though some nights we don't get too much sleep. When the weather is bad we aren't bothered and it doesn't make us mad either.

The war news sounds very good again. The war in Europe is progressing and we are doing pretty good out here. The darn weather has been so bad lately it's really slowed things down. The ole infantry is still plodding along and making good progress too. Every time I see a bunch of those guys, I respect them more. Theirs is the toughest job in this war. I think of them often at night when it's raining and cold. We sleep in a tent on canvas cots and live fairly comfortable. They spend the night in a fox-hole half-filled with water and can't even breath regularly for fear of giving their position away. You can't imagine what the jungle is on a dark rainy night. You can't hear and it's so dark you actually can't see your hand before you—I've tried it. We see quite a few of these boys coming and going to the "front".

Been thinking of us too. Damn it all Legna—wish I would get busy. When I think of you, I long for you—kind of like star-picking. Sure miss your letters, Honey!

All my love,
Howard

Phillippines

December 12, 1944

Darling Legna,

We still haven't received any mail —must be something wrong. This is the longest our outfit has gone without mail since we've been overseas. It has been exactly a month now and there is no hope of a delivery in the near future. Wish something could be done about it, but there isn't!

I'm convinced now that it rains here every day. Three days of sunshine and six days of rain. Much worse than New Guinea ever was.

Legna, so you remember my mentioning our Red Cross representative, Pop Glunt? He is going home in about a month. Seeing as how he lives near Washington, DC and expects to be there quite a bit, I asked him if he would give you ring. So sort of be on the lookout for a call from him. He will be able to answer any questions you have concerning "yours truly". The old boy's mother is pretty sick and his son is overseas so he thinks he should go home. Then again he has done "his part". He's too old for this hot climate and the living conditions. The year has kind of burnt him out. We are going to miss him; he has done more for the outfit than anyone else. The boys love him like a father.

We are still hacking around doing nothing. Can't figure why "the coach" doesn't put us in the game. Maybe he is saving us for the "victory dance". We will probably get our fill before long, but I wish to get started. There is a lot of bitter fighting going on all around us, but so far we've done nothing. Had some exciting moments but they never really materialized into much of any "consequence". Maybe we should be happy about it, but guess we are never satisfied.

Bennert is sitting on my left pulling his hair trying to think of something to write his wife. Our toughest job is exactly that right now. It used to be a letter a day from him. Now he gets one off about every three days.

Sunday is quite a big day here. All the natives get cleaned up, put on their best clothes and visit around. A large number of them go to church and appear to be devout. In the afternoon there are cock-fights. Most of our boys go to that. We even have a few roosters in the outfit. Whenever we get a fight, the whole squadron backs our chicken. Some boys win a lot of money and also "lose".

Legna, I'll be thinking of you on Christmas Day and I'll be hoping that we will have the following one together.

All my love,
Howard

Phillippines
December 25, 1944

Dearest Darling,

Got a Christmas present this year—had two letters from you yesterday. The first mail I've had since November 12. These letters were postmarked November 30th and December 1st. Guess there is a lot more mail for the outfit around the Pacific "somewhere". The boys we left in New Guinea said I had a package from you. It was forwarded by boat, so that means I might not see it for a month.

Legna, I've been complaining off and on about us not doing much to really fight this war. Well I had "it" coming and believe me I got "it".

In fact, I'm swimming in this mess and the water is rather treacherous. Like Fischer said when I first saw him in the Philippines, "I've seen enough war and want to get out of it." I'm not anxious to get out but I've seen all I care to see. Kind of a "rough-go", but we are doing alright. 'Tis better though when you are right in the thick of things, at least you feel as though there is a job being accomplished. Makes you a little nervous at times but the morale is high.

Believe it or not, but we are having turkey for dinner tonight. It was delivered by airplane yesterday. Guess we are going to have a pretty good Christmas after all. Had a celebration last night between air raids.

Can't remember the last time I wrote you. Things have been happening so fast lately. We've been busier than any time since coming overseas. You hit the sack whenever there's an opportunity and there aren't many. We aren't allowed to have lights at night so therefore the writing situation is in bad shape. I'll manage to get a letter in once in a while.

Legna, right now I would like to meet you and then just the two of us go to some nice quiet place and take life easy for a month or so. A thirty day leave and "you" would be about the best thing that could happen to me right now. We will have to take a crack at that, when I get back.

Yes, I remember the sweater I liked on you. Nice looking "profile" there and it's a good looking sweater. There are so many things I remember, but they seem so far and remote from what is happening now, till it doesn't seem as though it actually existed. Just part of the war that we called hardships, I guess. But damn I wish this thing would come to a rapid conclusion. It's wearing me down.

Honey, don't know when I'll get to write again. My APO has been changed to 321 again. Wish they would make up somebody's mind.

All my love,

Howard

Phillippines
December 31, 1944

Darling Legna,

You will probably be hopping mad by the time this letter arrives. I haven't written a single line since Christmas Day. Well, I was complaining because of our inactive status a couple of weeks ago but "my my" things certainly perked-up. For the past ten days we've been working 18-20 hours a day. The damn Nip bombers won't let you sleep when you're not working. Most of us are a little beat out right now. One thing though, we have really accomplished a lot and the morale is perfect. Before long we will hit a steady routine and I'll have some spare time for writing. Have a lot of sleep to catch-up.

Legna, in the past 15 days I've seen more war than all the rest of my time overseas. It's a little rough. Makes you realize what a horrible business it can be. We play for keeps out here and somebody always gets hurt. Sometimes I'm so damn nervous I jump at the slightest noise, but I think the worst of our battle is over and we will have smooth sailing for a while. I think all the outfits at this base have run the gauntlet of everything that the Japs could possibly dish-out. I can say they will have to do much better in the future if they expect any satisfactory results. Persistent devils though; they don't give up easily.

Got a couple more letters from you yesterday —the 200th and 201st. That's a lot of letters and I don't think I've written that many since I left. Ray Wood brought them up from our former "Philippine" base. Also had a letter from Stanley Trott. Guess he was kind of surprised to hear from me. He seems to be doing alright and is sweating out the "home trip". I was glad to hear from him. Think I'll write him again.

Understand we are going to have turkey for dinner tomorrow, which will be mighty nice. I could stand a good meal and right after take a 24 hour nap. I could take you up on that tucking-in affair too —can't recall as ever having been tucked in but it should be a rather pleasant experience. Any "pleasants" would be welcome now and you are just the one to do that where I'm concerned. I've thought of you a lot these past few weeks even though I was busy and it helped a lot Honey. More than I could ever put in words.

The outfit performed wonderfully the other night. In fact they saved our necks. The pilots were given a job that was as tough as anything that's come out of this war. Believe me, I'm really proud of the outfit and think we all did a marvelous job, though my part and the rest of the ground crew was small, we did the job and it was an excellent one.

All my love,
Howard

P.S. Will write when I get a chance.

Philippines

January 2, 1945

Darling Legna,

I just knocked off today and decided to take a rest. Thought I'd better write a letter, too. Worked until the wee hours this morning bombing up planes. Went to bed around nine last night, with everything all set for today. Ten o'clock I got word the mission had been changed, so I had to gather my men, go to the "line" (air strip) and load up with bombs. The men hate to work on the line at night and I don't blame them. We have a constant red alert beginning at dark. You have to depend on the ack-ack firing at a close Jap plane for a warning that the devils are near. Doesn't give you much time to find a hole, in fact sometimes they get in and drop their load before the ack-ack finds them. We've also gotten a few strafe jobs and they are the worst. The men are so scared they don't think of what they are doing. I don't blame them for feeling the way they do; I feel the same way. But I'm the guy that has to remain cool and calm, say when to knock off and hit the dirt —also when to go back to work. I'm just as scared as they are. It's all in the days work though, but "somehow" you just can't accustom yourself to these conditions. (Becoming fairly acclimatized though.) There are many others doing the same things. We take it in stride.

Schwen has finally made captain. He should have had it long ago. The "wheels" held back on it. Why I don't know, guess they wanted to make him sweat a little. I'm glad Bob got it. Would also be kind of glad if I made it. Maybe I will, if I stay over here another year or so.

Honey, do you realize that I'm getting kind of old? Will be 26 on the 19th. That's getting up there towards manhood, don't you think? I was 11 when I established that beach-head on Shady Side, almost fifteen years ago. Time certainly passes fast. Wish I could do all of that over again. Sure hope I don't spend that much time on this beach-head though.

Wish we would get some more mail. Haven't received any packages yet. I think we will get some when the rear echelon catches up with us. Legna, I don't know what in the hell I would do, if I didn't get mail from you. I'm not saying this to make you write more letters —you write often enough. They really keep me out of the ruts.

Say, I think you might start planning for the house we are going to build or buy. I'm positive we are going to need one. What a great day that will be! "I'm eager."

Honey, the going is pretty rough now and probably will be for a while. Don't worry about me. Shenton can take care of himself. In a way I kind of like it, but in more ways I don't. Better go now.

All my love,
Howard

Philippines
January 4, 1945

Darling Legna,

Had another letter from you today. Surprised me. So far I have most of your December letters but the November ones are still on their way. Sure wish those packages would arrive. Could use a little of that canned food.

Say, what's this all about, everybody is reading everybody's letters I write? One of these days I'm going to cross my wires probably and somebody will read something they shouldn't. I'm only kidding Legna, seems though they are getting a lot of publicity. Doesn't matter, I never say anything personal about anyone.

My work has slowed down a little now. Everything is organized and running smoothly. That is everything but transportation. That just can't run smoothly —'tis an impossibility. Finally had a shower which lasted long enough to settle the dust. It sure was a great help. Thought for a while there we would have lung trouble. Also, we have good roads in now and that helped speed things up.

Honey, the squadron is sure doing a good job now. We are right in the "middle of the caper". Yesterday we had four victories in the air and shot-up a few Nips on the ground (planes). So far today, the boys have knocked another out of the sky. Long as they keep doing that I'll sleep in my fox-hole all night and learn to love it. 'Tis true that the morale is better on the fighting front, makes you a little nervous though. Our pilots are doing a great job and believe me, they are "eager". We should pile-up a pretty good record from here on out. All of us will be glad when it's over though, that's for sure! My boys are mighty busy breaking out ammunition. We all needed a work-out.

The Nips are still hitting us at night but they've slowed up a bit. If I could get a hold of one of those Jap pilots, I'd keep the sun-fish awake for three weeks, to pay for the sleep we've lost. Our sacks take quite a beating with us jumping in and out of them all night. Expect my air mattress to spring a leak at any time.

So Miss Grace had another crying jag. Guess she just can't help it. But it does make a person feel bad when she breaks. Tell her to forget the tears and make with the letters.

Legna, if you can get ahold of a fruit cake, how about sending a couple of lbs? Wait until the Christmas rush is over. Our APOs are swamped right now so wait for a month or so.

Better shove off now. Will have more opportunity to write now. I'm still loving you.

Love,
Howard

Philippines
January 6, 1945

Darling Legna,

Haven't much to write about but while I had time, thought I'd knock out a letter. We are still pretty busy but my section chiefs can carry the load now. Everything is all set and we don't hit many snags. That's the way I like it. You can spend more time on personal things.

Getting a pretty good night's sleep now. The Nips have slowed up considerably on their bombing forays. Believe me, there's nothing like a good night's sleep after a hard day. It is a mad house around our shack when we don't get one. Some of the boys stay in the sack until the ack-ack cuts loose, then they make a dive for the fox-hole. If you are already in, you are subject to a terrific pounding from flying heels and elbows. Somebody is going to break their neck one of these days. The fox-hole is right alongside of my bed. All I have to do is roll over, catch my helmet and strap it on while I'm going down. By the time I hit bottom, I'm all set, except for flying bodies. I'm glad things have quieted down a little. We were all losing a little weight from the strain.

Woke this morning and gazed out of my tent on a domestic scene. A herd of cattle had wandered around during the night and were nibbling grass and chewing their cuds. You wouldn't have thought there was a war going on just around the block. We also have chickens and pigs. The natives bring a few chickens to the camp. Usually somebody buys one, then bribes the cooks to clean and cook them.

The laundry system is much better now. We get regular service. Still a mystery to me how the natives get our clothes so clean. They pound the clothes with a club and it sue does the job.

Legna, I haven't written to Australia yet about sending my clothes home. So don't expect them for a long time yet. Should have taken care of it but guess it's just one of those things. The rascals are charging us too much money for storage. Will have to take care of the matter pretty soon.

So a lot of people back in the States think we are going to be fighting indefinitely. Well, I hope not, don't see how it can last for more than another two years at the most. Should be over long before that. What happened to the terrific optimism that prevailed not so long ago? We are hitting the Nips at a pretty rapid pace right now; sure hope we can maintain this speed.

Honey, I'd better go back and tend to my work. I'm still loving you as much as ever.

Love,
Howard

Philippines

January 9, 1945

Darling Legna,

The war seems to have left us a little behind again. Everything is fairly quiet and serene now. The cattle grazing in the field looks quite typical. We haven't had an air raid for the past two nights. Somehow we just can't get accustomed to a full night's sleep. However, I'm happy about it all and hope we remain in this present status for a while anyway.

Looks like the tail end of our outfit will be delayed catching up. Thought sure they would be in by now. Understand it will be some time before they arrive. Of course the reason we are so interested is because they have all of our mail. Should be getting delivery direct before long. Sure hope so, this going without mail is no good. Tis rumored though that a shipment of fresh meat and beer came in. That will help a lot. Could stand some fresh meat and a couple of beers along about now. Wouldn't be surprised if the Wacs invaded pretty soon. When that happens it's time to move on. So far we've managed to keep a little ahead of them.

The pilots are getting a little rest now. The missions haven't been too rough the past day or so. They are moaning because they haven't seen any Nips. Probably they will be going on leave before long. I could take one of those too —in fact, I'd like to. San Francisco wouldn't be bad. You could rush out and meet me there. There I go, day dreaming again. Don't think there's the slightest chance of that ever happening. Been wondering where the leave area will be now —Australia is a long way from here. In fact it's so far I don't think I'd take the ride. The pilots still like Sydney though and would jump at the chance to go. If we get much action though, they want to fly.

Our camp is coming along pretty nicely now. We have more time and men to work on it. The showers are installed and tis a pleasure. The dust makes it a real treat. Before long we expect to have a mess hall. One that is screened in and tables. By the time this is accomplished we should be about ready to move out again. Sure hope we aren't here when the rainy season starts. A little over 33 inches of rainfall a month is too much. The water won't soak in the earth here. The ground is solid.

Legna, you might just as well start looking around for our house. Roosevelt says, the war should be over in "45". I should be home shortly after. Hope that's true. Will round out my time overseas to about thirty months. (That's enough for me.) Even a year from now seems like a long time to me. I'm almost ready to come home right now. Have to go now "Honey".

All my love, Howard

Philippines
January 12, 1945

Darling Legna,

Had a change in the weather today. There's no work to do. It's been raining hard all day, so no flying, no work. I'm trying to wrack my feeble-mind in an attempt to get off a letter. Sure isn't much a fellow can write about. I'm getting desperate!

Life is really back to normal now. We are contemplating electric lights and movies. Soon as the Wacs arrive we'll probably have dances.

We will have lights and movies when the rear echelon gets here. Also some mail which we need and want the most. A few letters would make us quite happy.

Things are getting so slow here! I'm ready to move out. Luzon, China or home —preferably the latter. The pilots say Luzon is a wonderful looking place. Real towns with paved streets and roads, even railroads. Hope we get over there before long. Our present base isn't so nice. The darn rats and snakes are about to annihilate the entire outfit. They are getting worse than the Nips. King Cobra inhabits this island and far as I'm concerned he can remain King. I'll have nothing to do with either him or his court. The bloody rats carry germs too.

Couple of the pilots got leave. They left this morning for Sydney. If they stop in Brisbane, I'm having them send my clothes home. (Much better than working the deal by mail!) Lucky devils, wish I could have gone with them. My next leave will be to Manila, no doubt. That's no good. The Japs have probably wrecked the place since they took over. Shouldn't take us long to renovate the place though.

Honey, the way the war is progressing we should have control here pretty soon. Then we will probably start sweating the China campaign. Maybe we will get home before we go. Nice to look forward to anyway. We could do a lot if I got back to the States for a while.

All my love,
Howard

479

Philippines

January 15, 1945

Dearest Darling,

Yesterday was an interesting day. Reckseit and I went visiting. We went all over the island, stopped at different outfits and had lunch on a PT boat. It is surprising how much you miss when you are confined more or less to your own outfit. I saw many things I had heard about but didn't have time to see them. Also we met a lot of fellows, some we knew from other bases. The Navy offered to take us on a patrol mission in a PT, but the army frowns on this so I guess we won't go. Sure would like to take one of those excursions. Usually they run into a little excitement and that's what we need right now. Just to keep in the groove.

Our boys got another Nip yesterday. They were escorting bombers at the time. The 311th is still leading in number of victories. Hope we stay out front. The pilots were pleased with the guns, no stoppages. They are firing their guns quite often now, plenty of strafing targets and they like to do the job.

The outfit is going all-out for rat warfare now. The darn pests were about to carry us away. We trap and shoot them. Got seventy the other night —also about ten probables. Wouldn't be surprised if we have a few casualties ourselves. The boys are a bit reckless with their pistols.

Legna, you still haven't told me what you got for Christmas or were contemplating. Our packages still haven't arrived. Expected a few in today but doesn't look like they are coming in. Wish to hell the first class mail would get in too.

Have to go now, Honey.

All my love,
Howard

Philippines

January 19, 1945

Darling Legna,

Today is the day. I'm just one year older. Been wondering lately, just how many more of these years are going to find me in the army. In fact, sometimes I think maybe I'll never get out. (Guess a million fellows think the same thing.)

Bennert and I have been experimenting with the manufacture of ice cream "tropical style". We have some mix the Red Cross donated. You add water or milk if you have it, stir it up and freeze it in the ice compartment of the Frigidaire. Had it two nights in succession now and it tasted pretty good. Gave one of the boys a belly-ache and he couldn't sleep. Well, he's just one less we have to share with now. Guess the reason we like it so, is because it's something cold. I like it!

Almost had another victory yesterday. One of the boys chased a Nip and got a pot shot at him. The Nip's plane was smoking and his landing gear fell down but the sun-fish escaped into some cloud cover. We'll get a "damaged" for it, I guess. The pilot was certainly disappointed —he wanted that Jap mighty bad. The air opposition is almost nil over Luzon these days. Every so often they find a stray. (Usually that Nip will stray no more.)

Not much excitement around these days. Haven't had an air raid for a long time. Hope we never have another one.

Honey, I don't have anything more to say for now. I might tell you I still love you, but you know that.

All my love,
Howard

Philippines

January 20, 1945

Darling Legna,

"Be darn", we got some mail today, but no letters from you. Had a letter from Whitey and a card from Gilbert L. It was postmarked back in November. Not bad though, the situation is so bad now, we'd even appreciate a newspaper.

Yesterday, I had the surprise of my life. Bennert and the boys knew it was my birthday, so they decided to "pull one out of the hat". I made the ice cream yesterday afternoon thinking we would have it for the evening as usual. (It can't be frozen until after dark, as the generators aren't turned on until then.) About 10 o'clock last night, I said, how about somebody getting the ice cream. Two of the boys went and came back not only with the ice cream but a "cake" about two feet in diameter, as well. Imagine my surprise! We had a little party. One of the boys had the cake made in some other outfit so I wouldn't know about it. They even wacked me about 26 times. We have quite a scramble. Even had me making a speech. Guess good speech-making is accompanied by the flow of wine. Mine wasn't so good. The ice cream and cake was a wonderful treat. Somebody even whipped-up some chocolate to go over the cream. (And they say, we are suffering from combat fatigue.) Little things like the above mentioned really mean a lot under our present circumstances. The boys were sure swell.

Today we have an issue of beer and pretzels—4 bottles per man. Legna, we are living in the lap of luxury. Beer should go good around these parts—settles the dust in one's throat. Wish we were getting a case. Maybe we will later on.

Reckseit and I are going to try and build an ice box. One large enough to give us ice water for the whole squadron —also large enough to make ice cream for the whole outfit. Will be nice if we can do it. Awfully short of materials though. Takes a month or so to get the stuff together. If we can take it with us when we move it will be a great asset to our morale.

We have heard that the War Dept. is fixing things so that everyone that has been in the combat zone 18 months will get a 30 day leave to the States. Looks like an awful big program to me and I don't see how it can work. Seems like everybody over here has been around for darn near that long and many for 30 months. Well, it's something nice to think and talk about.

Think you and I could put 30 days to advantage? Damn Legna, we could make it seem like a lifetime (of Bliss).

All of Me,
Howard

Philippines
January 22, 1945

Dearest Legna,

Some more old mail came in yesterday, dated early November. It is coming in slowly but it is coming, that's what we want. Even had an issue of the Home News. See you contributed some money. An excellent idea; the paper is worth something. I never have written and thanked the

Mayor of Galesville for putting me on his mailing list. Maybe I'll get around to it someday.

Everybody has gone wild around camp. We are really constructing. The officers are building a club. Reckseit is building an ice box. Everybody's building. I'm wondering if we will be here long enough to derive some benefits from these engineering feats. Just about ready to move again. I don't like our present base too well. We want "Manila".

By gosh, you did exactly what I thought you would do with the money I sent for Christmas. Honey, maybe you did want that silver or whatever it is, but I wanted you to buy something for yourself with that money. It was your Christmas present, not ours. I'm not angry about it, but I wish you had bought something for your "little personal self". We can get those "other things" later. (I call them "things" Honey, I don't know any name for them, so don't get peeved about that.) Maybe I'll get to buy you something next year, "all by myself".

Ray Wood has been having quite a laugh lately. His sister writes him often. In every letter she mentions "rotation". In fact she is an authority on the subject. Tells him to do this and that and how to do it. Rotation is a word we whisper out here and as for its definition, we don't know but it certainly doesn't seem to affect your time limit in the combat zone. The eighteen month rotation plan was evidently designed for soldiers that are too ill to swallow an atabrine pill. Either that or they are paralyzed. Ray will probably be in both of those states when his eighteen months are up. But he still won't be rotated! (Anyway, it gives us something to joke about.)

No, I don't expect to find things dull when I get home. I'm sure there will be lots to do. Whatever that "lots" will be, I'm just the guy to be doing them. Number 1 is to be with you and just about a million others. I want to eat, drink and be merry—that I intend to do. Won't take me long to get my fill though.

Someone said we have a stack of mail today, so much they haven't finished sorting it. I hope there is some from you. Think I'd better rush over and check on that right now.

All my love, Howard

Philippines
January 24, 1945

Darling Legna,

I'm kind of happy today, even though I am a little tired. Lots of mail has come in —got about twelve letters from you the past three days — dated all the way from November to the 8th of January. Not bad at all, exactly what I like the most! Also had a nice letter from Miss Ethel and one from Miss Grace. The ole gal used air-mail this time and the letter came thru in "record time". (January 8th, it was.) Our packages are still back at our first Philippine base. The rear echelon is still in the rear. Wish they would hurry and catch us, we can't even get paid now, all the records are with them.

Well, I see by the Home News that some of the "deferred boys" that were working in vital war industry have been drafted. That's too bad. They've stayed out of it this long, should think they could stay out altogether. I feel a little sorry for boys being drafted now. Guess everybody going in now has their choice of one branch of the service (the infantry). But I didn't have any choice either when I came in. They gave me three none of which were the infantry, so I got put in with the "doughboys". Another thing, the fellows coming in now won't have much of a chance when we start to demobilize. Anyhow this is a rough time to be a recruit in the army.

Think our refrigerator will disintegrate of dry rot before it's completed. It's so darn hard to get working materials; we have to make practically every nut and bolt we use. Lot of fun though. Hope it works.

Legna, I can't think of anything you could send me. If you can get a box of cigars, I like them. But from the poop we've been getting, tobacco is very hard to get. Don't bother about it too much. If you can get a box, send it but don't worry about it.

Legna, if you want to check-up on my whereabouts, get a January 8th or 12th edition of Time and read about the Thunderbolts and Mitchells. Damn magazines print more things —information that would never get past an army censor. Understand the story is not really up to par (what actually happened) but it should be pretty good reading.

Our new flight-surgeon and I had a chat the other evening. His name is Hartman. Darn if he didn't go fishing a number of times with Cap'n Bob Lee. This was back in "25", so it was before my time. He remembers Shady Side quite well. Says he intends to go back again when the opportunity presents. (Me too, the very first opportunity!)

Honey, thanks for the many letters. They help an awful lot. Damn, but I love you Legna!

Goodnight Darling,
Howard

Philippines

January 26, 1945

Darling Legna,

More mail came in today. Got seven yesterday and nine this afternoon. You were knocking out quite a few in the month of November and December. Guess I have just about all of them to date now. Can't say for sure, I destroy all my letters, after about the second reading, will save Bennert a lot of work in case anything happens. Besides I don't have room to keep them. These are wonderful days. It's great to get mail.

So you think you'll be embarrassed when Pop Glunt calls. (If he does, I think he will.) You needn't be. Pop is a regular guy and he doesn't know about the wallet and Calox. Wish he was here now. Could use some of the ice cream mix the Red Cross issued. Pop did more for the morale of this outfit than any other man, officers included. Hated to see him leave but it was for the best. He's too old to be hacking around this part of the world. Also he did more than his share.

Legna, you'd better let politics and the running of this war alone. Just take it easy. Because we are out here having a few hardships, is no reason why people back home should stand on their heads. I'm not allowed to discuss politics in any form but I think Roosevelt is doing a wonderful job. I hate to think of labor strikes, when we are taking a few of our hardships. But that's human nature, people are never satisfied. We are the same way. We have everything we need out here, except an air-compressor. I've been trying to get one for months —need it for my transportation shop. So slow down Honey. Be patient. Don't get upset by what happens. Doesn't do any good to get hot under the collar. Wish I could get that air compressor though.

You say we have a $1000 in bonds. That is enough for the time being. Maybe we'll get some more later on. Legna, I never did get an answer from the allotment bureau. How about checking with the bank to see what they know. Possible that the statement you sent me did the trick. (Don't get excited about it now, the army likes to take a long time to get administrative matters straightened out.)

How about those two "ll's" in Philippines. Hell of a note, isn't it? There have been lots of he-lls out this way though, I can prove that! Guess I'll have to get Bennert on the ball. Neither he nor I knew for sure and were too lazy to find out.

Wrote the Honorable J.E. Smith, editor of the "Home News" yesterday. You know I never met the fellow, but I wrote as though our acquaintance had begun many years ago. I spread it pretty thick about Galesville being a Metropolis and supporting a Mayor. Maybe he won't like it. I told him to let me know if he didn't. I would still write and thank him for his paper. Also knocked out a letter for Norman Linton today. (Got his address out of the paper.)

Billy Crandell is coming home how about that? Knew I should have been a bloody pilot, they get all the breaks. Seems like he just went overseas. We should be sending some boys home pretty soon. They need 300 combat hours or 18 months flying in the combat zone. They even get a leave every three months. Poor fellows, I feel sorry for them. But they deserve it. They have a rough-go of the war at times. Most of them do a good job, but it's a job!

Honey, this is one of my longer letters. Wish I could write more of them but there isn't much to write about.

Love,

Howard

P.S. Haven't received any packages yet.

H.

Philippines

January 29, 1945

Darling Legna,

Today is the first time I didn't get any mail. It has been coming in very nicely lately. Think I'm about up to snuff on your letters now. You sure put them out in the past two months.

There isn't much to write about these days. Must be that when things slow-up, my mind gets sluggish. Haven't done much the past few days. Spent most of the time working in the area. Fixing the officers club and messing around my tent. My Ordnance boys built a beautiful desk out of ammunition boxes and gave it to me for my tent.* Reckseit has a swivel office chair he picked-up off a ship. They really go well together. Even installed the phone on the desk. Guess we are just big-time-operators. It is nice to fix your tent; makes it comfortable and also keeps you busy.

Honey I want you to note the little Filipino in the pictures (The one with just a shirt on). His name is Felix, what a little devil! I taught him to play baseball and he was pretty good after a week. In return he taught me how to ride the breakers into shore. Gosh, that little tiny boy is like a fish in the water and they love it. The picture was snapped when we were enjoying the beach life. One of the enlisted men took it, sent the negatives home and got the pictures back. Thought he'd make me a present. (Incidentally, I do have a pair of shorts on. The Filipino gals didn't mind so you shouldn't too much.) Our camp was just about twenty five yards from where I'm standing. Looks great, doesn't it?

Wood wants me to hurry and finish this letter. He wants to try out the new desk. Tell you Legna, it's a pretty good desk. He'll have to sweat-out one more page.

We are supposed to have a party on Friday night. The nurses came in a few days ago and the boys are giving them the rush. The flight surgeon has a date for everyone. I turned mine down. Most of them aren't too sharp. Besides, I don't feel much like hacking-around out in the wilds. Maybe I'll be host at the festival.

Say, I'm glad you finally told me who the person named "Buck" is. I had no idea it was Ethel L. Thought it was one of your kinfolk though. How about that "Tea", and it Shady Side! Guess there are some other big-time-operators around.

Honey, I'd better let Wood have the desk. He must write or else his wife will probably be furious.

I love you Legna, and I too am looking for the day when we can get together.

All my love, Howard

Editor's note: When a plane landed with a bomb still attached and the bomb came loose and bounced down the runway, Howard refused to order any of his men to disarm it, but took care of it himself. That is probably the reason his men built him the desk and gifted him with the picture of Howard with Felix.

Philippines

January 31, 1945

Darling Legna,

Nothing much to write about, but I just feel like writing to you. Got a January 15 letter from you today —darn good service. Also had a card (birthday) post-marked Washington, DC, but there was no name on the damn thing. I think people use cards as an easy out, figuring well, I should certainly let so and so hear from me. Then they buy a card and all they have to do is address an envelope and sign their "bloody name". It's such a lazy careless way of expressing one's self. I shudder every time I get one. And then to forget to sign it —that alone shows how much interested the person really is.

Honey, I'm glad to hear Billy Crandell got home and that he hasn't changed much. The pilots in the European zone seem to get rotated quicker than our boys. Must be that their missions are tougher. We have boys with over a hundred missions and they haven't even started to "sweat-out" going home. Hope some of them get a break soon. There aren't many of the old boys left. Most of them have been sent home for medical reasons. I hate to see the old boys leave. They've been in the outfit a long time and if they go home they won't be coming back to this squadron. But they deserve everything coming to them.

We aren't doing too well with our frigidaire. Reckseit is slowing down on the job. I took a half a day yesterday and built a volley-ball court. Tried to get Rex to help me, but he insisted that he had to work on the box. I kept my eye peeled and he didn't do either. Maybe we'll move to a cold climate, then we can have an ice-box. These boys work with too many theories.

Legna, I think I have all of the "T" shirts you sent me. I received two boxes, all told an even dozen. Thought sure I wrote and told you about them. (You know this war might be affecting me, maybe I'm getting absent-minded.)

If I was home tonight, I would want to take you to dinner. A real good and big meal, cocktails and all. Then I'd like to see a good stage show —something musical and funny. On the way home we could have a couple of Budweisers just to make us sleep well. Then go home and hit the "ole sack". Wouldn't that be nice? Darn I'd like that. (What's "that"?)

Fuzz, I have to go and knock-out a shower, before dark.

All my love,

Howard

Philippines
February 3, 1945

Darling Legna,

Our party came off very nicely last night. There were only about eight girls present. 'Course that made quite a "rat race" with about thirty fellows around. Think everybody had a wonderful time. We had beer, whiskey, gin, coca cola and fruit juices to drink. For food, we had chicken sandwiches. Pretty nice for being in the country, isn't it? The club was decorated and looked better than any beer-joint back home. (We will have another party pretty soon, lots of fun.) I had to leave and go load-up bombs for an early mission today, but I'd had enough by that time.

492

Some of the boys were starting to feel good by that time, so I didn't miss anything.

After reading today's war summary in our local newspaper, I'm beginning to get a little optimistic about the war in Europe. Things are going real well and we aren't doing bad out this way. We are wondering which will fall first, Berlin or Manila? Out here Manila will be just a stepping rock, hope it doesn't take more than another year for the job.

Had two letters from you today. Fairly late ones, too. Looks like you don't have much to write about either. Just so I get them, I don't care about their length. Your talk about ice skating seems a bit fantastic to me. I haven't seen snow or ice since the winter of "43". It is getting a little warmer out now. Summer is about here.

Can't get the boys to play volley-ball. Guess I built the court for nothing. Guys don't have too much energy.

Darling, there's nothing more to write for now. Incidentally, I still love you, same as ever and always.

Love,
Howard

Philippines
February 6, 1945

Legna Darling,

What in the world can I write about? Nothing! I'm getting a bit desperate on the subject. You can't even talk about the weather, it never changes. Tell me, "little one", what to write about. This thing is about to whip me.

Drew another beer ration today. Five bottles. Now for five evenings we can sit and swig a little after supper! All we need now is an issue of cigarettes; they have been scarce at our base for the past month. Must be a "transportation problem". There are plenty of smokes at our rear bases. Maybe you'd better whip over a box of cigars if you can get them.

Honey, no packages yet. We have a report that a lot of packages were thrown overboard from a ship while enroute to our base. Seems rats and insects were about to assume command. They had to get rid of the packages to save the ship. 'Tis a likely story, most of the packages contained foodstuff.

So Billy Crandell did the inevitable —isn't that something? I often wondered why it is that so many marriages take place before a fellow goes overseas. If he doesn't get hooked the first time, then he gets the "ole shaft", the next time he comes back then has to go over again. Ah, but love and its perplexities. Guess if we knew all the answers, there would be no romance, adventure and damn tomfoolery. Fun though, isn't it?

Either ignore or take that last paragraph as a joke. It has nothing to do with (we), I love you with all of me heart Legna.

All of it,

Howard

Philippines

February 11, 1945

Legna Darling,

Yesterday we had some rain. It wasn't much but settled the dust anyway. Makes about the third shower in almost two months. Freshens things considerably. In fact, it's probably a good thing I didn't write you, was feeling a bit fresh myself.

The outfit is all together again. First time for a long while. The boys just arriving are hearing some of the most fantastic tales you ever heard. Everybody is telling them "how rough" we had it and the stories have surpassed all proportions. Yes, everybody has returned now and we are all pretty happy. I'm all set to go again. Feeling pretty darn crowded. Funny isn't it? Three weeks ago I wanted a long vacation but now I'm raring again.

Got my first package today —the one your Dad sent. Honey, in case I don't get a chance to hack out a letter, thank him for me. Those cigars are wonderful —I'm inhaling one right now. Also gave one to the C.O. I don't know why —he can't promote me —but it doesn't hurt to maintain friendly relations. They are really superb! (Cigars)

We expect to have a movie tomorrow night. I hope so. Haven't seen a show in over two months. "Hardships". Don't guess I've missed much. Shows haven't been too good lately, so they tell me.

Bennert is running wild. He's taken to reading "bloody Wild West stories". That's certainly no way to keep up with his education. Of course, he and I argue about the sheriffs and outlaws of the West. I read all of Zane Grey's books, so we are right in the caper. I just finished reading a very good book, by a gal named Davenport, titled "The Valley of Decision". Good reading.

You know, right now I wish I were in Shady Side for about a thirty day leave. Guess I'm getting kind of homesick for you, Legna. Those spells hit me every so often and it makes me wonder how much longer it will be before I get to see you. Damn but it seems a long time since we had that goodbye in New York. Sure hope we never go thru one of those again. The army has certainly never committed any great favors toward us. The set-up at Bolling was tops, but it didn't last long enough. I'm still living those days in memories. "The best of me life."

Honey, I'd better go now. Wood is hacking around the desk. Think he wants to write "sweet nothings" to his wife.

All my love, Howard

Philippines
February 12, 1945

You, "you Darling",

I love you woman, so help me, I do! I think you are the "bestest gal" in all the world. Just received three of those five packages you mailed. The contents were wonderful. The food will sure go good. Honey, don't bother about sending me any more cigars like I mentioned in one of my recent letters. I have the box your Dad sent and also one from you. That will last me for a long time. Thanks for everything Legna. I mean what I wrote at the beginning of this page and not just because you sent me those packages. For the past three days all of our mail has been packages, no first class at all. Guess we can't have everything. But I do like to think I have you, Honey. It keeps my morale <u>high</u>!

Nothing exciting happening these days though I am finding quite a lot of work. We are going over all the equipment and whipping it into shape. Our equipment must be good, because it certainly takes a beating. If you take care of it, it will last a long time. The vehicles get more abuse than anything and as time goes on, we have to pull more "maintenance" to keep them going.

The blooming Wacs came in today. The outfits (311th) rear echelon just managed to beat them by a nose. Wouldn't be surprised but what the Wacs won't beat us to the front yet, on one of these moves.

Legna, I've changed my mind about coming home for a leave. At first I thought I'd rather stay here till it was all over but now, all they need do is say the word and I'm on my way. Of course, I don't expect to be presented with a leave for a long time yet but if I get the chance I'm going to jump at it. If it happens Legna, look out, 'cause I'm going to be after you!

All my love,
Howard

Philippines
February 16, 1945

Darling Legna,

I haven't written for three or four days; there isn't anything to write. Haven't had any first class mail during that time. The postal dept. must be trying to get rid of all the packages they have on hand. You never saw such a mess. Usually the boys open theirs right by a trash can and tis very little they salvage. All of yours came through fine, nice wrapping job, Honey! I have received several and had to throw every damn thing away.

Saw a show last night —first time since the later part of November. Pretty good too. Had a very good cast—Cooper and Bergman— "Saratoga Trunk" was the title. During the show I was inhaling the smoke from the good cigars you sent me. Afterwards we had a late supper in the tent, fixed with food sent from home. Then none of us could sleep; we ate too much.

I've managed to pick-up a picture of every officer in the squadron. That is, every officer that was with the outfit when we were based at 704. Been of lot of changes since then. I'm going to send a few home each time I write. Assemble them and stow them away for me, will you?

We have been doing a lot of bombing lately; in fact our work has been nothing but bombs for the past few days. Keeps my boys busy and working pretty hard but we like that. Sure would hate like hell to be a Nip on Corregidor. We have been pounding that island to pieces.

Honey, I hope there's a letter for me from you today. Could use one nicely.

All my love,

Howard

Philippines

February 18, 1945

Darling Legna,

Had a letter from you yesterday, first time for a week or so. The "permanent base commandos" are here now. They don't work on Sundays, so we don't have mail anymore on the Sabbath. Can't say too much about that though, our outfit had today off. We were scheduled for "maintenance and training". Maintenance is alright but I don't know so much about this training business. I supposed everyone was trained before they came overseas. Little late in the game to start training. But it's nothing to think about, just another way for higher Hqs to say, "Take a day off".'

I'm enclosing more snapshots of the 311th officers. Put them on file for me. It will be pretty nice having pictures of all the boys in the outfit. I'm going to try and get a set for Fischer —I'm sure he'll appreciate them.

How about the harangue of a fur coat? A $100.00 and our love. Honey I'd never let a fur come between us, if you want the coat go ahead and borrow the money. I told you to buy yourself something with the money I sent you for Christmas, but you bought silver ware. You women! Tell you what to do. Take the $100 if you still want the fur and we'll let it go as a "birthday present". How about that? Sounds alright to me! As for my still loving you, I do and always will. Would take a very drastic measure to dissever those feelings. (The ones I have in me heart, Legna.) These thoughts and feelings really enfold you Honey. Don't let this engulf you though. Getting kind of sticky and deep here, better give it the "gun and go around".

Don't know what I said about China and my getting a leave. However, I hope we do go to China. If I have to stay overseas I want to be right in the middle of the caper. Course Manilla shouldn't be such a bad place. Shady Side is <u>my place</u> though.

All my love,
Howard

Philippines

February 20, 1945

Dear Legna Darling,

Had another nice package from you today and it came thru in fine shape. Contained tuna, shrimp and chocolates. The boys went for the comics too. Kind of went for them myself. The candy is in excellent condition. I have already placed the cans in our frigidaire. You know we have a kerosene job in our tent, sometimes it freezes, sometimes it does not. Do manage to keep water cool anyway. Right now our tent is well stocked with foodstuffs and we are living high! The G.I. rations are improving. This morning we had a fresh egg for breakfast. So we are having such a rough time, would like to have a leave though. (To the States.)

Our work is dropping off steadily. Of course I'm real busy only when we are using bombs. Incidentally, we did a good job working Corregidor over. The pilots put "them" where they counted the mostest —dropped a lot of eggs on that little island. Right now we are back on the milk runs, but the pilots can stand a little rest. They've earned it.

Were you paying me a compliment when you said I was all the movie stars in one? Damn, Legna, what a comparison. I don't want to be like any movie star. They are no different from anyone else—just make more money, *that's all.*

Sorry to hear you had so many children fail the first term. Anthony had better sharpen-up somebody. I didn't think anyone ever failed a class, at least it seemed that way when I went to school.

Don't get too restless Honey. There are times when even I chomp the bit. Control, that's what it takes.

All my love,
Howard

Philippines
February 23, 1945

Dearest Legna,

Had another package from you today. Guess I'm lucky. This must be all you sent (5). Everything came thru in good condition too, thanks to the way you did the wrapping. You are a darn good "wrapper" Honey. My packages came thru in better shape than any of the others I've seen in the squadron. Course, I'm quite a wrapper myself. Wish I could prove that point to you, right this moment!

Quite an ingenious act, the one of you using comics for packing. I enjoyed the Annapolis papers too. Everybody in the tent reads the funnies you sent. Legna I got a package not so long ago and it evidently "had contained" some funny books because there were two of them left in the package. The darn thing had been in water for about a month or

501

so. The water had eradicated the return address so I don't know from whom it was sent. Couldn't recognize the handwriting, just could make out my name. Had to throw the two books or remaining books away; they just fell apart in <u>me</u> hands.

I'm enclosing a few snapshots Bennert took while we were in Guinea. They aren't so good. Seems like something was wrong with the film. Also a negative that Reckseit snapped the other day. That's me in the darn thing. Take a look and if you like it, get an enlarged print made. (Reckseit likes it.)

Honey, I think I know what you mean by saying, "you are getting restless". I've been that way and it isn't because of combat fatigue. I don't mind this war too much; it is just one of those things you run into during a lifetime. The worst part of it is being so far and so long a time from everything you love. I want to come back and be with you, to be together and do the things we like. I want to make love to you and have you, all mine, for the best or worst. These are the things I want, and I think about them more every day. (You "thing" you.) All of this makes a fellow realize what he is out here for. It makes you want to do a good job, accept whatever comes along no matter how rough it gets. But damn Honey; wish we could get it over in a hurry. I've lots of personal duties to perform.

Talked with an officer the other night who has been out here for three years. He's married and hasn't seen his wife in all that time. That Legna is a "rough go" as the Aussies will say. Hell, he will have to court that gal again, probably have to get introduced. Wouldn't be so bad for a single guy to be away from home that long; ah, those poor married

502

people! After reading this over it sounds like I'm getting involved. Better get out.

All my love, Howard

Philippines
February 28, 1945

Darling Legna,

Had a couple more packages from you, or I should say "your family". One was from Miss Ethel. The Andrews family went "all out" with Christmas packages this year. Tis wonderful, I think all of them arrived and I didn't have to throw a thing away. The five or six I got from other folks went right in the trash barrel. Contents completely ruined. You did a marvelous job of packing Honey. My packages came thru better than any of the other boys. Usually they take a large package to the trash pile, open it and come back with a handful of stuff. The cigars are the best I've ever had. You sent so many. Don't send anymore until I ask for them. I'm living like a Wall Street broker on what you all have sent over. Legna, you are a darling. I love you with all me heart. Thanks for everything, and tell your Mom and Dad I appreciate very much what they sent me. I've got enough food to last me six months.

This base is beginning to wear on me now. I want to hit the road again. Without a doubt this is the worst place the outfit has ever been. The dust makes it unbearable. The stuff is in the air all the time, even in camp it is getting bad now. Before "the line" (our installations on the strip) was terrible. I don't know what to say about it except that it is worse than terrible. When the rains come, will have mud up to our necks. Guess this just isn't a nice place. "Ready to leave it anytime".

Wish you could see what is going on in our tent right now. It is a little after ten o'clock and the boys are fixing a midnight snack. Bennert and Reckseit are doing the cooking. I was "it" last time. Bennert picked up some eggs today so we are going to have bacon and egg sandwiches, probably to go with them. Every so often Bennert drops his utensils and grabs a camera to take some snapshots. Don't think they will turn out so good but if they do, I'll send some to you.

So the Mayor called you and spoke of my letter. I expected some comments, but didn't think they would be flattering. I kind of ruffled the "Honor's" feathers a little but it was all in fun. Guess he has a pretty good sense of humor.

How about giving me some news on Norman W. It isn't like the Navy to remain silent. The lucky devil, he must have had a "break", to get home so soon. The Navy certainly looks out for their men, but they probably think the same of the Army.

Honey, tis chow time. Goodnight. Wish I could be sitting across the table from you.

All my love, Howard

Philippines
March 5, 1945

Darling Legna,

We have installed a radio speaker in our tent. It runs from the radio in the club. There is a broadcasting station on the island and the programs are really swell. Right now there is a spot light band on and the music is beautiful. When a swing tune is played we usually have to tie Wood down, he's a jitterbug. Don't mind him dancing so much but we have a gravel floor and he kicks the stones out of the tent. I like to lie in my sack with some sweet music playing. Puts me to sleep. Also brings back memories. We also get the latest war news. Our tent is complete with electricity, radio and frigidaire. "Filled the foxhole in."

Not much doing these days. I'm really beginning to get bored. Never wanted to leave a place as bad as I do this one. Have to go searching for something to do, wish I had a hobby. If it wasn't for the gay banter we throw at each other in the tent, life would be pretty dull. It's even getting so I hate to try and write a letter, there isn't a thing you can think to say that hasn't been told a thousand times.

Haven't had much mail lately. In fact no one has. Got two letters from you today. First time I've had mail in a week.

So you search, or find I should say, recreation by shopping. Must be an "All-American pastime with the women. Every time one of the fellows gets a letter from his wife, she has just bought something. First they tell how beautiful the item or article is, and then they quote the price. The latter brings on a mighty groan.

Legna, how about sending me some snapshots of you. I want to take a reading. I love you Honey.

All my love,
Howard

Philippines

March 8, 1945

Dearest Legna Darling,

The Finance Dept. finally came thru and payed us, first time for over three months. I wired $350 to you thru the Finance Office. It should come thru in about four or six weeks. Let me know if you <u>don't</u> get it.

The wind is whipping the dust around fiercely today. If we don't get out of here soon, somebody is going to get T.B. Beats anything I've ever seen. You can see the darn stuff in the air, sometimes as high as 500 feet. Wish to hell it would rain a little, the dust is making me very disgusted.

You asked if I was wearing your ring. Honey, I wear it all the time, in fact I never take it off, except when handling something quite messy.

Legna, I'm surprised to hear you and Norman didn't have a good time together. Thought you two would have a wonderful time. Not that I approve of it 100%, tis only natural that you should though. I don't like young fellows hacking around too much with the gal I love, especially the Navy. Those boys are smooth operators with the women; at least that's what they tell me. I want you to go out and have a good time, no reason in the world why you shouldn't. But save "the all of me" part of yourself, for Shenton. (Sounds funny, doesn't it? Doesn't make sense.) Honey, I'm talking about "Hector and Oscar". I claim exclusive rights. There is more but I can't tell you that in a letter. Anyway, save yourself for me Honey; I'll need it all.

Have to go sweetheart!

All my love,
Shenton

Philippines
March 12, 1945

Darling Legna,

The weather is really nice here now. We had rain three days ago. It was welcomed with open arms or something. Today we have no dust and tis cool, just like a spring day at home. Won't last long though, the wind and sun will dry things up in no time.

Had a letter from you and Miss Grace yesterday, dated early in December. They must have been lost somewhere. I usually get your letters in 15 to 18 days.

Legna, did I ever tell you that your letters would never be censored. It is only mail going to the States that go thru the censor. I didn't know but what you thought your letters would be censored. Occasionally I detect a guarded sentence in your letters. Say anything you like Honey.

The Colonel (Group Commanding Officer) left yesterday for a thirty day leave in the States. He deserved it. Wasn't so long ago that he bailed out in enemy territory. Took him quite a while to get back. He had some pretty rough experiences. Guess this leave is about the best thing that could happen to him. It would be for me, of that, I'm positive.

Honey, I just happened to think of something concerning the pictures I'm sending home. I realize it must be a slight shock, seeing so many men and people scantily dressed. To us it doesn't mean much, in most instances there weren't any women within hundreds of miles and we ran around camp in shorts or draped with a towel and thought nothing of it. Please don't think it degrading or obscene. We are the same as we ever were; besides it fits the climate. Of course, I realized the pictures aren't as bad even as what you see on a beach at home. I just want you to know that our morals are still as good as <u>ever</u>. Better not show any of those shots to the ladies of the "Temperance League", they would probably gasp! Why don't you go ahead and paste them in the scrap book? Some of the pictures might get lost or mislaid.

I like the kisses you put at the end of your letters. Too bad I can't reciprocate but censorship rules say nix. Tell me though, do you have to use those damn "Ha, ha's" in your letters? I hate them. No offense Honey. I'll even take the "ha, ha's" just to get your letters.

Say, I'd better get out of here. You might be getting sore. I love you Legna, guess that's what really counts.

Love,

Howard

Philippines
March 16, 1945

Darling Legna,

Everybody in the squadron is pulling their hair. We haven't had any mail for five days. Haven't the slightest idea what is holding it up, but I wish the darn mail would come in.

We aren't doing much work these days. I'm so tired of doing nothing, I'm going nuts. Every day is an eternity. Wish to hell we would get going again. A leave would come in mighty nice about now. I could take a month and I don't think anyone would miss me. However, all leaves have been cancelled. Guess I'll be darn lucky if I ever get another, while overseas. Could use thirty days in the States very nicely now or anytime for that matter. We all talk a lot about going home, but I think it will stay in the talking stage and not materialize for a long while.

Understand we are drawing a beer ration today. Eleven bottles per man. That should perk things up considerably. That's the largest issue we've ever had.

Fischer flew up to see us the other day. He has been promoted to Captain. Hasn't changed much —still running around making contacts and trying to swing deals. Stayed with us two days. It was just like he had never left the outfit. Bert is a darn good radio man, wish he was back with us.

Honey, if I don't find something to keep me busy and stop me from thinking so much, I'm going to be in bad shape. It's you that occupies most of my thoughts. I'll be reading and sort of hit a trance; when I wake up it's always you I've been thinking of. (No good, Honey.)

All my love,
Howard

Philippines
March 18, 1945

Darling Legna,

Here it is Sunday morning. Today even feels like Sunday. The P.A. system is broadcasting church music right from the States. Everything seems so quiet and peaceful. There aren't many planes flying. You can even talk in a normal tone and be heard. Yes, even here you can realize that today is Sunday, but far from being like what they are at home. I remember Bud K. and I would take off about 11:00 and run up to

Woody's for a quick beer. In the afternoon we would visit Shady Side or hack around the river, sailing or swimming. Great life, that!

We finally had some mail yesterday, first in a week. The boys had started sweatin' the darn stuff. I had a letter from you. (Happy day.)

You mentioned our party. No, I didn't dance with any of the gals. Didn't even have a date, nor was I deep in wine, but I did have enough to drink. There are only a few boys in the outfit dating nurses. It isn't worth the bother. Those gals are so popular they drag nothing below the rank of Major.

Legna, we are getting a book made. It's about the Group and Squadron. Understand it's going to be pretty nice. Will be printed in the States. I'm going to have a copy sent to you. Won't be ready for about six months but thought I'd tell you before I forget. Something else, Cpl. Loomis, one of my transportation boys is having his wife get some colored snapshots made. She is going to send a copy of each to you. They are beautiful.

Honey, no elaborations today, but I do love you.

All Me Love,

Howard

P.S. Better not show all of those pictures to everybody.

Philippines

March 20, 1945

Legna Darling,

There sure isn't much a fellow can write about these days. We do the same things every day, the dust is getting much worse—damn I've never seen anything like it.

Fischer was over for supper again last night. He's leaving today. Guess he'll wind up around Manila. Wish I was going with him. He asked about you, talked about the time you were in New York.

Had a couple of swell letters from you yesterday. You mentioned leaves and marriage in one. Yes, Honey, I think I could bear us not being married if I came home on leave. There's no sense in rushing now, we've already waited so long. I was a darn fool for not getting married before I left the States. (I think I am.) But we will talk about marriage when we get together again.

Looks like you are going to be very busy this spring with the operetta, student council and all those other meetings. You know I never did see any of the operettas at Southern. Was wondering where you found the singing talent. Must be a job with such few students. Mr. Bischoff could take the part of a mad bellowing bull, quite easy, I imagine. How come you get mixed up in all those things? Seems to me you are always working on something of the sort.

Honey, I'm enclosing a couple negatives of some snapshots Bennert took. Have them printed. One of them makes me look like a farmer. Tis the effect created by the Filipinos straw hat. We can't wear them anymore. There's a regulation against it. I like them too.

511

Legna, don't pay much attention to what I said about marriage. We'll take care of that when I get home. I love you Darling. "Understand that's grounds for marriage".

All my love,
Howard

Philippines
March 22, 1945

Darling Legna,

Hit the jackpot today, got four letters from you. This is the first mail we've had in four days. You mentioned something about not hearing from me for a week or so. Can't understand that. I usually write every other day or every third day. Must be a tie-up somewhere in the service. Damn Legna, I've written a lot of letters! I get dates mixed, most of the time I just guess, so don't pay much attention to them, but I still write about three letters a week. Maybe the censor is delaying some of my letters.

Honey, I don't understand this "fresh controversy" that I started in one of my letters. I can't remember what I write. The whole thing sounds like I was trying to make a wise crack, left out a few words and the sentence lost all meaning. Usually I leave out a few words when I'm writing and thinking at the same time. Guess you know that by now. But that "fresh business", I can't imagine what it's all about. Don't suppose it matters greatly! Never fear, my dear, I let you in on everything, "pardner". You know that reminds me of an act Wood, Bennert, Reckseit and I put on some weeks ago. We were playing cowboys. Every time the Doc would come in the tent we would go into our act. I think the Doc thought we were crazy at first but he "sharpened up" after the third or fourth try. We were trying to make him think we were crazy, maybe we'd get a homer. Don't know why we picked a cowboy act, must have been because of the caribou atmosphere. Those animals create an awful smell. Every day we whip out our 45s and chase the buggers away from camp. (This is probably as clear to you as water in a caribou wallow.)

I'm having a little trouble with my teeth again. The dentist says our diet is no good for teeth, too much soft, mushy food. The gums are taking a beating. Have to spend 5 or 10 minutes every night and morning giving them a work-out.

Wood has a Jap sword. It came from Corregidor. We have a lot of friends in the outfit that took the island. Those boys did a darn good job —had a pretty tough fight. The sword isn't too good. Guess it's better than nothing though.

Honey, we aren't doing much these days, just hacking around on odds and ends. Doing quite a bit of bombing, but nothing extraordinary. Want a leave, bad!

I'm loving you as always, never changes.

Love,
Howard

Philippines

March 25, 1945

Darling Legna,

Today is Sunday and there isn't a thing I can say about it, except that another week has passed. The weeks aren't passing so fast lately. Time is certainly dragging. Guess that's the way it will be from here on out. The first year goes the fastest; the third will probably be a century.

Got that lock of hair yesterday. Don't know what to say about it. Honey, I hope you aren't getting your hair cut too short. I like a gal with plenty of hair on her noggin. If you cut anymore off you'd better save it, so I can make a toupee when I get back. My hair is thinning rapidly; the fellows tell me I'll be bald before long. I will put your lock with the pictures I have of you. (How about sending me some snapshots?)

Been listening to the radio almost all day. We get some wonderful programs on Sunday, right from the States. Good music flavored with the latest news, we are fortunate to have a radio. The boys in Europe are making good progress. I'm going to lose money though; I bet that the war would be over by the 1st of April (European). I wouldn't dare make an estimate as to how long it will last out here.

Darling, that is about all for now. Wish to hell we'd get busy. Too much constant thinking of you going on these days.

Send some pictures!

All my love,
Howard

Philippines

March 30, 1945

Darling Legna,

Nothing much doing today. We have maintenance and training on the schedule. In a way I'm glad we aren't working today. For the past week we have dropped a large tonnage of bombs. Our planes have been supporting the infantry. It is interesting work for the pilots, but they sure use a lot of munitions. It's a break for the infantry boys; cuts their casualties down considerably. When they want to take a town, we are called in to soften it. Usually we run the Nips out and the doughboys meet little opposition.

Had a letter from Whitey; he expects to come home within the next six months. Lucky him. He wanted to know when I was going back. Haven't answered yet, but it won't be in the next 16 months, unless I get so I can't move my fingers or toes. Legna, if I thought I would get home by this time next year, it would make me very happy. That would be two and half years. No, I don't think I'll make it. Can't figure how the Navy manages to send their men home after 18 months or 2 year overseas. (I'm all for adopting their system.)

Honey, I miss you an awful lot these days. Sometimes it seems like I've been away for several years. I think of you constantly, in fact more now than ever before. Damn, but I'll be glad when I can come back and be with you, for keeps.

War news from Europe sure is good.

All my love,

Howard

Philippines

April 1, 1945

Legna Darling,

Today is Easter. Seems just like another Sunday. I was busy this morning and didn't go to church. First Easter I've missed in a long time. We had a big bombing day; our boys are really dropping the tonnage. Getting to be a real bomber outfit.

It started to rain early this evening. I think tis the start of the rainy season. The rain doesn't come straight down; it hits you horizontally, at almost 90°. Surprisingly how cool it gets when the rain comes. Glad I bought a poncho a few days ago. I'll be sleeping in the darn thing before long.

Haven't had any mail for four days now. All we've had is packages and a few V-mails. Thank goodness I don't get any V-mails. Most of the boys hate them. Lately, you are the only one I've had mail from. When I get them from you Honey, I don't care about the others.

Wish I could whisper sweet-nothings in your ear, Honey. Guess I will have to start reading poetry again —I seem to get inspiration from literature. The sight of you though would be all that's necessary. Damn Legna, I hope that I'll be home by next Easter, more and more each day I think of coming back to you. If absence makes the heart grow fonder, I'm crazy! It makes the heart lonely and starved. Mine is "yearning" for the day we can be together.

I wired $100 to you today. When you get the check, keep the money, it's a birthday present. (I know it's May 20th.) You can get "Hector and

Oscar" a sweater. I think they like a sweater as much as I like you <u>in one</u>. (Show-off)

Honey, I'd better get out of here. Getting nasty.

All my love,
Howard

P.S. Send me some pictures!

Philippines
April 4, 1945

Dear Legna Darling,

There isn't a damn thing a fellow can write about. It's awful, really! I don't think I have ever felt so dull and monotonous. We do the same thing every day and time goes so slow. If it wasn't for playing poker and reading, I don't know what we would do. I've read so much my eyes begin to pop. Maybe a leave would fix me. Could take 15 or 20 days just to get away from it all. Don't know why I'm complaining; there are thousands in the same boat.

A few of the pilots have received orders to be sent home. Probably will be a month or so before they can get transportation, but they are quite happy. I'm glad to see them get a break; some of them need to go home. From what some of the pilots write, boys that were sent back on physicals, they want to get back over here. I think they are trying to keep <u>our</u> morale up to par. I wouldn't mind it here if I could keep busy and interested. Guess war is a dull business sometimes!

Had a letter from you yesterday. It was an oldie, must have been tied up somewhere. First mail we've had in four days. It seems to come like

517

that these days. You are writing quite a few letters these days, Honey. I love them! Sorry I can't write more than I do.

How about the latest doings in the Pacific? By gosh, the war is sure humming, even though I can't find much to do. Bet there are any number of guys out here that would be glad to swap jobs with me. I should be happy, but I'm not. Looks as though the E.T.O. [European Theatre of Operations] has entered the finale. Our progress over there seems phenomenal. I don't see how the Krauts can take the terrific barrage. They should have collapsed long ago.

Legna, I hope the operetta turns out alright. You should give Bicky the leading role. I'm sure he wouldn't need a microphone—save the state some cash. I thought perhaps Anthony would be drafted by now. He'd make a good soldier—he is so neat in appearance, that's an indicator.

Guess the rainy season is about starting in Shady Side. Hope it isn't as bad as out here.

Darling, keep your fingers crossed and hope or wish a lot. The way things are going, I might be back in another year. Oh yes, keep loving me too, that's vital.

All my love,

Howard

Philippines
April 9, 1945

Darling Legna,

No doubt I am being cussed and you are madder than the dickens. In fact, I've probably lost a few thousand feet in the height of your estimation. Sorry Honey, but I couldn't write. Haven't had the facilities and I've been busy setting up a camp. Had to carry the load by myself this time. Bennert and I usually work together on these things but he was left with the rear echelon. I don't mind it a bit though. Confusion and work seem to agree with me. I've had lots of mail from you. Wood came up yesterday and brought my mail along. Good boy! It will probably be a long time before I get any more.

Sweetheart, I wish you wouldn't keep saying in your letters, "Shenton, if you find you don't love me anymore, please notify me first." Out here of course, there is no one I could possibly fall in love with, but if I meet anyone while crossing the country on my way home, I'll wire you right away. Have no qualms my sweet, I don't think anything like that could possibly happen. (Positive!)

As you will notice in the letter, there's a new APO, it's 70. Sure have had quite a few. Hope I keep this one for a little while; maybe my mail won't be so messed-up.

I enjoyed your telling me about Mrs. Phipps and the new choir leader. She's quite a character. She sure could use her finger to aid her talking. Was always afraid she was going to put someone's eye out with one of the emphatic thrusts.

We have started to send some of our pilots home. Gosh what a bunch of happy boys. Wouldn't it be wonderful if we would start getting "30 days leaves" soon? (Nice dreaming.)

I better go now Honey.

All my love,
Howard

Philippines

April 13, 1945

Dearest Darling Legna,

I'm about set now, so you should be getting a few more letters. Our mail has been coming in fairly regularly, they are shuttling it from our last base. Though today I didn't get anything but a copy of the Home News. Bennert is still at the last base, so I can be sure of getting my mail. I've missed him on this job. You know we usually work together on all moves but this time we were split and I sure felt the increased load. I'm alright though, a little tired but the ole morale is top-notch. Hope Bennert is with me on the next jump, we make a good team. He and I argue like hell and fuss a lot but we get results and that's what counts. By the way, Bennert and Wood made their captaincy. Wood's here with me but I haven't seen Bennert yet. Guess I'll come home still a 1st Lt. That's as high as I can go in a fighter squadron. Wish I could get transferred from Ordnance to the Air Corps; then I'd have a good chance for promotion. Just so I get home, that's the main interest.

I have a darn nice camp built, as good, if not better than any before. I've been able to hire a lot of Filipino labor and it has helped me lots. Of course, the first time it rains, we will be under water but that can't be helped. The rainy season is getting pretty close now.

The outfit is dropping more bombs now than ever before so you see I'm pretty busy. Supervising the construction of the camp and operating on the flight line keeps me at a high pace. Sure glad I have good enlisted men. They know how to do the job. Been working them 18 and 20 hours a day, and handling 1,000 lb. bombs isn't a job for boys. Makes men sleep rather soundly at night. But they say our planes are doing a good job. That's good enough for me.

Now to talk about us. What is all this talk about you going to kiss me many times when I get back? I'm going to hold you to that so don't disappoint me like you did at Aberdeen some few years ago. Of course I don't expect to be standing idly by. I'm going to be right in the caper. (Right in the middle of it.)

You know Norman L. wrote me—a typewritten letter—he didn't even sign his name. Hacked it out with the damn machine. (Last time he'll hear from me.) Guess I'm <u>peculiar</u>.

Legna, I'm still loving you Honey. Wish I could get back to you, soon and I mean real soon.

Heard about the President this morning. Tough break.

All my love, Howard

Philippines
April 20, 1945

Darling Legna,

First chance I've had to write. Been shifting around quite a bit, as you can see by another new APO. Kind of hope we settle down for a little while. Moving the outfit is a mess, unless you have time to do a little planning. The planes didn't stop operating for any of our moves; makes it much harder when you are operating and moving. Our outfit is sure piling up the bombing missions. We are still giving support to the infantry. Those boys are having a rough time, they are fighting in mountainous country and the Nips are really dug-in. Takes a 1,000 pounder to knock them out. We are gaining quite a good reputation with our good bombing. My Ordnance men are sure catching hell though. Sometimes they put in 18 & 20 hours. Long as our work is doing some good, we don't mind. We will work 24 hours if we have to. As I was saying, seems like weeks since I've written, but it just couldn't be helped this time Honey.

Made this last trip by train, almost like in the States. The train traveled about 10 miles per hour and the scenery wasn't too good. In fact, I've taken my last train ride, unless of course, I'm ordered to go. The dust is much worse there than any place we've been yet, wish the rainy season would start. Haven't made Manila yet but expect to visit it before long. Reckseit was down there yesterday. Didn't seem to think much of it. The Filipinos are really giving us a shafting on fresh food. They want a fortune for their fruit and fresh vegetables. Laundry service is still darn good, even get starch now.

I'm still getting my mail. Had one of yours today dated April 5. Our transport has been keeping us supplied. Think I'll whip down to see Bennert tomorrow, also have to pick up some spare parts for vehicles.
Sounds like you are in for a lot of work this spring with the operetta and Bischoff in the hospital. Read all about the Service Men's Plaque presentation in the Home News. Can't understand why the sermon was subjected "The Dignity of Man". Just the word dignity makes me think immediately of unfriendliness, of course that subject is as good as any, I guess. You know courtrooms are inhabited with a dignified atmosphere, hence the "severity and reprimand", that's why I don't like the word.

Darling, the feeling you have of seeing me soon, would be wonderful if I had it, but I'm not being optimistic about coming home. Don't want to be disappointed, it sure would be a let-down to think you were going home, and then found out you couldn't. Keep on feeling that way Honey, it boosts my morale. Damn, but Shady Side must be beautiful about now. You are what I want though Legna, more than anything in this world.

All my love,
Howard

P.S. APO 74 (NOW)

Philippines
April 23, 1945

Darling Legna,

Still pretty busy these days, at least though, we are organized now and the work isn't so far. I flew down and picked up Bennert yesterday. He was having a wonderful time fat-catting with the rear echelon. (Fat-catting is taking life easy and eating good food.) I stayed overnight, managed to get a few supplies and brought back some mail. We have B-25 and a C-47 in the Group. I went down on the B-25 and came back on the transport. Flew over Manila and Corregidor both ways. Looking at Corregidor from the air you wonder how in the world our paratroopers ever landed there. The island looks as small as a table top from 5,000 feet. Don't think I would like to bail out and try to hit it. Air travel is pretty good around here, scenic and fast.

Our camp is just about finished. If it wasn't so darn dusty it wouldn't be bad. This is the first time we've been situated far from the ocean and it's awfully hot, even hotter than New Guinea.

Legna, how about those three long days I let go by without writing to you? My gosh, what will you say when I didn't write for over a week during our moving? Hope you don't write many letters or address the letters, I should say, to APO 70, use 74! But Honey, I think a letter every three or even four days is darn good for me to write. Wish I could write more often but I just can't.

Wood and I are going on a little trip tomorrow. We will only be gone for the day. Seems funny to say you are going somewhere. Before there was never any place to go, but here there are a few places a fellow can go.

Honey, I still miss you as much as ever. I'd better get back to you soon.

All my love,
Howard

Philippines
April 26, 1945

Legna Darling,

Tis awfully hot today, I just came in from the line. Decided to take a few minutes rest and to write you. The sun will knock you out. Don't think I've ever seen it as hot before. I try to arrange the work for my men so they can work early in the morning or late in the evening. Handling 1,000 lb. bombs is not work for boys; my men are getting pretty rugged.

Ray Wood and I went to Clark Field the other day. Ray wanted to look-up a friend of his, a doctor that practiced in his hometown. We found him, talked together for a few hours, had lunch at the hospital. (Steak about an inch thick.) This Doc is a surgeon and he's attached to an infantry division. He related a few of his experiences. Believe me

Honey, those pillrollers do a good job. Can you imagine a surgeon at home performing sixty four major operations in a single day? Wonderful work and I admire the man. Think we'll ship down and see him again soon.

The Nips are giving us a little trouble around here. They are coming out of the hills and infiltrating our camps, looking for food and a way to escape mostly. A few of the boys in the outfit have one or two Nips to their credit. We keep a pretty tight guard around the airplanes at night, also around camp.

Legna, the outfit is winding-up its 18th month overseas. In some ways it doesn't seem like such a long time —others make it a hell of a while. Would sure like to get a thirty day leave to the States around June or July. However, we shouldn't think of such things. Would be great though. A lot of the pilots are on their way home. They will probably be reassigned and stay in the States, lucky boys, but they've earned it.

Darling, I think of you with every conceivable thought for a happy and lovely future, "the both of us."

Love,

Howard

Philippines

April 28, 1945

Darling Legna,

Nothing much doing out of the ordinary these days. The boys are going out on patrols with the guerillas and infantry; they are killing quite few Nips. Most of them are pretty close to camp, within two or three miles. So far we haven't had a casualty. The boys act like they are going duck hunting. They have brought back quite a few souvenirs, swords and things.

I haven't been working much the last few days. Picked-up a "damn cold" and it is knocking me out. Think I caught it while sleeping. The temperature is over 100° during the day. At night it gets cold enough for two blankets, but when you turn-in, it is still hot and you use nothing. Around 2:00AM you wake-up stiff, just like being on a desert. Amazing how cold it gets at night.

Legna, I feel sorry for Jeanne H. too but if you think she is having a rough time, think of Ernie. If Ernie is at sea and out this way, he has plenty to worry him. The Navy boys are not in a comfortable position in these waters. Women have had babies for years; seems to me without undue hardships. I hear so many stories from our married boys, about their wives having babies while they're overseas. Looks like all the "little women" are martyrs, at least they give that impression. Maybe I interpret the situation wrong. I could say more about it if I were in the same boat. I'd better shut-up anyway. I don't know anything about marital wars.

Darling, would you get me four baseball hats, size $6^{7/8}$ (two) and $7\ ^{1/8}$ (two), color doesn't make too much difference, blue preferred. (The squadron color is blue.) Maybe you can get them thru the sports section at school. Bennert's and Wood's wives can't get the darn things.

Still love you, Honey, much too much, I'm afraid.

All my love is *yours,*

Howard

Philippines
May 4, 1945

Darling Legna,

I wrote a very nice letter to you yesterday, took it to the mail-room for mailing. Arrived just in time to see a new censor regulation posted. My letter contained quite a bit of material pertaining to the regulation. So I had to tear the letter up, thank goodness it didn't get in the mail. The Group C.O. has little patience with men breaking censorship regulations.

We are going to have a few days off pretty soon. Maybe I'll get a chance to visit Manila. Wood and I want to look the place over. If we could get some lumber we could build a shack. It would be nice to get off the ground before the rainy season starts. Something tells me we will all don bathing suits and swim the area instead of walking. The rain really comes down. Have had a few healthy showers already. 'T'ain't nice!

The news from Germany sure has us enthused. Can't wait until we get some of those airplanes out here. Possible that some of us might get to go home. That would be nice!

Our food is darn good these days. We have some new cooks and they are doing a swell job. Haven't had anything to equal it for some time. Hope we have continuations. I could still go for a soft crab with a hot roll, wish I could even catch a few.

Honey, you will have another year of teaching behind you soon. I will have another year of army life at the end of this month. Four years is a "hell of a long time". Hope I don't have to stay and draw another fogey; that would make six years. Was wondering if you were going to school this summer. You mentioned it some time ago. If you do, you should pick some place in New England where it won't be so hot.

Legna, I hope I get home pretty soon, not just to be home, but to see and be with you. I'm lonesome for you Honey.

All my love,
Howard

Philippines
May 6, 1945

Dearest Legna Darling,

Had a letter from you yesterday, first in many days. I think we will start getting good service again. After no mail for three or four days it sure is great to get a letter from you. I love them "and you".

The last letter was chocked with ultimatums for my leave. (I might say here, what leave?) Honey, if I were to come home for thirty or forty days, I expect to have some fun. By that, I mean move around, see and mix with old friends. Can't very well do that by staying in one spot. Of course I expect you to accompany me on most of these sojourns. If I should happen to come home during school, you might not stay off all the time I'm there, but "by damned" you will take some time off, no matter what. My main reason for coming home is to see you and after an absence of two or two and half years, nothing is going to stop me from being with you as much as possible. You talk as though the school can't get along without you, and that's not true.

Honey there is such a remote possibility of getting a leave. I don't know why we even talk about it. I wouldn't dare say whether or not we would get married. We will know soon enough, in fact very soon after I get home. Another thing, I would definitely have to come back here, even if the war was to end while I was in the States. Unless of course there is something wrong with me physically and at that, I would probably have to be paralyzed. Tell you one thing I'm going to do and that is "drink lots of cold beer." Maybe you had better cultivate a taste for the stuff and keep me company.

Legna, Bob Schwen is in the hospital, nothing serious, but he may be there quite some time. Don't say anything to Gloria about this. Bob might not have told her. I hope he gets to go home—don't get this last statement confused now. Gosh, we are sending lots of pilots home now. Glad to see the boys get a break.

Legna, how much dough am I saving these days? What is the status of my savings? Is the bank having any trouble with my allotment? From the price of things around here, I probably won't be saving as much money.

I opened the last box of cigars you sent me. One of the pilots made captain so we had a little celebration. I rationed the cigars, they have to last me a long time.

Don't forget to see what you can do about those baseball hats. Oh, yes, send me some wrist bands for watches. Preferably cloth and the kind where you have the band between your wrist and the watch. This type keeps sweat from harming the watch and is good for the wrist.

Please don't get excited about this leave business; I'll be here for a long time. It wouldn't matter much except I want to get back to you. Glad you got the film!

Love,

Howard

Philippines

~~Apr~~ **May 7, 1945**

(I've got April on the brain)

Legna Darling,

From the tone of your letter it seems I'm not writing often enough. I'm sorry but I don't think there is going to be any improvement. Honey, writing is getting to be a real task, after 18 months of doing and seeing the same things every day, a fellow can't be very interesting. It's hard to explain, but t'is true.

How about the specs you mentioned in your last letter. What's wrong with those beautiful orbs? Maybe you are doing too much work at night without the proper light. Damn Legna, you are a bit young to be wearing glasses. I wear sun glasses practically all the time, the sun will knock your eyes out if you don't. A bit inconvenient with all the perspiration.

Had a visitor yesterday, a fellow that was transferred out of the outfit some months ago. He left us in New Guinea and I saw him in Leyte for a short time. Now he is only a few miles from us. We went to Clark Field, snooped around and had dinner in one of the surrounding towns. Chicken and ice cream, but talk about exorbitant prices. I never eat out unless it is necessary. Anyway, we had a pleasant day. I was glad to see the "ole boy" again. (Lt. Stern from the 310th)

Still haven't made my excursion to Manila. Can't say I'm so enthused about going now. We have a club for the officers up in the hills. It is a beautiful place, called "Hacienda Dolores". Has a fairly good size swimming pool and that's what interests me. It's wonderful to take a dip in the late afternoon. All we need is a golf course and that would top everything. This club is going to be nice for me. I never go out at night (or travel around very much) so it will be a good way to work off some spare time. We will probably have plenty of that before long.

Honey, if you run across a book (any kind) you think I might like, send it over.

For now sweetheart, all my love!

Howard

Philippines
May 13, 1945

Dearest Darling Legna,

Had a slew of letters from you yesterday, one dated May 1st. T'was about time some mail came thru. Course I admit I haven't written for several days. Wood and I went on a little trip and for the past three days we've been working on our shack. This house is going to be a good one, it takes a lot of work but we made up our minds to do a good job.

About the "little trip"—went to Manila—was there for two days! You know honey, when you look at a city like Manila after war has passed thru, you think of how "blessed" we are by not having the same devastating machine move thru our cities in the States. It is quite impossible to imagine how destructive war can be. War has left a terrible scar on that beautiful city that will take many years to erase. We took lots of pictures. I had Bennert's camera—just hope they turn out alright. Even the harbour is a grave yard, never saw so many sunken ships in my life and I've seen a few. After a day and half of sight-seeing, I don't care to go

531

back. There isn't much to the city now. (I did go to an air-conditioned theatre, neon lights and cushioned seats, "the Nips slipped-up".)

Say Honey, what is this business about my being the ole Shenton when there is work to do? Did I raise hell in one of my letters before we moved out? It is true that we get along better here when we are busy, because we don't have time to argue and play tricks on one another. But I didn't think my letter writing was being effected, especially my letters to you. If I did it might be a good thing for you, maybe you learn things about me that will be a benefit. I have no false make-up Legna, whatever there is about me is just me, so what you see and know about me is just Shenton. By that, I don't mean I can't be changed, always could listen to reason and facts. I know that I love you as much as any man could love a woman. With that, we have enough to get married. T'is what I want to do. But Honey, there are so many things we must consider. We want something that will last forever, come what might. (Love alone does not speak permanency.) Don't worry about it Darling, everything will work out. We must be practical, you know! Legna, did you ever think of how much you mean to me? I want to come home right now, but it's not just to be coming home, I want to come back because of you. I could live most anywhere but not without you. Look over my lifetime before meeting you; I should say "fell in love". See if you can find anything that I would like to contact again. Any memories revolve around one thing— "Legna"—and that's good enough for me.

All my love, Howard (APO is now 74)

Philippines

May 15, 1945

Darling Legna,

Had a busy day, worked on our shack from early till late. Been raining like a sun-fish all day, but we manage; even tho we did get a bit wet. Should be able to move in about two days, hope so, because the rainy season is upon us. This is going to be the best house we have ever had, complete with (1) each, porch. Wish we could get a radio; there is some good music on the airways around these parts. Going to try and arrange a water system.

Legna, the Air Corps boys are fortunate in this theatre of war. Here I am writing about building a nice shack, when only a few miles from us the infantry boys are living like, I would say animals, but nature takes care of animals. If you could see the way it rains out here and then think of the boys fighting in the mountains with only the equipment they can carry on their backs. Yes, we are quite fortunate in the Air Corps, but sometimes I feel a bit uncomfortable, when I'm sitting in a chair, with a dry roof overhead. T'is the fortunes of war, I guess.

I'm enclosing a money order for $135. Stow it away for me, Honey. Had to use money order this time; the cabling set up isn't completed at this base. A few more trips to Manila and it won't matter to me what system is being used for sending money home. A trip to Manila is worse than a squadron poker game, don't think I'll be taking many trips.

So you and Anthony B. don't get along too well. You are probably driving the poor man to exasperation. No, Honey, maybe he's just a hard man and should be leading an outdoor life, instead of haggling with women over room temperatures. You know, he once called me a sugar baby because I wouldn't walk to the bus in a pouring rain and missed a day at school.

Legna, that's about all. Wish I could say I'd see you in another twelve months. But I don't see how! (Miracles!)

All my love,
Howard

Philippines
May 18, 1945

Dear "Legna Darling",

Mail came in today and I had two letters from you, one postmarked the 8th. Seems like the mail is getting through pretty fast now. Ten days from the East Coast is darn good time. Was wondering how long it took my letters to reach Shady Side. I was glad to hear you got two letters from me, all in one week! That guy Shenton is on the ball!

Honey, the pictures are wonderful, just what I needed, and wanted. You are looking pretty sweet these days. The satin dress is sure nice. Fits very well too. Tell Miss Ethel she hit the jack-pot. I love the profile pose. It stirred up that longing feeling though; that isn't so good when we are 12,000 miles apart. Looks as though you were talking when the time exposure was taken. Thanks for all of them Legna, they are really nice.

Finished our house today and I must say it's pretty sharp. We'll have to send you a few pictures of the place. I installed the sink this afternoon, all I have to do now is figure out how to catch and store the rain when it runs off the roof. The boys say they wouldn't take a thousand pesos for the shack. I wouldn't either, we have put in a lot of hard work. T'is worth the work tho, we have already had a taste of the rainy season. It isn't nice to be on the ground when the rains come.

Schwen isn't in the squadron anymore. He came back from the hospital and was transferred to Group Headquarters. I don't think Bob wanted to leave either but we will see him as much as ever. I'm sorry he didn't get a homer! Could use one myself.

There is something going around the outfit now about going home and getting out of the Army. Evidently it is a point system, time of service, overseas time and things like that. Everybody has been adding up their points, that's as far as it goes. I'll be back when the war is over, <u>for sure</u>.

So you've been having dreams, Darling, sweet dreams! I don't dream very often but when I do you play a very important part. It's alright to dream about "stuff", just natural or nature, I guess. Long as it's just you and me!

Went up in a bomber yesterday as an observer. Saw our pilots work over some Nips. It was ground support work and I can see why the infantry likes the Air Corps. It was very interesting to watch and I sure had a ringside seat.

Guess that's all sweetheart. We'll try to better that twice a week record. I sent a money order for $135 in my last letter. Keep an eye peeled for it.

All my love, Lovely Legna,
Howard

Philippines

May 19, 1945

Darling Legna,

We moved into our new house today. Sure is nice. It is screened-in and the floor is about two feet off the ground. Wish you were here with me tonight, the place is clean and cozy. I'm sitting at the table writing with my pajamas on, real clean and white they are, even starched. Put clean sheets, pillow-case and blanket on my bed. The laundry service makes living conditions a lot better. Back in N.G., laundry cost an exorbitant sum. Then it wasn't very clean. Smelled clean anyway. I think we are going to appreciate our little house, especially when it's raining. Haven't rigged my water system yet, but expect to have it in by tomorrow.

Bennert isn't here for the house warming. He went to Manila and will probably R.O.N. there. (That means "remain over night".) We moved all his equipment to the new shack. He might be back yet. Hope he can locate a radio for us. I had a lead on one and he's following thru on it.

Couple more of the pilots are about to take-off for home. Keep on this way, there won't be any of the old boys around. I would like to be going with them. Wouldn't even regret leaving our new house.

Wood & Bennert are making remarks about the way you wear your hair in the pictures. What is that thing called, a puff or bangs? Looks alright to me, naturally!

Honey, I don't want those baseball hats to play ball in. Over here the sun is so bright you must have a hat with a long bill, to shade your eyes.

The hats we brought over have worn out and we aren't allowed to wear straw hats anymore. But we can wear baseball hats around camp and on the line. Do the best you can. We need them pretty badly, especially the 7 $^{1/8}$ size—that's for me—but send the others, even if you can't get my size.

You are mistaken about me not loving you when I was in the States. (Sounds like some of the psychology you picked-up in school.)

Love,

Howard

Philippines
May 25, 1945

Dearest "Legna Darling",

There isn't much doing these days. But I'm not complaining. I can stand a few months of this life, maybe I'm getting lazy. The climate is conducive to such a reaction. A siesta goes quite well in the afternoon, even the pilots get a break. They do most of the flying in the morning.

It was mighty nice of Anthony B. to requisition the hats. Guess he's a pretty nice guy after all. The boys were glad to hear of the possibility of getting them. Would you see if you can find a couple of wrist-watch straps to send me? My one and only is about to drop off my arm.

What's wrong Honey, are you getting impatient because I don't rave about us getting married? You know, your last letter was almost a proposal of marriage. Keep trying, Legna, I'll weaken sooner or later. Honey, I must keep telling you, I love you and have every intention of us getting married. What is it any way? Must be one of the things women like to be reminded of (often). Just sit tight and hold your fire, everything is going to come out alright. Let's get this <u>war</u> over first.

Tell your Mom that is a swell poem she wrote for the boys in the service. When I saw the name Miss Ethel at the end, I had visions of the schoolroom in Shady Side with me crouched behind a book, glancing up once in a while to watch Miss Ethel work someone over. Also the plays we used to put on. Never realized then how much work it was for the teacher. We had some good ones, too. You know, Legna, if I had a guiding hand at home in those days, I might have gone places in school.

Darling, don't get impatient with me, in the things that matter with just us. I want you more than anything in this world.

All my love,
Howard

Same ole place
May 28, 1945

Dearest Darling Legna,

I don't know, but is there something the matter? I haven't had a letter from you in five days. Though your last letter didn't intimate that there was anything wrong. But perhaps I wrote something, course you could be busy. Guess it's about final exam time. Teachers are probably busier than the students. (T'was true in my case.) Whatever it is Honey, sit down and write me a sweet letter. (Maybe you are just lazy.) Look out Shenton; you will suffer for that one!

Wood and I are going to Lingayen tomorrow. He has to go; I'm going to see if I can locate the Placido boy. Wish I knew his name, first and last. I'll find him though if he's still around. I know his outfit, ran into them at Leyte a long time ago.

Have had the pictures I took in Manila developed. Should be printed in a few days. I might have to send the negatives to you for printing. Each of us in the shack want a set and we can only get one set printed here (Paper shortage).

The squadron has a new C.O. again. The former has gone home. This makes about eight since I've been in the outfit. This fellow is a West Pointer. He joined the outfit when we were at Bradley Field. Remember?

Say, our food is really good these days. Getting lots of fresh stuff, meat and eggs once in a while. Hope it continues, I could stand a little weight added. We have a new ice machine, which makes enough ice to give us a cold drink at noon. That really goes good.

Tonight, I would like to sit real close to you Legna and talk. There wouldn't have to be any point in my conversation. Just want to be close to you and feel you there. Course that wouldn't last long, I'm sure it would lead to other things. Maybe not stuff, but good old fashion loving. I'd better get home soon, 'cause I'm thinking more about "us" as days pass. Honey, if we could be together tonight, I wouldn't want anyone around. Just you and me—we'd be happy too.

All my love,
Howard

Philippines

May 31, 1945

Darling Legna,

Arrived home last night, late last night. Had a good trip, excepting for the ride. Darn, I hate to ride in a Jeep. Accomplished a few things, got some vehicle parts, and a load of lumber for the squadron. Didn't see the Placido fellow, his outfit has moved. You know Legna, we were operating from the same strip for about a month. But that's the way it goes. I had the same experience with Junior Trott. In fact I was at the same base with Junior for six months and didn't know he was there till after we had moved.

There was a letter from you on my bed when I came in. You said the caps were in the mail—fast work Honey. I might say, you are indeed efficient. You're a real sweetheart too. I love you!

The pictures I took in Manila came out pretty good, with the exception of the one I wanted most. It was of a Japanese bathtub that some high ranking officer had installed amid all of the modern plumbing at the Army-Navy club. Darn I wanted that one, more than any.

Honey, I'm afraid now that it will be another year before I get back to the States. We hear so many things about leaves, rotation and going home in general. Guess we really shouldn't talk about it, there's nothing definite, never will be, I think. I don't like to raise false hopes —yours or mine.

Met a couple of boys yesterday that just came over from the States. Talking with them made me a bit homesick. I'd give anything to get back.

Tomorrow we start driving on the right hand side of the road. Think I'll stay put for a few days, won't be safe on the roads. You know, it's rather funny, but driving on the left is as natural to me now as driving on the right back in the States. It will take a few days to get straightened around.

Don't worry about that Teachers Convention in July. I won't be home then, but if I should, you wouldn't be attending. There would be a convention maybe, but just you and me.

Love,
Howard

Philippines
June 5, 1945 (So Wood says)

Dearest Legna Darling,

I thought something was ailing you. I didn't get a letter for a week or so. Must be a slip somewhere. I can't recall saying anything about "not writing". Maybe I'd better start reading my letters two or three times before mailing. Your 290th letter was a "sizzler". You can sure make a noise when you think you are hurt. O.K. Honey, so I'm not your darling any more. You're still mine, whether you want to be or not. I'm firm on that score, Legna. Perhaps though, you shouldn't be wasting your love on a guy that can't or won't show that he appreciates it. Please, don't do like some of our boys' wives are doing, Seems the boys wrote home and said they had gone out a few times while on leave in Australia. That really did it. One of the boys hasn't heard from his wife for two months, and she with their baby that he has never seen. Nice going, isn't it? Don't pull anything like that on me Legna. I'm afraid I'd burst several blood vessels. I don't know what in the hell people back home think we are doing over here. They must have no imagination or think some of the horror pictures they see in books and on the screen is all propaganda. Well, for myself, I can say that I haven't suffered or had undue hardships. But some of our boys risk their lives every day. What makes it so tough is the things you see happen and know it is quite possible that same can happen to you. Let you and me forget the whole thing, I'm speaking of what I just said above. I love you Legna and I've always been true to you. That's the way I want it to be. (Some nice-looking gals around here.)

I've been traveling a lot the past few weeks, getting a little weary. Been drawing supplies and equipment, things are so spread out, it takes days to find and get what you want. I was supposed to make an airplane trip today but begged off. I want to enjoy my "little house" for a while. Wood and Bennert greeted me like I'd been gone for a month when I get home. The silly buggers. Well, we do have a little fun.

Legna, there's a deal on the fire about me transferring from Ordnance to Air Corps so I can be promoted. The "wheels" want to give me a break. I'm stepping careful. Don't want to get tied up in case there is an opportunity to get home. Honey, I want to come home more than I could ever hope to say or write. I want to so badly that I lose sight of the fact that there is still a war going on and that isn't the right way. I shouldn't feel bad if I don't get back until the show is over. There are so many men that have been out here much longer than me. Of course they want to go home too, and they should have first crack at it. I wouldn't let a promotion stop me though.

Honey, how about some more pictures of you? I love them. Try to keep your "yapper" shut when they are snapped though. It will be a long time before you get the Manila shots. Was down there again yesterday getting some vehicles.

All my love, Honey!

Howard

Luzon

June 8, 1945

Dearest Legna Darling,

No letters today. Shenton isn't getting much mail these days. I'm not complaining though, guess I haven't been writing many. In fact, I expect I'll be writing fewer still. There sure isn't much to say. But don't worry Honey, I'll always write to you, whenever possible.

Wood and Bennert are getting a stock question in their wives' letters. It is, "When are you coming home?" What a remarkable query. I think the point system has the civilians in a lather. You know Legna, everybody can't go home; there's still a war on out here. There won't be many from the Air Forces getting out, until the show is over. I'm afraid points aren't going to help us very much. T'is probably just as well to stay and see the darn thing thru. I'd better not get any offers though, 'cause I want to come home so much, I'd accept. Maybe we will get leaves to the States.

Been raining almost all day and it's pouring right now. I took Wood to Manila today. Had some business to take care of and Wood has a doctor friend in the infantry. We found the doc, had a nice chat for a couple of hours. We ate lunch at Nichols Field, came right back to camp. Neither of us felt like hacking around town.

If we could live for six months as we are living now, things would be pretty nice. The food is very good and with a good waterproof shack we are doing alright. I could put on a little weight, could stand a little of that too.

Legna, didn't you say something about going to summer school? With the convention coming up, I don't suppose you will make school. And I always thought a schoolteacher was fortunate in having a long vacation. If only I could get back to the States, we've have one —just you and me (H.C. Shenton).

Honey, I don't mind too much about mail, but don't be too persistent with "your vengeance".

All my love,

Howard

Luzon
(We can mention it now, the censors say)
June 9, 1945

Dearest Darling Legna,

I didn't intend to write tonight but I'm going on a trip in the morning and I may not be back for a couple of days. Thought I'd better keep peace by writing tonight. Honey, something happened to the mail from May 8th to the 15th. I know darn well seven days didn't go by without my writing you a letter. Bennert and Wood have the same difficulty, Bennert's wife thought he was on his way home because she didn't hear from him in over a week. So I was right about you being angry because

544

you weren't getting any mail. Honey, your surmising about the reason for not getting mail was incorrect at the time. But will be true in the near future. Try to remember your 292th letter so you will know what the *score* will be. Shame too, we have such a nice house.

All of us went to the club for dinner tonight. The meal was excellent. Wish I could have stayed around a while after eating but had to get back, write you and prepare for my trip. The club is really beautiful Legna. Wish you could have been there with me. I think you would have enjoyed it very much. Had fruit cocktail, salad, steak and two vegetables, topped off with pie and coffee. Ate so much I was a bit uncomfortable, had a good cigar after the meal too, one you sent me.

Rained again today, all day, didn't think so much water could fall from the sky. The roads are just about washed-out; the vehicles are taking a beating.

Gosh, I'm sorry to hear about Cap'n Will Lee. Didn't we call him Cap'n Blink? He was a wonderful man. I think he was the kindest and sincerest man I'd ever known. Remember, I spent so much time over at his house when Snip was living with them. Miss Liza will have a tough time with him gone. Perhaps Sam will get on the ball though.

The picture of you isn't so bad. How about that wind-blown hair, Honey? What's wrong, don't you like to reveal that broad forehead of yours? Do something with those bangs! I love you though, Legna, bangs and all. I even love you when you're angry.

Will write soon as possible.

Love,
Howard

Philippines (Luzon)

June 12, 1945

Dearest Legna Darling,

Came back from my trip yesterday, was going to write, but felt pretty beat-out. Guess I will be busy for a while now, things are picking-up. If you don't hear from me for a week or ten days, please don't get angry.

Legna, you never told me what was wrong with my letters, when I was at Mindoro. How about enlightening me? Perhaps I can refrain from doing the same thing again.

Understand the outfit is going to start sending men back to the States on leave. That will be wonderful, 45 days at home! I don't stand a chance of getting it at first. Too damn many married men among the officers. Seems like they get first choice. We should have married, Legna! Probably be eight or ten months before it gets around to me. 'Course I stand pretty high on points, maybe it will help me out. It is surprising how few men in our outfit have above 85 points, I've got exactly 85. That is one reason they are in no hurry to send me home on leave. If I was to get in the States I might not have to come overseas again. Wouldn't that be nice??

Honey, I wrote another letter to the "clothes storage" firm in Australia. Hope they send my clothes. Been hacking around with those guys long enough. About time I was getting a little action. Told them to send the clothes C.O.D. or rather the most expeditious way. They will no doubt send me a bill for storage and shipping charges and wait till they get the money before releasing the goods.

546

Legna, what do you hear from Derwill? Is he still in Hawaii? Let me know how he is getting along and tell me what he is doing. Always a possibility I might run into some of the boys. The Galesville News keeps me posted on most of the boys' whereabouts, but so far it hasn't helped.

Think I'll whip-up to the club for a swim this afternoon. I need a little sunshine and a little cooling off.

How's your attitude sweetheart? Are you still angry or back to normal?

I'll be glad to get some more pictures.

All my love,

Howard

P.S. Honey, I received a package a few days ago. Contents: shrimp, sardines, and comic sheets. Thanks, you darling!

Luzon

June 15, 1945

Dearest Legna Darling,

Had two letters from you today, kind of surprised me. I went to Manila this morning, to take Fischer, who was visiting us and to pick up a few supplies. Bert wanted me to stay overnight, his outfit has a house there and Bert is staying for about a week. Just think, had I stayed, your letters would have laid on my bed unopened until tomorrow. Glad I decided to come back this evening.

Legna, you mentioned about my letter being held by the censor. Tell me, has anything ever been cut from my letters? I would like to know because I really try <u>not</u> to break censorship rules. Wood has had things cut-out of his letters and he's the squadron censor!

Yes, I have enough points to come home, the critical score is 85 and that's exactly what I have. 'Course there are many men here with higher scores than that and naturally they will be first. Not even sure yet that officers will be affected by points, there are only three of us in the squadron with 85 or about. (The married men beat me out again.)

It was nice seeing Fischer again. He asked about you and mentioned "our day" in New York. He doesn't look too well, just got out of the hospital, was in for about a month. I had lunch with him at his squadron house. It was great. They served some kind of Chinese dish, looked good and tasted good. Filipino house boys served us and they know their job.

No Legna, I don't think we should buy a house. In the first place, we have no idea where we are going to live. Then again, we'd better wait until we are married. Who knows, maybe I'll be changed so much, you might not want me.

Honey, I comb my hair straight back. Fact is, I don't have much to comb. When "that picture" was taken I had just come from the shower.

Love,

Howard

Luzon
June 16, 1945

Dearest Darling Legna,

I'm glad the Prom was a success. It pleases me to have you say you had a good time. My only regret is that I couldn't be there with you, but our time will come. Seems to me I danced with you for the first time at a

Prom. No, it was just a dance at Southern. A Friday night, I whipped down from Washington and met you at the school. Miss Ethel was there too, having a wonderful time dancing! Honey, I wish you could have more good times. We'll have good times and happy times when I get back. (Both together at the same time.)

Wish the hats would get here. If I don't get them soon, it will probably be sometime before I see them. Dierlein (he is my other tent-mate) got three from home and gave me one, but it's too small. About time yours were arriving, isn't it?

I've been working pretty steadily lately, not overworking but keeping busy. I've done an awful lot of traveling; getting so I hate to sit in a Jeep. Don't want to ride in airplanes either.

We are having a good argument in my tent tonight. The boys are talking Jeeps —where they should be assigned and the best way to take care of them. I say, send all the Jeeps back to the States or give them to the Filipinos and we could operate a lot more efficiently. I have no great liking for the darn Jeep.

Been reading a book, supposed to be a "best seller", entitled *Forever Amber*. I didn't finish it. What a story. It jumps from one bedroom to another. Sure would hate to think that sex could rule our country the way it did during the Restoration Period. 'Course I realize it's just a story. (About sex.)

Honey there isn't much more I can write about. Had a letter from you yesterday, pretty nice too.

How about that hair, Honey? I like bangs, but aren't yours getting a little long?

All my love,
Howard

549

Luzon

June 20, 1945

Darling Legna,

Had a letter from you yesterday. The watch strap was in it. Nice work, you are pretty sharp Legna; it's a nice strap, too.

Wood, Bennert and I went to Manila yesterday. Met the doctor friend of Wood's then went over to see Fischer. Fischer's outfit has a marvelous house in town, complete with servants. All of us were invited for dinner and the meal was great. Even had ice-cold cocktails before dinner. Wood's friend enjoyed himself. He is in the infantry and those boys don't have any luxuries. Bert wanted us to stay all night, but we had to refuse, so we drove back rather late in the evening. If a fellow could go to a place like that, once or twice a month, overseas duty wouldn't be too bad. Wish we could do it more often.

Honey, when you added my points, naturally you didn't get 85. I have four campaign stars, at 5 points per star. I'll no doubt have a couple more before we are thru. My 85 doesn't mean too much, will take about 8 or 9 months to get down to that score. I'd like to get a 45 day leave right now, that would fix me perfectly.

Whitey certainly didn't stay out here very long. Couldn't have been more than a year. If he's been to the places you mentioned in your letter, why he deserves to be home. Some of those were mighty hot spots, especially for the Navy!

So school is completely over. Now you can have a long vacation! I bet though, you work more during the summer months than when you teach school. How about the convention? Are you still going to decide the fate of the Maryland student? I'd like to sit-in and hear what goes on; sounds as though it would be interesting.

Honey, three watch straps will be enough and I'm sure you can pick-out a couple of books I might like.

I'm still loving you Legna. That is one thing that hasn't changed. I'm not sure about the rest of me—some think I've changed and some say not. I can't see any difference.

All my love,
Howard

Luzon
June 24, 1945

Darling Legna,

The second watch strap came yesterday. Pretty good strap, but they won't stay white very long. I also had a letter from Miss Grace. She's been writing quite a bit lately.

The boys have been playing a little volleyball the past two days. First time we'd played in months and we played a terrible game. Our game is not so rough now. Someone whipped out a rule book. We abide by the rules with a few modifications, of course.

Wish I could share Carrie's view on my coming home, but it will be sometime yet, Honey. Gosh, if we had two babies I'd be getting back pretty soon —that's 24 points! Would raise my ante to 109 and those with that score should make it in a couple of months. Legna, we should have married and started a family. One of our officers has 118 points. He should be going home within a month. (Many babies, a lot of service.)

Each man was issued a case of beer yesterday. This "fat-cat" life is getting me down. This is the best place we have ever been. Wish it would last. Even had fresh eggs this morning. Should say egg though, there was one per man. Had a fresh orange too!

Honey, I haven't heard anything about my clothes. Wrote the storage company another letter and told them to ship the stuff. No, I don't expect to go back to Australia. Hope not anyway. From here on out I want to travel north and then east.

The war news is very good, certainly was a shock to hear of the mass surrender on Okinawa. Looks like the Nips are getting a little sense. I hope more of them follow the same thought. There is a lot of betting going on, that the war will be over in three. (A bit fantastic, I would say.)

Sounds like you are going to have a busy summer with the convention and work about the R.H.H. Wish I could be in on it, but am afraid we wouldn't accomplish much work.

All my love,
Howard

Advancing

Western Pacific Area

"I hate war as only a soldier who has lived it can, only as one who has
seen its brutality, its futility, its stupidity."

—General Dwight D. Eisenhower

ARMY AIR FORCES

DROP-STITCH

"On Board,"

Darling Legna,

July 2, 1945

Well I'm living with the Navy again and find it a high standard, it's awfully high compared to Army's. The food far surpasses anything we have ever had, and the Navy can't understand why we rave about their food. After the loading detail was over; there is nothing to do but read, eat and sleep, have a show every night too, weather permitting! I am in charge of loading and I must say it's quite a job, these Navy fellows are very particular about stowing cargo. I've loaded several ships and every one has been different, the Navy gives us a hand though, which is more than I can say for the merchant marine, those guys stink!

Legna, we have been getting a little mail while waiting and I must say, I've been getting darn little. If it wasn't for the Rome News I'd be mailess, got all of the watch straps, wish the caps had come thru before I left. Gosh knows, when I'll get them now, I guess I can't complain much about mail tho, I haven't been writing much lately. Sometimes writing gets to be a damn nuisance, it's nice to get letters tho, maybe I'm lazy.

554

"On Board"
July 2, 1945

Darling Legna,

Well I'm living with the Navy again and find it a high standard. (T'is awfully high compared to the Army.) The food far surpassed anything we have ever had, and the Navy can't understand why we rave about their food. After the loading detail was over, there is nothing to do but read, eat and sleep, and have a show every night too, weather permitting! I am in charge of loading and I must say it's quite a job. These Navy fellows are very particular about stowing cargo. I've loaded several ships and every one has been different. The Navy gives us a hand though, which is more than I can say for the merchant marine. Those guys stink!

Legna, we have been getting a little mail while waiting and I must say, I've been getting "darn little". If it wasn't for the Home News I'd be mail-less. Got all of the watch straps. Wish the caps had come thru before I left. Gosh knows when I'll get them now. Guess I can't complain much about mail tho. I haven't been writing much lately. Sometimes writing gets to be a damn nuisance. T'is nice to get letters tho. Maybe I'm lazy.

I sent $150 by wire last month. Don't remember if I mentioned it before. Was kind of late getting it off. Let me know when it arrives. Have to cancel a receipt held by the squadron.

I've been reading some good books on board. The ship has a darn good library; in fact I think perhaps I read too much. My eyes can't stand the strain. Hate to think of wearing glasses though. Guess I'll slow down on the reading.

Legna, you're surmising that I might be home by December or January shouldn't be too wrong. I expect to be back in January. I can come home now but would have to come overseas again for another year. The Army sure drives a hard bargain. I should certainly be home by next summer anyway.

Darling, there isn't "anymore" to say now. I'm getting damn homesick or perhaps it's lovesickness. I want to get back to you.

All my love,
Howard

Western Pacific Area

Dearest Legna Darling,

There isn't much a fellow can write about here. I could give you the "old tourist job" but censors won't allow it. Too bad we can't use postcards. I think you could say all they want you to say and have space left over.

Well Honey, Bennert, Wood and I are building another shack. Nothing super this time, just have enough room and that's all. We put in too much work and money in our last house and didn't live in it long enough to pay for our trouble. We will have electricity in this one, but no running water. Course we always have a telephone, that's essential. Wish we could get a radio; there is a very good broadcasting station here, good music and all the latest news events.

Right now, I could use some mail. Haven't had any since the latter part of June. I've been thinking of those baseball caps. Hope they get thru alright. Speaking of mail, you won't be doing so well on your end either. Don't get angry about it though. Just couldn't be any other way.

By now, you and your colleagues should have decided the fate of "educational progress" for the state of Maryland. Honey, I hope you find your work interesting. Still, I know mine isn't. Wish I could break the routine, but guess the Army is built on routine.

Haven't heard much about the "point system" lately. At the rate they are going in this theatre, I'm beginning to think less and less of my meagre 85. Wish I had about 120 or even 100 — then I'd be getting home pretty soon. We have sent a few enlisted men home on points but their score is much lower than officers. I figure about another year or slightly less for me, that isn't so bad, but when you say "year" to fellows out here it seems like eternity.

Sweetheart, I intended to write more but there isn't anything to say. If I could only whisper a few sweet-nothings in your ear!

All my love,
Howard

Western Pacific

Dearest Darling Legna,

It has been an awful long time since I've written. Sure hope you are not perturbed about it, because nothing else could be done. Course it works about the same way on this end. We won't get any mail for weeks now. You have been writing though and quite a few letters should accumulate, I hope. Whereas, I haven't been able to hack out a letter! (I'm being called a liar.)

I've been pretty busy for the past few days, building a camp. Don't know why I always get stuck with these jobs, but looks like I just can't get around it. I'm so damn tired of building, tearing down, loading and unloading ships, till I can't think straight. Honey, I'm getting weary and it isn't combat fatigue. Guess I've been overseas too long. There was a time when I built camps with enthusiasm, now all I do is ask for enough material, which of course I never get. Think I'll take a course in "civil engineering" when I get back to the States. The army has given me a pretty good background. Either that or stevedoring. I could almost apply for a commission in the Navy with my present "ship experience". Shipped with a swell crew this time, swellest bunch of fellows I ever met. Gosh, these people do get good food.

Now sweetheart, how about "us"? Are you still loving me as much as ever? Been so long since I've had a letter, guess I need a reminder — should I? It's a darn good thing I have you to think about Legna, otherwise there are times when I'd probably blow my top, so to speak. You are the only "one" I have who really cares and believe me that counts! I can tell you Honey, if it weren't for you, I wouldn't care whether I got home this year or in the next two. It's just that you are all I have to come back for (better or worse). My best thoughts are of you and me, 'course some of them may not be the "better thoughts" to some people's way of thinking, but to ours they are wonderful! (Hope I'm right on that score.) Could be too, as the boys say about me, "Shenton isn't always right, but he's never wrong!" Love is a great thing, I'm told and I believe that, but Honey I want to get with it, right in "the middle of the caper."

There isn't much a fellow can write, but I'll be writing my usual quota. (Don't misunderstand that Honey; I'm not being drafted into writing letters.)

All my love,
Howard

Western Pacific Area

Dearest Darling Legna,

Things are kind of rough now —haven't had any mail for almost a month. Makes it darn hard writing, without incoming mail. Then again censorship regulations are strict; a fellow can't say much.

Finished building our new shack yesterday, not a bad bit of construction, but it isn't as good as the last. Hardly pays us to build a nice place, we move too darn often. The camp is coming along. Most of the main installations are finished. Got a swell shower and kitchen, food isn't bad now either--much improved since our arrival. I expect everything to be completed in a few more days. Will be darn glad when it is, too. This camp building is getting terrifically boring. Wood and Bennert gave me a lot of assistance on this one, for which I am quite happy. There have been times when I was alone. (I feel lonely quite often but that has nothing to do with camps.)

My old skin disease came back, only this time it's on my legs and I've got it bad. Thought perhaps a cooler climate would rid me of the stuff for good, but t'is worse than ever. Isn't bad enough for a "homer", but very uncomfortable. There is no specific remedy, sometimes a certain lotion will clear it up, then you try it again, with no effects whatsoever.

Night before last we had a great experience. T'was raining hard in the evening. Along about midnight a strong wind came up and blew our tent down. We had a time getting the thing up again, everything we owned got wet, including us and our sacks. Got a lot of laughs out of it. We looked so miserable it was funny.

Next month will be two years since we had our day in New York. I didn't have much fun that day. I kind of figured it would be our last time together before I shipped-out. Long, long time Honey, and as each day goes by it seems a lot longer. I hope another year will do the job, and I think it will. Gosh, all the fellows think about now is going home. (Would be nice.)

Legna, give me the story on what you accomplished at the convention. Should be interesting. Maybe someday I will have a personal interest!

About all I have for now.

All my love,
Howard

Western Pacific Area

Darling Legna,

I'm not feeling too sharp tonight, hardly enough to write a letter. But I want to write you, even though there's so darn little to say. Don't know what ails me; just have a slight headache, maybe I got too much sun today. Then again I have been working, been worrying about getting the darn camp set up. Wish we would move just once and I could tag along, instead of being a "wheel". We move so often till I'm getting "jammed to the gills" (Poor fish)

We have a nice site except for the dust. There's a road running along the edge of camp and the vehicles really dust us. Won't be so bad if we get a good road in, but that all takes time. Course, we do have plenty of time! However, we do live a lot better than some outfits —takes a little work but 'tis worth the trouble.

Honey, if you see Emma Jean ask her for Carroll Smith's address. I had the darn thing but lost it. I think Carroll is around the vicinity and I'd like to meet him. If I do meet him, he will be the first guy I will have run into from around home. (Think I messed up in my grammar.)

Legna, that's about all I have for now. If I could only get some mail from you!

All my love, Howard

Western Pacific
July 23, 1945

Dearest Darling Legna,

As you have probably noticed, I can date my letters now. Can't see why it makes much difference though, no one ever knows the date, sometimes not even the month. I do know that it has been a month since I've received any mail, that's bad! The whole outfit is just crying for "that morale booster"!

I have a new job now, in addition to my other duties, Ordnance, Transportation, CWS and camp builder, I now have the adjutant's job to perform. Our adjutant left this morning for home. Yes Honey, "home"! He has 118 points and his number was called. Lucky boy. Wish they would hurry and get down to my meager 85. If I get this adjutant's job permanently, there's a possibility of a promotion in it. But Legna, I'm not interested in being a captain; I just want to go home. In order for this deal to go thru, I have to be transferred from Ordnance to Air Corps and it might not go thru higher headquarters. (Transfer I mean.) Frankly I don't much care a damn, I'll do my job whether I'm a 2nd Lt or a Major. Rank has ceased to be important. Oh Honey, why didn't we get married and have a thousand kids? (I wonder!)

The camp is still under construction, believe me I'll be glad when it is finished. Guess I'm not as eager as I used to be. I don't think anyone is after 20 months over here. Just think though, some fellows have been out 36 months or more. It murders me every time I think of it. This outfit has sure left a long trail behind since we came overseas. Some of it was a little rough and some quite smooth. Wish we had a portable camp though. Hit the beach and wham, your camp is set up. Would save a lot of headaches, if anyone mentions a camping trip to me when I get back to civilian life, I'll do something drastic, quite devastating too.

The news is certainly great. The Nips are sure taking a pounding. How in the world they stand it, beats me. We sure are pouring it on them. The Navy is certainly tearing things up around the Nips' homeland. The navy has done a real job in this theatre of war. Those boys are alright.

Sweetheart, I haven't made any plans for when I come home. Guess you know though, that you are going to be in them, A-No.1 priority! Gosh I want to see you so bad. Kind of makes me get goose pimples whenever I think of looking at you and talking together. Hope we can get a little farther than that!

All my love,
Howard

Western Pacific Area

July 25, 1945

Dearest "Darling Wench",

I am so happy right now, probably will go outside and broadcast it to the island. The boys sent some mail up today and I had sixteen letters from you and Honey, I love them. Expect to read them all at least twice. Gosh, it's been so long since we've had mail—an even month. Now I should be able to hack out a few letters without any trouble.

Honey, about that trip you are planning when I return. I'm all for it. I want to go someplace where just you and I can be alone (together) for a couple of weeks at least. How about the married or single business though? Just wondering if you would go thru with it if we weren't married? (That word "married" makes me jump!)

Sounds as though the convention is interesting for you. I guess it would be at first, but give it time, will be a little monotonous before you are thru. Hope you accomplish something, seems like a pretty important detail to me.

From the pictures you sent, I would say Mr. Bischoff is looking like a pretty old man. Looks like the kids are wearing him down. Guess he is getting pretty old at that. Teaching is a tough racket, must be!

Legna, I understand absolutely nothing about the stock you mentioned. Guess you know what you are doing. I don't say a word. I've never tried to make heads or tails of the returns published in the papers. Looks like a complicated affair, but you are good at math, so you shouldn't have any trouble.

From the background of the picture with Henry and Peadie, I would say their lot is next to Miss Marquette or the old steamboat pier lot. I remember a cluster of small locust trees up in that corner of Cap'n Ed's lot. I used to flush quite a few rabbits and quail up there. Lot of underbrush laying around. Sam Crandell used to trim the roadside and throw all the brush over the fence. A lot of sparkin' took place there back in the old days. Sure is a nice location for a house. I'm glad Henry and Peadie could get it. Hope we can do as well, when _____! Peadie looks as full of devilment as ever. You'd think she'd wear Henry down but he looks big as ever.

Got Aunt Jenny's letter. Will try to answer soon as possible. Haven't checked for sure yet but I think Livingston's outfit is here. I'm going to look for him soon as I have a "free moment". Oh, and I have written to Miss Grace, in fact quite frequently. Had a letter from Gilbert. He's sure a bird, isn't he?!

Sweetheart, those chills and bumps you get when you think of us, I get them too. I was looking at the sunset over the ocean this evening. My, what a beautiful scene, the sea and sky merging so you couldn't tell one from the other, with the sunlight beams dancing over all, touching everything with beautiful colors. The P.A. system was playing soft and sweet music. I would have given everything to have you standing with me arm in arm watching it all. Wood came up while I was watching and said, "Makes you feel homesick, doesn't it?" I didn't even answer, just nodded my head. 'Tis things like this that make a fellow think of the real life. Know what I mean? Someone to love and share it all with, a home and all the things that go with it, comfort, security and the fun of living, laughter, tears, taking things as they come, give a big sigh and say to yourself, "It's great to be alive and I wouldn't miss it for anything." Honey, I'd better hack this letter off, getting deep.

All yours,

Howard

Western Pacific

July 28, 1945

Darling Legna,

Meant to write you yesterday but I didn't get time to even take a shower. Things should slow down a bit now, at least to a steady rhythm. I have a lot to learn about this new job. Frankly Honey, wish I didn't have it. Hope it's just temporary. Damn paperwork, I hate it. Too much sitting in one spot for me. I like to get out and roam around. Course I still get around; I have my regular duties on the flight line and transportation.

Legna, if you didn't get "the drop-stitch" I put on the stationery gal, why, I give up. Either you're too naïve or I have a terrible dull sense of humor. (Was pretty good writing paper though.) Col. Odren gave it to me, was all he had. He thought it was pretty good too. [See July 2, 1945 letter]

Some news about Billy Crandell and Mac Hardesty getting discharged. How in the heck do they fall into beautiful set-ups like that? Must be a lot of pilots back in the States, plenty here too. Speaking of pilots, what in the world is Norman Wilde buying a lot and house for? Must intend to get hitched. He's the marrying type, don't you think? Every darn one of those guys left home after I did and by gosh, they are way ahead of me getting back. No.1 to leave S.S. and probably the last to get back. (Fortunes of war, I love it.)

Legna, those campaigns I told you about, there is no ribbon for each campaign. You get a bronze star to wear on your theatre of war ribbon, a star for each one, a silver star for five of them. Just don't want you to think I'll be coming home looking like a Christmas tree. Speaking of medals, our pilots were awarded the DFC [Distinguished Flying Cross] for the mission they pulled, that wild night at Mindoro. They sure had that award coming; those boys did a job that night. As for me, I was crouching low in a fox-hole, sweatin' it out.

This month has passed in a hurry, that's what keeping busy does for a fellow. The trouble is when we get busy, it's too damn busy. The camp is completed now, no medals either! Just hope we don't move too soon. Want to get a little compensation on this one.

Went out looking for Livingston day before yesterday. Still not sure he is here but I'll give it another search someday.

The Nips turned down the Truman and Churchill surrender terms. Kind of knocked my calculations off a bit. Thought for a while the terms would be accepted. Don't know what to think now. I'll give up guessing and thinking about things like that. Reckon I was <u>hoping</u> on that "ticket to the States".

Don't know whether I told you in my last letter or not, but the baseball caps arrived, believe I did. Anyway, they are sure good ones, just what I wanted. Thanks Honey, they will help take care of my poor eyesight. They look much better on me than do glasses.

Sweetheart, your ring is wearing thin, guess it gets rough treatment on my hands. I always wear it—hope it lasts till I get home.

All my love,
Howard

Ryukyus (What a name!)

August 1, 1945

Dearest Darling Legna,

I'd better get some mail pretty soon. Don't think I'll hit "that rut" again. That wouldn't be good either, for then, you get angry and I get a reprimand, and I don't like them. Even if I do write a nice letter to smooth out the ruffles. Guess though if I stayed on the ball, I wouldn't be on the receiving end of your explosive ~~burts~~ bursts. Can't spell tonight worth a darn, maybe I've been reading too many "poop sheets" today, the words kind of run together.

I've been busy for the last few days with the adjutant work. At the ending and beginning of the month, there are a lot of reports and things to go in; in addition to pay-rolls and the normal paperwork we have every day. AT is all interesting to me though and that helps. I still want to come home, no matter how interesting a job can be.

Our food has certainly been good for the past week, just hope it continues. Fresh eggs we've had three mornings in succession, fresh meat for supper too. All we need now is a "beer issue" and we'll be all-set. Wish I had a cold bottle right now.

Legna, don't send me anymore cigars for a while yet, not until I ask for them anyway. Been getting a few thru the PX and I want the civilians back in the States to have some.

Nasty day today, been raining hard and the ground is awfully muddy. Rains more here than it did in the Philippines. Thank goodness we have a good shack.

Sweetheart, how's your health these days? Give me a little information about yourself. I'm curious to know if you've put on any weight since I left. (Bet you haven't.) With a good cook like Carrie around, I should think it an easy matter to put on weight.

How about it, can you cook anything yet? Something tells me you should be learning.

All my love,

Howard

Ryukyus

August 4, 1945

Dearest Darling Legna,

The mail came thru today, mail forwarded from the old APO and one letter to 901. That's darn good service. Wasn't expecting it for another week.

Your "guess" about my whereabouts is fairly accurate, right on the head. That globe of yours must tell you things.

Honey, you certainly are "smitten with the marriage bug". What happened all of a sudden? For a practical person you sure go haywire. Legna, you should know enough about the army by now, to know you can't make plans. (That doesn't give you the answers, does it?) Since you are pinning me down, I'll give the answers to your questions "a go". I can't see why you are in such a hurry to get married. Remember Honey, almost three years will have passed since we've seen each other. How do you know you still want to marry me? Perhaps I've changed so you won't want anything to do with me. Three years is a mighty long time and people can do a lot of changing in that period of time. Sure, I want to marry you, that's all I think about but thoughts are based on what I knew three years ago, not what I know at the present. It is quite possible neither of us has changed but let's wait and find out for sure. You are acting like an eighteen year old gal about to elope. We aren't going to a party you know, you can call it a game if you like, but the stakes are high and I play for keeps. You have already said, we will have to make compromises. How do you know I will accept yours and you, mine? Legna, can't you see, I love you more than anything? You are the only gal I've ever given a second thought about marrying. Honey, but there's more to it than that. Sure we love each other, but we don't know if we are meant for marriage. I think we are, I want to be for sure, positive!

Sweetheart, we've been waiting a long time for this, let's not mess up now. There will be time for planning when I get back. We've been waiting since the night in August 1940 (Saturday, 29th to be exact). A fishing trip, no fish, a storm, car with radio and the Hit Parade. Fumbling of hands, hesitation then a kiss, but the kiss was wrong because of a career; in fact this case was hopeless. I felt almost like a criminal, but what was this great offense? I was a lonely boy, who had been kicked around ever since he was six years old. Had never had anything he wanted, a home, love, not even an education which he wanted badly. He had sense enough to know what an education meant but wasn't given a chance to get it, because of brow-beating, bickering, many arguments which left him tearless but sad within, also a feeling of despair. Figured what the hell was the use, but damn it, he knew he could go places with a little encouragement but the case was hopeless. But he didn't give up entirely. He took it and grinned —what difference did it make? Just another knock-down in the great fight of life. Maybe if he kept plugging he'd get a chance. This blow didn't make him bitter, and consider the world was against him. Legna, this kid had felt many hard knocks, had sat at a table with ten or twelve people and was ribbed about eating too much and always getting the rear end of the chicken. While sitting there taking it, his hands would clench beneath the table and he would fill-up and want to bawl his head-off but no, would just grin and laugh it off. (Oh, pride, what a beautiful sting, just like a high velocity bullet.) Sometimes it was quite a wonder, "why he had ever been born." Then he was growing up and in the summer of 1940 met a girl whom he liked very much but had never thought about before. He had never thought about her before because it was another hopeless case. He couldn't meet this gal on her standards or level of life. But then something happened. This boy fell in love with the girl from the other side of the tracks (the high side). There was a warning, but love doesn't heed warnings. It rushes in no matter what the odds, triumphant, the victor. She told him that Saturday night it was hopeless. Mom, Daddy, a teacher's career. (A revolution on that career, I believe.) Well, another knock-down, but his eyes were open, should have known better, hadn't it happened before? Stubborn cuss, this guy. There was a gal he thought, that could give him something that he wanted all his life — companionship, being treated like a real human being, and greatest of all, "love"—he was starved for that. Not the cheap, gaudy, bawdry affairs that a young fellow runs into learning about life, but something that was deep as the ocean, strong-bound as the rock of Gibraltar, or the mountains which make up the world. So that's why he thought he had committed a great offense. Later something happened. The girl took him back and it wasn't stubbornness that made him go, it was love! Damn it,

Legna, can you understand that? For the boy was sure that this girl loved him equally as much. Then what? Along comes the Army and war. He saw her a few times but never for any single "length of time". They fell deeper in love, if that was possible. He goes overseas, for two, possibly three years, and she wants to get married as soon as he comes back. A bit of recklessness, I'd say. No Honey, let's don't jump before we know what lies at the end of that leap. That is his idea because who knows, something might pop out of the past, no more knock-downs, especially where she is concerned, because Legna, he loves this girl with all his being, afraid the knock-down would be a complete knock out. Probably wouldn't hurt him as much as it would her. You see Honey, he doesn't want this to happen to her, and remember his beautifully stung pride.

Legna, I hope you understand all I'm writing. Was never so earnest or sincere in my life. Read it two or three times and then let me know what you feel!

For instance, would you be willing to go with me and meet my Dad? He's a rough, tough boy—drinks, runs with wild women and raises merry hell. He gave me some hard knock-downs too, but he's still my father and I'll always treat him as being just that. He can have the shirt off my back if he needs it. You see, Honey, he had some knocks too and though he passed a few on to me, I'll still treat him right. I don't want to give what I had to take, it isn't in me. I know what the score is on that type of treatment and never intend to be on the giving out side. Tell me, would you be willing to do what I asked in the first sentence of this paragraph? I have a family, you know, even though you have never seen or heard much about them. Would you do this and accept me or take me, as I am? There's a past over me Legna, and if you take me that cloud might envelope you at times. If you can take it, fine, but if you couldn't and something broke us apart, I'm afraid of the consequences. It would leave an awful wound and there aren't many "Purple Hearts" in that league.

Been keeping busy with my "jobs". Gosh, how the paperwork piles up. Always some darn report that has to go in. I'm still interested though. I say that as though I could be any other way and I couldn't be, not in the Army!

I'm hoping for January too, if it could be! Possibly we will get a break this time.

Honey, I'm not reading this letter over because I'm likely to tear it up. Read it carefully, will you, before you open up with your barrage of heavies?

All my love,
Howard

Ryukyus
August 7, 1945

Dearest Darling Legna,

Don't know if it is safe for me to write now. After the last one I expect an explosion heard 9,000 miles away. Can't wait until I get an answer.

Bob Schwen has been transferred to another outfit. I think he's bucking for a "Majority". Last time I saw him (in early June) he was in the hospital. Nothing serious just needed a little medical treatment. I wish him luck, but he's sure a politician.

Legna, don't think I'll take that leave. The set-up has changed again. You no longer sign an artificate stating "you will return and remain in the combat zone for a minimum of one year." But the C.O. is the boy that approves or disapproves the request for leave and mine won't go thru. Guess I'll just have to sweat-out my points. Under the new leave policy, everybody wants to go home, quite a bit of clambering.

Some of the Navy boys we made the last trip with came in today to see us. We were glad to see them. Sure are a nice bunch of fellows. Had them for supper. Was the first time they had ever eaten out of mess-kits full of food. Think I'll whip-out to their ship and grab a real good meal. Understand Louis Hartge's ship is around here. By the way, who is he? I don't remember him. I picked-up his address from the Home News.

I was mistaken about Livingston. Found the 2nd and not the 4th Wing. Well, maybe I'll run into someone yet.

Honey, how is, or I should say, what is the marital status of "one Lt. Shenton and Miss Andrews"? Just remember one thing, Honey, I love you and always will.

All my love,
Howard

Ryukyus
August 8 or 9, 1945

Dearest Darling Legna,

Got two letters from you today, both addressed APO 901. I'm glad the mail has started to come thru. Honey, the letter you received from me postmarked July 14, was mailed quite a few days before that. Guess it was held by the censors. Can't kick on that, those boys have a job to do. Sure is nice to be getting mail regularly again. Now maybe I can hack out a few more.

Sweetheart, I can see you don't remember what you read in my letters. In that last letter you mention going to see "Valley of Decision" and said maybe I had read or seen the darn thing. I distinctly recalled writing you and mentioning the book. It was around February or March. Think I commented on it rather profusely. Oh well, doesn't matter, but sharpen up Honey, you are making me think you're day dreaming. Let's keep that head out of the clouds, you might stumble and twist your ankle.

Speaking of shows, I haven't been to one for a week. We have them just about three a week, but I've seen our last few features, besides I have homework to do now. I must have seen "Valley of Decisions" about the same time you did, since I've been here anyway.

Say, the atomic bomb sure caused a lot of commotion, didn't it? Everybody is talking about it and every time we turn on the radio we hear a broadcast about "the bomb".

So you polished the glittering diamond and it sparkled like a star. Seems to me, it is an awful small diamond, considering the cost. But all nice things come in small packages, they say, (Somebody said anyway. Maybe it's just a rumor.) Honey, I'm afraid I'll have to stop wearing your ring. It is wearing rather thin and it's loose on my finger. I'm worried because it might drop off and I don't want to lose it. My finger wouldn't look natural without it, there's a mark, a white or un-sunburned mark around my finger. I'm going to keep wearing "H", 1941 as long as possible.

Legna, I don't care if you have a big wedding, but I don't know what a big wedding is. If it is anything like the one you and I went to, then let's not have one like that. I couldn't stand a sad job like that thing. Never saw so many long faces in my life.

Just heard some good news. Russia has declared war on Japan. From the way events are taking place, this war should be over before long. That's going to be a great day, just so a fellow can come home and stay!

All my love, Howard

Ryukyus
August 11, 1945

Darling Legna,

A bombshell loaded with news of Japan's "request for surrender" hit camp last night. Talk about a 4th of July celebration. The fireworks here were a display, the likes of which has never been seen. Don't know why everyone got so excited. We are still fighting the war. Course I admit, it was great news but I'll celebrate when the signatures go on the dotted line. Sure does make a fellow feel good though, to know that victory is so close. Now we can think about coming home and staying there.

Legna, I wrote you a letter two days ago and gave it to Wood for mailing. He forgot to mail it, so you'll probably get this letter the same time as the other. Wish to heck some mail would start coming-in, we are sure about due.

Bennert and I are burning the midnight oil, working on reports. Almost convinced I got the adjutant's job at the wrong time. We are backed up in most of our paperwork; the orderly room doesn't function too well on a move. Hope we get things cleared-up by the end of this month. Guess we will, if Bennert holds out. I'm really putting him thru the paces. He knows more about this type of work than I do, course I'm learning. In a way, I'm sorry I had to take this job, if I was interested in a post-war Army career, it would probably be a help to me, but Honey, I just want to do my job, to the best of my ability as long as I'm in the Army. First chance I get after it's over, I want to get out, but fast! I know you don't agree with this policy, but that is the way it is going to be, on that score, I'm definite.

Can't wait till I hear what you have to say about the answers I gave you. Concerning us, remember? Whatever you think I'll still love you sweetheart, nothing can change that either. (Do I sound stubborn?)

All my love,
Howard

Okinawa

Our sinewy sons were sent over seas

Far from their families and far from their dreams

They never wrote letters of hardships, despair

Only of love, yearning that one day soon:

They would come home,

They would resume

And carry on with the rest of their lives.

Excerpt from *A Tribute to Veterans*
Written by Jerry Calow
Used with permission
©2003 by Jerry Calow

Somewhere on Okinawa

August 15, 1945

Dearest Darling Legna,

Today is "the day", at last the war is over and believe me, everybody is happy. Funny thing though, when the announcement was made there were no cheers or even much comment. Guess we did our celebrating the night we heard Japan had made a "request for peace". Sure were a lot of fireworks around here that night. Honey, I didn't feel any different when I heard the news. Perhaps if I were in the States, or on my way there, I would have really felt like raising hell. But, there is still a job to do out here, my work will continue, only difference, no bomb-handling. I realize that we must carry on with our work as before. There is no doubt in my mind that every effort will be made to get the men out of here and home, as quickly as possible. It will be a little hard to take, staying out here when the war is over, but there is still work to do, so I guess we'll be hacking around for a little while.

Captain Ergen, one of our pilots, is coming home on leave. His home is near Pittsburgh, he promised to call you for me. Hope this one doesn't fizzle out like the one with Pop Glunt. Ergen will be able to tell you all about me, so ask him anything you like (about me).

Legna, we aren't getting any mail. Can't figure it out, damn but I'd like to have some mail. Things are getting critical, just got to have some letters.

Expect to be doing some night work tomorrow and the next day. There are reports that must be in, course I'm going to have Bennert in there pitching with me, though he doesn't know it yet.

Guess that is about all for now, Honey. Sure could have appreciated the peace or cessation of hostilities if you and I were together.

Love,

Howard

Okinawa
August 17, 1945

Dearest Darling Legna,

Happy day, Honey! The mail started to come in, had seven from you, two Galesville Home News. I'm glad the mail is arriving; the boys' morale was getting a little low. (Mine too.)

Bennert and I worked on poop-sheets until 9 o'clock tonight. This paper battle is getting rough. I will really need a rest when I get home, especially if the present pace is maintained. Darn good thing Bennert is around, he has 92 points and will no doubt go home before me. I'm going to miss him.

Too bad I missed Chauncey L. Would like to have seen him. He must have arrived there, right after I left. The deal I had on Livy sure fizzled-out. I don't think he was ever here.

Sorry to hear about Bud Rogers. Guess he's is having a good time, compared to what most of the boys are going thru. Just one of those things I don't pay much attention to.

Can you imagine, we haven't had a "red alert" (blackout) for two nights now. Seems funny to spend a full evening with lights on. Now we can see uninterrupted shows, which is a help.

Honey, honestly, I'd better get home soon; I think I'm love-starved. I need a lot of that, guess I've been thinking too much of you, lately. Just want to warn you, if I seem over-powering or something when I get back. Don't be shocked, I'll get over it.

Legna, I haven't the slightest idea what we will do when I get back. But I want to be alone with you for at least a week. Don't want anyone around to bother us; we should have a lot to talk about.

I can't get a leave now, before when getting a leave, you had to sign a certificate that you would return overseas and stay for a minimum of one year. That clause is out now, you first take a leave, but now the C.O. won't recommend me. Just have to wait for the point system. Could use 12 most graciously. Can't we have a 12 pointer by proxy? Doesn't sound like a good idea, does it?

We have a bunch of new officers, just in from stateside. (Pilots). They are all set to go back, but I'm afraid they will be a bit disappointed.

Sweetheart, I can't send any of those X & O kisses, against censor regulations.. But damn I could use quite a few real ones.

You sound as though you are mighty busy this summer!

All my love,
Howard

Okinawa

August 21, 1945

Darling Legna,

First chance I've had to write in about three days. Been working on some terrific reports. The C.O. and I started work at 8:00 in the morning, this was yesterday, and we kept at it until 11:30 last night. This damn paper work is getting rough; sure have been busy since I took over this new job. 'Tis a bit interesting though, at least it's different.

What's all this talk about me being difficult to know? Thought I was a frank person, guess you are right though about people only knowing me to a certain point. There are a lot of things I keep to myself, maybe I have a reason, or perhaps it is just my nature, I don't know.

Honey, I just can't believe you weigh 110 lbs. You sure don't look it in the pictures you send me. I think you'd better check those scales. I think I've lost a little weight lately, guess I've been working a little hard. Feel O.K. though; ready to come home at a moment's notice.

How about this fur coat? What in the world is Indian Lamb? Never heard of it. Bennert says his wife bought some kind of a lamb coat, but it wasn't Indian. Sure, I'll like it; I think you have very good taste in clothes. Imagine they're pretty expensive, too.

Sure is a lot of talk out here about getting men back to the States. Heard some very good stories, but wouldn't repeat them because I don't think the situation is that good.

Gosh Legna, wish I could write you and say, "Honey I'll be home by Christmas". There wouldn't be any way to hold me down. Things do look pretty good though, I'm hoping.

All my love,
Howard

Okinawa

August 21, 1945

Darling Legna,

I wrote to you this morning, in fact, just before lunch. The mail came in this evening and I had two letters from you, so thought I'd give you tit for tat. Besides I took a shot this evening and my arm might be sore tomorrow.

Legna, you are certainly going all-out on this marriage deal, aren't you? Please don't get high hopes of me coming home in two or three months or even by Christmas. You must not forget, peace doesn't alter the Army too much. Just because the fighting is over, there is still lots to do. I can't explain them to you, but if you think about it for a while, you'll get the answers. Let's put it this way, I'll be back as soon as I can possibly get there. Nothing will prevent me from achieving that goal. (Nothing personal, I should have said.) By that I mean a promotion or staying here because I want to. T'ain't likely the promotion would happen anyway, but sweetheart I want to get back to you as soon as it's possible. Gosh, I want to go home more and more every day. Maybe I'm sick for love, never was homesick, you know. Thing that gets me though, is why you are so eager for this marriage. Sure are leaving yourself wide open, Honey.

I wish you wouldn't mention things like the atomic bomb. You people sit 12,000 miles from the fighting and you don't know a damn thing about what's going on out here. Yet you make comments and form opinions on how war should be conducted. Leave that to the military leaders, that's what they are for. So far, they have performed a wonderful job, with I would say, superior results. The fellows up top know what the score is and as long as they keep the enemy away from our shores and accomplish the purpose, "everything for which we are fighting", well, that's good enough for me. Seems to me a lot of people think war is just a big adventure trimmed with medals and ribbons that make a uniform look dashing. Just in case someone drives-up in a vehicle, leans out and asks you, it isn't. I don't intend to tell you what it is like, because even I don't know the complete story, but I do have an excellent idea what it is like, so I do speak with a fair knowledge. Six months after the peace is signed, I'll bet you wouldn't know there was a war going on, a short while previously. That's as it should be according to my way of thinking, because I don't want any reminders. You all just sit back and let us do the fighting. We know the hows and why-fors, because we are right in "the middle of the caper". Don't take offense at what I've said here, Honey, but I'm being frank. (I realize freedom of speech is one of those things we are out here fighting for.)

So Scoop is going to get married this month. Sure hope her husband doesn't have to go overseas again. From what you say about him, he must rate pretty high on points. Near as I can remember he was overseas when I was back in the States. Honey, if you catch any bouquets, don't get superstitious. I want you to catch it though, if you can —from the tone of your letters I'd say you'd try anything. Darling, if I were to give you a performance rating on courtship, you would get a "superior" on perseverance. Don't weaken though, Legna. I love you and everything you have to say. But Honey, hold your fire until the target is in sight. What do your Mom and Dad have to say about all this? Not that it should make any difference, I'm just curious.

How about that new green suit? You must have quite an extensive wardrobe Legna. How about the new style bathing suits? From the pictures I've seen, there isn't anything left for imagination, especially the top part. Daring, aren't they?

All my love, Darling,

Howard

Okinawa

August 23, 1945

Darling Legna,

Had two letters from you today and in one you said you had received two from me in one day. Good shot, Shenton, you are doing pretty good! It's a cinch tho Legna, I didn't write two in one day, did that day before yesterday, was quite a job. You said something today about me not writing as often as before. Doesn't seem that way to me, thought I was writing just as often.

Legna, I don't know how they expect a fellow to take on a lot of additional duties but in the Army you don't ask questions and do as you're told. However, I have been relieved of some of my duties. I don't have transportation and Chemical Warfare anymore and now we have a new Ordnance officer so all I have is the adjutant's job. My transfer from Ordnance to Air Corps hasn't come through yet, but I expect it to. Don't know about the promotion. I can't be promoted until I've had the adjutant's position for three months. Then if I get promoted, I'll have to stay here three months after that. Honey, I'm not letting anything keep me from coming home (repeat: nothing). Course, if I see I'm going to be here that long, well enough.

Speaking of Billy Crandell and Mac Hardesty, reminds me, I saw in the Home News that Bob White of Annapolis was home and discharged. You know, I was supposed to be drafted same time as he was, I didn't make it then, he went in during January '41, I followed in May. Another is Mervin Hardesty, he and I went in together. Understand he's been discharged for some time. I was first to leave S.S. and no doubt I'll be last to come home. It has been a long tour, Legna, don't know whether I'm any better or worse because of it. I'll let you decide that when I get back.

There isn't any doubt about the fact that all of the boys have changed since they came overseas. You are right about me having a high forehead. Legna I don't know where my face and head meet, and don't think the boys are nice about it either. I'm taking a real ribbing, but I like it. Then again look how much older I am. Gosh I was a kid when I came in. Guess I've reached full maturity by now. I feel that way anyhow. If I haven't, I'd better start all over again, well, I should be out in another year, guess I can sweat it for that long.

Honey, I've only been in "one" theatre of war. There were three you know, European, Asiatic-Pacific and North African. I'm A & P, that's enough —-covers a lot of territory.

I hope Stanley Trott didn't get headed over this way, because if he hasn't started, I don't think he will have to come. He mentioned coming out here a long time ago.

Our new Ordnance officer left the States in early July. He's already talking about going home. Yep, he has a wife and she is going to have a baby before long. He said if it weren't for the baby he wouldn't mind so much. I agree with everything he has to say about the matter, but he shouldn't let it bother him. He darn sure couldn't have expected to stay in the States forever. These boys should think about things like that when they get hitched. Another thing, all the folks back home seem to think now that the war is about over, everybody will be coming home immediately. T'ain't so Legna, there's much more to it than just that. I do feel confident that we will get back as soon as it's humanly possible to get us released.

Have a big ceremony coming-up; the pilots are going to be presented their medals, by our immediate Commanding General. They will get their DFCs and Air Medals. We don't have many boys left to get the DFC. The fellows that flew the "hot mission" were our old boys, and most of them have gone home. 'Course they still get the decoration, but won't have it pinned on by a General.

Legna, I still haven't got it straight about your weight. Doesn't matter, just don't fall way to nothing. Honey, I'm glad you are taking good care of Oscar and Hector. I love them, so help me! Just don't let anyone mess-around. I have a long lease there and I know that Oscar wouldn't like it.

Honey, I'd better go. Wood and Bennert are waiting for me. We are going to see a show.

All my love,

Howard

Okinawa

August 26, 1945

Dearest Darling Legna,

We sure are having a heck of a time with our mail. It comes in spurts about every five days.

Honey, my job was indeed a pleasure last night. Gosh, I had a swell time, though it was work. Had a call around 10 o'clock to get all the enlisted men with 85 or more points, ready to leave for home by 10 o'clock in the morning. We had nineteen men in that bracket, wish we had a thousand. Honey, if only you could have seen those boys when I told them they were going home. I think at first, that they couldn't understand, just stood dumbfounded, then when it dawned on them, gosh, it was wonderful to see. We had them processed and ready to go, at five this morning. They took-off for Manila. Some of the boys were so excited they couldn't spell their names nor repeat their serial numbers. I hope my orders come thru like that, what a thrill!

There isn't much being said about officers with 85 or more points. But after last night, I'm sure a hopeful cuss. Looks to me like I stand a pretty good chance. 'Course, I could hang around for a promotion, I won't! The squadron's morale must have taken a 200% leap last night and I'm all for it. Sure would like to think I'd be home by Christmas, right now, I'd say anything was possible. Bennert and I are the only officers in the squadron, eligible in points.

Today is Sunday and the Sundays around there are getting to be like they were back in the States. I still want to try breakfast in bed on Sunday, just once. I don't think I'd like it. Maybe I would though, if you made it.

Honey, there isn't much left.

All my love (that's a heap)
Howard

Okinawa

29 August 1945

Dearest Darling Legna,

The mail has started to come in again. I hope it continues that way. Guess there's nothing quite like mail. Haven't seen anything to beat it *yet*.

According to one of your letters, you got the one I wrote about *why* we shouldn't get married as soon as I hit the beach in the States. After getting your letter, I would say, yes Honey, perhaps you are a practical person. 'Course, I realize there isn't much practicality where love is concerned, but we shouldn't lose our senses entirely. I say this because I know Legna, sometimes when I think of you, loving you, it's like a huge fire consuming just you and me, but nothing else matters. Guess you could almost call it a wild dream. After I get back and we get together again, we will know for sure, whether to add fuel to that fire or else stomp it out. Sweetheart, I'm not sure but you are likely to find a few changes in me. Nothing drastic or devastating, I hope, but you might find a few you don't like. I can't tell you what these changes are because I don't know myself. When I get back, I'll find out, been out here quite a while Honey, and it's a different world from anything you know about. I'd better let this drop here; I'll have you believing I'm something out of a fantasia.

Legna, I don't think you'd better send any packages at all. Don't get excited now, by that I don't mean I'll be home. You know how it is, we move around so darn much, it takes forever for the packages to catch me. 'Course, there are possibilities of my coming home soon but I'm not saying anything, because I have nothing definite to go on. Don't want to have a terrific let-down either. Disappointments are hard to take on the subject "of going home". So, don't send me anything unless I ask you to.

There's only one thing I really want for Christmas and I can't get that when we are 12,000 miles apart. Damn it Legna, I'd even come down a chimney to get to you.

I can't for the life of me figure how you think I've nothing to do since we've ceased hostilities. I've been just as busy if not more so, since this

588

thing was whipped to a halt. When you mentioned it in your letter I instantly thought of what you said in a letter when I was at Fort Jackson. Remember? It was when the Armed Forces were granted free mail privileges. You said, "With mail service free you should be able to write very often Shenton". So help me though, I love you Legna.

Honey, don't get too many extra duties in connection with your school work. Don't want you to be tied-up, just in case!

All my love, Darling,

Howard

P.S. New APO, 180

Okinawa

2 September 1945

Dearest Darling Legna,

Today is V.J. Day. I'm kind of glad it came today. This is Sunday out here and everything is so quiet you can hear a pin drop. No airplanes taking off or landing; that in itself makes it nice around here. Our camp is right beside a strip and most of the time you can't talk over the phone because of so much racket.

Three more of our pilots are leaving for the States today. That only leaves two of the old boys, and I guess they will be going pretty soon. One of the boys leaving today has been living with Bennert, Wood and me for over a year. He is quite happy about the whole thing, and who wouldn't be? Wish something would come thru on ground officers. Lately things have been pretty silent as far as we are concerned. Can't even find a good rumor.

Honey, in your last letter you mentioned the fact that we would be single for the rest of our lives. That is, according to Shenton's way of thinking. Don't know how I ever indented you with that impression. Damn it, you are either getting married right away or else you are never going to get hitched. Slow down, Honey. There is a medium you know. A happy medium some say. Another thing, you wanted to know if there was someone else. I can answer that readily enough. There couldn't be anyone but you, unless it was a New Guinea native, Filipino or one of these Okie gals. Sort of elimination, you see. I haven't gone native yet, though I have been here long enough to be naturalized. Guess you are it Legna, whether you want to be or not.

Think I'd better tell you again about being overseas and staying overseas, in war and peace. The people back home are crying because their Johnny isn't home from the combat zone and also yelling about the draft. Legna, so far as my job goes, it hasn't changed a mite since peace has been declared. Not only that, but it won't change, we all have as much to do now as before. In fact, paper work is going to get heavier. The government is doing all it could possibly do to get us home. I guess you've heard of a unit in the army being compared with a football team. (You know, the old teamwork line.) Well, when the whistle blows in the Army you can't dump off your equipment and take a walk. In the first place people at home can't visualize the enormity of this part of the world, with all of its islands. It will take a lot of men to occupy this territory and every one of them will be busy doing his job. I want to come home though Legna, just as quick as possible but someone will have to take my place. Wish we could get something definite on going home from higher headquarters. I'm eager!

Love,
Howard

Okinawa

5 September 1945

Dear Legna Darling,

I knocked out a good day's work and I'm pretty tired. Had to make several trips to the finance office today —the boys were paid. This converting dollars and cents into yen and sen is quite a job, especially when the money runs into the thousands. Each man brings a bag when he gets paid now. I counted so darn much dough today I got dizzy. It's tedious work, you are so afraid of making a mistake. Kind of keeps you on your toes. Bennert and Wood went to a show. Wanted me to go but I thought I'd write you, then hit the sack. In addition to other duties, I had to take calisthenics. I must be getting old, sort of knocked me out. In fact, I couldn't get my leg muscles to respond when we quit. Bennert was the instructor and he likes to put a man thru the paces.

Honey, another of our pilots left for home yesterday. This boy's name is Johnny Dierlein (Dear-line) and he lives in New Rochelle, New York. He is going to give you a call when he gets back. Ask him anything you like. Johnny has been living with us for over a year, so he should know quite a bit about me. 'Course, maybe you aren't curious.

Someone is sure making a big secret out of ground officers in the Air Forces going home. We can't find out a damn thing and we are slowly going nuts waiting to hear something. Wish they would come out with some kind of information, I expect to come home fairly soon and if I'm not, I'd like to know about it. However, that's the Army way of doing things and I should know better than to even think about it, but it's an important issue with me. Guess that's why I'm frettin'.

Honey, how about this being stubborn affair? Fancy you thinking I'd like to be stubborn. Really I can't understand that. Besides, you don't have to tell me that stubbornness is silly and by no means a virtue, I know that. But, sticking to a point when you think you are right isn't exactly a crime either.

I was surprised to hear about the bus line to Shady Side. Looks like the old town is going to break-down and communicate with the rest of the world. Shouldn't be long before the town is sporting a mayor (should have one anyway, just to keep up with Galesville) and a Chamber of Commerce. Guess things are quiet around there now with the summer gone. I'd give anything to be there though, now or anytime.

Sweetheart, I do love you. Keep wishing I'm home by Christmas, will you?

Love, Howard

Okinawa

6 September 1945

Legna Darling,

What in the hell can I write or say to make you believe I want to come home? In all my experiences, I haven't run across a man who has been overseas for over eighteen months, that didn't want to get back to the States. No matter what was offered to make him stay. Honestly, I've about given-up. You think I don't want to come home and you seem to think that now the war is over all a person has to do is run down to the beach and catch a boat. Think I'll just forget the whole thing and say no more about it. The more I write and try to explain the more confused you are. So I'll end the whole thing by saying, I'll be there as soon as I can possibly make it. If I have to go to Japan, then the gig's up. I'll be a long time getting my orders, of that I'm pretty positive.

Honey, forget about us going to the Army-Navy game at Philadelphia unless they are selling tickets for 1946. I'll never make it by 1 December '45. I don't know why you can't go though. Seems to me you get a gang together and whip along with them. I sure would like to see a game, the Army-Navy doesn't enthuse me too much but I'd like to see them play.

Speaking of coming home, Bennert's wife is sitting by the phone waiting for him to hit the coast. What a long vigil that gal has in store and Bennert has more points than me.

Had a letter from Miss Grace today. She doesn't write too often. Evidently though, she has been busy entertaining the family. Say, how come you didn't tell me Capt. Noah Hazard passed away? Didn't you know he was an old buddie of mine? He was kind of young, must have had heart trouble.

Legna, you wench. I'm not afraid of you, or anything for that matter.

I love you Honey!

Howard

Okinawa

8 September 1945

Dearest Darling Legna,

I haven't much to say tonight, but just feel like writing. Everything is quiet. Seems like the Sunday atmosphere has invaded Saturday night. I imagine quite a few of the boys are at our club having some drinks. I can't go for the liquor they serve. Just a bit too powerful for me, leaves a bad taste in my mouth. Sure could go for a cold beer though. Either that or a glass of milk. (Milk sours awfully fast in this climate, might not agree with me.)

From what you say about Chauncey, I would say he is in Japan. His job must be evacuating allied war prisoners from Japan. That's one of the first things accomplished when we moved in. Gosh, I hope I don't have to go in there. 'Course it shouldn't make much difference if I have to stay overseas. All of these islands are about the same. But it will hold me up from going home that's the real reason I don't want to make the trip. Bennert is in the same boat, he doesn't want to go either.

How about old man Bischoff getting married again? Looks like everybody gets hitched, one and many times. Wonder if he cleared his throat while repeating the vows. He's getting kind of old for this marriage-business, I think!

Honey, if they make Southern a Junior High School, what happens to the High School? Sounds like you might be leaving Mt. Zion or are you going to teach Junior? (High School, I mean, don't get that last sentence wrong.)

Bob Schwen came down to see us today. I think he's going to spend the night. He doesn't look too good, guess he isn't over the sickness he had while we were in Luzon. Otherwise, he's the same, like me and the rest of us, he wants to go home. Bob has a lot of points, just 12 ahead of me. I'm hoping we all go back together—be terrible though for whatever port we hit in the States.

Legna, from what I hear about the Navy and its discharge system on points, looks as though Derwill is stuck for a while. That Navy sure drives a hard bargain. According to the news tonight, they are going to use warships to transport Army men to and from the occupied zones. Sounds like a good shot. An aircraft carrier can carry a lot of men.

Honey, remember what I told you about sending Christmas packages. That still holds. I'm afraid I'd never get them. Save-up "everything" you have for me. I'll get it when I hit home. Think you can keep it until then? Hope so, cause I intend to collect.

That's about all for tonight, Honey.

All my love, Howard

Okinawa

16 September 45

Dearest Darling Legna,

Today is Sunday, but things are a little different. There is a typhoon howling around here, gustful winds and rain that comes horizontal. 'Tis a good day to drink beer and shoot pool, I might add, any day is good enough to drink beer. Hope this weather doesn't hold very long. We have 26 more enlisted men leaving for Manila tomorrow and the next day.

Manila is the first lap of the trip back to the States. These men all have 85 points as of the 12th of May, we just picked-up another battle star that was ending since June 1944. They are sure eager to get out of here.

Bennert and I are still sweating our orders. The Air Force seems a bit reluctant about letting the officers go. I've got 98 points now and expect to pick-up 5 more pretty soon. Gosh, I'd like to get out of here before the 1st of October. The last thing I think of at night and the first thing in the morning is going home. I shouldn't let it bother me, but just can't help it. I'm pretty certain now that the trip to Japan is out, that is a big help. I didn't want to go up there, guess it's because I'd have to build another camp and I've had my fill of that.

Legna, I think I mentioned sending $400.00 home by wire. It didn't go, the Finance Office wouldn't send it, and so you don't have to keep your eye peeled. Think I'll get a couple of checks made out and carry it myself. Probably need a little dough for that trip to the States.

No mail again yesterday and of course we never get mail on Sunday, now that the war is over. This is getting to be a hell of a place. Food's no good and no mail. Sure wish we'd get some fresh meat. I'm losing a little weight and it doesn't agree with me.

Sweetheart, you said "you wanted me home". I want to be home with you! Hope this waiting doesn't drag-out much longer.

All my love,
Howard

14 September 1945

Still at Okinawa

Darling Legna,

I should have waited until after the mail came in today before writing this letter. But I have an opportunity this morning so I'd better take advantage of it. Something must be wrong. I haven't had a letter from you in about five days. The thing that has me puzzled is the fact that I got your 351st and 354th letters that last time I had mail. Never have received the 352nd and 353rd, something is messing-up.

Sweetheart, I think that this is it! I think I'll be on my way home before the 1st of next month. Have received information from higher headquarters that all company grade officers with 85 or more points can plan to be sent home shortly. Wish I had told you to go ahead and buy tickets to the Army-Navy football game. The way things are stacking-up I believe I'll be home by that time. The boys are sure sweating this thing out, transportation is holding-up the procedure. I'd like to get on a ship right here and head directly to the States. Everyone has been going to Manila on the first leg of the journey. I'd like to go directly.

Legna, I don't know whether I'll land on the West Coast or not. Understand they are routing men living on the East Coast thru the Canal. If I land on the West and can arrange it, I would like you to meet me in Chicago. If on the East, how about meeting me in New York? 'Tis possible I'll hit New Orleans. You can still meet me, anywhere. Wood and Bennert will be with me, they are going to have their wives meet them in Chicago if we land on the West side. You could bring a couple of my uniforms with you and we would be all-set. Honey, if something takes place now and keeps me over here for three or four more months, I'll blow my top, me and about a thousand men. I'm confident this time though, looks like the real business. Just waiting for the word to move and I'm off. Can't sleep at night for thinking about it. Everybody is hep-up, would be a terrible disappointment if this deal didn't go thru, but I'm sure it will go thru, at least I'm getting packed. 'Course, I could stay here another three months and make captain, but it will never happen!

I sure hope there is some mail for me today. Honey, just in case I don't have a chance to write, you'd better not write me after 1st of October, if I think I won't be leaving then or get held-up for some reason, I'll let you know. As it stands now, don't write after 1st October.

Damn, I can hardly wait to get moving. This thing is worse than sweating-out a Nip bombing raid. The move to Japan might hold this going home up a little. If it does, I'm going to hate that little chunk of coral.

All my love, Howard

Okinawa

10 September 1945

Dearest Darling Legna,

Got two great big letters from you today. First mail we've had in four days. The mail gets more static every day. Maybe the situation will improve after the occupation of Japan. Most of the airplanes are tied-up now; if we get mail and fresh food once in a while things aren't so bad. But even the food has been bad for the past two weeks.

I managed to pay myself this month, first pay I've drawn since May. We didn't get here early enough to submit vouchers for July and in June I was on an LST at Subic Bay waiting for the ride up here. Anyway, I'm sending $200 by wire, so keep an eye peeled for it. This damn currency is enough to drive a man crazy. In yens, $200 is 3,000 yen with the largest denominations 100, so you just take a bag when you get paid. 'Tis hard to count too.

Say, I remember the friend of Pert Lee's, the one you called Ernie. He's short and quite chubby, smiles and laughs quite a bit. He used to hang around Miss Mary's a lot.

I almost forgot, we don't have censorship anymore. The enlisted men sure appreciate that. It isn't so nice writing when you know someone is reading everything you say.

Legna, I'm surprised you didn't know I was in the Fifth Air Force. (Should make that <u>was</u> an <u>am</u> because I think I will be for a while to come.) The 5th is occupying Japan you know, being the oldest outfit (Air Force, I mean) in the Pacific. 'Tis only fitting and proper" that we have the honor of entering the homeland. I want to enter a homeland but not where the Nips reside. I don't want to see Japan either. Far as I'm concerned it's just another group of islands in an ocean; they are all alike. Besides we'd go up there and put on a great show, parades and inspections all the time. That's not for men who have been in the combat zone. The stateside boys could do a better job at something like that. We don't like to dress-up and get formal. Home is the place for me!

About the High School going to Annapolis. Will you live in town or commute? You know, I can't remember that lady's name, the one you lived with in Annapolis. Guess Miss Ethel will want you to stay home and commute if you go to Annapolis.

I just met a captain from that Stange fellow's outfit. Our medical officer came overseas with them and their captain was paying a visit. He told me that Stange had gone to Clark Field to act as an instructor. There is a unit there that trains pilots fresh from the States for combat. Also said that Stange would be going home as soon as his tour is up down there. That means he should be on his way within the next thirty days. Stange is pretty lucky; his outfit just came over last November. It's funny, but his outfit camped right alongside ours at Leyte and also at Migalden and Luzon and I didn't know he was around until we left them at Migalden. He went to Lingayen and we went to Porac, then he went to Lanog which is on the northwestern coast of Luzon.

Legna, we have recounted the points as of 2 September this time. Right now I have 98 and stand to get 5 more in the very near future. Lots of points but they aren't doing me any good. Maybe they will before long. I sure hope so. We will do alright if we don't have to make the Japan trip. Honey, I'm sweatin' that one out, but profusely!

Honey, you really think you can handle that overpowering urge I spoke about! I hope so, but thought I'd better warn you. The longer I stay here the worse it gets too. Maybe I'd better stop-off somewhere on the way home and get it out of my system. No, I'll have you meet me, that's what I want.

All my love,
Howard

Okinawa

20 September 1945

Dearest Legna Darling,

Finally got some mail yesterday. Understand the post office blew away with the typhoon last Sunday. I believe the wind was higher that day then any time before. Whipped-up to about 80 miles an hour or so. We lost a lot of canvas; darn near lost our shack. The rain just beat in; I mean thru the tents, everything got soaking. Was quite an experience, the sacks got wet but we crawled in anyway and lay there waiting for the tent to blow away. If only we had the house I built in Luzon, that thing would have survived a typhoon. This one we just threw-up.

Sweetheart, I'm about worn-out with waiting for news or "poop" as we call it, to come in from higher Headquarters, about us going home. One day we think we are all set and will be on the way in a short while. Then the next day we hear another rumor and the bottom falls out of our hope basket. Can't get anything official on the business, everything is <u>mum</u> far as officers are concerned. The enlisted men are getting out, but I won't complain about that, first real break those boys have had so far. But I'm sitting on dynamite, this business of thinking you are going home, then have nothing happen, is really getting me down. I go to bed at night thinking about it and have a terrific hangover from it the next morning when I awake. All of us are sitting around snapping at one another like a bunch of wild animals. We weren't this way, even while in combat when the going was a bit rough. Wish something would come out giving us some definite information. If we have to stay for a few more months, that's alright, we will resign ourselves to that. I'm beginning to feel like the mouse trapped by a playful cat. Every night Bennert, Wood and I have a "discussion" on the whys and why nots of being sent home. Right now I am on the Army's side; they have a problem to solve. They just can't let everybody go now. There will have to be an Air Force in the Army of Occupation and until such time as the occupation is finished and running smoothly, they want to keep all the experienced men to do the job. After all, you're old experienced men are the only ones eligible to go home. Damn but I'm getting tired of waiting for the answer though. Really sweating it out Honey, so far. I have a grand total of 98 points right now, with a possible 10 more on the way. That's too many; I want to be on my way.

How about the date with the Chaplain? From what you say, sounded like a vicious circle. It must have been embarrassing, even for you, when the brethren would enter the cinema. (Must have been amusing too.) I've met some nice chaplains in the Army. We have a fine one in the Group. He's a priest and lives with the officers of the 311th. Wood and I tease him a lot. I'm afraid he thinks we are a pair of morons. Getting so he won't sit at the same table and eat with us, but we still give him the business. In a way, I feel quite sorry for the fellow, only been overseas about 10 or 12 months and he has lost 40 lbs. Looks terrible. Guess his health is pretty bad. We have a tussle with him though; he can take it and dishes out better than we give (sometimes)!

Honey, you are trying to pin me down again. Still can't figure out why you think I'm afraid to marry. Legna, I think of you constantly, of loving you and being with you. Sometimes it hurts, why do you think I

602

want to come home? It isn't because I like to travel. I want you, Legna. Don't know how to explain this "wanting", but that is what I <u>want</u>.

All my love,
Howard

Okinawa

22 September 1945

Darling Legna,

Haven't much to say, but have a few idle hours, so thought I'd say it anyway. Everybody is lying around doing absolutely nothing. We have worn ourselves out starting and gathering rumors about going home. Even that is getting to be a dead subject. We've heard all the news from the States about the point system. The critical score doesn't have to be lowered like they talk about doing. The thing to do is, get the men with 85 points on their way home. No damn sense in cutting the score when there are thousands of men over here that have been eligible ever since the point system was initiated last May, I think it was. It goes back to what I said before about the point system. Supposedly it was devised and its primary function was to get men home from overseas, to get home and be discharged. The way the darn thing is working now, the men in the States are benefitting, the boys overseas are still there and there doesn't appear to be any particular rush about moving them out. You know, Honey, I was under the impression that the Navy point system was rough, but talking to some Navy men this morning I find it isn't as bad as ours. I would be more eligible under their system, looks like points don't mean a thing far as we are concerned.

Honey, about that new-fangled bathing suit. I wouldn't mind but maybe Hector and Oscar might not like being exposed. After all, I would classify them as secret and confidential material and must be kept from the <u>enemy</u>. Do as you like, what's good enough for Hector and Oscar is sure good enough for me! I'm a bit particular though, but they know that.

The group commander pulled an inspection this morning. Everything was O.K. He seemed to be fairly well pleased with our area. The son-of-a-gun even inspected our living quarters. This is another reason why I want to get the hell out of here. It's a little difficult to go from combat conditions to this present G.I. setup. I don't think much of it, but have to follow orders. Even starting a strict enforcement of military courtesy. Most of us have forgotten all we ever knew. Nobody ever saluted in the field, that has always been stateside and rear area stuff, but we are doing it now. Our squadron commander is a West Pointer and he kind of goes for that business. I think he feels I'm not giving my all for the cause. I managed to talk him out of saluting while in the immediate camp area.

You really sound as though you are a busy person this season. Just be sure you put me on your schedule, in case I get home this year.

All my love,

Howard

Okinawa

25 September 1945

Hello, you "Beautiful Wench",

Today is a day that will go down in the history of my life. Legna, there is no more 311th Fighter Squadron, or 58th Fighter Group. The outfit has been disbanded. We are still in the process of breaking up, started this morning. It is the screwiest deal I've ever been thru; have already transferred men with the required points to le Shima, to stay until we get transportation home. Afraid though, there might be a delay of about a month. I'll blow my top for sure, if I have to sit on the beach for a month waiting for a ship to come-in. All men not having the required points are being transferred to outfits that are going to "occupy". As usual, Bennert and I are stuck again. We will join the boys at le Shima but we don't know when. We had to stay here and clear the squadron. Clean out all the administration work and turn-in all the organizational equipment. It shouldn't take us more than 10 days or 2 weeks to do the job. This is one boat we can't miss. It is going to be mighty hard on the men if we have to wait around for a month. Sure hope it doesn't take that long.

Honey, after what I've just mentioned, it is obvious you shouldn't write anymore. Got the 358th letter today, so that makes a grand-total of 359.

So Norman W. ran into a gal in Providence that remembered me. That doesn't sound so good. People usually only remember those with bad reputations and I thought I left with a clean slate. Quite a coincidence though, at that! We boys spent a lot of time in the Officers Club; they served a good brand of Scotch. The only thing wrong up there was the Navy. They always wanted to run the place. Practically did too, had us out numbered 10 to 1. I thought Norman would be out of the service about now, or is he going to be a regular? More power to him, if he is, I don't want any part of it. By the time I get back to the States I will have had more than my share, all I care about anyway.

Sweetheart, you don't have to tell me to save myself for you. I've been doing a lot of saving these past two years. Afraid though, I won't be any prize. I feel like I'm 50 years old sometimes. Maybe it's the food. Hope so, because I want to "still be eager". You can help me there; a lot of you should fix me-up. Damn, I think about it enough, so it should help me when we get together.

Will write whenever I can. Don't look for many letters though.

All my love,

Howard

Okinawa

29 September 1945

Darling Legna,

I'm still hacking around this damn island. Bennert and I have been pretty busy the last few days. We are about finished now and can take-off for Ie Shima, but there is no hurry; the ship isn't scheduled to pull-out until the 15th. Yes Honey, there is no more 311th, at least for all intents and purposes there isn't. We still have a few things to do to make that act official.

The weather sure looks black around here this evening. We have been warned there is a typhoon on the way and should hit us tomorrow morning. After the last one our tent is in sad shape and won't stand another, I'm thinking. Hope we don't have to evacuate though. That means you get solidly wet.

Honey, if our ship leaves Ie Shima on 15 October, I should be home around the middle of November. The thing I'm afraid of is, the sailing date might be set-back. The Army is sure flexible; they can change their plans overnight. I'm not going to enjoy sitting around the beach waiting, even until the 15th. Bennert and I are going to stay here long as we can; at least living conditions are a little better. Sure am in a sweat to get on that ship though, the next few weeks will seem like years. Looks like the outfit will be overseas for two complete years. Most of us thought we would only be out here 18 months when we came over. That was supposed to be the normal tour of duty overseas, but there are lots of men that have been here for over three years.

Sweetheart, kind of get prepared for my coming home. Don't get enveloped in things that will keep you too busy. I'd like to have a little of your time, if you don't mind.

All my love,

Howard

Okinawa

3 October 1945

Darling Legna,

The 311th has finally been deactivated officially and otherwise. All of the equipment has been turned-in, the records brought up-to-date and passed to higher Headquarters. All we need now is a ship to bring us home.

There seems to be a terrible mess somewhere about shipping the men back. Over a week ago we sent most our men to Ie Shima to be processed and await shipment with the few remaining here to join them. Well, it seems that isn't the procedure. Everybody that went to Ie Shima is being sent back to this island. So it looks like I won't have to make the trip to Ie Shima. Soon as our men get over here again, Bennert and I will join them and stay with them until we hit the States. Rumors are going around that we should be sailing around the 15th. At the rate things are moving now, with all this damn confusion of jumping back & forth on these islands, I don't know what to believe about the sailing date. I would like to get the hell out of here though, this sitting around waiting is getting me down, I want to get home! If we make it by the 15th I'll be quite happy, but so many changes take place in the Army a fellow never knows what the score is. Should make it by Christmas, that's all I can say now. Nothing to do but hope for the best.

Honey, I might not get a chance to write again. This replacement camp is at the northern end of the island. Think I'll take the enlisted men and go up there tomorrow morning. The boys from Ie Shima should be in there sometime today. If I get a chance I'll drop you a line before we take-off, but don't count on it.

All my love,
Howard

Okinawa

16 October 1945

Darling Legna,

Still sitting on this damn island, waiting to come home. All of us are in a Casual Camp waiting for the ship. We've been here since the 5th and it has been nice living. A bitch of a typhoon hit us a week ago and laid everything low. There wasn't a tent standing in this camp. Most of the island was in the same shape. What a mess. The tents blew down long before the typhoon subsided and it was raining. Everyone got wet, in fact everything got wet. The mess-halls all blew down, so we ate infantry fashion for a week.

Honey, this darn boat was to sail on the 15th; here it is the 16th and we know nothing as to when we will leave here. I personally think we will be out of here around the 20th, but that's just a good guess. If we have another typhoon, things will be delayed again, probably for a week or so. Hope we get out of here before another typhoon, they are wicked.

From the information I can gather here, I don't think you will be able to meet me anyplace. There's a possibility the ship will dock on the East Coast; no matter where it docks I will travel to Meade by troop train. So that leaves all "meetings out" until I get to Meade. Everybody will be split according to their state when we dock. I'm still hoping the ship goes to the East Coast. I'd rather not ride a troop train across country. 'Course to get off this island I'd land anywhere in the U.S. It wouldn't be too bad around here if there was something to do but we are lying around with time heavy on our hands. If we get out of here by the 20th, I'll be quite happy, anything over that will be hardships.

Still think I'll be home by December 1st!

All my love,
Howard

Epilogue

Howard arrived safely at Fort Meade, Maryland, to out-process before he could go home for good. Glorious's parents forbade her to drive to Fort Meade to meet him because they were afraid for her safety when she encountered all those love-starved soldiers who had just arrived home from overseas. Their reunion would have to wait a little while longer.

As my Uncle Howard told it to me, he hitch-hiked home from Fort Meade to Shady Side and went straight to the Rural Home Hotel and to Glorious. When he walked in the door, Mr. A and Miss Ethel, her parents, told him Glorious wasn't ready yet, she was upstairs in her room and would be down soon. Howard would have none of that. He bounded up the long staircase three steps at a time and rushed into Glorious's room. There she sat at her dressing table with curlers still in her hair. He didn't care; he gathered her in his arms and kissed her with abandon. They were together again after two long years of forced separation caused by a war fought on the other side of the globe.

Capt. Howard C. Shenton (yes, the Army Air Corps finally promoted him to Captain at the 11th hour) married Glorious Legna Andrews on June 22, 1946, at Centenary Methodist Church in Shady Side after a 6 month engagement. Her brother Derwill was unable to get home in time for their wedding from Pearl Harbor where he was stationed in the Navy. Howard & Glorious lived in Shady Side their entire married life, first residing in a suite of rooms at the Rural Home Hotel until they built a red brick house on West River where they lived together in marital bliss for the rest of their married life.

Mr. and Mrs. Howard Shenton celebrated 50 years of marriage in 1996, surrounded by loving family, including Miss Ethel, who would leave this earth at the age of 108 the following year, Glorious's brother, Derwill and his wife, Anita, their daughter, Jacqueline and her husband, Rev. Jerry Grace and their son, Richard. Howard and Glorious never had children of their own. I, Jacqueline, am their niece and god-daughter. They gifted me with the old suitcase full of letters when Uncle Howard was in the last days of life, suffering from metastatic melanoma brain cancer. He died in their home on October 30, 2003. His beloved wife, Glorious Legna, had already begun the long slow journey into the dark recesses of Alzheimer's disease. In her last days she resided at Heart Homes at Bay Ridge in Annapolis, a facility for patients with dementia, close to her brother, Derwill and Anita, where they visited her almost every day. She died in July of 2008. Howard and Glorious are buried side by side in the Galesville cemetery. They were married for 57 years.

Glorious continued to teach at Southern High School and eventually became a guidance counselor then an instructional supervisor at the school for many years before she retired. She was a Southern Bulldog at heart.

Soon after the war, Howard and Derwill bought an oyster boat and oystered together for a few years. Eventually they gave that up. Howard started work for the Natural Resources Marine Police, then called the Tidewater Fisheries, on the Chesapeake Bay. He eventually became the Chief of Marine Police. In order to accept the position, he needed a high

611

school diploma, so during middle-age he studied for the GED and passed with flying colors. They both retired and lived a happy life together helping out their neighbors and friends in Shady Side and stayed active in Centenary United Methodist Church.

Glorious grew beautiful flowers in her many gardens and Howard complained about having to cut around them when he mowed the grass. Howard grew vegetables, especially tomatoes, in a large garden in their backyard. They enjoyed many hours with family and friends on their 43 foot Chesapeake Bay built wooden workboat, *The Glorious.* They were instrumental in founding the Shady Side Heritage Society where Glorious served as the librarian until her Alzheimer's got in the way of that, and Howard spoke about the Chesapeake Bay to children's groups who visited the museum.

In later years, Howard's brother Shim found him and they renewed their ties. Often when Shim visited Howard they would go fishing out on the boat. On one of those fishing trips, Shim suffered a massive heart attack while in the middle of the Chesapeake Bay. There was nothing that could have been done to save him but being out on the water so far from help made it a traumatic experience for Howard. He had just found his brother again after so many years of separation and now he was gone. At least Shim had the comfort of dying in his beloved brother's arms.

Those of us who had the privilege of knowing Howard and Glorious Shenton can still hear his big booming laugh and her gentle giggles. We can still see the love for each other in their eyes. They epitomized marital happiness and were an example for all of us. One can't help but wonder how those long years of yearning for each other during the war must have built up a store of love and commitment that would carry them through so many blissful years together.

It has been my privilege to offer their love story to the world.

Glorious in front of the living room fireplace on her wedding day, June 22, 1946

Howard & Glorious Shenton on their 50th Wedding Anniversary

Discussion Questions

1941-42

August 31. 1941 Howard writes:

I can't understand why you haven't written. It had been three weeks since I've heard from you. Maybe you didn't get my last letter, so many of the boys say their mail doesn't get through. I'm really starting to worry about you.

Why do you think Glorious didn't write back? Is there something Howard wrote that could have upset her? What do you think that could have been? If you had been Glorious, how would you have handled it?

October 31, 1941 Howard gives Glorious some advice on how to discipline the students who misbehave in her classroom.

As I told you once before you should take a few lessons from some of these old army sergeants. They would have them straightened out in no time. Don't let them get you down and when you tell them to do something make sure they do it. If they don't, there should be some way to punish them. But

616

don't ever let them get away without punishment, or let them think they are putting something over on you. And be calm; Goodness yes, "do be calm".

What do you think of his advice?

In the same letter, Howard says he doesn't suffer from want of letters and gives Glorious permission to stop writing. **What do you think caused him to write this? Do you think his attitude toward receiving letters might change in the future?** [Apparently he stopped writing to Glorious for a while because his next letter was dated December 1, 1941, over a month later. He began that letter "Dear Miss Andrews".] **Why do you think he did that?**

Jan 31, 1942

Howard writes: *We certainly are losing the best years of our life now.*

What are the ramifications of war time on young men and women? What are the long term effects? Glorious and Howard were in their early twenties at the time. Why are those the "best years" of their lives?

March 27, 1942

What do you suppose is "The Promise" that Howard writes about? Why do you think he can't make that promise?

May 27, 1942

When Howard went before the Officer Candidate School Entrance Board, he was asked to define *character* and *reputation*. **How would you define *character* and *reputation*?**

July 18, 1942

Howard refers to "our moon". **Why does the moon play such a big part in long distance relationships?**

September 27, 1942

Howard is describing his weekend with Glorious and says this about the movie they saw together:

First we went to a show & that was alright because she seemed to enjoy the picture. Personally, I thought the picture a bit on the silly side. There were too many love scenes and they weren't carried through with the right spirit. It was obvious the boy didn't love the girl & equally as obvious that the gal was crazy about the boy. But I don't think a girl in true life could throw herself at a guy who didn't love her. There would be no point to it. (Love is something which must be shared mutually.) So much for the show.

What do you think about Howard's wisdom on "love"?

October 10-11, 1942

In Glorious's letters to Howard she cites some reasons how she knows she loves him. **What are those reasons and do you think they signify true love? Why or why not?**

October 20, 1942

Glorious writes this about her day of teaching:

If I had been a person who acts on impulse I'd have handed my resignation to Miss Motley at 3:15 this afternoon. I had a very nice day teaching my own classes, every one ran very smoothly, but I had to take a class for an absent teacher the last period. They were holy terrors and I really took a beating. I was ready to quit, honest. That is how it goes though, some days I love it and wouldn't stop for the world and others I just want to give up. That's life I guess.

How do you keep perspective when you are having a bad day to prevent making an impulsive decision that could affect the rest of your life?

October 25 & 28, 1942 from Glorious to Howard, Glorious outlines the plans to meet in Baltimore at the train station**.**

How was the situation so different from today that made it so difficult to arrange a meeting in advance?

1943-44

June 6, 1943

Howard and Glorious had their serious discussion about marriage when he was home on leave. He writes this in the next letter:

Honey, I wish you had come back with me, I thought about you all the way up. Legna, we don't want to get married though. Everything is so uncertain and in a state of more or less confusion. I love you more than anything in the world but we mustn't rush into marriage and make a mess of it.

What would be the disadvantages of them getting married at this point in the war?

January 18, 1944

Howard writes: Have you ever heard the proverb, *"Life is like a spear which some seek to escape: I would prefer impalement on the shaft."*

How would you interpret the meaning of this proverb?

March 9, 1944

Howard writes: *I think a person should be content. I am now even though not too happy.*

What is the difference between being content and happy? What seems to make Howard content? What makes him not happy?

March 12, 1944

Howard writes: *The weather has been very nice this week, lots of rain. The moonlight at night is beautiful and it's so cool you really enjoy them. There are about a 100 nurses around here and "ole Shenton" can't get a date. There isn't much you can do if you get a date, talk and drink coffee.*

Later Howard explains he was joking but how would you have taken his comment if you'd been Glorious? Remember they couldn't talk to each other and the delay between letters was often several weeks, if the letter got there at all.

Easter Sunday (April 9, 1944)

Howard writes: *We are having an egg-hunt but we are hunting for a place to hide them. The place isn't so hard to find but the accessibility is slightly hazardous. Also we have a few eggs hunting us every so often but we don't make such good hunting.*

What do you think he means by this and why didn't he just write it without the 'code'?

April 14, 1944

Howards writes about some changes in the men since arriving in New Guinea:

Legna, there's been quite a few changes in some of the boys since we hit New Guinea. I just hope I'm not following suit. The men are touchy, irritable and pretty hard to get along with. My training in the infantry is standing me in good stead. I've expected everything we've encountered and a little more. The going hasn't even been bad so far. I get sore because some of the guys lose their sense of humor. Better not say too much, I might lose mine. I think I can take a year and a half or two over here right in my stride though. Course you can't predict in the army.

Why do you think some of the men changed? How do you think Howard's infantry training prepared him for the conditions more than officer training? In what ways do you think people's temperaments and upbringing effect how they respond to unpleasant, even dire, circumstances?

April 21, 1944

Howard begins his letter with:

Can't for the life of me think of what to write about. Letter writing is getting to be quite a chore. Just about getting ready to hit the ole routine again. There's plenty going on, but it's all "old stuff". Maybe I'll be getting another APO pretty soon. That's what I like, in that way, time doesn't drag.

Even though Howard is in an exotic place with beautiful scenery, he suddenly is having difficulty thinking of things to write Glorious about. **What do you think is causing this? In wartime there are restrictions on what members of the military can write about. How do you think this affects his ability to write letters home? *See the Army pamphlet WHEN YOU ARE OVERSEAS in the appendix for reference.**

April 25, 1944

Howard writes in rather strong language about a painful letter that Glorious wrote to him. Long distance relationships are difficult enough without a world war separating couples for years at a time. Obviously Howard wrote something that upset Glorious in a previous letter.

What would you have done in Glorious' place? How could Howard have handled the situation differently? Do you think they truly understood the impact the war was having on their relationship?

April 29, 1944

Howard writes: *Legna, you mentioned something about censorship of your letters. Incoming mail isn't censored. The army doesn't give a hoot what is said in the mail coming in, it's just the outgoing and all of those aren't given the third degree.*

What would it be like writing to your sweetheart knowing your letters could be opened and read by Army censors?

May 6, 1944

Glorious' birthday was coming up and Howard writes this to her:

Thinking about your birthday this month, I sort of took inventory on the ages of the fellows around me. You know, with the exception of about one man, I'm the youngest screw-ball in this outfit by a few years. Would like to be with you on the 20th. We could celebrate the occasion quietly, sober—and have a lot of fun. What's the meaning of that word fun? I'll learn when I get home. Shouldn't be too much of a job. Maybe I'll learn before then! What could we do on the 20th to have a good time? Take a drive, have dinner, a show and maybe a dance later. Oh, we could go for a speedboat ride, if there was one available. Water is kind of cold yet for swimming but we wouldn't necessarily have to take a dip. We could have fun though, Legna! Right now I could have fun sitting around the house drinking milk all day. I'm going to cherish a "cow" when I get home. How I miss that vitamin.

How do our circumstances change our view of what is fun? How would being in a war zone impact fun activities?

May 10, 1944

Howard writes: *My "one hitch" in the army is drawing to a close, three years the 30th of this month. Seems like 23. Looking back it's kind of startling, almost a jumble, but I don't think it has changed me in any way. I still think the same about life, wonder if my perspective will change? The whole thing has been a great experience.*

How do you think Howard's perspective may have changed if he'd stayed in the infantry? What do you think has made this a great experience for Howard?

August 17 or 18, 1944

Howard writes in reference to Schwen's and Wood's 15 day leave to Sydney: *Those two married boys are going to find a tough go of it down south. It's no place for married men.*

What do you think he meant by that? How might their time on leave affect their marriages?

September 19, 1944

Howard introduces two films in his August 17/18 letter. Howard critiques and elaborates on the plot of two "pictures" (films) that were shown on base: *Christmas Holiday* and *Gaslights.*

Do a search on the critiques of both films from the 1940s and discuss the similarity and differences of Howard's critique. How does casting enter into both Howard's and the newspaper's critique of Christmas Holiday?

What do you think of Howard's stance that nobody would actually fall for the diabolical psychological strategy used in Gaslights? [Gaslighting has become a commonly used psychological term. An online search will produce a lot of information on it.]

September 26, 1944

Howard writes: *Understand from all the reports that the Home Front isn't what it's cracked-up to be. Returning soldiers from overseas are a bit disappointed, mostly with their women. Too bad, the boys should have something nice to come home to. Seems to us though, most of the fellows want to get back in the fight. I think a lot of this was caused by hasty marriages and "good times" as people call it. People aren't happy nowadays unless they are always doing something wild. After what I saw in Sydney, I'm convinced most people don't know how to have a good time. A good time to them is comprised of drinking and sex, and the emphasis is on the latter. All of this looks and seems wonderful for a few days, especially after having been in some remote spot for few months. But after a few days it becomes nauseating and you feel like running away from it all. Well, the adjustments will be made I suppose, but some people are sure going to suffer from them.*

What do you think about Howard's assessment of the reasons returning soldiers are disappointed when they get home? How could changes in both the men and the women affect their reunion? How do individual expectations play into it?

September 29, 1944

Howard comments that he'd like to do high school over again. **What would you do differently if you could do high school over again? If you are still in high school, how would you change your current attitude toward your situation?**

October 17, 1944

Howard is on New Guinea again going to school. The Wacs are there. He expressed the opinion that they shouldn't have to put up with the climate, implying that women can't handle it like men can.

What do you think of his opinion? How have cultural opinions changed about women since WWII?

Christmas Day, December 25, 1944

Howard wrote: *Legna, I've been complaining off and on about us not doing much to really fight this war. Well I had "it" coming and believe me I got "it". In fact, I'm swimming in this mess and the water is rather treacherous. Like Fischer said when I first saw him in the Philippines, "I've seen enough war and want to get out of it."*

War is so often glorified and young men want to be part of it but when the reality of war faces them, they often change their minds when it's too late. **Discuss the difference between the "glory of war" and the "reality of war".**

Then he goes on to write:

I'm not anxious to get out but I've seen all I care to see. Kind of a "rough-go", but we are doing alright. 'Tis better though when you are right in the thick of things, at least you feel as though there is a job being accomplished. Makes you a little nervous at times but the morale is high.

Why do you think men and women volunteer to go to war?

1945

January 2, 1945

Howard writes about his Ordnance men hating to work at night loading bombs on the planes due to enemy planes dropping bombs and strafing them. He describes their fear like this:

We have a constant red alert beginning at dark. You have to depend on the ack-ack firing at a close Jap plane for a warning that the devils are near. Doesn't give you much time to find a hole, in fact sometimes they get in and drop their load before the ack-ack finds them. We've also gotten a few strafe jobs and they are the worst. The men are so scared they don't think of what they are doing. I don't blame them for feeling the way they do; I feel the same way. But I'm the guy that has to remain cool and calm, say when to knock off and hit the dirt—also when to go back to work. I'm just as scared as they are. It's all in the days work though, but "somehow" you just can't accustom yourself to these conditions. (Becoming fairly acclimatized though.) There are many others doing the same things. We take it in stride.

How so you think this affected Glorious when she read this letter? Why are people in leadership roles able to stay cool and calm when everyone else is scared? How do they do that?

At the end of this letter he writes:

Honey, the going is pretty rough now and probably will be for a while. Don't worry about me. Shenton can take care of himself. In a way I kind of like it, but in more ways I don't.

Why do you think he added this part?

January 4, 1945

Howard writes: *Say, what's this all about, everybody is reading everybody's letters I write? One of these days I'm going to cross my wires probably and somebody will read something they shouldn't. I'm only kidding Legna, seems though they are getting a lot of publicity. Doesn't matter, I never say anything personal about anyone.*

Why do you think the people back home are reading all of Howard's letters to each other?

January 24, 1945

Howard writes: *Legna, if you want to check-up on my whereabouts, get a January 8ᵗʰ or 12ᵗʰ edition of Time and read about the Thunderbolts and Mitchells. Damn magazines print more things —information that would never get past an army censor. Understand the story is not really up to par (what actually happened) but it should be pretty good reading.*

What is your opinion about the press printing information during war time that could jeopardize the safety of the military? Do the people back home have a right to hear the truth whether or not the information could put our military or the war strategy in jeopardy?

February 20, 1945

Howard writes: *Were you paying me a compliment when you said I was all the movie stars in one? Damn, Legna, what a comparison. I don't want to be like any movie star. They are no different from anyone else —just make more money, that's all.*

The Golden Age of Hollywood spanned from the 1920s to the early 1960s. Hollywood actors and actresses attained major celebrity status and were revered by many people. **Does Howard's reaction to Glorious comparing him to movie stars surprise you? Explain why. Why do people revere celebrities? What have they done to deserve their heightened status in society? How do celebrities compare to ordinary people who have not gained fame and fortune?**

May 15, 1945

Howard writes: *Legna, that's about all. Wish I could say I'd see you in another twelve months. But I don't see how! (Miracles!)*

How did the uncertainty of when the war would be over affect their communication and their relationship, as well as their future plans? Little did Howard know at the time that his word, "Miracles!" was actually foreshadowing of what would come to cut the war short.

June 5, 1945

Howard addresses something Legna said about being hurt. He wonders if the people back home understand what's really going on in the war.

I don't know what in the hell people back home think we are doing over here. They must have no imagination or think some of the horror pictures they see in books and on the screen is all propaganda. Well, for myself, I can say that I haven't suffered or had undue hardships. But some of our boys risk their lives every day. What makes it so tough is the things you see happen and know it is quite possible that same can happen to you.

If the people back home really understood the conditions during war, how should that affect the way they react to letters from those serving in combat zones and how they should respond? What are the reasons they don't really understand the actual conditions of the war zone?

July 15, 1945

Howard writes about the beautiful sunset on the beach:

Sweetheart, those chills and bumps you get when you think of us, I get them too. I was looking at the sunset over the ocean this evening. My, what a beautiful scene, the sea and sky merging so you couldn't tell one from the other, with the sunlight beams dancing over all, touching everything with beautiful colors. The P.A. system was playing soft and sweet music. I would have given everything to have you standing with me arm in arm watching it all. Wood came up while I was watching and said, "Makes you feel homesick, doesn't it?" I didn't even answer, just nodded my head. 'Tis things like this that make a fellow think of the real life. Know what I mean? Someone to love and share it all with, a home and all the things that go with it, comfort, security and the fun of living, laughter, tears, taking things as they come, give a big sigh and say to yourself, "It's great to be alive and I wouldn't miss it for anything."

Why do you think witnessing such beauty in nature makes people think of love?

August 4, 1945
As Howard responds to Glorious' desire to get married as soon as he gets home, he opens up about his past.

How does this new information explain some of his previous reactions to marriage? Why do you think he reverts to using third person when explaining his painful past? What issues does he think will be a challenge if they do get married? Do you agree with his counsel to Glorious? Why or why not?

August 8 or 9, 1945

Howard writes: *Say, the atomic bomb sure caused a lot of commotion, didn't it? Everybody is talking about it and every time we turn on the radio we hear a broadcast about "the bomb".*

Later, on **August 21, 1945**, he responds to something Glorious wrote about the atomic bomb.

I wish you wouldn't mention things like the atomic bomb. You people sit 12,000 miles from the fighting and you don't know a damn thing about what's going on out here. Yet you make comments and form opinions on how war should be conducted. Leave that to the military leaders, that's what they are for. So far, they have performed a wonderful job, with I would say, superior results. The fellows up top know what the score is and as long as they keep the enemy away from our shores and accomplish the purpose, "everything for which we are fighting", well, that's good enough for me. Seems to me a lot of people think war is just a big adventure trimmed with medals and ribbons that make a uniform look dashing. Just in case someone drives-up in a vehicle, leans out and asks you, it isn't. I don't intend to tell you what it is like, because even I don't know the complete story, but I do have an excellent idea what it is like, so I do speak with a fair knowledge. Six months after the peace is signed, I'll bet you wouldn't know there was a war going on, a short while previously. That's as it should be according to my way of thinking, because I don't want any reminders. You all just sit back and let us do the fighting. We know the hows and why-fors, because we are right in "the middle of the caper". Don't take offense at what I've said here, Honey, but I'm being frank. (I realize freedom of speech is one of those things we are out here fighting for.)

The perspective on war strategy can be very different whether a person is in a combat zone or on the home front. What influences a person's opinion on war? Why do you think Howard mentioned freedom of speech?

August 15, 1945

Howard writes about the end of the war.

Today is "the day", at last the war is over and believe me, everybody is happy. Funny thing though, when the announcement was made there were no cheers or even much comment. Guess we did our celebrating the night we heard Japan had made a "request for peace". Sure were a lot of fireworks around here that night. Honey, I didn't feel any different when I heard the news. Perhaps if I were in the States, or on my way there, I would have really felt like raising hell. But, there is still a job to do out here, my work will continue, only difference, no bomb-handling. I realize that we must carry on with our work as before. There is no doubt in my mind that every effort will be made to get the men out of here and home, as quickly as possible. It will be a little hard to take, staying out here when the war is over, but there is still work to do, so I guess we'll be hacking around for a little while.

What did you think about Howard's reaction?

633

August 26, 1945

Howard writes about a happy job he had:

Honey, my job was indeed a pleasure last night. Gosh, I had a swell time, though it was work. Had a call around 10 o'clock to get all the enlisted men with 85 or more points ready to leave for home by 10 o'clock in the morning. We had nineteen men in that bracket, wish we had a thousand. Honey, if only you could have seen those boys when I told them they were going home. I think at first, that they couldn't understand, just stood dumbfounded, then when it dawned on them, gosh, it was wonderful to see. We had them processed and ready to go, at five this morning. They took-off for Manila. Some of the boys were so excited they couldn't spell their names nor repeat their serial numbers. I hope my orders come thru like that, what a thrill!

What does it say about Howard's character that it was such a pleasure for him to see the enlisted men so excited to be told they were going home when he wants to go home so badly himself and must stay longer?

September 2, 1945 V.J. Day

Howard writes that he still has a job to do overseas even though the war is officially over. **In subsequent letters he mentions some of the jobs the military still has to do. What are those duties?**

September 10, 1945

I almost forgot, we don't have censorship anymore. The enlisted men sure appreciate that. It isn't so nice writing when you know someone is reading everything you say.

Why do you think the censorship regulations were lifted?

September 25, 1945

Howard writes: *Got the 358th letter today, so that makes a grand-total of 359.* (From Glorious to Howard)

How did Howard's and Glorious' letter writing help their relationship? How did it challenge it? How would you compare the pitfalls of letter writing during WWII to the issues with social media communication today?

General Questions:

1. What are some of the things Howard wrote that amused you?

2. There is a great deal of discussion between Howard & Glorious centering on the use of trains and buses. How is public transportation different in the United States now compared to then? Given what you know from their letters about transportation during WW2 what changes would you make to today's public transportation situation?

3. Howard makes frequent references to Glorious and other women's weight, inferring that weighing too little wasn't attractive. Did this surprise you? In what ways?

4. Discuss the importance of receiving mail to men and women serving in the military during WWII. How did it affect their morale? What specific things caused the mail service to be so erratic, besides the obvious, being at war?

5. Howard often mentions how hard it is to think of something to write. Knowing that there are certain things they are not allowed to write about and probably don't want to worry their loved ones, they were most likely trying to avoid certain topics. If you were in that position, what would you write about? What do you think the people back home wanted to hear?

6. What were some things that surprised you about life in the service overseas during WWII?

7. Howard mentions music frequently. Why is music so important during wartime?

8. Howard writes about books he reads while overseas. *Elmer Gantry* by Sinclair Lewis, *Merchant of Venice* by Shakespeare, *Crescent Carnival* by Frances Parkinson Keyes, *The Valley of Decision* by Marcia Davenport, Zane Grey's Westerns, among others. How did reading help Howard's morale?

9. Howard repeatedly writes that he doesn't think he has changed. As an outside observer, in what ways do you think he changed from his first letter to his last? How did he stay the same?

10. The generation that served during WWII is called "The Greatest Generation". What evidence in Howard's and Glorious' letters supports their generation being called The Greatest Generation?

Appendix

Army Pamphlet No. 21-1
When You Are Overseas

WHEN YOU ARE OVERSEAS

THESE FACTS ARE VITAL

PAMPHLET NO. 21-1

WRITING HOME

THINK! Where does the enemy get his information—information that can put you, and has put your comrades, adrift on an open sea; information that has lost battles and can lose more, unless you personally, vigilantly, perform your duty in SAFEGUARDING MILITARY INFORMATION?

CENSORSHIP RULES ARE SIMPLE, SENSIBLE.—They are merely concise statements drawn from actual experience briefly outlining the types of material which have proved to be disastrous when available to the enemy. A soldier should not hesitate to impose his own additional rules when he is considering writing of a subject not covered by present regulations. He also should be on guard against false rumors and misstatements about censorship. It is sometimes stated that censorship delays mail for long periods of time. Actually all mail (with certain nominal and very unusual exceptions) is completely through censorship within 48 hours.

THERE ARE TEN PROHIBITED SUBJECTS

1. Don't write military information of Army units—their location, strength, matériel, or equipment.

2. Don't write of military installations.

3. Don't write of transportation facilities.

4. Don't write of convoys, their routes, ports (including ports of embarkation and disembarkation), time en route, naval protection, or war incidents occurring en route.

5. Don't disclose movements of ships, naval or merchant, troops, or aircraft.

6. Don't mention plans and forecasts or orders for future operations, whether known or just your guess.

7. Don't write about the effects of enemy operations.

8. Don't tell of any casualty until released by proper authority (The Adjutant General) and then only by using the full name of the casualty.

9. Don't attempt to formulate or use a code system, cipher, or shorthand, or any other means to conceal the true meaning of your letter. Violations of this regulation will result in severe punishment.

519309°—43

10. Don't give your location in any way except as authorized by proper authority. Be sure nothing you write about discloses a more specific location than the one authorized.

INCLOSURES IN LETTERS.—Do not inclose anything in a letter that would violate any of the foregoing rules.

PHOTOGRAPHS, FILMS.—Special rules apply to the transmission of photographs and films. Do not send them until you have ascertained what regulations are in effect in the area.

POST CARDS.—The use of post cards may or may not be authorized. Find out first, and then be sure that the picture or printed part of the card does not violate censorship regulations.

LETTER ADDRESSES

ADDRESS.—Always leave room for a forwarding address to be written in.

On mail to civilians.—Use normal address and form.

On mail to military personnel.—Give name, grade (rank), Army serial number (if known), unit and organization, and location if in United States. If addressee is also overseas use his APO number c/o Postmaster ——. If in the same general locality as the sender see Army Postal Service for authorized address.

On mail to prisoners of war held by enemy.—Obtain full information from local Army Postal Service.

RETURN ADDRESS.—Every letter or post card must have a return address. Place it in the upper left-hand corner, leaving a margin of ½ inch for resealing in case of censorship beyond the unit censor. The ½-inch margin rule applies equally to mail from officers and from enlisted men. Both are subject to examination by base censorship detachments.

```
Sgt. John Smith, 6740318,
Co. C, 299 Inf., A. P. O. 1005,                    Free
c/o Postmaster, New York City, N. Y.



                        Mrs. John Smith,
                        123 First Avenue,
                        New York City, N. Y.
```

The return address must include (1) full name, including grade (rank), (2) Army serial number, (3) unit (company, battery, etc.), (4) organization (regiment), (5) APO number, (6) % Postmaster (city assigned).

Return addresses on mail written to prisoners of war are subject to specific regulations. Obtain information locally.

No geographical location of sender may be shown on an envelope or other outside cover.

OFFICIAL MILITARY MAIL

Special regulations are provided for official military mail. They are not covered herein.

MAILING YOUR LETTER

Reread your letter to be sure you have complied with all regulations. This will protect you and assure the most expeditious delivery of your letter. Five minutes now will save later delay and prevent possible suppression of the letter. It will protect you from punishment for unintentional violations.

ENLISTED MEN.—Place your letter unsealed in your organization mail box, never in any civil post office box. *You are required to use the Army Postal Service, and the Army Postal Service only.*

OFFICERS.—Seal the envelope, sign your name without comment in the lower left-hand corner to indicate your compliance with censorship regulations (your letter is subject to further censorship examination by base censorship detachments), and deposit in the organization mail box. *Use only the Army Postal Service.*

V-MAIL

This is an expeditious mail program which provides for quick mail service to and from soldiers overseas. A special form is used which permits the letter to be photographed on microfilm, the small film transported, and then reproduced and delivered. Use of V-MAIL is urged because it greatly furthers the war effort by saving shipping and airplane space.

Censorship rules apply to V-mail with such adjustments as are necessary due to the form used and special processing features.

BLUE ENVELOPES

Enlisted men who wish to write of private or family matters and who feel that censorship of a specific letter by their unit censor would cause embarrassment may be authorized to use a blue envelope which will allow censorship action to be taken by the base censor rather than the unit censor.

Blue envelopes should be obtained from your organization and must be addressed to the final intended recipient. Only one letter may be placed in each envelope and the envelope should be sealed prior to mailing.

Censorship regulations apply to blue envelopes as well as to all other communications.

WARNING

Written communications may be sent only through the facilities of the Army Postal Service. Any attempt to avoid this restriction by mailing letters in civil postal systems or by having travelers transport communications will result in severe disciplinary action against both the sender and the intermediary.

CABLES; RADIOGRAMS

Every cable message goes through the hands of at least 12 people. Radiogram messages are available to all who wish to "tune in," including the enemy!

Constant effort is being made to provide you with approved, rapid, cheap electrical communication.

Under no circumstances can cables be sent over commercial or foreign outlets until their use is authorized by proper military authority. "Safe Arrival" messages, identifiable as such, are prohibited at any time. There are two types of electrical messages generally available: Senders' Composition Messages (SCMs), which are like the cablegrams and radiograms you know at home, and Expeditionary Force Messages (EFMs) which are fixed text messages sent at a very low rate, much like Christmas and birthday telegraph messages in use in the United States, but with set messages composed to meet your normal requirement.

As soon as safety allows you will be assigned an APO *cable* address. Until it is assigned only serious, emergency messages may be sent, and then only if first approved in writing by the theater or area commander or his authorized representative. The Red Cross can handle certain extremely urgent personal matters by cable.

Ask your unit censor how to send messages, either SCMs or EFMs.

CABLE ADDRESSES

Outbound.—First give *your* cable address; next, the full name, street address, city, and State of the person for whom the message is intended; then the message, and finally sign your full name. Example:

```
AMTRAG (typical APO cable address)
Mrs. John Smith, 1616 Main St.,
Zenith, Ohio:
     XXXXXX   Message   XXXXXX
     XXXXXXXXXXXXXXXXXXXXXX
                    John T. Smith.
```

Note that there is no Army serial number, no unit nor organization, and no mention of your location.

Inbound.—Cables and radiograms should be addressed to you, giving your full name, Army serial number, and *cable* address, but not your unit nor organization.

TALK

SILENCE MEANS SECURITY.—If violation of protective measures is serious within written communications it is disastrous in conversations. Protect your conversation as you do your letters, and be even more careful. A harmful letter can be nullified by censorship; loose talk is direct delivery to the enemy.

If you come home during war your lips must remain sealed and your writing hand must be guided by self-imposed censorship. This takes guts. Have you got them or do you want your buddies and your country to pay the price for your showing off? You've faced the battle front; it's little enough to ask you to face this "home front."

CAPTURE

Most enemy intelligence comes from prisoners. If captured, you are required to give only three facts: YOUR NAME, YOUR GRADE, YOUR ARMY SERIAL NUMBER. Don't talk, don't try to fake stories, and use every effort to destroy all papers. When you are going into an area where capture is possible carry only essential papers and plan to destroy them prior to capture if possible. Do not carry personal letters on your person; they tell much about you, and the envelope has on it your unit and organization.

BE SENSIBLE; USE YOUR HEAD

U. S. GOVERNMENT PRINTING OFFICE: 1943

Glossary

Names, places, and things related to Shady Side and personal references in the letters:

Cap'n: Abbreviation for Captain. A colloquial title given to waterman, men who owned their own boat, and anyone who was well-respected in the Chesapeake Bay communities. An expression of respect.

Derwill: Glorious' younger brother who was at Massanutten Military Academy while too young for the draft. Glorious called him Drilk or Frère (French word for brother).

Ivan: Glorious' old Model A Ford

Leatherbury Well: Some of the Leatherbury brothers owned a well-drilling company in Shady Side

Miss Grace was Cap'n Charlie Hartge's wife who was Howard's foster mother

Miss Mary's: Miss Mary Hartge had a dance hall/bar across the road from the Rural Home Hotel so they could hear the music all summer long until late in the evening.

Rhode River: A lovely sheltered river on the other side of West River from Shady Side

Roomy, also called **Scoop:** Glorious' roommate at Hood College. Her real name was Ruth Duff

R.H.H.—Rural Home Hotel in Shady Side: A summer boarding house owned and operated by Glorious' parents, Mr & Mrs AW Andrews. Mrs Andrews was known to everyone as Miss Ethel. She taught at Shady Side Elementary School.

Wobble Bump and Ache: Washington, Baltimore and Annapolis train that ran locally between the three cities

World War II Stuff

ack-ack: Anti-aircraft fire

Atabrine: anti-malarial drug

AT-6: The North American Aviation T-6 Texan is a single-engined advanced trainer aircraft used to train pilots of the United States Army Air Forces(USAAF)

B-25 Mitchell: A medium sized bomber used during WWII

Bully Beef: Corned beef in a tin issued by the Australian government to US Soldiers similar to SPAM
http://www.ww2incolor.com/forum/showthread.php/3537-Food-of-different-armies

Caduceus: Symbol of Medicine

Calox Tooth Powder: a form of dental hygiene product used to brush teeth

Christmas Holiday: A WWII era film
https://en.wikipedia.org/wiki/Christmas_Holiday

Cycad tree:
https://en.wikipedia.org/wiki/Cycad

Daisy Cutter High Explosive Bombs mentioned in July 13, 1944 letter

Doughboy: member of the Army or Marines, replaced by G.I. during WWII

Elmer Gantry by Sinclair Lewis: a book and WWII era film about a hypocritical preacher who was addicted to alcohol
https://www.npr.org/templates/story/story.php?storyId=19288767

E.M.: enlisted men

Gaslight: a psychological term for making someone believe bad things did not happen when they actually did occur in an attempt to make the person doubt his or her sanity. Also a 1944 film of the same name.
https://en.wikipedia.org/wiki/Gaslight_(1944_film)

Goldberg inventions: A complex imaginative machine designed to do a simple task. Named after Rube Goldberg, an American Pulitzer prize-winning cartoonist who began his career as an engineer. He drew Goldberg machines in his cartoons but allegedly never actually built them.

Kick the gong around: Smoking opium or dope

K.P.: Kitchen Patrol or Kitchen Police

New Guinea WWII information
http://www.history.army.mil/brochures/new-guinea/ng.htm

Sunfish: a derogatory term, [probably a euphemism for son-of-a-bitch]

Thunderbolt P-47: One of the main fighter-bombers used by the US Army Air Forces during WWII. The aircraft was equipped with 8 .50-calibre machine guns and could carry a bomb load of 2500.

Tojo: Japanese army officer who initiated the Japanese attack on Pearl Harbor and who assumed dictatorial control of Japan during World War II

USO (United Service Organizations Inc.): Nonprofit charitable organization founded during WWII to entertain and support American troops during the war.

V.J. Day: Victory over Japan Day. Japanese representatives signed the terms of surrender on September 2, 1945 aboard the USS Missouri, in effect ending the war.

Waac—WAAC: Women's Army Auxiliary Corps

Zero: Japanese fighter plane